CELEBRATING
50 YEARS
Texas A&M University Press
publishing since 1974

David Crockett in Texas

THE TEXAS EXPERIENCE

*Books made possible by
Sarah '84 and Mark '77 Philpy*

DAVID CROCKETT IN TEXAS

HIS SEARCH FOR NEW LAND

ALLEN J. WIENER

Texas A&M University Press
College Station

♾ This paper meets the requirements of ANSI/NISO
Z39.48–1992 (Permanence of Paper).
Binding materials have been chosen for durability.

Library of Congress Cataloging-in-Publication Data

Names: Wiener, Allen J., 1943– author.
Title: David Crockett in Texas: his search for new land / Allen J. Wiener.

Other titles: Texas experience (Texas A & M University. Press)
Description: First edition. | College Station: Texas A&M University Press,
  [2024] | Series: The Texas experience | Includes bibliographical
  references and index.
Identifiers: LCCN 2024027569 (print) | LCCN 2024027570 (ebook) | ISBN
  9781648432156 (cloth) | ISBN 9781648432163 (ebook)
Subjects: LCSH: Crockett, Davy, 1786–1836—Homes and haunts—Texas. |
  Crockett, Davy, 1786–1836—Last years. | Crockett, Davy,
  1786–1836—Family. | Land tenure—Texas—History—19th century. |
  Texas—History—Revolution, 1835–1836. | Alamo (San Antonio,
  Tex.)—Siege, 1836. | BISAC: BIOGRAPHY & AUTOBIOGRAPHY / Adven-
turers &
  Explorers | HISTORY / United States / 19th Century | LCGFT: Biographies.
Classification: LCC F390 .W64 2024 (print) | LCC F390 (ebook) | DDC
  976.8/04092 [B]—dc23/eng/20240723
LC record available at https://lccn.loc.gov/2024027569
LC ebook record available at https://lccn.loc.gov/2024027570

On the cover: *David Crockett*, by James Hamilton Shegogue, watercolor on paper, 1831.
Courtesy National Portrait Gallery, Smithsonian Institution; Gift of Algernon Sidney
Holderness, NPG.84.231

Cover and interior designed by Noah Van Soest

To all the librarians, archivists, and research
specialists around the globe—
Without you, there could not be this.

" . . . these were shadows of the things that have been.
That they are what they are, do not blame me!"
— The Ghost of Christmas Past, from
A Christmas Carol by Charles Dickens (1843)

"It's the only way it makes sense."
— Nick Charles, *The Thin Man* (MGM, 1934)

Contents

Acknowledgments

I am indebted to many people for their help in completing this book. My friends Tom Kailbourn and Jim Boylston have been steadfast supporters from the beginning. Both provided valuable feedback on draft manuscripts. Jim also gave generously of his time in researching Crockett's letter from Texas. Tom's military insight, key translations of Mexican documents, and editing skills were of great value in recreating events at the Alamo. Gert Petersen provided valuable information about Crockett's Tennessee years and devoted time to reviewing manuscripts. Wade Dillon lent unflagging support to the project and located the valuable *Niles' Weekly Register* of August 20, 1836, indicating where Crockett's nephew, William Patton, was after the war. James E. Ivey shared archeological information about the Alamo structure, including some of his unpublished work. Stuart Reid shared information regarding James Grant and the Matamoros expedition, and the nature of Bowie's illness. Todd Hansen responded to my many emails with valuable information and insight regarding Alamo documents. Larry Jones generously shared his photo collection. The late Kevin Young, a bottomless source of Alamo information and wisdom, and the most generous of friends, lent valuable insight and shared his extensive collection. Ronnie Atnip contributed maps and other information regarding geography and Crockett's movements through the Red River country. Gary Pinkerton helped locate period maps. William Chemerka, founder of The Alamo Society, provided valuable articles from his collection and the *Alamo Journal* archives. Courtney Tucker provided valuable comments on the manuscript.

Kevin Klaus of the Texas General Land Office Archives and Records guided me patiently through the GLO's online land records database and other documents that were crucial to the completion of this work. I am grateful to Dr. Daniel Feller for his support of this project and my earlier research into Crockett's life, particularly his expertise in Jacksonian era land policy. Many thanks to Karen Kraycirik, chief operating officer and minister for stewardship at Christ Church Cathedral in Houston, for use of the portrait of William Fairfax Gray. Terri Hoover Mirka arranged permission to use the portrait of John Swisher. I am very grateful to Mike Harris for creating a drawing of the 1836 Alamo for this book and to Mike Boldt for adding labels that I requested.

I am indebted to the staff at Texas A&M University Press for their assistance throughout the publishing process. Special thanks go to Editor in Chief Thom Lemmons, Managing Editor Katie Duelm, Editorial Assistant Nicole duPlessis, and my copyeditor, Matt Joyce. Many thanks to my indexer, Teri Greenberg, for her meticulous work.

This book is dedicated to the countless librarians and archivists who continuously serve researchers. I am indebted to the entire reference staff at the Library of Congress, but especially archivists Valerie Haeder of the Periodicals Reading Room, Lewis Wyman of the Manuscript Division, reference librarian Will Elsbury, and Michelle Cadoree Bradley of the Science, Technology and Business Division. Others who provided assistance include Ronald A. Lee, Juanita Bradford, Veronica Sales, Allison Griffey, and Heather M. Adkins at the Tennessee State Library and Archives; Sean McConnell, Rosenberg Library archivist at the Galveston and Texas History Center; Kate Mersiovsky and Dennis Michael Edelin at the National Archives; Dr. Gerry W. Beyer, Texas Tech University School of Law; Elizabeth White, Dunedin Public Library in Florida; Ashley C. Armstrong, Lawrence County Archives in Leoma, Tennessee; Jerry Limbaugh, Franklin County Tennessee Historical Society; Ken Barr, Alabama Department of Archives and History; April Jones, register of deeds in Weakley County, Tennessee; Lauren Waite, deputy clerk, Hood County, Texas; Deirdre Coslow, chief deputy clerk, Johnson County, Texas; Jody Mitchell and Ruthann Miller of the Lilly Library at Indiana University; Casey Edward Greene, head of Special Collections at the Rosenberg Library; Erin Harbour, Marisa Jefferson, Kendall Newton, and Aryn Glazier of The Dolph Briscoe Center for American History at The University of Texas at Austin; Chris Cotton, East Texas Research Center at Stephen F. Austin State University; Tim Hodgdon of the Research and Instructional Services Department, Louis Round Wilson Special Collections Library, Wilson Library, University of North Carolina at Chapel Hill; Melissa Nesbitt, archival manager, Southwest Arkansas Regional Archives; Leslie Sitz Stapleton, Archives and Special Collections manager, Texas A&M University-San Antonio; Cynthia Wilder, chair of the Daughters of the Republic of Texas Library Collection Committee; Dr. Ana Krahmer, director of the Digital Newspaper Program, University of North Texas Libraries; Joanna Bouldin, archivist at the McClung Historical Collection, East Tennessee History Center, Knox County Public Library System; Lisa A. Struthers, director of the Albert and Ethel Herzstein Library, San Jacinto Museum and Battlefield Association; and LaShun Hall, archivist at *The Dallas Morning News*. I am forever in your debt.

Any errors or oversights are entirely my own.

DAVID CROCKETT IN TEXAS

Introduction

On April 29, 1828, David Crockett rose from his seat in the US House of Representatives to speak about a land reform bill, and he used the opportunity to advocate for the relief of poor farmers in his Tennessee congressional district. Crockett emphasized the public good that came with private land ownership and suggested that people were far more likely to fight for land they owned, which was the tie that bound them to country. "Why does a man [take] pride in his country? Why does he defend it?" Colonel Crockett asked. "It is, sir, because in so doing he fights for his home—for the spot upon which all his affections are fixed—and which stands identified with ten thousand endearing recollections. I cannot be mistaken, Mr. Chairman, when I assert, that to make of your citizen a landholder, you chain down his affections to your soil and give him a pride and elevation of character, which fires his heart with patriotism and nerves his arm with strength." The War of 1812 was still fresh in the nation's memory, and Crockett alluded to the sacrifices the war had wrung from the poor farmers who willingly defended their country and what little land they owned or occupied. "When your country was invaded, and the flag of its honor insulted, they shouldered their guns and fought in its defence [*sic*]; and, not to pay myself a compliment, I had the honor to fight, side by side, with them."[1]

Crockett's speech summarized the crucial connection between land and citizenship in a democracy, and he phrased it much as Thomas Jefferson had. In his book *Notes on the State of Virginia*, Jefferson proclaimed, "Those who labor in the earth are the chosen people of God." In a nation of mostly small farmers, Jefferson saw land ownership and cultivation as essential to a thriving democracy. The importance Jefferson applied to land ownership set the tone for the nation's land culture. His belief that the country's future lay in farming and that farming was the most virtuous of human activities encouraged generations of Americans to seek their own fortune in land ownership.[2]

More land was essential to a country of farmers with a growing population. Jefferson understood the United States was destined to expand, that available land in the east would diminish, and that Americans would move west to claim the vast lands there. Indeed, Benjamin Franklin predicted the country's population would double every twenty-five years and saw it as a necessity in an expanding country with vast unclaimed lands, unlike in Europe, which lacked such land resources and had grown overcrowded. Jefferson shared these views and, as president, doubled the size of the country in one bold step when he purchased the huge Louisiana Territory from France in 1803. Like Crockett, Jefferson thought the nation's fate was tied to the prosperity of its citizens, particularly the yeoman farmers who were its backbone, even if that figure was largely a myth. Despite Jefferson's vision of yeoman farmers as honest, hardworking men who were content with their small plots of land, many of those small farmers were in it for the money as much as any large speculator or urban investor and saw land as a means to financial improvement. Contrary to Jefferson's idyllic image of them, small farmers often labored as hard as workers in the eastern factories he abhorred, and they did not necessarily see their independence linked to remaining small farmers. Jefferson thought the government would sell public land to farmers at reasonable prices, but he failed to anticipate their desire to own ever more land and to engage in speculation, which often required credit and debt. Jefferson thought debt robbed men of their independence, and he failed to see that landowners, large and small, would inevitably embrace it.[3]

Daniel Feller, author of the book *The Public Lands in Jacksonian Politics*, suggests, "There was something magnetic about land in Americans' imagination: it was the pot of gold at the end of the rainbow, both for 'actual settlers' and for speculators (two categories whose antithesis I believe begins to melt the minute you start looking at actual cases). Land (not corporate shares or bonds) was the main vehicle for financial investment/speculation; land ownership also had an ideological allure as the purported basis for everything noble in American character and everything sound in the American polity. People chased it compulsively and even irrationally. Just about every politician who had any means speculated in land."[4]

As early as colonial days, Americans looked longingly toward the seemingly limitless acreage of western land. But following the French and Indian War, Britain closed the West to colonists in an effort to maintain peace with Native Americans—an act that became a major grievance among colonists in the run up to the American War for Independence.

George Washington, for one, was particularly chagrined by the prohibition since he had explored and surveyed thousands of acres of land in the Ohio Valley and expected to claim much of it for speculation.

Anyone willing to take the risks that exploration and resettlement incurred might claim sizable tracts of land for themselves. The federal government retained ownership of the public domain, which, along with tariffs, provided most federal revenue. The government used its vast land resources as a political tool to regulate the flow of people westward, often by offering cheap land to anyone willing to live on it. Many settlers swept west and claimed land or simply occupied it as squatters with little concern for the letter of the law. Neither the states nor the federal government had the resources, or perhaps the will, to remove squatters from public lands. Some states even provided occupant claims to squatters who might live on the land indefinitely, improve it, and even sell their improvements to someone who might claim it with a legal warrant. New territories, eager for statehood, and states with small populations welcomed new settlers who would increase their numbers, qualify them for statehood, or increase their representation in Congress.[5]

No sooner did open land become available than legions of well-heeled land speculators sprang forth to snap up huge, low-priced tracts, which they could then sell at a profit. Profits could be used to buy up more acreage and repeat the process. Money could be made by leasing land to those able to pay rent, which sometimes took the form of crops and livestock, and who might earn enough on the land to eventually afford a plot of their own. Land could be developed for commercial or residential use. The lure of open land enticed thousands of Americans westward, both to farm and, ultimately, to use as a base to engage in land speculation themselves. Scratch a poor squatter and you just might find a speculator wannabe. Crockett's proposed land reform legislation would have provided poor occupant farmers with up to two hundred acres of land at prices as low as $0.125 cents per acre, when public land was selling for no less than $1.25 per acre. Crockett intended to give occupants enough land to farm but also enough more for speculation or to develop. This was a sure avenue to social reform and upward mobility, which Crockett knew from his own experience. Without land of their own, the poor were likely to stay that way.

Andrew Jackson used his authority as a wartime general and later president to enrich himself and his associates with vast acreage. "He would stop at nothing when he saw an opportunity to advance his financial interest or that of his friends. Land was the way to wealth on the frontier, and that drove Jackson's elaborate scheme to capture immense Indian lands south and north of the Tennessee River."[6] As president, Jackson pushed through legislation that moved southeastern Native American tribes across the Mississippi River and seized their vast lands, much of which fell into the hands of speculators, including Jackson himself. Jackson also realized that land wealth led not only to social status but political opportunities too.

So did David Crockett. He understood that land was the key to all his ambitions—the way to build wealth, achieve social status, and win public office; the way to "take a rise" in the world, as he put it. In the early nineteenth century land was all, and Crockett chased it across hundreds of miles and seven Tennessee counties. At his most successful, he owned hundreds of acres, won a seat in the state legislature, and was on course to win one in Congress. He was a militia colonel and an entrepreneur who turned his land into business ventures—and he would lose it all. In November 1835, he decided to carry his pursuit of land into Texas. But to fully understand that journey it is first necessary to revisit Crockett's years of land pursuit in Tennessee.

Author's Note: This book draws heavily on historical correspondence and news accounts written by and about David Crockett in the 1830s. The direct quotes cited in the book appear exactly as Crockett and his peers wrote them, including their original punctuation (or lack thereof), misspellings, and all.

CHAPTER 1
Tennessee

Born into poverty on August 17, 1786, David Crockett struggled throughout his economic and professional life. Lacking formal education, he scratched out a living by hunting and hiring out as a laborer, sometimes to pay off his father's debts and later in exchange for a rudimentary education that at least taught him to read and write.

After marrying Mary "Polly" Finley in 1806, the twenty-year-old Crockett rented land at Finley's Gap in Jefferson County, Tennessee, where his sons John Wesley and William were born in 1807 and 1809, respectively. Crockett soon realized there was little future in working rented land. Prosperity was found in *owning* land. He scraped together what money he could to buy five acres in Lincoln County on Mulberry Creek and moved his family there in the fall of 1811. Crockett leased another fifteen acres in April 1812. It was the start of Crockett's lifetime pursuit of land. Within months he planned to move his family to Franklin County, but Polly was pregnant again, and they remained in Lincoln County until after their daughter, Margaret, called "Little Polly," was born on November 22, 1812. Early in 1813 they made the move to Franklin County, setting up a homestead on Beans Creek, about ten miles south of Winchester, the Franklin County seat, and a few miles north of the Alabama border. Legend has it that Crockett dubbed the new home "Kentuck" for reasons that are vague at best. The place may have been called "Kentuck" before Crockett lived there, and he may have referred to it by that name.[1]

The family had not been settled long before an Indian uprising upended their world. By mid-1813, a faction of the Creek nation called the Red Sticks broke with tribal leaders and embarked on a war against white settlers and other Creeks who opposed them. Shortly after fighting broke out, the Red Sticks attacked Fort Mims, north of Mobile, Alabama, on August 30, killing some three hundred people in the fort, some white and some of mixed blood, including women and children. Outrage over the attack's brutality led to militias being called out to crush the Red Sticks, since most federal troops were busy fighting the British and other tribes. When the call went out for volunteers, Crockett was among the first to step forward, much to his young wife's dismay.

Polly's tears and entreaties to her husband to remain at home were understandable. She was a young wife and mother of three small children living in a strange place without a friend or relative in the neighborhood. In going off to war Crockett left her to fend for herself with few resources. He doubtless felt obligated to join other men in the region to defeat a dangerous foe that might threaten his family with far worse than Polly would face living on her own for a few months. His neighbors were going, including James Patton, who also left his wife, Elizabeth, and their two children behind. Staying safely home while others did the fighting did not go down well with Crockett and off to the front he went. Polly resigned herself to remaining at home, apprehensively waiting for his return, never certain that she would ever see her husband again. Oral history tells of a friendly Cherokee named Lightfoot living nearby who shared his food with Polly and her children when they had little to eat.[2]

Crockett began his ninety-day enlistment as a volunteer on September 24, 1813, and served under Gen. Andrew Jackson, a man who would become a major figure in Crockett's career, and not for the best. He soon saw war's cruel realities and, in addition to undertaking risky scouting missions and often hunting to feed his hungry comrades, faced a tenacious foe. In his autobiography, Crockett describes a particularly grizzly encounter at Tallusahatchee, a Creek town full of Red Stick warriors. When the Creeks realized the town was surrounded and they had no chance against the soldiers, many of them surrendered. But some forty-six warriors took refuge in a house and chose to fight from there. When a Creek woman seated in the doorway fired an arrow that killed a soldier, the troops became incensed and, according to Crockett, shot the woman multiple times. Then, he later wrote, "We shot them like dogs; and then set the house on fire, and burned it up with the forty-six warriors in it. I recollect seeing a boy who was shot down near the house. His arm and thigh was broken, and he was so near the burning house that the grease was stewing out of him." Crockett later took part in Jackson's November attack on Fort Talladega, where "Old Hickory" trapped the Red Sticks between two lines of fire. Crockett later wrote that after a "considerable number" of Red Sticks were killed they "broke like a gang of steers, and ran across to our other line, where they were again fired on; and so we kept them running from one line to the other, constantly under a heavy fire, until we had killed upwards of four hundred of them." The Red Sticks actually lost three hundred dead. Although hundreds more of them escaped, some later died of wounds suffered in the battle. Jackson's force lost fifteen men, and another eighty-five were wounded, one of them James Patton, Crockett's Franklin County neighbor, was badly injured in the battle and died two weeks later, leaving a widow and two children.[3]

Although he had volunteered for ninety days, Crockett later concocted a yarn in his autobiography that claimed he had only signed up for sixty days and, when that time was up, took part in a mutiny so that he and other men could return home. Although a mutiny did take place, Jackson put it down and Crockett took no part in it. He was among the men who were given a furlough in November to return home for fresh horses and warmer clothing. By the time he returned, very little of Crockett's ninety-day enlistment remained, and he was discharged on Christmas Eve. He was paid $65.59 for his service, including expenses.

In his book, *A Narrative of the Life of David Crockett of the State of Tennessee*, Crockett padded out his account by claiming he took part in other action that occurred after his discharge, no doubt to exaggerate his military experience when he wrote the book in 1834 during the runup to his 1835 congressional campaign. Politicians then, as now, understood that military experience impressed the hoi polloi. But he missed the final victory over the Creeks in March 1814 at Horseshoe Bend, where Jackson crushed their resistance and followed up with a negotiated settlement in the Treaty of Fort Jackson. Signed in August, the agreement cost the Creeks twenty-two million acres, more than half of all Creek lands and equal to about three-fifths of present-day Alabama and a fifth of Georgia. Much of that land belonged to Creeks who fought on Jackson's side, but that made no difference to Old Hickory, who claimed that whites and natives could never live peacefully together and the sooner the Indians were removed the better for everyone. Nor did it escape him that all that former Indian land would be opened to speculators, including Jackson himself.[4]

Crockett returned home and remained there for nine months before reenlisting in pursuit of more military adventures and, perhaps, a bit of glory. Little is known about his months at home, but the twenty-eight-year-old Crockett, a husband and father, seems to have found little that appealed to him in the life of a family farmer. He always seemed happier when out hunting, often for extended periods, than following a plow. Although the Creek War was over, the War of 1812 was still ongoing. It must have beckoned to Crockett with the promise of something more exciting than reaping crops, and he enlisted for another six months. Polly again begged him to stay but her pleas again fell on deaf ears, and she was once more left to fend for herself and her children. Polly spent those months wondering where her husband was, whether he was alive or dead, or whether he might return to her badly wounded and disabled. None of this seemed to weigh on Crockett. He made only passing reference to it in his autobiography, and he gave no justification for his decision to reenlist and leave his family behind. Unlike the Creek uprising a year earlier, the current war offered no imminent threat to the frontier or his family, yet he felt compelled to enter the fray saying only, "I wanted a small taste of British fighting, and I supposed they would be there." There is no record of how Polly survived or if Lightfoot the Cherokee or someone equally generous provided her any help. All that Crockett tells us in his *Narrative* is: "Here again the entreaties of my wife were thrown in the way of my going, but all in vain; for I always had a way of just going ahead, at whatever I had a mind to."[5]

Crockett's seeming callousness in taking this step for no greater reason than seeking new adventure is disturbing. Although he remained an active member of the militia and rose to the rank of colonel, most of his energy in the years that followed were devoted to seeking public office, engaging in business ventures, and acquiring as much land as he could. These endeavors seemed not to factor into Crockett's inexplicable decision to go to war once more. However, Crockett, now a 3rd sergeant, missed the main action, notably Jackson's successful defense of New Orleans in January 1815. Crockett's company was also too late to join Jackson's attack on Pensacola, Florida, and his victory there over British, Spanish, and some still-hostile Creeks who refused to accept the terms of the Treaty of Fort Jackson. The recalcitrant Creeks had been sheltered, armed, and trained by the Spanish and British. But after the Europeans fled, the Creeks scattered into the swamps and countryside. Crockett, who had only gotten a glimpse of the departing British ships, was part of a force sent to flush the Creeks out and end their resistance for good. While Jackson moved on to New Orleans and glory, Crockett and his comrades plodded endlessly through the swamps and countryside in search of Indians who always managed to vanish ahead of time. Crockett's unit spent most of this tour trying to fend off starvation, marching to the point of exhaustion, and never facing a hostile force. Fed up with the business, he returned home in February 1815, and when the call came again to resume the pursuit of elusive Indians, he paid another man to serve out the final month of his enlistment.

Crockett expressed joy at being free of war and his dislike of the endeavor, writing in his *Narrative*, "This closed my career as a warrior, and I am glad of it, for I like life now a heap better than I did then; and I am glad all over that I lived to see these times, which I should not have done if I had kept fooling along in war, and got used up at it." It would be a long time before Crockett reconsidered his distaste for war.[6]

Returning to Beans Creek, Crockett found Polly seriously ill; she soon succumbed. Neither the date nor exact circumstances of her death have survived, but there is little doubt that she suffered during Crockett's long absence, possibly with a prolonged illness, and lacked effective care while being burdened with the upkeep of a farm and the care of their children. Crockett may have blurred the circumstances of her death in his autobiography, and he says only that his wife died after his return from the war. However, Crockett may have cut short his enlistment because he learned of his wife's illness and hurried home to be with her. Indeed, Polly may have died before Crockett arrived home. It is only certain that she died within a very short time of the end of Crockett's enlistment. He tells us little about Polly's death except how badly it impacted him and how it left him to care for his farm and children. It was a task for which he was distinctly unsuited but one that Polly had been forced to undertake during his months at war. A brother and sister-in-law moved in for a time and helped relieve the burden, but the arrangement proved untenable and Crockett soon found himself searching for a new wife.[7]

The 250-acre farm adjacent to Crockett's "Kentuck" tract, lying on the Rattlesnake Spring Branch, was owned by James and Elizabeth Patton and had been gifted to James by his father. James was killed in the Fort Talladega battle that Crockett survived. It is no surprise that Crockett, a twenty-nine-year-old widower with three children, and the twenty-seven-year-old widow Patton with two youngsters of her own found a solution to their difficulties in marriage. They wed in 1815 and Crockett moved onto her "snug little farm." In addition to her property, Elizabeth brought some $800 ($15,391 in 2022 dollars) to the marriage, both highly welcome to the ambitious Crockett, who used his new wife's wealth to fuel those ambitions. In addition to the five children from their previous marriages, David and Elizabeth would become parents of three offspring of their own in the first six years of their marriage.[8]

Crockett proved himself a capable military leader during the war, and in May 1815 he was elected lieutenant in the state's 32nd Regiment of the Militia. Crockett planned to seek political office and knew military status would help him. But first new land beckoned, and Crockett was eager to explore it.[9]

In the fall of 1815, Crockett set off to explore Alabama land formerly held by the Creeks, but he was brought down by malaria during the journey and nearly died. Indeed, a passerby stopped at the Crockett cabin to tell Elizabeth that David was dead. But Crockett eventually made it home—much to his family's relief—and he put off further exploration until the following year. By the fall of 1816 he was ready to set forth again and set out to explore the Shoal Creek area, which was part of land ceded by the Chickasaw in September 1816, located in what would soon become Lawrence County, Tennessee. Here, he again fell ill, but he found a site to his liking on the Beeler Fork of Shoal Creek. He and some friends built a cabin and cleared some land before Crockett moved his family there. By the following January he and Elizabeth had leased her thirty-eight-acre farm to James Penn for two years at $2.50 per acre, or ninety-five dollars per year. Crockett reduced the first year's rent to seventy-six dollars in exchange for Penn paying half the rent in advance in cash, a good deal for the Crocketts as public land was selling for a minimum of $1.25 per acre.[10]

It didn't take Crockett long to begin accumulating land in Lawrence County, starting with 160 acres on the Beeler Fork site on Shoal Creek where he had built his cabin, likely paid for with some of Elizabeth's money. At the same time, Crockett gained prominence as a political figure and leader. Concerned with lawlessness in the area and a lack of any government to control it, Crockett and a few other residents formed the Shoal Creek Corporation, which functioned as an ad hoc government, and Crockett was designated one of its commissioners. The corporation successfully petitioned the government to create a new county where they resided, and the Tennessee legislature obliged, creating Lawrence County in October 1817.[11]

A month later the legislature named Crockett one of twelve justices of the peace, and he was soon appointed a court referee as well. The following March he was commissioned lieutenant colonel in the 57th Tennessee Militia of Lawrence County, and his men elected him to serve as their lieutenant-commandant. He commanded the regiment and was responsible for holding a regimental muster each year. The title of colonel was not merely a ceremonial honor but a real title that Crockett kept for the rest of his life. Around the same time, he was appointed a Lawrenceburg town commissioner and was also called upon to serve other legal functions. His star was clearly ascending and so were his land holdings. Early in 1819 he bought a small plot on the Military Road, near what became the center of town, where he built a cabin that served as his office.[12]

The importance of land ownership was brought home to Crockett when he decided to run for a seat in the Tennessee legislature. State law required that prospective candidates own at least two hundred acres of land to qualify for election. As Crockett searched for a new home site, he aimed to accumulate enough additional land to make up the required two hundred acres. Still more land was needed for a business venture he planned that would include a gristmill, powder mill, and distillery. There were other potentially lucrative lands with iron deposits, and still more land might be leased or developed. In 1820 Crockett purchased a warrant for 454 acres from Ralph Graves and made twelve separate entries for tracts of various sizes, bringing Crockett's total land holdings to 614 acres. He doubtless saw this as a good start in his quest to become a large landowner, agent, and speculator, while his land holdings also served to support his political ambitions.[13]

The new home was completed in the spring of 1820 on forty acres located on the Crowson Fork of Shoal Creek. The family moved in around June, renting out their home on Beeler Fork to Reuben Tripp and Thomas Pryor. Crockett chose a thirty-acre plot on Simonton Fork of Shoal Creek for his mill-distillery complex. He borrowed heavily to come up with some $3,000 ($78,657 in 2022 dollars) to fund the enterprise, a major investment for him and a heavy debt, but he hoped to retire the debt once the complex began paying off.[14]

Crockett did not lose a step in his pursuit of political office. Although he resigned his commission in the militia and resigned as a justice of the peace in November 1819, by the end of the month the legislature again appointed him a town commissioner, one of five men chosen to select a suitable place for a permanent seat of justice for Lawrence County.

They were to procure fifty acres on which to locate the town, which was to be called Lawrenceburgh (later Lawrenceburg) after Capt. James Lawrence, commander of the US frigate *Chesapeake*. Lawrence had famously uttered "Don't give up the ship!" with his dying breath after being fatally injured in a battle during the War of 1812.[15]

Work on the mill complex moved slower than Crockett anticipated, and he wasn't earning as much from it as he expected, but he was still anxious to acquire more land. He had contracted for sixty acres of land from John C. McLemore, a major landowner, and in October of 1820 sought another 320 acres from him. Crockett expected to pay McLemore by the first of November but later told him he needed more time as his "powder factory have not been pushed as it ought" and he was having difficulty settling an older claim. Still, he urged McLemore to send him a warrant for three hundred acres and promised to pay him by the following spring with interest payments until then. Crockett asked McLemore to respond immediately as he had two occupant claims that he could apply to the warrant, otherwise he could lose those claims to someone else who held a warrant. It appears Crockett never secured the warrant or the land as the records show he never owned more than the 614 acres he already had in Lawrence County. When Crockett later liquidated his Lawrence County lands, he still owned only those 614 acres. Nevertheless, Crockett's efforts emphasize his interest in building wealth through land ownership, just as he knew McLemore had done.[16]

On New Year's Day 1821, Crockett launched his campaign for a seat in the lower house of the Tennessee General Assembly seeking to represent Lawrence and Hickman counties. Before beginning his campaign, he spent three months driving a herd of horses to Elizabeth's father, Robert Patton, in Swannanoa, North Carolina. Along the way he stopped in Morristown, Tennessee, to pay an old debt to the widow of a man from whom he had borrowed one dollar fifteen years earlier. Although the surprised woman had long forgotten the debt, Crockett had not.[17]

Despite his success in public life, Crockett chose to campaign in a way that would suggest he was ignorant of government process, was unprepared to speak in public, and was as simple and plain as most of his constituents. But he was pretending. It is likely that voters were aware of Crockett's experience, may have seen him presiding in court, or served under him in the militia. But they still enjoyed his stump speeches, which were laced with jokes, hunting stories, and jibes at his opponents. His campaign style worked, and in August 1821 he won election to the first of two consecutive terms in the legislature. It was a major step in Crockett's political career, which complemented his steady accumulation of land and budding business endeavors. As he later put it in his autobiography, "I just now began to take a rise. . . ."[18]

Crockett arrived in Murfreesboro, then Tennessee's capital, in time for the opening session of the legislature on September 17, 1821, and soon began a lifelong advocacy for the poor and landless, particularly squatters in West Tennessee, by voting for a bill to regulate the surveying of the area. He voted for a constitutional convention but agreed to a postponement until an expected special session; voted against a bill to suppress "the vice of gaming," which he enjoyed and did not regard as a vice; and against several applications for divorce, a practice he staunchly opposed.[19]

But only twelve days into the session he received the horrifying news that his mills and dam had been swept away in a flash flood, requiring that he shut down his distillery as well. In his autobiography, Crockett conveyed the severity of this tragedy, which literally washed away all of the economic advances he had made in Lawrence County. He accurately noted that the misfortune "made a great change in my circumstances, and kept me back very much in the world." He had invested "upwards of three thousand dollars, more than I was worth in the world" in the venture and said the disaster "just made a complete mash of me." He was not exaggerating. All that remained to him were "some likely negroes, and a good stock of almost every thing about me. . . ."

The mill tragedy plunged Crockett into hopeless debt. He had borrowed heavily to pay for its construction and now found himself with no income from the venture and many creditors to pay off. The bitterest pill would come with the realization that he would have to sell all the Lawrence County land he had accumulated to pay his debts. The lawsuits against him began in October, less than a month after the disaster, when he was ordered to pay three creditors a total of $184.73. A fourth creditor was awarded $71.40 the following January and a fifth granted $72.13 in April (totaling $8,606.69 in 2022 dollars).[20]

Then, one by one, each of the tracts of land he owned fell under the sheriff's auction hammer, beginning with the 160 acres on Beeler Fork, which was sold to pay off three creditors to the tune of $264.32, bringing the total cash judgments against him to $593.08 ($15,550 in 2022 dollars). Crockett couldn't bear to witness the loss himself and granted power of attorney to Mansil Crisp, one of his creditors and a fellow justice of the peace, who oversaw the liquidation of his lands. This spared Crockett the spectacle of watching the 454 acres he had purchased earlier that year conveyed to more of his creditors: fifty acres to James Welch, another fifty to Bradley Halford, eighty to Enoch Tucker, ninety more to William Tucker—and so it went until all of it was gone. The land included Crockett's home on Crowson Fork, the site where his doomed mill had stood on Simonton Fork, Crockett's office at 43 Military Road, and other plots he had invested in, some containing iron ore deposits.[21]

Little remained beyond the rent he and Elizabeth continued to collect on that "snug little farm" back in Franklin County. And, of course, Elizabeth had faithfully tended the farm and children in Crockett's frequent absences, operated the mill, and most significantly, provided her husband badly needed support and encouragement. Unlike his seeming insensitivity to Polly, Crockett showed genuine appreciation for the strength he drew from Elizabeth. In his *Narrative*, he mentions what little remained to him at this low moment, but adds, "Best of all, I had an honest wife. She didn't advise me, as is too fashionable, to smuggle up this, and that, and t'other, to go on at home; but she told me, says she, 'Just pay up, as long as you have a bit's worth in the world; and then every body will be satisfied, and we will scuffle for more.' This is just such talk as I wanted to hear, for a man's wife can hold him devilish uneasy, if she begins to scold, and fret, and perplex him, at a time when he has a full load for a rail-road car on his mind already." [22]

Elizabeth's support was of crucial importance to Crockett, and not only at this low point. In addition to the money and land she brought to their marriage, Elizabeth also provided motivation and guidance that spurred him toward higher goals he might not have otherwise contemplated. It was only after their marriage that Crockett began to pursue land and public office in earnest. Even when they lost nearly everything, she maintained her resolve and bolstered Crockett's spirits, helping him find the will to start over. Crockett clearly had powerful ambitions of his own and a drive to succeed and advance socially and economically, but Elizabeth deserves more credit than she has been given for facilitating his ambition with genuine affection and support. By most accounts theirs was a marriage of convenience—a widow and widower with children to raise—but it clearly grew into something deeper with the years. Indeed, they would "scuffle for more" in West Tennessee.

Even before his debts were settled, Crockett was planning his next move, which would take him and his family into the Obion River country in West Tennessee. Despite his economic setback, in October 1821 he purchased eight hundred acres on the Obion River from his father-in-law, Robert Patton, for $1,600 ($42,000 in 2022 dollars). The acreage was part of a one thousand-acre tract owned by Patton in Carroll County, land that would become part of the new Gibson County in October 1823. Patton deeded the remaining two hundred acres to his daughter Ann Cathey McWhorter, Elizabeth's sister and wife of Hance McWhorter. Surveying was an inexact science, if not a dodgy practice at the time, and the survey of Patton's one thousand acres inadvertently added two hundred more acres adjoining McWhorter's two hundred acres, which they claimed as part of their property, giving them questionable title to four hundred acres in all. It was on this disputed piece of land that Crockett chose to live, rather than on the eight hundred acres he had paid for, perhaps anticipating that it, too, might be claimed by his creditors, leaving him little incentive to build on it. Instead, he moved his family to a cabin on the disputed two hundred-acre site claimed by the McWhorters. Within months, Crockett sold his own eight hundred acres to John C. McLemore and James Vaulse (or Vaulx) for $1,600, exactly what he paid for it. He may have needed the ready cash or had yet more debts to pay off. In any case, it left him without profit or land title. He was, in fact, squatting on McWhorter's disputed tract.[23]

After the legislature adjourned on November 17, Crockett set out to explore the Obion tract, traveling west with his oldest son, John Wesley, and a hired man named Abram Henry. The land was still wild and largely unsettled and Crockett found a pleasing location for a new home. His nearest neighbors were seven miles away, the next fifteen, the one after that twenty. Crockett never owned this land and remained a squatter on it for the next six years. He and his companions erected a cabin, cleared a field, and planted some corn before he trod the 150 miles back to Lawrence County early in the spring of 1822, just in time to face the grueling settlement of his debts.[24]

Crockett arrived home to attend a special session of the legislature in April 1822, during which he introduced a bill "for the relief of Mathias, a free man of color" and similar bills. He unsuccessfully opposed extending the time for filing and adjudicating North Carolina land warrants, an ongoing battle that he continued fighting for years.[25]

The legislature adjourned on August 24, 1822, and soon after Crockett packed his family and what little they had left and moved to the Obion, continuing his pattern of exploring new land to the west before moving his family there. By October he was settled and out hunting. That winter he fell through some ice while crossing a river and nearly froze to death while on a journey to retrieve powder from a brother-in-law who lived nearby. Heavy storms and snow caused rivers to flood and widen, making them difficult and dangerous to cross. Crockett later said that four inches of snow covered the ground when he started, and that the river looked like an ocean. Elizabeth had vehemently opposed his embarking on this risky errand but, like Polly before her, found her entreaties ignored. Crockett went anyway.[26]

*　*　*　*　*

Crockett wasted no time making a new start and soon after arriving at his new home he won a seat in the legislature from his new district and thus did not miss a session. His opponent, William E. Butler, was married to Andrew Jackson's niece, marking the start of what would become a habit of pitting himself against Old Hickory. The legislature convened on September 15, 1823, and Crockett now represented five counties, compared to the two he had represented in Middle Tennessee.

He again opposed Jackson when the general was put up as a candidate for the US Senate and Crockett supported the incumbent, Col. John Williams, a longtime foe of Jackson. Although he didn't really want the office, Jackson narrowly won by a vote of 35–25. The Tennessee political faction headed by John Overton had nominated Jackson as a first step toward running Old Hickory for president, believing the general needed a higher political profile. Crockett was already allied with Overton's adversary, Andrew Erwin, one of Jackson's most bitter opponents, and Crockett's association with him placed him on Jackson's enemies list.[27]

Crockett also opposed Felix Grundy's move to sell the remainder of the Hiawassee District for up to $1.50 per acre and for cash only. Crockett knew his poor constituents did not have that kind of cash and relied on credit, which he advocated for rather than legislating for "ready money men." His stand placed him in opposition to James K. Polk, who represented a district near Crockett's and who was later a leading Jackson supporter. The issue may have seemed minor at the time, but it marked the beginning of Crockett's opposition to the Jackson forces in Tennessee and a career-long effort to protect the interests of the poor, especially when it came to land ownership. Overton was instrumental in negotiating a settlement with North Carolina regarding the cession of lands in the Western District of Tennessee and agreed to recognize warrants issued by North Carolina to its Revolutionary War veterans redeemable for land in the Western District. Tennessee was required to honor these warrants under the terms that ceded North Carolina land to the federal government that became part of Tennessee. By 1818, however, that land was exhausted, and Congress opened the western portion of the state to continue satisfying the warrants, even though that land had been acquired from the Chickasaw, not from North Carolina. Crockett moved to cut off the application of these land warrants, but his motion failed.

The use of these warrants was rife with fraud and corruption, and they were more typically found in the hands of speculators than war veterans. Crockett, Polk, and others advocated unsuccessfully for a cut-off date to end the use of these warrants, while Overton and others saw the warrants as a lucrative opportunity for land speculation. For the next dozen years Crockett would fight a losing and increasingly desperate battle to secure land reform for poor settlers in West Tennessee. He took the fight from the legislature to Congress, where he served three terms that were almost entirely consumed by this issue. The fate of Crockett's career hung on the issue of land reform, often tenuously.

Crockett also voted to remove poll taxes, which he saw as a cynical tool to prevent the poor from voting. He voted against using prisoners as free labor for river navigation projects in West Tennessee because he recognized that many prisoners were simply debtors. He also proposed releasing them from imprisonment. Each of these votes established a pattern that Crockett adhered to throughout his career, particularly his advocacy for the poor, and increasingly placed him at odds with Jacksonian forces that worked to defeat him and frustrate his legislative initiatives.[28]

When the legislature adjourned on November 29, 1823, Crockett returned home and resumed engaging in land deals. He and several others signed a lease for a tract of land on the Obion River, which may have been intended as a hunting preserve. He was still borrowing money to fund his land speculations and accumulating debt.

Governor Carroll convened the second session of the legislature on September 20, 1824. It would be Crockett's last. He continued battling the North Carolina land warrants and shady practices surrounding them without success. The House adjourned October 22, 1824, and Crockett, seeing little possibility of changing the legislature's mind on land reform, decided to take his case to Washington by running for Congress in 1825. Lacking sufficient funds and political connections, he lost to incumbent Adam Alexander, who benefitted from the high price of cotton at the time. Crockett returned to his farm and civic duties while pondering his political future. Toward the end of the year, he embarked on a long bear hunt, something he relished and which helped clear his mind. Crockett's fondness for hunting, particularly his pursuit of bears, is evident throughout his autobiography. He boasts of having killed 105 bears in one winter alone and notes that the meat was shared with his neighbors.[29]

By January 1826, Crockett resumed his land hunt, buying occupancy rights to a two hundred-acre tract from James Atkinson for eighty dollars. Atkinson's father-in-law, Yarnell Reese, had given the claim to Atkinson, who sold it to Crockett, who attempted to establish his claim by spending the better part of a day on it under a makeshift lean-to with some of his furniture, thus establishing legal "occupancy." Crockett sold the grant rights to Edwin Warren on October 10, 1826, for $205, but he retained title to the land itself and was found delinquent in paying taxes on it in 1828 and 1829. By 1830 that delinquency had been transferred to Reese, who apparently paid the taxes to restore his own claim to the land, but the case wound up in court where it dragged on for years. In May 1835, Crockett lost the case and was ordered to pay Reese's court costs. The court found that Atkinson never had legal right to sell the land to Crockett in the first place and reverted ownership to Reese. Such was the fast and loose nature of land dealing in Tennessee.[30]

Business enterprises still occupied the Colonel's mind, and in September 1825 he laid plans for a venture to transport barrel staves down the Mississippi River to New Orleans. He arranged construction of two boats for the job and the cutting of thirty thousand staves. By January 1826 they were ready to ship. Crockett, who had no boating experience, hired a crew that wasn't much better at it. The crew quickly lost control of the boats when they entered the Mississippi's swift current, and they drifted rapidly downstream through the night. The men decided to lash the boats together, which only exacerbated the problem and they eventually crashed into some sunken logs and driftwood. The boats took on water and Crockett, who was below deck at the time, barely escaped when he was pulled out through a small window, most of his clothing stripped off in the process along with a bit of his flesh. The boats and staves, and Crockett's entire investment, were lost. The hapless mariners found themselves soaked in Memphis, where Marcus B. Winchester, the city's postmaster, took pity on them and provided them fresh clothing and some pocket money. He also took an interest in Crockett and, after chatting with him, encouraged him to try again for the Ninth Congressional District seat in 1827, even offering to anonymously fund Crockett's campaign. That was all the encouragement Crockett needed and he soon laid plans for another run for Congress.[31]

The barrel stave disaster brought Crockett more debt and financial woes. George W. Gibbs was trying to eject Crockett from leased property that April but withdrew his action, even paying Crockett's court costs, after learning of his economic hardship. Nonetheless, there was a silver lining in Winchester's offer to back Crockett politically, and he would remain one of the Colonel's strongest supporters. Even as late as 1831, when Overton pressured Winchester to stop supporting Crockett, Winchester remained loyal to him. With his help and Crockett's effective campaigning, the Colonel won a seat in Congress in 1827 and easily won reelection in 1829, both victories coming over Adam R. Alexander.[32]

Following his 1827 victory, Crockett brought his wife, Elizabeth, and his eldest son, John Wesley, with him on his journey to Washington, DC, where Congress was to convene on December 7. On their way to Swannanoa, North Carolina, to visit Elizabeth's family, Crockett fell seriously ill, likely a recurrence of the malaria he first contracted years earlier and which had troubled him ever since. He spent four weeks recuperating before he was finally able to continue to Washington. Elizabeth and John Wesley returned to Tennessee, bringing with them three slaves given to them by Elizabeth's father, Robert Patton.[33]

While recovering in Swannanoa, Crockett witnessed a duel between his friend and fellow congressman Samuel P. Carson and Robert B. Vance. Carson had defeated the incumbent Vance in the 1825 congressional election and defeated him again in 1827. During the latter campaign, Vance accused Carson's father of supporting Britain during the Revolutionary War, which led to a duel between the two rivals that took place on November 6, 1827. Crockett was close enough to the scene and had recovered sufficiently from his illness to witness the duel, in which Vance suffered a fatal wound. According to family history, Crockett was the first to bring the news of Carson's victory to the Carson family. The Carsons and Burgins were close to the Patton family in North Carolina. Captain Alney Burgin delivered Sam Carson's challenge to Vance, and Crockett's brother-in-law, Abner Burgin, who later accompanied Crockett to Texas, was married to Elizabeth's sister, Margaret. Like Crockett, Carson was on his way to Washington to serve in the twentieth Congress, which was Carson's second consecutive term. They served together in Congress for years and both travelled to Texas after their congressional careers ended. Carson would play a key role in Crockett's decision to explore Red River land in Texas.[34]

Although Crockett was never a committed Jackson supporter or aligned with Tennessee's Overton faction, he campaigned as a Jackson man in 1827. Old Hickory was far too popular, especially in Tennessee, for a newcomer like Crockett to oppose him. Nonetheless, Crockett soon broke with the solidly pro-Jackson Tennessee congressional delegation led by James K. Polk and was thereafter seen as unreliable by the Jacksonians. He narrowly lost his congressional seat to William Fitzgerald in a bitter and hard-fought campaign in 1831, during which personal attacks and hard feelings overshadowed Crockett's usually affable electioneering style. The Jacksonians also pounced on Crockett's 1830 vote against Jackson's Indian Removal Bill, which most of his constituents supported. Nonetheless, Crockett bounced back in 1833, returning to his more agreeable campaign stump speeches and narrowly defeated Fitzgerald by a mere 173 votes. Jacksonians tried to ensure that Crockett would never win election again by gerrymandering his district to include Madison County, which Crockett lost in 1831, while removing areas where the Colonel was popular. He knew the move was designed to "make a mash of me" and he would struggle to hold onto his congressional seat. Crockett also was aided by reduced support for Jackson in Tennessee and the growing popularity of Henry Clay, Jackson's leading foe. Many Tennessee residents disapproved of Jackson's endorsement of his vice president, New Yorker Martin Van Buren, as his successor in the White House. The Tennesseans, led by Congressman John Bell, preferred one of their own, and Crockett joined them in endorsing Judge Hugh Lawson White for president in the coming 1836 election. Jackson's hatred of Crockett was visceral as was Crockett's displeasure with Jackson and outright hatred of Van Buren. Crockett had lately focused on Jackson's refusal to recharter the Second Bank of the United States, and he took every opportunity he could to lambast the president for removing federal deposits from the bank. Old Hickory told his ally James K. Polk that "Mr. Bell, Davy Crockett & Co. had placed judge White in the odious attitude of abandoning principle & party for office.... Political demagogues, hypocrites, and apostates, may delude the people for a short time, but the moment the deception, and abandonment of principle, is discovered, the people will hurl them from their confidence, and the recoil is overwhelming. Just so with Mr. Bell, Davy Crockett and Co." Jackson intended to do whatever it took to end Crockett's career.[35]

Politics did not prevent Crockett from continuing his land ventures. On June 12, 1826, he and William James purchased two hundred acres in Weakley County on the South Fork of the Obion River. James initially owned only seventy-five acres of the tract, but Crockett soon bought out his interest and gained title to all two hundred acres. Crockett sold the land to Henry Flowers for $500 cash on October 25, 1830, only a year after securing his grant. However, this same tract somehow came back into Crockett's possession, although there is no record of how that happened, and he sold it a second time to Enoch Tucker, a Weakley County neighbor, for $505 on October 22, 1835—ten days before leaving for Texas.[36]

Only weeks after he and James purchased those two hundred acres, Crockett entered another claim for twenty-five acres from William R. Davie located on the South Fork of the Obion River in Weakley County. The Colonel purchased a North Carolina land warrant from Davie, entered his claim on June 30, 1826, and secured a grant for the acreage on October 12, 1829. As usual, real life outpaced Tennessee's land bureaucracy and Crockett likely rented this land out for two years before finally moving onto it with his family in 1828, when McWhorter moved onto the two hundred-acre section where Crockett had been living as a squatter since 1822.[37]

Throughout his years in Congress, he sought land and new business opportunities. But, despite all of his efforts, Crockett's financial balance sheet remained in the red. After his 1831 loss to Fitzgerald, Crockett was hard-pressed to pay his campaign debts and was soon delinquent in payment of property taxes. To get his hands on some ready cash he sold his twenty-five-acre homestead to his stepson, George Patton, for one hundred dollars, along with a ten-year-old slave girl named Adeline for another $300. Crockett never owned more than a few slaves, but he did not oppose the "peculiar institution."

Desperate for a place to live, Crockett wrote to Calvin Jones in August 1831 asking to lease twenty acres of Jones's land and cited his need to sell his home to pay campaign debts. Jones offered him a six-year lease, but Crockett does not appear to have executed it. Instead, he scraped up eighty dollars to buy an occupant claim for two hundred acres from Joel Henry Dyer on November 7, 1831, which was located south of the twenty-five-acre plot Crockett had sold to George Patton. It was his last home in Tennessee and there he built a house where he and his family lived until Crockett left for Texas in November 1835. In September 1833, he and Elizabeth sold their 250-acre Franklin County property, the "snug little farm" she owned prior to their marriage, for $1,225 ($43,207 in 2022 dollars).[38]

Crockett's chronic financial woes were always worse when he lost an election and his congressional pay. Members of Congress earned eight dollars per day and his total salary during his three terms was $6,696, equal to nearly $230,682 in 2022 dollars. A good bit of that salary was likely eaten up by his cost of living in Washington, but some vanished at the city's gambling tables where Crockett spent many an evening, sometimes losing heavily.[39]

Although Crockett spent considerable time at the gambling tables, he was serious about his work in the House and labored to level the economic and social playing field, which he saw as a stacked deck that gave unfair advantage to the nation's wealthiest and thus most influential citizens. On February 25, 1830, he introduced a resolution to abolish the US Military Academy at West Point, claiming that the institution favored the wealthy and their sons and was not accessible to the poor, although their taxes helped pay for it. His resolution may have been partly motivated by his experience in the Creek War when he felt that volunteers were scorned by professional officers. He claimed ordinary soldiers did most of the fighting, not West Point graduates. He believed that those officers were guilty of class prejudice and that they judged Crockett not by his deeds but by his class. He saw the academy as an example of the wealthy gaining advantage at the expense of the poor. Although some of Crockett's claims were mistaken, and West Point did not serve the sons of the rich exclusively, many shared his opinion. The Tennessee legislature even considered directing its representatives in Washington to oppose further funding of the academy, and Crockett found support for his stand among his constituents. He also was supported in the press—the *Jackson Gazette* agreed that West Point was "a depot for favoritism."[40]

Crockett continued his efforts to secure land reform for squatters and poor farmers in West Tennessee. At first, he sought to work with the rest of the Tennessee delegation, but he abandoned that strategy when it became obvious that Polk and the other Tennesseans had no sympathy for squatters. They were determined to push the federal government into ceding the land directly to Tennessee, where the legislature could dispose of it as it saw fit and at any price. Crockett knew the legislature had no more interest in giving land to the poor than Polk did and would sell it at the highest possible price, putting it out of reach for most of Crockett's constituents. Polk claimed land sales would fund schools, but Crockett had good reason to doubt that much of the money would go to his district, and he received complaints from his constituents about a lack of school funding. Having staked his career on securing a land reform bill and seeing that his fellow Tennesseans had no intention of helping him, Crockett sought support from anti-Jackson congressmen, trading support for their legislation in exchange for pledges to back his bill. The tactic failed and, despite coming close at times, the bill was doomed. Crockett's courting of anti-Jackson forces alienated him from the entire Tennessee delegation, and he became a pariah who was politically isolated in his home state.[41]

Crockett's eroding political career did not slow the rise of a mythology that had been growing around him since he arrived in Washington. The press had created an outsized alter ego of Crockett, perhaps based on his outlandish campaign speeches, which were spiced with backwoods hyperbole and tall-tale imagery such as "Davy" describing himself as a "half-horse, half-alligator" wild man. Even before he arrived in Washington, newspapers reported that he had waded the Ohio River while towing a steamboat on his way to the capital. That was only the beginning; although such caricatures enhanced Crockett's popularity, they also provided fodder to his enemies who sought to cast him as a crude, ignorant bumpkin who was not to be taken seriously.[42]

Of course, Crockett's constituents knew the yarns he spun and the jokes he told were just an act intended to seal his bond with them—and everyone was in on the joke. It showed that he really was one of them, shared their dreams and frustrations, and could truly speak for them in Congress. But once the national press got hold of the image there was no controlling the extremes to which it might be taken. Crockett could control his image on the campaign trail but not in the national press or among the purveyors of popular culture. In the Jacksonian "age of the common man," the public was anxious for such fictional frontier figures and Crockett was tailor-made for the role.[43]

In April 1831, James K. Paulding's play *The Lion of the West* opened in New York starring James Hackett as Nimrod Wildfire, a frontier character clearly patterned on the "Davy" caricature. The play was an enormous success in the East and in Europe. Although Paulding took pains to deny he had intentionally lampooned Crockett, and the Colonel accepted his disclaimer, there was no mistaking Crockett's influence on Paulding. Crockett even attended a performance in Washington during which he and Hackett momentarily held up the play by bowing to one another, a gesture that brought down the house.[44]

James Strange French later anonymously published *The Life and Adventures of Colonel David Crockett of West Tennessee*, an 1833 biography based on French's own experiences visiting the Crockett cabin mixed with jokes and yarns attributed to Crockett and embellished with material lifted from Paulding's play. It was a runaway bestseller. Later editions were retitled *Sketches and Eccentricities of Col. David Crockett of West Tennessee*.

Excerpts appeared in newspapers throughout the United States, accelerating the speed with which Crockett's alter ego was outpacing him. The book was published in England in 1834, by which time Crockett was becoming nearly as well known in Great Britain as he was in America. *Sketches* captures the outsized "Davy" more accurately than the real Crockett, but also the tone of his campaign speeches. In one scene Crockett regales a stranger with this description of himself: "I'm that same David Crockett, fresh from the backwoods, half-horse, half-alligator, a little touched with the snapping-turtle; can wade the Mississippi, leap the Ohio, ride upon a streak of lightning, and slip without a scratch down a honey locust; can whip my weight in wild cats . . . hug a bear too close for comfort, and eat any man opposed to Jackson"—the final comment reflecting Crockett's early support of Old Hickory.[45]

Although French embellished *Sketches*, his 1833 visit to Crockett's Tennessee home enabled him to capture life at the Crockett cabin and offer a brief sketch of Crockett himself:

> It was in appearance rude and uninviting, situated in a small field of eight or ten acres, which had been cleared in the wild woods; no yard surrounded it, and it seemed to have been lately settled. In the passage of the house were seated two men in their shirt sleeves, cleaning rifles . . . and there walked out, in plain homespun attire, with a black fur cap on, a finely proportioned man, about six feet high, aged, from appearance, forty-five. His countenance was frank and manly, and a smile played over it as he approached me. He brought with him a rifle, and from his right shoulder hung a bag made of raccoon skin, to which, by means of a sheath, was appended a huge butcher's knife. . . .
>
> His free mode of conversation made me feel quite easy; and a few moments gave me leisure to look around. His cabin within was clean and neat, and bore about it many marks of comfort. The many trophies of wild animals spread over his house and yard—his dogs, in appearance war-worn veterans, lying about sunning themselves—all told truly that I was in the home of the celebrated hunter.
>
> His family were dressed by the work of their own hands, and there was a neatness and simplicity in their appearance very becoming. His wife was rather grave and quiet, but attentive, and kind to strangers; his daughters diffident and retiring, perhaps too much so, but uncommonly beautiful, and are fine specimens of the native worth of the female character; for, entirely uneducated, they are not only agreeable, but fascinating. There are no schools near them, yet they converse well—and if they did not one

would be apt to think so, for they are extremely pretty, and tender to a stranger, with so much kindness, the comforts of their little cabin.

The colonel has no slaves; his daughters tend to the dairy and kitchen, while he performs the more laborious duties of his farm.[46]

The Colonel was soon celebrated in song as well. Blackface performers in minstrel shows were popular acts at the time and several of them adapted new lyrics to old songs like "Zip Coon" and "Pompey Smash" to include references to Crockett. While in New York the Colonel saw a performance of "Zip Coon" by Thomas Rice, who added the Colonel's familiar motto, "Be sure you're right, then go ahead," as a coda to the song. He then bowed to Crockett, who bowed to Rice in return, just as he had to James Hackett.[47]

At first Crockett didn't know quite how to deal with his growing celebrity, but the publication of *Sketches* was a clear warning that "Davy" was getting out of control. Although the book was based partly on what Crockett told French, it was also laced with bogus stories and quotations attributed to the Colonel. While not entirely unflattering, it wasn't the image Crockett wanted to project and he feared it could be used by his enemies to paint him as uncouth and incompetent. Crockett was equally miffed at the income these purveyors of his image were gaining while they paid him nothing. He decided to address the issue by penning his own autobiography, *A Narrative of the Life of David Crockett of the State of Tennessee*, which was published in 1834 by Philadelphia-based Carey & Hart. Crockett received considerable help from his Washington roommate and fellow anti-Jackson congressman Thomas Chilton of Kentucky. The Colonel provided the facts, stories, and jokes, but Chilton edited the manuscript, and his work was substantial enough for Crockett to assign him half the book's royalties. Crockett said he would "accomplish two objects" in publishing his memoir: "First, I shall vindicate myself from the spurious work sent abroad [*Sketches*]; and secondly shall get the means of going ahead, just now." That meant earning some serious money from book sales. He vowed "never to go home until I am able to pay all my debts and I think I have a good prospect at present and will do the best I can."[48]

The book became an instant bestseller in America and England and has never been out of print. Excerpts from it appeared in newspapers throughout the country. Crockett soon embarked on a promotional tour of northeastern states where huge crowds met and cheered him at every stop, attesting to his growing celebrity. He hastily slapped together a book documenting his tour, *An Account of Colonel Crockett's Tour of the North and Down East,* which consisted largely of edited newspaper accounts of his appearances and quotations from his speeches. The book failed to repeat the success of *Narrative* and unsold copies would clog Carey & Hart's warehouses until after Crockett's death. Although the tour demonstrated how popular Crockett was, it hurt him politically when he sought reelection the following year. His opponents gained traction with voters by accusing the Colonel of ignoring his duties in Washington while touring for personal gain.[49]

Crockett's time away from home was also felt by his family. Years later his daughter Matilda recalled, "Father spent so much of his time hunting, electioneering or at Washington City that it seems now like I was never with him much." Matilda was only six years old when her father began his first term in Congress and fourteen when he went to Texas, which left little time for Crockett to spend with her. Matilda's recollection lends insight into Elizabeth Crockett's life as well. Although she knew what was in store for her as she watched and encouraged Crockett's political rise and witnessed his long absences, she understood that her husband was never much of a homebody or family man. He had always enjoyed hunting in all kinds of weather, scouting land, and campaigning. During Crockett's long absences Elizabeth took on the responsibilities of tending their farm and home and caring for their children, and she understood that it was an unavoidable part of life as a politician's wife.[50]

Crockett had barely defeated William Fitzgerald in 1833, after which his congressional district was gerrymandered, further hindering his chances. He faced an even tougher fight two years later when he squared off against Adam Huntsman, a foe every bit as adept as he in backwoods campaigning, joking, and firing off clever rejoinders. Like Crockett, he was a veteran of the Creek War and had lost a leg in the conflict. Crockett made sport of his opponent's "timber toe," which may have backfired on him as it denigrated a man who had lost a limb in the service of his country. Huntsman squeaked through, beating Crockett by a mere 252 votes out of more than nine thousand ballots cast. Crockett accused Huntsman of buying votes and turning the Jackson machine on him, but Huntsman kept his sense of humor and reminded Crockett that he lost because he simply didn't get enough votes. Still, it was clear the Jacksonians had succeeded in torpedoing the Colonel's campaign.[51]

Ironically, for the first time there was a significant drop in the election of Jacksonian representatives in Tennessee in 1835. The success of four such candidates was a decrease from eight in the previous election. Also, for the first time, there was a significant number of Anti-Jacksonians elected in Tennessee, nine in all, an increase of eight. This was also the moment when most of the Tennessee delegation, including Crockett, issued a petition drafting Hugh Lawson White as a presidential candidate in opposition to Jackson's hand-picked successor, Martin Van Buren. So why did Crockett lose? Several factors contributed to his downfall. Huntsman got the jump on him on the stump while Crockett was still in Washington, where his final effort to bring up his land bill failed. Crockett had little to run on after the Jacksonians stifled his attempts to get a hearing for the bill on the House floor—part of their efforts to prevent him from achieving any gain that might help his reelection bid.

Huntsman hammered away at Crockett's book tour, which took him away from his congressional duties and, according to Huntsman, should require Crockett to refund his congressional pay for each day he'd missed. Huntsman cast doubt on Crockett's honesty and suggested he was more a national celebrity than a common man of the people. Worst of all, Crockett had failed to deliver his promised land reform bill and had little to show for his six years in Congress. The Jacksonian press piled on and hit the same points, adding the charge that Crockett had sold out to the Whigs but ignoring to mention that he had long been allied with the Erwin faction in Tennessee that opposed Jackson and had never really been a Jackson man anyway. Nor could Crockett compete with Jacksonian spending on Huntsman's campaign. Thus, despite unprecedented gains by anti-Jackson forces in Tennessee, Crockett lost his seat by a narrow margin.

But the defeat may not have stung Crockett as sharply as it seemed. Matilda later remembered that it didn't seem to matter much to the Colonel and recalled that he had been anxious to go to Texas for some time. "I remember the day my father came home after his last race. He came in and said to mother, 'Well, Bet, I am beat and I'm off for Texas.' I don't think Father cared much for his defeat, he wanted to go to Texas anyhow." In fact, Texas had been on Crockett's mind for years and, being an avid reader of Washington newspapers, he kept up with events there. On March 30, 1830, he'd risen in the House to speak on behalf of the proposed Buffalo and New Orleans Road project, pushing for the road to terminate in Memphis, rather than New Orleans. Crockett pointed out that it would then be on the direct route from Washington to the province of Texas, "which I hope will one day belong to the United States, and that at no great distance of time."[52]

Indeed, Crockett appears to have been planning a complete break with Tennessee and permanent move to Texas for some time. Shortly before leaving Tennessee he sold the last two of his properties. First, he liquidated the two hundred-acre plot that he and William James purchased in 1826 by selling it to Enoch Tucker for $505 on October 22, 1835, only ten days before leaving for Texas. Second, he sold the two hundred acres he bought from Joel Henry Dyer for eighty dollars in 1831 to his brother-in-law, Hance C. McWhorter, for $300 on October 31, 1835, literally on the eve of his departure for Texas. Crockett was thus landless as he prepared to depart for Texas and at the same economic low point he had reached before leaving Lawrence County thirteen years earlier. But there was something different about the sale of this land only days or hours before Crockett's departure for Texas. The Colonel was ending all of his connections to Tennessee. He wouldn't need any land there because he didn't plan to remain in the state much longer. The $805 he gained from these last land sales would equal $27,103 in 2022 dollars, a tidy sum to leave his family while he was away, with some left over to bankroll his journey.[53]

Crockett saw no future for himself in Tennessee and had lost or sold the land he had accumulated over two decades. There was little hope of winning public office again in his gerrymandered district, and a loss would run up his debts. Although those were major factors in his decision to leave the United States, his gloomy view of the country's future also played a prominent role in that decision. The political winds stirred him, and he became frustrated with what he saw as Jackson's abuse of power and, worse, the willingness of US citizens to approve it. Jackson's designation of Van Buren as his heir was the last straw. If Crockett had come to dislike Jackson nearly as much as Old Hickory hated him, he truly despised Van Buren. "I have gone so far as to declare that if he martin vanburen is elected that I will leave the United States for I will never live under his kingdom Before I will Submit to his Government I will go to the wildes of Texas." He thought Jackson a tyrant and was disgusted by what he saw as the nation's blind loyalty to him. "I do believe Santa Ana's kingdom will be a paradise, compared with this in a few years," he wrote to *The National Intelligencer*. "The people are nearly ready to take the yoke of bondage, and say Amen! Jackson done it—it is all right!" He expressed the same views in a letter to his son John Wesley on Christmas Eve 1834, referring to Jackson as "the poor old fool." He charged that Old Hickory "does not know what he is about: he has destroyed the circulating medium of the country and destroyed all the prospects of internal improvements; he has destroyed the commerce and wants to bring on a war and go out with a Blaze of glory, and I am afraid that the people will say amen as usual. They will say it is all right, Jackson done it. If the people is ready to sustain him in this I am ready to give up the ship. I still say as I have for the last four years, that if Martin Van Buren is elected I will leave the United States as soon as I can get out." He wasn't exaggerating—Crockett was truly fed up, not only with Tennessee but with the United States and what he viewed as a blind personality cult that had grown around Jackson. Exploring Texas was not merely another adventure for Crockett—he was moving out for good.[54]

Crockett's cynical comparison of Jackson to Mexican President Santa Anna, a real dictator, may have been political hyperbole. Crockett was aware of the growing discontent among American expats who had colonized Texas and were strongly opposed to Santa Anna's centralized government. No doubt Crockett's friend and fellow congressman Sam Carson, who owned quite a bit of Texas land, bent Crockett's ear with glowing descriptions of the vast, fertile lands in Texas's Red River country that were there for the taking. Although he was aware of the threat of war in Texas, Crockett was not interested in fighting and planned only to explore the land. For decades he had settled in one place after another, moving steadily westward in a continuing search to increase his wealth and grow a land empire—from Jefferson County to Lincoln; from Lincoln to Franklin; from Franklin to Lawrence; from Lawrence to Carroll and Gibson; and finally, to Weakley. A move to Texas was simply one more effort to start over on new land, this time in a new country.

Matilda later remembered that her father "wanted to move right away but Mother persuaded him to go first and look at the country and then if he liked it we would all go. He seemed very confident the morning he went away that he would soon have us all join him in Texas." Crockett was eager to move but deferred to Elizabeth's sound judgment and went along with her more cautious approach, agreeing to explore the place on his own before making a decision about moving there. If Texas didn't pan out there were other places to explore. Either way, he was finished with Jackson's United States. Crockett made his intention clear on the eve of his departure when he wrote to his brother-in-law, George Patton, "I am on the eve of Starting to the Texes—on tomorrow morning myself Abner Burgin and Lindsy K Tinkle & our Nephew William Patton from the lowar country this will make our Company we will go through Arkinsaw and I want to explore the Texes well before I return."[55]

Several days before his departure, Crockett celebrated by throwing a party, hosting a bran dance and barbecue at his home, which attracted a large crowd. Matilda later recalled, "Everybody far and near were invited. I tell you they had a glorious time. The young folks danced all day and night and everybody enjoyed themselves." It was a last hurrah for Crockett in Tennessee, and he was happy to put the place behind him.[56]

Crockett knew that trouble was brewing in Texas and fighting between colonists and Mexican troops had broken out even before he left Tennessee. But Texas might offer him a new beginning and if there was one thing that Crockett knew about it was starting over.

CHAPTER 2

Texas

The Texas that Crockett aimed to explore was a place in chaos and revolt. The territory had long been a problem for colonial Spain and then for Mexico when it became independent of the mother country. Texas's remoteness and tales of raids by Comanche and other tribes frightened off most prospective settlers and made the territory difficult to govern from far away Mexico City. Like Spain, Mexico sought to secure Texas by colonizing the place and building its population, but they found few Mexicans willing to face the risks.

The Spanish had attempted to bring some order and control to Texas through missionaries sent to convert native tribes to Christianity, backed by troops to compel any who resisted. A system of missions and presidios—fortified bases—confined native people under the watchful eyes of troops, who also kept out hostiles. Intermarriage among the natives and Spanish gave rise to a unique local population called Tejanos, a reference that eventually applied to all Mexican nationals in Texas. None of these efforts improved Spain's control over Texas, and the Comanche continued to raid there with impunity. But some hardy souls residing in the United States were courageous (or daft) enough to take the risk, and Spain was willing to try anything that might lead to control of the province.

In 1819, Missourian Moses Austin cut a deal with Spanish officials that allowed him to bring settlers from the United States into Texas, provided they agreed to become loyal Spanish subjects. The colonists received large tracts of fertile land and perhaps a new start in life. Alas, Moses Austin died before he could pursue his plan but, following Mexican independence, his son, Stephen F. Austin, took up where his dad left off. The younger Austin became the first empresario to establish a colony in Texas, promising to recruit only respectable folk who would make solid citizens. Immigrants were required to swear allegiance to Mexico and convert to Catholicism, although the religious requirement was never really enforced. In exchange, colonists received large land grants: 320 acres for farming and another 640 acres for grazing land. Those who brought families received thousands of acres more. Austin stood to gain from the colonists, who paid him a $12.50 survey fee for each one hundred acres they claimed. Native tribes posed less of a threat in eastern Texas, where the colony was located, while the feared Comanche roamed and raided much farther to the west. Still, other tribes lived closer to colonists, roughly between the Sabine and Trinity Rivers, including the Karankawa, Wacos, and Wichita, who did clash with the settlers. However, Austin was able to maintain peace with most of the tribes and remained neutral in disputes between them and Mexico. He formed alliances with the Cherokee, Shawnee, and Delaware, and remained at peace with the Tonkawas and the Lipan Apaches. The colonists also formed militia for defense. Austin found some three hundred enthusiastic families that began moving into Texas late in 1821, the same year Mexico achieved independence from Spain. Crockett's exploration took him to the west of these colonies, closer to the Comanche, but still some distance from their territory.[1]

Initially a monarchy, Mexico became a federal republic in 1823 and a year later adopted the federal Constitution of 1824, which included key features of the US Constitution and the liberal Spanish Constitution of 1812. Catholicism became the official state religion, and the church was supported by public funds. A president and vice president were elected to four-year terms by the state legislatures and the president's powers were limited. Although the central government had power to make laws, implementation of them was left to the states. Anglo settlers assumed the new government would embrace the same level of personal freedom and local government power they had enjoyed in the United States. Provinces could adopt their own constitutions as long as they did not conflict with the federal document. But the constitution did not bring stability, and within a few years Mexico would see one president after another ousted from office and replaced. The struggle over the presidency reflected a broader conflict between supporters of the new constitution and those who favored stronger central government, the latter backed by large landowners, the military, and the church.

Local militias gave the colonists greater independence from central authority and created a kind of self-contained Americanized territory. Colonists adopted their own American-style legal system, including pro-tection of slavery despite Mexico's opposition to the institution. Austin lobbied to exclude Texas from the slavery prohibition, and Texians ensured they'd keep their slaves through a system of long-term "indenture agreements" between slaves and their owners, running anywhere from seventy to ninety years, which provided a clumsy but effective fig leaf for slavery in Texas. The colonists had come to Texas to grow cotton and slave labor was essential to its cultivation. It was the source of income for most colonists and the reason why they, like Crockett, wanted as much fertile Texas land as they could get. By 1825 Austin's colony included 1,357 whites and 443 slaves. Both numbers increased as more colonies were established, including one in Nacogdoches, which soon rose in rebellion against Mexico's authority and declared itself the Republic of Fredonia, a move that soon fizzled and saw its leaders scurry back to the United States just ahead of Mexican troops. Austin was anxious to maintain good relations with the central government and emphasized the need for colonists to remain loyal Mexican citizens.[2]

But American settlers brought with them an independent nature, distrust of government, hunger for land on which to grow cotton, and slaves to work that land. They tenaciously guarded their land and freedom and, ironically, their slaves—regardless of the legal regime they were living under. It was not long before illegal immigrants were moving into Texas from the United States in violation of Mexican law. By 1828, the central government became concerned about Texas and dispatched Gen. Manuel de Mier y Terán on a fact-finding mission. Mier y Terán observed that the American colonists "all go about with their constitution in their pocket, demanding their rights." He also raised alarm in Mexico City when he reported the Americans now outnumbered native Mexicans in Texas by ten to one, and not all were the upstanding folk Austin promised to bring. He reported, "Among the foreigners there are all kinds: fugitive criminals, honorable farmers, vagabonds and ne'er-do-wells, laborers, etc." He thought the place somewhat bizarre and observed, "The total population is a mixture of such strange or incoherent elements that no other like it exists in our entire federation." Although he found the Americans industrious, he also observed their resentment of the government and heard talk of revolt from some of them. As a precaution, he recommended that more soldiers occupy Texas and that immigration from the United States be ended. Observing that Anglos outnumbered Mexicans in Texas by some twenty-six thousand, Mier y Terán recommended flooding Texas with more Mexican colonists to correct the imbalance, an idea that proved unworkable since Mexicans remained reluctant to move there. It also riled colonists that

Texas was not an independent Mexican state but joined with Coahuila to form the state of Coahuila and Texas, which was governed from its capital in Saltillo, placing Texians at a considerable distance from their state government and even more distant from the central government in Mexico City. The Texas city of San Antonio de Béxar, for example, lay about 350 miles from Saltillo. This further fed Texian desire for self-government and, later, independence.[3]

By 1830 Mexico became sufficiently alarmed by the influx of American colonists to adopt the Law of April 6, 1830, which barred immigration from countries bordering Mexico, effectively prohibiting US citizens from entering. The law also ended generous tax exemptions granted to colonists, and Mexican tax collectors soon set up customs houses in Texas to collect duties. A prohibition on Anglo coastal settlements was reinforced and new forts were to be built in Texas, manned by soldiers who would enforce the new crackdown and establish a stronger government presence in Texas. Most threatening to Texas cotton growers was a prohibition on importing any new slaves into Mexico. All in all, it was an ominous harbinger of things to come. Although many long-term colonists disapproved of these measures, most of them recognized the government's right to impose them and, as Mexican citizens, felt obligated to accept them. Nonetheless, regardless of other Texian grievances, Mexican threats to slavery were taken seriously by colonists concerned about the future of cotton growing in Texas and, thus, the economy and the very survival of the colonies.

The smoldering issue of slavery always simmered beneath the surface of other colonist grievances. Texas cotton planters battled continually to stave off the Mexican government's efforts to curtail or abolish slavery altogether. Although the government made several attempts to restrict slavery in Texas, it lacked the resources necessary to enforce such restrictions. The government worried about losing control over Texas as increasing numbers of US immigrants settled in the territory, many of them slave-owning cotton planters, who soon outnumbered the native Tejanos. Immigration became a more significant issue with the global boom in cotton prices during the early 1830s, which led to a massive expansion in American migration into northern Mexico, doubling the region's Anglo population in four years.

Although the colonists nominally agreed to adhere to Mexican law and convert to Catholicism, few actually did the latter, and they went along with the former only as long as it didn't interfere with their business.

Throughout the colonial period, the government's efforts to control Texas and the Texians' desire for more autonomy created tensions. Texians were troubled by the instability of the Mexican government and alarmed by frequent regime change. They feared that policies adopted by one Mexican government might be reversed by the next. Texians were united in their opposition to the Law of April 6, 1830, and although most of its provisions were eventually repealed, colonists worried the central government might make similar efforts in the future.

It is not clear how serious Mexico was about abolishing slavery in Texas, which was the only Mexican territory that relied on slavery. Mexico's continual flirtation with abolition seems to have been intended primarily to gain control of Texas by discouraging immigration rather than reflecting a major concern with slavery. In fact, the Texian indenture agreements, used to circumvent bans on importing slaves into Mexico, were not unlike the peonage practices in Mexico and the United States, which remained in place long after Texas independence.

Regardless of the Texians' other grievances, they saw Mexican threats to slavery as threats to the future of Texas. Immigrants came to grow cotton, which required large numbers of slaves, thus Mexico's suspicion of the "peculiar institution" endangered the economy. Nonetheless, the ease with which colonists circumvented Mexico's slavery restrictions suggested slavery would remain secure in Texas. This explains why few slave-owning colonists took part in the revolution and indicates that slavery was not the primary cause of the revolt, although it was a powerful underlying issue. The colonists who hesitated to join the rebellion hoped that most political issues could be resolved and any threat to slavery removed, particularly if Texas was granted separate statehood.

Although most slave owners rejected revolution, radical war hawks used threats to slavery to drum up support. They raised often hysterical alarms that, ironically, equated threats to slavery with threats to freedom. Radicals spread fears that abolition would lead to violence by slaves against their masters and violation of white women by liberated slaves. These efforts were not unlike similar anti-abolition campaigns among slave states in the United States a few decades later. But it was only after Mexico invaded Texas and annihilated the Alamo and Goliad garrisons that support for the war spread throughout Texas and drew in panicked slave owners.

If slave owners were slow to rally to revolution's banner, they later ensured that slavery was institutionalized in the Texas Constitution, which denied citizenship to non-whites, including Blacks and Native Americans, and restricted it to "all free white persons who shall emigrate to the republic." The constitution also protected slavery by allowing white immigrants to import slaves and by prohibiting emancipation. Owners could free their slaves only with congressional approval and by agreeing to send them out of Texas. Even a provision that would have empowered Congress to require slave owners to treat slaves humanely was defeated. Free Blacks could only reside permanently in Texas with congressional permission, but only two slaves were granted legal emancipation by Congress in the entire history of the Texas republic. These measures leave no doubt about the importance of slavery and white supremacy to Texians, whether or not slavery sparked the war. Attempting to determine how great a role slavery played in causing the uprising requires asking whether or not the colonists would have revolted if Mexico City had granted permanent protection of slavery, rather than constantly edging in the other direction. This may be impossible to answer, but it is nonsense to suggest that slavery was not an important factor in the Texas Revolution.[4]

More Americans kept arriving in Texas, many with diminishing regard for Mexican authority, all with dreams of land empires based on the amazingly large tracts of cheap land that Mexico offered to them. Mexico was slow to see the danger in this, perhaps believing that in time the Americans would assimilate into Mexican society. Austin encouraged such thinking by cultivating good relations with Tejano leaders and the state government in Saltillo. The Anglo and Tejano populations shared common interests in developing the area, cultivating foreign trade, and gaining more local political power. Mexico's new policies only fed the fires of rebellion among both groups.

Texians weren't the only Mexicans unhappy with President Anastasio Bustamante's oppressive regime in the early 1830s. Opposition to his rule grew into open rebellion in January 1832, ultimately led by Gen. Antonio López de Santa Anna. The revolt raged throughout the year and ended in December with Bustamante's downfall and the election of a liberal government. Santa Anna was elected president and assumed office on April 1, 1833, but left day-to-day governing to his vice president, Valentín Gómez Farías. Meanwhile, Santa Anna's federalist revolution influenced events in Texas.[5]

Santa Anna began his military career at age sixteen as an infantry cadet and served under the command of Joaquín de Arredondo, with whom he spent five years fighting insurgents and keeping an eye on native tribes. In the aftermath of rebellions, he witnessed Arredondo's brutal mass executions of insurrectionists. It was a lesson that stayed with him. Always a mercurial opportunist, never an ideologue, he was first loyal to Spain and opposed Mexican independence, but later switched sides. During an 1821 campaign against insurgents led by Agustín de Iturbide, he suddenly joined Iturbide's rebels. However, a year later he broke with Iturbide and advocated for a republic. In 1829 he beat back a Spanish invasion at Tampico and became a national hero.[6]

Mexico established a fort at the Texas port city of Anahuac to enforce collection of customs duties, which incited Texian outrage and resistance, even when Austin managed to put off enforcement. Anahuac's commandant, Juan Davis Bradburn, an expat from Kentucky, carried out the collections, enforced the ban on importing slaves, sheltered runaway slaves escaping from the United States, rejected the farcical indenture agreements, and held up approval of new land surveys—all moves guaranteed to anger colonists. In June 1832, Bradburn arrested William Barret Travis and Patrick Jack following an armed confrontation between soldiers and colonists over the rape of an Anglo woman by a Mexican soldier. Jack and Travis were jailed for nearly two months, making them martyrs and heroes to some colonists, but most had no sympathy for the two and viewed them as malcontents. Nonetheless, about one hundred armed Texian radicals marched on Anahuac and threatened to release the prisoners by force. A peaceful release of the pair was negotiated after Bradburn was replaced and the Mexicans backed down, but the incident fueled the fires of rebellion and turned Travis and Jack from pariahs into heroes.

Travis, a lawyer and one-time newspaper publisher in his native South Carolina, arrived in Texas in 1831 after abandoning his pregnant wife and their son. Local legend suggests that he suspected his wife of infidelity that resulted in her pregnancy and that Travis may even have killed a man as a result, but the story has largely been discounted. He set up a law practice in Anahuac, on Trinity Bay, and became fluent in Spanish. During his legal work throughout the area, he fell in with a radical group that became the War Party.[7]

Around the time when Travis and Jack were released, a group of Texians attempted to smuggle a small cannon into Anahuac by boat but were intercepted by Mexican troops from the fort at Velasco. A short battle ensued, ending with a Mexican surrender and abandonment of Velasco, an easy Texian victory.

In July 1832, Nacogdoches colonists formed a militia in support of federalists throughout Mexico. When the Mexican commander in Nacogdoches,

José de las Piedras, demanded the colonists surrender their arms and disband, he met the same resistance that Bradburn faced in Anahuac. The *ayuntamiento*, or municipal government, not only refused the order but organized its own militia and dispatched requests for aid from other settlements. Before long upwards of three hundred Texian volunteers arrived on the scene. When Piedras refused Texian demands that he switch allegiance to Santa Anna, a battle ensued in which the Mexicans lost thirty-three dead and more than a dozen wounded, while the Texians suffered ten casualties. Piedras then sneaked his forces out of town by night. Under the leadership of James Bowie, the colonists pursued the larger Mexican force and through stealth and ambush fooled them into thinking the Texian force was much larger than it was. Most of the Mexicans mutinied and then surrendered, agreeing to throw in with the federalists, at least nominally.[8]

The easy Texian victories at Anahuac, Velasco, and Nacogdoches were not open revolt; they were actions in support of Santa Anna's federalists and similar to other pro-federalist actions elsewhere in Mexico. But radical Texians continued to call for independence from Coahuila, if not from Mexico altogether. Travis was among this group, which would come to be called war hawks, or the War Party, who eschewed all pretense of being Mexicans and expressed themselves as Americans who were entitled to the same rights they had enjoyed in the United States. At least some Mexican authorities interpreted the rhetoric as a call for independence from Mexico. By the same token, some Texians distrusted Santa Anna and feared that he would revert to the pattern of military men seizing power in the name of liberal government only to clamp down with a totalitarian fist once in power. General Mier y Terán eventually lost all hope for the future. Strongly opposed to the federalists and convinced that Texas was already lost to Mexico, he committed suicide on July 3, 1832, the day after Travis was released from his Anahuac cell.[9]

Texians met in convention during the first week of October 1832 to consider their options, a move that was strongly opposed by Tejanos. San Antonio de Béxar—known as San Antonio today but commonly referred to as "Béxar" in Crockett's time—refused to send any delegates and considered the gathering illegal. The convention called for the repeal of the Law of April 6, 1830, and demanded Texas's separation from Coahuila. It created a central committee that could call such meetings in the future and formed committees of correspondence in each township, which would enhance communication should any new flareups occur. Mexico declared the entire proceeding illegal and annulled its resolutions, but Texian reformists were encouraged by Santa Anna's advances and called a second convention in April 1833, which made the same demands and met the same resistance within Coahuila and Texas. The convention designated Austin and two others as emissaries to carry Texian demands to Mexico City. In the end only Austin went, setting sail on June 1 and arriving in Mexico City in July, but his mission was soon overtaken by other events.[10]

Santa Anna had left government in the hands of Vice President Farías, who planned to cut the size of the military, redistribute land, and confiscate church property. Farías was thus a threat to the centralist elites—the Catholic church, army, and large landowners—who pressured Santa Anna into stopping his runaway vice president. The largely unprincipled Santa Anna had no problem in making a 180-degree political pivot and marched into Mexico City in April 1834, ousted Farías, disbanded the national congress, and replaced it with unelected centralist supporters. He all but abolished the 1824 Constitution and replaced it with a centralist document that placed power squarely in Mexico City, not the states. This marked the end of Mexico's stab at federalism, while Santa Anna's measures led directly to renewed federalist hostility toward the government, notably in Texas. Turmoil was already underway when Austin loped into Mexico City planning to lobby for greater Texas autonomy. But he represented a province that had engaged in open confrontation with government forces and seemed on the cusp of rebellion, having also convened two conventions that Mexico regarded as illegal. Austin couldn't have chosen a less propitious time for such a mission.[11]

However, Austin's views were already shifting in the direction of complete separation from the mother country. His thinking had changed in the face of continual political turnover and chaos in Mexico, a country seemingly in an endless cycle of revolutions, coups, and unstable government. While in Mexico, Austin foolishly wrote to the Béxar *ayuntamiento* suggesting that it seek cooperation from other towns to organize a state government, appearing to ally himself with the radicals. It didn't help Austin's case that several Mexican states were already in rebellion and battling government troops. Texas was considered particularly dangerous because it was populated by Anglo colonists who had openly resisted Mexico's authority. Nonetheless, Austin supported separate statehood for Texas and when he met with Santa Anna drew the false conclusion that the new president also backed the idea. With that in mind Austin confidently headed back to Texas in December but he was arrested when he reached Saltillo. His letter to the Béxar *ayuntamiento* had alarmed Tejano leaders, who considered Austin's mission illegal and accused him of fomenting treason. They reported Austin's letter to Mexican authorities, and when it landed in Mexico City Santa Anna ordered the empresario's arrest. Austin remained imprisoned through most of 1834. Even while in prison, he tried to maintain allegiance to Mexico, but his pleas fell on deaf ears in Texas. Although he had secured a repeal of the ban on immigration, it was not enough to quell colonist grievances and outrage over Austin's arrest.

The Texian cause was aided by demands in other Mexican states for more autonomy as well as unrest in the Mexican military, which was alarmed by government instability. However, in Texas and elsewhere disagreement took root between federalist factions that favored more state independence and those that supported the centralists. In Béxar, Santa Anna's betrayal of federalism drove reluctant Tejanos into alliance with the Anglo anti-centralists, and they were soon joined by citizens elsewhere. The rising hostility pushed Santa Anna to back down and loosen restrictions. He instituted land reform, eased immigration, enlarged the size of Texas's legislative delegation, approved trial by jury, and recognized English as a legal language. It all came as a relief to Austin, who remained ever the peacemaker and now felt comfortable abandoning the push for statehood. The reforms gave colonists confidence in their economic well-being and cooled Texian anger. Fewer colonists continued to support the radicals, and plans for another convention fizzled. Travis ruefully observed, "As long as people are prosperous they do not desire a change."[12]

Santa Anna thought things had calmed in Texas, but he took the precaution of dispatching Col. Juan Nepomuceno Almonte on an inspection tour of Texas to assess the political situation. *El presidente* was taking no chances and, if Austin didn't fully trust him, neither did he trust the Texians. What he learned from Almonte was unsettling.

Almonte's nine-month tour from February to November 1834 raised concern about the government's hold on Texas, and he advised that "some action be taken as soon as possible by the Supreme Government that will safeguard the integrity of the territory." He was suspicious of colonist motives in their early clashes with troops, faulted them for taking up arms, and suspected their grievances were contrived and really aimed at removing troops from Texas. He also faulted the Mexican government for removing nearly all troops from Texas claiming that it only encouraged further rebelliousness. Almonte mentioned that the one hundred soldiers in Béxar were the only troops to be found in Texas. He regarded Texas's demand for separate statehood as aggressive and found that in Texas "no law is respected unless it serves the interests of the colonists," and he thought lawlessness would grow unless troops were dispatched to the province immediately. With importation of slaves continuing unabated along with defiance of Mexican civil authority, he predicted the repeal of the Law of April 6, 1830, would increase immigration and bring at least a thousand new families to Texas during the current year alone.

Almonte suspected that even the most moderate colonists sought separate statehood for Texas to lend it some degree of sovereignty and hoped to later declare it independent of Mexico in order to join the United States. He predicted the colonists would use the outbreak of more turmoil in Mexico's interior as justification for seceding and that Texians who opposed such a plan were powerless to act unless troops were present to support them. He warned that colonists were unlikely to shed their ways and that "compatriotism, similar customs, laws, religion, language, and [the form of] government under which they have been educated and whose institutions are so familiar to them, can have a great hold on their spirit and nothing, in their view, could compensate for those advantages." He mentioned that similar observations were made earlier by Mier y Terán, and he suspected the United States was encouraging rebellion in Texas to cajole Mexico into selling the province.

Almonte advised securing Texas ports and garrisoning Nacogdoches and Béxar with three thousand troops under a commander answerable only to Mexico City. He met with Cherokee and other US tribes that had been forcibly removed from their native lands by Andrew Jackson's Indian Removal Act, which Crockett had voted against in Congress. Almonte thought the Cherokee continued to harbor ill feelings toward Americans, including the Texas colonists, and was certain that were "these Indians given the lands that were promised to them seven or eight years ago . . . I believe that the Government could rely on them at any time. They can bring together 500 [men] all armed with *American carbines*, that they call 'rifles.'" He found the Indians more trustworthy than the Anglo settlers and thought them less likely to cause trouble and that they "do not understand intrigue to the degree that the Americans of the North do." Almonte's experience with Anglo colonists convinced him they would never accommodate themselves to living equally among Mexicans, and he painted a picture as dire as Mier y Terán had. Nonetheless, he recommended releasing Austin, but only after the Texas garrisons had been beefed up. Austin was released from prison in December 1834 but was forced to remain in Mexico City until finally being allowed to leave in July 1835. He began making his way home in August.[13]

The political winds shifted again in 1835 when Santa Anna's centralist Congress, dominated by conservative elites, took a sledgehammer to the recent Farías reforms and voted to raise a large national army while reducing the size of state militias. This gave the central government more control over the states, many of which soon denounced the move and began building up their local forces. In Zacatecas the governor called out the militia and prepared for attack by centralist forces. In a portend of things to come, Santa Anna marched on Zacatecas, smashed the rebellion, and permitted rampant looting by his soldiers, sending a blunt message about how he would henceforth deal with rebellion. He assumed dictatorial powers and strengthened centralist control. He disbanded state legislatures and began drafting a new constitution that would, effectively, make the states powerless nonentities that would be ruled from Mexico City. In the proverbial wink of an eye, Santa Anna had made himself dictator of Mexico.

Mexican actions reawakened the Texas war hawks. In June 1835, trouble again flared in Anahuac, and again Travis was at the center of it. When the local commander renewed collection of customs duties, Travis led a group of twenty men with a small cannon in an attack on the post. The Mexicans again retreated and ultimately surrendered. Travis again thought he'd be greeted as a hero, but he was met with the same scorn from most colonists that followed his actions three years earlier and further polarized Texians into war and peace factions, with James Bowie and Travis among the more prominent members of the former. In July, Bowie led a raid on the Nacogdoches armory and seized its weapons. There, he found the militia formed up in fear of a Mexican attack, but Bowie's efforts to rouse the colonists to rebellion again fizzled. Bowie later intercepted Mexican documents that included charges of treason against Texian colonists, an arrest order for Travis, and information about a military force being sent to Texas. But Bowie's attempt to stir up a fight again met with tepid response. Texians remained suspicious of him and other land speculators who were working with Agustín Viesca, governor of Coahuila and Texas. They believed Bowie and others were motivated more by Mexico rescinding fraudulent land grants than military threats and saw Bowie's move as an attempt to create fear of an imminent Mexican attack. But some Texians were legitimately concerned about Mexico's repeal of the Farías reforms, particularly the renewed seizing of cargoes arriving at Texas ports, although these were seizures of illegal imports. The government considered this smuggling, but Texians, perhaps spoiled by the years of lax enforcement, saw it as illegal confiscation and even piracy or theft. The situation was further heated when rumors spread that Texians would be denied citizenship and the ban on immigration reimposed. Travis called the government a "plundering, robbing, autocratical, aristocratical jumbled up govt. which is in fact no govt. at all—one day a republic—one day a fanatical heptarchy, the next a military despotism—then a mixture of the evil qualities of all." These were the same concerns that troubled Austin, who wondered how Texas could ever be secure as part of such an unstable country. Santa Anna's sudden takeover of the government reinforced his fears.[14]

Back home again, Austin went so far as to suggest that Texas secede from Mexico and join the United States, and he sought to draw more American immigrants to Texas, hoping that might discourage Santa Anna from attempting an invasion. By July, proclamations appeared in the United States declaring that Texas could not remain part of Mexico for long and must inevitably join the union. Mexican tactics only fueled these flames, which would grow throughout 1835 as American newspapers beat war drums ever louder and urged Americans to take up arms and rush to Texas. Mexico had feared US designs on Texas for some time, fears that were stoked by American attempts to buy the place. In 1827, US President John Quincy Adams offered Mexico $1 million for Texas, and two years later President Andrew Jackson upped the offer to $5 million. Mexico steadfastly refused and remained wary of American interest in Texas.

Travis's latest action in Anahuac resulted in Mexican Gen. Martín Perfecto de Cós ordering his arrest, a move that backfired when peace advocates who had earlier condemned Travis now rushed to his support. Rumors of Santa Anna sending a large military force into Texas further enraged colonists and empowered the war hawks. Texians refused to carry out orders from Mexican authorities and Travis was never arrested. Ever the grandstander, he warned Mexican authorities that the Texians "shall give them hell if they come here." Columbia residents called for Texians to meet in a "consultation," but avoided calling the gathering a convention, which would have been illegal. A similar meeting in Nacogdoches passed resolutions opposing centralism and endorsing the call for a consultation. These renewed stirrings of Texas rebellion were widely reported in the US press and doubtless seen by Crockett long before he left for Texas.[15]

Austin supported the consultation, which was to convene on October 15, and proclaimed Texas must be "forever free from Mexican domination." Word soon came that General Cós had moved troops into San Antonio de Béxar to reassert Mexican authority. Austin called for all *ayuntamientos* to send delegates to the consultation and raise their militias, which soon swelled to full strength with volunteers. Austin had finally abandoned all hope of a peaceful outcome and proclaimed that the Texians were united in favor of war.

Indeed, Mexican artillery landed at Copano Bay and five hundred fresh troops under Cós soon followed. This drove US newspapers to ramp up Texas war talk and outrage over Mexico's action, as if Mexico had no right to govern itself as it saw fit. Cós arrived at Copano on September 20, and a week later led his troops into Béxar. Santa Anna had played into the hands of his enemies. By opting for force, he brought on the very rebellion he sought to suppress.

It is certain that Crockett was aware of some of these events although press reports were often distorted and lacked balanced coverage. Much published information was second hand, passed on by travelers arriving from Texas and then heavily editorialized in the press. There is no way to know how critical an eye Crockett cast over these reports, but whatever he knew did not alter his plans to explore Texas.

Mexico had given a cannon to the citizens of Gonzales for protection against Indian raids but now feared that it might be used against its soldiers. Béxar commandant Col. Domingo de Ugartechea demanded the cannon's return, but the Texians resisted and secretly buried the piece. Ugartechea sent one hundred mounted troops to retrieve it, but some 160 volunteers soon arrived in Gonzales to face the Mexicans. Austin proclaimed the citizens' right to keep the cannon and urged Texians to avoid violence, but he privately admitted that war was now inevitable. The Texians brought the cannon forward, loaded it with scrap metal, and hoisted a makeshift flag bearing the outline of a cannon and the words "Come And Take It!" They fired one volley and advanced but found that the Mexicans had retreated back to Béxar. The non-battle set off the spark that ignited full rebellion, rallied support from colonists formerly reluctant to join up, strengthened the case for independence, and fed the illusion that military victory would be easy. It also put an end to the peace faction. The war was on, but its goals would remain a matter of contention among the rebellious Texians.

Austin arrived in Gonzales and found more than three hundred armed Texians who soon elected him their commander. The volunteers formed their own companies, chose their own officers, and reserved the right to vote on their decisions or replace them at will. There was nothing to prevent them from leaving whenever they chose to, which many did throughout the war. Central command was tenuous at best, and no unified army or clear chain of command existed. Instead, individual units operated independently. They might join other units to form a larger army at times but could just as easily withdraw. Thus was Texas's "Volunteer Army of the People" born. Despite efforts to form a disciplined regular army, the war would be fought mostly by such citizen-soldier volunteers, which made discipline difficult and handicapped the ability of military leaders to formulate strategy. Nonetheless, Austin's force soon grew to five hundred, and he laid plans to march on Béxar, drive Cós back across the Nueces River, and begin the process of separating Texas from Mexico entirely, although he kept the last goal to himself for the time being.[16]

Crockett understood the independent-minded citizen-soldier volunteers. In 1830 he had introduced a resolution in Congress to abolish the Military Academy at West Point, claiming it was largely reserved for the sons of the wealthy and privileged. He claimed that "our western men choose, when they are compelled to fight, to elect their own commanders. They are wholly unwilling to trust themselves amid the fury of the battle, under the command of a "*Boy*," not of their own choosing—untried, except at the famous place called "West Point," where, like the ancient story, they march up the hill, and down again, but smell no powder. . . . This, Sir, is ARISTOCRACY with a vengeance."[17]

The Texians enjoyed another victory in October at Goliad where Cós had left about fifty men. A force of some 120 Texians attacked the Mexicans, killing three, wounding seven, and capturing twenty-one while twenty escaped. Goliad and its fortress, Presidio La Bahía, were a key strategic location between Béxar and the coastal ports. Minor as they were, the easy Texian victories at Gonzales and Goliad reinforced the belief that Texians could easily defeat Mexican military units. Meanwhile, Santa Anna doubled down and in October abolished all state legislatures, ending local rule and placing state government in his hands. He could not have aided the Texian rebellion more. He was now easily portrayed as a brutal, repressive tyrant who was smothering Texian freedom. Broadsides and newspapers in the United States happily pounded that message home and increased the cry for volunteers to join the Texian fight. Cós and the Béxar garrison became the focus of animosity and calls arose demanding that they be driven out of Texas, joined with praise for Tejanos who were fighting the centralists. "War is declared . . . against military despotism," Austin announced in San Felipe, and he moved the planned consultation to November 1 since many delegates were now in the field with him. His small army began marching to Béxar on October 14.[18]

Newspapers in the United States closely followed events in Mexico and printed countless reports full of Texas war talk, emphasizing Santa Anna's "deprivations" and determination to snuff out freedom. The reports and broadsides read more like recruiting propaganda than journalism, and Santa Anna had aided in the spread of such talk by effectively ending federalism and through his brutal conquest of Zacatecas. A typical US news report dated September 13, 1835, proclaimed:

> TEXAS IN REVOLUTION. It appears that the citizens of Texas, who have emigrated from the United States, will have fighting to do, and that before very long—to defend their lives, liberty, and property, from the tyranny and oppression of a military despot—Santa Anna.

Others printed Austin's September 19, 1835, "Circular of the Committee of Safety at San Felipe," warning:

> Gen. Cos was expected at Bexar, on the 16th of this month with more troops, that he intended to make immediate attack on the colonies, that there was a plan to try and foment division and discord among the people, so as to use one part against the other, and prevent preparation, and that the real object is to destroy and break up the foreign settlements in Texas.

Austin issued another broadside on September 22, reporting Cós's September landing and raising more urgent alarms:

> Gen. Cos landed at Copano with 400 men, arms and ammunition. An expedition is now raising in the lower country to take the field at once. . . . Every man in Texas is called upon to take up arms in defence (*sic*) of his country and his rights.

Sam Houston, former governor of Tennessee, who had migrated to Texas long before Crockett did and was active in Texian resistance, issued his own broadside in October. It was a call to arms aimed squarely at the United States and emphasized the land bounties that awaited volunteers:

> War in defence of our rights, our oaths, and our constitutions is inevitable in Texas!! If volunteers from the United States will join their brethren in this section, they will receive liberal bounties of land. We have millions of acres of our best lands unchosen and unappropriated. Let each man come with a good rifle and one hundred rounds of ammunition—and to come soon. Our war-cry is 'Liberty or Death.' Our principles are to support the constitution, and *down with the usurper*!

Houston, of course, had no authority to offer land bounties, nor was there even a Texas government that could provide any. Nonetheless, US newspapers continued to encourage rebellion, emphasizing the kinship between American citizens and Texian rebels. Crockett could not have missed seeing Houston's call to arms, but it did not alter his plans to explore Texas and avoid mixing in the war effort. However, valid or not, the generous offer of land bounties would have caught his eye.[19]

Not all US newspapers supported the rebellion, and some took a skeptical view of it. The *Alexandria Gazette* commented:

> It strikes us to be exceedingly improper to pursue the course some of our citizens seem disposed to take in aid of the revolted Mexican Province.... We are now at peace with Mexico and have no right to *encourage* any of her citizens to rebellion, or resistance, or revolution, by raising troops for them and sending them arms and ammunition. We may wish the Texians the enjoyment of American liberty but we ought not to act in a hostile manner to a friendly nation.

The same doubts pervaded the US Capitol. When a Texian delegation travelled to Washington to urge Congress to endorse the Texian cause, lawmakers were not persuaded and refused to intervene.[20]

Austin requested a meeting with Cós, but he was rebuffed by the Mexican general, who made it clear that the Texian actions were illegal and no meeting was possible with criminals. Throughout the war, Mexico would maintain that view of the rebellion and treat rebels as pirates and criminals, not enemy soldiers, especially when Texian ranks began filling with recent arrivals from the United States who were neither colonists nor Mexican citizens. Mexico would use the same argument to justify showing no quarter to rebels and executing prisoners. Cós fortified Béxar, barricaded streets, located artillery, and prepared the town for attack. His force was essentially a disciplined, professional army, unlike the Texians, whom Austin commanded largely in name only. Every decision or order he made was subject to repeated councils of war, which served as debating societies for the individual volunteer units. An initial disagreement about whether to approach Béxar ended when officers decided to leave it up to Austin, who then moved to within a few miles of the town, camped on Salado Creek, and awaited reinforcements and supplies. There, his force grew steadily.

On October 28, a Mexican force led by Ugartechea with three hundred cavalry and infantry and two cannons attacked Bowie and Col. James Fannin while they were on a scouting mission with about ninety men near Mission Concepción. Although outnumbered, the Texians held off the larger force, beating back several charges before the Mexicans broke off the attack and retreated to Béxar, leaving sixteen dead and abandoning a cannon. It seemed another easy Texian victory against long odds and further evidence the Mexicans would run if pressed. Austin laid siege to Béxar on October 24 and notified the Committee of Public Safety in San Felipe that the town could be taken within days with sufficient reinforcements.

On November 4, three days after Crockett left Tennessee, the Texians convened the long-awaited consultation in San Felipe where, with war in mind, discussed rewarding US volunteers with land grants, forming a provisional government, and creating a regular army. Despite the support of war hawks, the Consultation—as it came to be known for posterity—failed to adopt a declaration of independence from Mexico and emphasized that the body was protesting Santa Anna's actions as loyal Mexican citizens. However, the body expressed loyalty only to the *principles* of the 1824 Constitution, not the Constitution itself, and proclaimed Texas was a sovereign entity while also professing loyalty to Mexico. It was clearly a mixed message. The body formed a provisional government structure called the Organic Law which contained twenty-one articles. They called for election of a governor with full executive authority who would serve as commander in chief of armed forces; a lieutenant governor, and a General Council comprising one representative elected by the delegation from each municipality and presided over by the lieutenant governor. After the Consultation adjourned, the governor and council would operate as a provisional government until March 1, when the Consultation would reconvene. There was no dispute resolution provision to settle disagreements between the governor and council and no separation of powers, thus the two bodies were autonomous, a fatal flaw. The Consultation also dispatched a delegation to New Orleans to raise funds to purchase weapons. In December, the Goliad garrison went further by adopting a declaration of independence from Mexico, which served mainly to alienate Mexican and Tejano federalists who favored a return to the 1824 Constitution and were put off by the declaration, which was quashed by the embarrassed General Council.[21]

By now Crockett had travelled a long way from his Tennessee home and was happily exploring the Red River country and hunting buffalo, far from the scenes of battle and political action. It is not clear how closely he was able to follow these events, but word of them eventually drifted throughout Texas and Crockett must have heard some reports. Even before reaching Texas, he followed events in newspapers along his route and he was at least partly aware of what had been taking place. Still, he lingered in the Red River country throughout December, even as the Battle of Béxar raged.[22]

The Consultation envisioned a professional army commanded by a major general commissioned by the governor but subject to the General Council's instructions, leaving the commander vulnerable to disputes between the two. The commander was given authority over regular enlisted troops but not the many citizen-soldier volunteers who comprised most of the army. The Consultation also created a militia to serve under the major general but with authority to elect its own officers, which was certain to hamstring the commander. No chain of command was laid out, and there was no provision for resolving disputes among the various volunteer commanders—thus the major general was certain to face the same dysfunction that Austin did in Béxar.

The Consultation elected the cantankerous Henry Smith over Austin as governor. Even in a more carefully crafted government structure, Smith would have been a problematic choice, but the Organic Law almost guaranteed he would be an obstacle to smooth governance. It also further marginalized the peace faction since Smith was a strong proponent of war and complete independence from Mexico. On the other hand, James Robinson, who was elected lieutenant governor, was fully open to the peace party's views and accommodation with Tejanos and possibly other Mexican states. Those elected to the General Council represented a balance of war and peace factions. Smith distrusted all Mexicans, clearly favored independence, and did his best to scuttle the council's efforts to reach out to Tejanos. Houston was elected military commander, placing him in charge of regulars, but his authority over militia and volunteers was tenuous at best. Finally, unspecified land grants were provided for volunteers. Before adjourning on November 14, the Consultation called on all men to join Austin's force in Béxar, a move opposed by Houston. The debate between advocates of complete independence and those seeking restoration of the 1824 Constitution remained unsettled and further roiled the provisional government. Things were off to a confused and shaky start and would, alas, deteriorate.

There was no accounting for what would happen if the governor and council disagreed, as they soon did with disastrous results. The military was left almost equally impaired. Houston may have been the commander, but men were reluctant to join the regular army, commit to enlistments of two years, or accept army discipline. Thus, the regular army would exist almost entirely on paper throughout the war, although a small number of regulars did serve. On December 10, the provisional government formally issued a resolution calling for a convention to convene on March 1, 1836, in the town of Washington. Delegates were to have "unlimited, or plenary powers as to the form of government to be adopted," but any constitution they drafted would be subject to voter approval. The resolution was adopted by the General Council on December 13, overriding Governor Smith's veto. The Consultation did not commit to either independence or reconciliation with the Mexican government and that question would await resolution at the convention.[23]

Meanwhile, Austin continued to struggle at Béxar. His officers rebuffed his efforts to launch an attack on the town, and by November a stalemate set in. Although new volunteers regularly arrived, just as many were likely to pack up and go home. Austin again ordered an assault on the town on November 21, but his officers again overruled him and told him their men refused to undertake an attack. By mid-month Austin was relieved of command so that he might travel to the United States to gain support and raise funds for the war. Before leaving he warned that the army required a commander who could somehow overcome the difficult task of maintaining discipline. Upon Austin's departure, the soldiers elected Edward Burleson to replace Austin, and around four hundred men agreed to remain and continue the siege. On November 26, a group led by Bowie attacked a Mexican pack train thought to be carrying an army payroll. Driving off the Mexicans, Bowie found the wagons contained only feed for animals. Known as "the grass fight," the action cost the Mexicans three dead and fourteen wounded, while four Texians were injured.

Burleson's attempts to order an attack were no more successful than Austin's as more men "volunteered" to go home or occupied themselves with plundering and drunkenness. However, he was able to create a force of some 220 men built around a recently arrived unit of New Orleans Greys that was willing to launch an attack. He drafted a plan with Col. Benjamin Milam, who rallied the men by shouting, "Who will follow old Ben Milam into San Antonio?" stirring enough of them out of their lethargy to muster a force of some three hundred in all. The attack began on December 5, lasted five days, and consisted of bitter fighting from house to house. A sniper's bullet killed the charismatic Milam two days into the fight on December 7. Cós appeared to gain a great advantage when he received six hundred reinforcements the following day, bringing his force to some 1,250. But the new arrivals turned out to be prisoners bound in chains who were more of a threat than a help to Cós. By December 10, a combination of Texian advances and at least two hundred Mexican desertions led Cós to surrender. IIis force had suffered 150 dead, wounded, or missing, while the Texians lost forty dead and wounded. Although Cós flew a black flag throughout the battle, signifying no quarter would be given to the Texians, the surrender terms granted him and his troops parole and freedom to leave Texas if Cós promised not to oppose restoration of the 1824 Constitution. This showed that the Texians had not completely given up on remaining part of Mexico if the Constitution could, indeed, be restored. In any case, many Texians did not trust the general to keep his promise.

It had all seemed so easy for the Texian volunteers, undisciplined though they might be, as they piled up one victory after another, often against superior numbers. It gave rise to hubris in the Texian ranks and some boasted openly of being able to defeat any Mexican force, no matter how large, even claiming that one American could lick ten Mexicans. Indeed, most volunteers thought the Béxar victory marked the end of war and returned home. They left behind only a tiny force, which alarmed those who knew the Mexicans would return, likely under Santa Anna's command. The Texians would have to defend Béxar to stop the dictator from having a clear path through the colonies. Although the loose collection of undisciplined volunteers had won early victories, such an army was unlikely to sustain a long campaign or defeat a large professional force. That would take a disciplined army, but building one would require an effective government and, in the end, Texas had neither. Traveling through San Felipe in February, William Fairfax Gray met with Governor Smith and found him inadequate for the position he occupied. Gray also observed most Texians had "a Munchausen-like idea of Texas prowess and of Mexican imbecility and insignificance. I fear it will prove a fatal error."[24]

Smith and the General Council quarreled continuously. Although there was initial support for joining with other federalist states opposed to Santa Anna, Smith and Houston rejected the plan and feared involving Texas in a war in the Mexican interior. But the council pursued the idea, which included launching an ill-advised expedition to Matamoros, a port city that might provide revenues to defray the costs of war and a base from which to join with nearby federalists. The expedition also was partially prompted by men who had lost money in Monclova land sales in 1835 and sought to recoup their losses. At that time, the legislature of Coahuila and Texas sought to sell vacant public land in Texas, ostensibly to raise funds to pay the costs of war. But the sales were widely seen as little more than a scheme to sell thousands of acres of Texas land at low prices to speculators, who could then resell for quick profits. Although condemned by Mexico City, and later deemed illegal and nullified by the provisional Texas government, and in the Texas Constitution, the land sales lent credence to Santa Anna's claim that the Texas uprising was under the control of land pirates rather than patriots. At first Smith agreed to the Matamoros plan and ordered Houston to carry it out. Houston, in turn, tapped Bowie for the task, but neither could find enough men for the job. The council thought Smith and Houston were dragging their feet and directed Edward Burleson, the Béxar commander, to organize the expedition. Burleson, however, departed San Antonio on December 15 and placed Col. Francis Johnson in command with a force of about three hundred and the Matamoros expedition fell to him. Johnson thought it a great idea, despite the already depleted size of the Béxar garrison. His enthusiasm was matched by that of Dr. James Grant, who also had fought in Béxar, and together they set about organizing the mission. Grant, leader of a movement to form a new Republic of Northern Mexico with other federalist states, was among the Monclova investors and he also owned land in Coahuila, giving him good reason to promote the expedition.[25]

Grant and Johnson stirred up interest in the Matamoros adventure among the Béxar garrison by assuring the men easily won land and loot, and the promise of action was more appealing to many than idleness in Béxar. Despite a steady flow of communications, promises, orders, and handwringing, neither Smith nor the General Council provided the money, provisions, or clothing needed in Béxar. On January 1, 1836, Grant led two hundred volunteers out of Béxar toward Matamoros via Goliad, leaving behind a mere one hundred men under the command of Lt. Col. James C. Neill, while Johnson headed for San Felipe to formally receive command of the expedition. Just for good measure, before departing San Antonio, Grant stripped the post of most of its arms, munitions, provisions, and, most crucially, horses while absconding with most of the cattle owned by local farmers and ranchers, leaving Neill in an impossible position.[26]

In keeping with the seat-of-the-pants nature of the Texas government and army, Johnson suddenly resigned from the mission but later changed his mind and resumed command. However, by then the council had appointed Col. James Fannin to take over the mission but failed to dismiss Johnson, leaving both commanders free to raise troops. It seems likely the council placed Johnson in command only of the Béxar volunteers while Fannin was to have overall command of the entire expedition. All seemed oblivious to the fact that Houston had already tentatively assigned Bowie the task, completing a triumvirate of uncoordinated commanders leading a hopelessly inadequate number of troops on an ill-planned expedition. Disregarding everyone else, Grant placed himself in command, and the men who left Béxar followed him. In such an army, command relied only on whom the soldiers were willing to follow, and for the moment, they were following Grant. Paradoxically, Johnson had warned the council that at least fifty more men were needed in Béxar. Before leaving, he ordered the town defenses destroyed and the cannon removed to the Alamo, an abandoned Spanish mission located east of the city that had been converted into a fortress by General Cós. Apparently, the order was not carried out as Texians were still manning the town defenses in mid-January.[27]

Before long, Smith, Houston, and Bowie cooled to the Matamoros scheme and Smith tried to cancel the expedition. One rationale for the effort was that it would draw Santa Anna away from the border and toward Matamoros rather than San Antonio and the Texas interior. But Santa Anna had already dispatched a force of 1,500 troops to Matamoros, more than sufficient to turn back the small number of Texians. Nor did Mexico show any sign of diverting its planned invasion of Texas. All resources would be needed to face that threat, particularly in Béxar. Unfortunately, the tactless Smith issued a self-serving tongue lashing to the General

Council after receiving another dire report from Béxar and blamed the council for refusing to withdraw its order to invade Matamoros, which he now described as a "predatory expedition" even though he had supported it earlier himself. Smith capped off his tirade by ordering the council to disband. The council then moved to remove Smith and named Robinson acting governor, but Smith refused to leave office. The governor and General Council remained preoccupied with finger-pointing and infighting rather than dealing with the desperate military situation at hand. It was exactly the kind of breakdown that was almost guaranteed by the Consultation's hastily drafted Organic Law, which crippled both government and the military. For all practical purposes the government ceased to operate on January 17 when a quorum of the General Council could not be assembled, and an advisory committee was appointed to function in its stead until the convention convened in March. Texas was, in fact, without a government and no organized military. Aside from a small number of regulars, the provisional government left the army a loose, uncoordinated collection of scattered volunteer units under local commanders with no central direction or coordination. It also made it difficult, if not impossible, to efficiently and quickly respond to emergencies, such as forming a large reinforcement to relieve an outnumbered, besieged post.[28]

Unaware of these events, Houston and Bowie hastened to Goliad where they hoped to put an end to the Matamoros expedition, but they could not dissuade the men or their leaders. On January 16, Houston dispatched Bowie to Béxar to assess the damage done there by Grant and Johnson. Bowie took along the roughly thirty men he could lure away from the Matamoros adventure. Meanwhile, Houston played for time and accompanied Grant's men to Refugio, hoping to persuade them to turn back. By now Houston had not only soured on the Matamoros adventure but doubted the wisdom of trying to defend Béxar. His orders suggest that he preferred pulling troops east across the Brazos where he could build and train a credible army that might have a chance to defeat Santa Anna. Despite his doubts about defending San Antonio, he recognized that the place was in jeopardy. As early as January 17 he wrote to Smith from Goliad that he had ordered Captain Dimmitt to raise one hundred men and march to Béxar if it was in danger of invasion but otherwise to assemble in Washington. Houston told Smith that "I would have marched to Bexar with a force, but the Matamoros fever rages so high."[29]

Houston's orders to Bowie regarding his Béxar mission have been debated ever since they were issued. No written order survives, but in his

January 17 letter to Governor Smith, Houston wrote, "I have ordered the fortifications in the town of Bexar to be demolished, and, *if you should think well of it*, I will remove all the cannon and other munitions of war to Gonzales and Copano, blow up the Alamo, and abandon the place, as it will be impossible to keep up the station with volunteers. The sooner that I can be authorized the better it will be for the country" (italics added). Houston later claimed that he ordered the Béxar fortifications and the Alamo destroyed, and its cannon moved east, omitting the fact that he had left the decision to Smith, who rejected it. Nonetheless, Houston seems to have been facing reality much faster than the rest of the government. He knew the meager force in Béxar had no more chance of resisting Santa Anna's army than Grant had of taking Matamoros, nor did he see much chance of rapidly recruiting the necessary force to do so, given the meager turnout of men thus far. Better to move men and material east and play for time while a more credible military force might be built. Houston wrote to Smith enclosing Neill's letter of January 14, which warned that men were returning home and he would soon be left with a mere eighty fighters. Meanwhile, scouts reported that at least one thousand Mexican troops were marching toward Béxar. Neill, of course, could not remove the valuable Alamo cannons, then the largest collection of artillery west of the Mississippi, due to the lack of dray animals. Johnson and Grant had seen to that by pillaging everything in Béxar that was not nailed down. In any case, while Houston clearly favored abandoning Béxar, he left the decision to Smith, and the governor never endorsed it. Johnson, of course, also had ordered the town fortifications destroyed and all cannons moved into the Alamo. In his January 23 letter to Smith and the General Council, Neill also favored pulling his small force out of Béxar, having received new intelligence from Tejano scouts that Santa Anna had arrived at Saltillo, less than six hundred miles from Béxar, with three thousand troops plus another 1,600 close behind. Fannin gave similar orders from Copano in February. Houston's recommendation is consistent with those actions.[30]

Houston sent Green B. Jameson, a lawyer by trade, to serve Neill as Alamo engineer, and it was Jameson who directed its fortification, including the placement of its twenty-one cannons. Jameson boasted the Texians would whip the Mexicans ten to one once the Alamo was properly fortified, mistakenly believing that artillery alone would do the job. He also reported a lack of discipline in the garrison, as did Neill, whose gloomy letters to Smith, the council, and Houston painted a dire picture of Béxar's prospects. He wrote throughout January and early February strongly condemning Johnson and Grant and begging for food and clothing for his 104 men and especially money, if only so his men could buy basic necessities. The men had been in service for four months and had not received the monthly pay they were promised. He described them as nearly naked and complained that clothing intended for them was also carried away by Johnson and Grant, some of it given to newly arrived volunteers who had been in service as little as four days. Men had left the garrison in violation of his orders to remain, and he asked for immediate reinforcements to bring the garrison to at least two hundred to three hundred men. Both he and Dr. Amos Pollard, the garrison physician, found hospital stores were depleted, but Neill also reported strong support from the local citizens who shared what little they had with the garrison.[31]

The lack of horses also made it impossible for Neill to conduct reconnaissance missions, making him increasingly frustrated by the lack of response to his pleas. He warned that Béxar had no chance of withstanding a large invasion force. After receiving word that Santa Anna had reached Saltillo, Neill was willing to pull his men out of Béxar altogether, but there was no way to remove the Alamo cannons and he refused to abandon them. "If teams could be obtained here by any means to remove the Cannon and Public Property I would immediately destroy the fortifications and abandon the place, taking the men I have under my command here, to join the Commander in chief at Copanoe, of which I informed him last night immediately on the above information being Communicated to me." Time was clearly running out, and despite his earlier pledges to defend his post with whatever force he had, Neill now saw the situation as hopeless. He was even more despondent after learning of the government's breakdown. By January 28 he was a bit more optimistic having learned that Travis was on his way with some cavalry. He reported plans to have Travis cut off Mexican supply lines and destroy bridges in the army's path. Somehow, he held out hope of reinforcements and promised that "with 600 to 1000 men, I can [pose] an effectual resistence," and he urged the government to end dissension and effect a meaningful response to the imminent invasion. His pleas fell on deaf ears. Even when a team led by Austin raised $250,000 in New Orleans in mid-January, the money was not devoted to military needs, desperate as things were.[32]

While Neill drummed his fingers in Béxar, waiting for help, Houston arrived in Refugio with the two hundred men led by Grant and Johnson. There he learned that Smith had been deposed and that the General Council had undercut him by placing Fannin and Johnson in command of the expedition. Then, on January 21, 1836, he gave an impassioned speech to the men and pleaded with them to break off the misguided adventure. Most of them eventually heeded him, or so the story goes. Houston's pitch may have actually been more subtle and focused on planting the seeds of doubt about the expedition among one company at a time. In any case, the expedition broke up and most of the men agreed to continue serving, but only as volunteers, not in the regular army, some remaining in Refugio, some drifting back to Goliad. Although the men may have been persuaded by Houston's argument, they refused to serve under him. After all, he had been given command only of regulars and, in any case, many objected to a commander who had not fought in any of the Texas engagements thus far, as Grant, Johnson, Neill, and others had. It didn't help Houston when the men learned that Smith, Houston's most important supporter, had been deposed. On January 29, Smith furloughed Houston until March 1, when the convention would convene, and told him to carry out a previous order to negotiate a treaty with the Cherokee.[33]

Nonetheless, Houston's leadership defused the Matamoros fever and only sixty-four men accompanied Grant and Johnson on the doomed expedition, which they foolishly continued and which the General Council and its advisory committee continued to encourage as late as mid-February. Although Fannin briefly joined the march, he later turned back to Goliad after learning that those 1,500 Mexican troops dispatched by Santa Anna had arrived in Matamoros. Grant's small force was no match for them, but he and Johnson compounded their foolhardy effort by splitting their already meager force in two with thirty-four men joining Johnson in search of livestock and provisions in San Patricio, while Grant took the remaining twenty-six men south to Agua Dulce Creek, where hundreds of Mexican troops under Gen. José de Urrea had gathered. Urrea surprised Johnson's band in San Patricio on February 27, killing or capturing nearly the entire force, although Johnson escaped. On March 2 he caught up with Grant, who found himself outnumbered four to one. Only six Texians escaped, the others being killed or captured, including Grant who was run down by lancers.[34]

The Matamoros fiasco had fractured the Texas government and army and stymied any effort by Houston to build an effective force. The Béxar garrison never fully recovered from that. In the coming months, every Alamo commander would insist that Béxar must be held if the colonies were to be safe, and they pled continually for reinforcements and provisions. Granting those requests was one of the few things the governor and council agreed on, although they would prove incapable of providing such relief. It is fair to ask from where reinforcements were to come, and under whose command? At no time during the revolution did more than a few thousand Texians serve under arms, rarely at the same time or in the same place or under unified command. Even worse, at the very moment when troops were needed in Béxar, Texian numbers dwindled partly due to the widespread false belief that, once Cós had been driven out of Texas, the war was over.[35]

On January 18, Bowie rode into Béxar and immediately agreed with Neill's renewed contention that holding Béxar was not only possible but essential. Bowie was impressed with the defensive improvements Jameson had made and, like Neill, placed undue faith in the number of Alamo cannons. The Texian arsenal also included hundreds of Mexican muskets taken from Cós and around sixteen thousand rounds of ammunition. If Santa Anna could be held here, his advance would be stalled far from home and his supply lines. Meanwhile, Houston might have time to organize a more effective army while the convention met and declared independence. It was a lot to put one's faith in, but Bowie and Neill continued to shore up defenses in everlasting hope that their pleas for help would be answered.

Bowie wrote to Smith on February 2 without mincing words. He reported that he and Neill were "laboring night and day laying up provisions for a siege, encouraging our men, and calling on the government for relief. Relief at this post in men, money, and provisions is of vital importance and is wanted instantly. So this is the real reason of my letter. The salvation of Texas depends in great measure in keeping Bejar out of the hands of the enemy. It serves as the frontier picquet guard and if it were in the possession of Santa Anna there is no strong hold from which to repel him in his march towards the Sabine. There is no doubt but very large forces are being gathered in several of the towns beyond the Rio Grande, and late information through Senr. Cassiana & others, worthy of credit, is positive in the fact that 16 hundred or two thousand troops with good officers, well armed, and a plenty of provisions, were on the point of marching." Bowie reported that his scouts were uncertain whether the Mexican forces they spotted intended to attack Matamoros or Béxar, but Bowie was convinced "an attack is shortly to be made." Bowie declared that "Colonel Neill and myself have come to the solemn resolution that we will rather die in these ditches than give up this post to the enemy," adding for good measure a reminder that "again we call aloud for relief . . . a large reinforcement with provisions is what we need." He added a postscript with more devastating intelligence that at least two thousand troops were headed for San Antonio with five thousand more close behind, intending "to make a decent on this place particular, and there is no doubt of it," adding that the Béxar garrison numbered only 125. Perhaps expressing second thoughts about dying "in these ditches," or emphasizing the urgent need for reinforcements, Bowie now mused that it "would be a waste of men to put our brave little band against thousands."

Only ten days, earlier Crockett had enlisted in Nacogdoches and was making his way to Washington where he expected to receive orders. He didn't know Houston was on his way to Refugio or about the turmoil created by the Matamoros expedition and the desperate situation in Béxar.[36]

Meanwhile, Travis, the war hawk radical of Anahuac fame, was looking for a place in the evolving revolution. On December 19, 1835, the General Council created a Legion of Cavalry and gave Travis command and a commission as lieutenant colonel, which was confirmed on Christmas Eve. While the measure called for 384 men to form the cavalry, like most of the government's fanciful military plans, this one would exist only on paper. Travis was barely able to wrangle some thirty men. Like Houston, he urged the creation of a regular, disciplined army, but no formal recruiting service existed for such a force and commanders of the various volunteer units had to raise their own men and often bear the expense of outfitting them. Their efforts typically proved futile because the needed volunteers simply were not forthcoming. Travis wrote to Smith on January 28 expressing his readiness to go to Béxar, but he also conveyed more bad news regarding his anemic recruiting effort. "Our affairs are gloomy indeed—The people are cold & indifferent—They are worn down & exhausted with the war, & in consequence of dissentions between contending & rival chieftains, they have lost all confidence in their own Govt. & officers. You have no idea of [the] exhausted State of the country—Volunteers can no longer be had or relied upon—A Speedy organization, classification & draft of the militia is all that can save us now. A regular army is necessary—but money, & money only can raise & equip a regular army. Money must be raised or Texas is gone to ruin. . . . The patriotism of a few has done much; but that is becoming worn down." He was forced to use his own funds and credit to outfit his men but had "barely been able to get horses & equipment for the few men I have." He added the names of nine men who had deserted, some of them taking horses, guns, and other equipment with them. Perhaps recalling the early skirmishes at Anahuac and Gonzales, Travis told Smith that a "mob can do wonders in a sudden burst of patriotism or passion, but cannot be depended on as soldiers for a campaign." His warning was prescient but went unheeded.[37]

Many Texians who fought the early battles returned home, and the army would rely increasingly on volunteers like Crockett, recently arrived from the United States, rather than long-term colonists. Roughly 63 percent of the 1835 army that fought at Béxar had lived in Texas for at least one year, while 30 percent had been there for six years or more and had moved to Texas between 1825 and 1834. However, by February 1836, volunteers who arrived after October 1835 comprised nearly 80 percent of the army. The figures suggest that either support for the revolution deteriorated among long-term colonists or they saw no imminent military threat. In any case the number of soldiers was insufficient to mount an adequate defense against an invasion. The breakdown of government left everyone waiting for direction, support, and leadership that might come from the convention in March. Unfortunately for the Texians, Santa Anna didn't wait that long to move on Texas.[38]

Travis was slow in advancing toward Béxar, halting several days at Beeson's Ferry, only twenty miles from his starting point in San Felipe. He dawdled there, writing letters to Smith, finally asking that he be relieved of the assignment. He felt diminished by being placed in command of such a tiny force, called the mission pointless, and said it risked damaging his reputation "which is ever dear to a soldier." Surely such a small squad did not require that a lieutenant colonel command it. He had done all he could to outfit the men, and they could move on to San Antonio under the command of Capt. John Forsyth. He saw inevitable calamity in such an expedition with so few ill-equipped men and insisted that he would be more useful in San Felipe recruiting badly needed volunteers. He ended his letter with a threat to resign his commission if he were not relieved of the assignment. He promised to lead the men as far as Gonzales and send them on to Béxar while he awaited further orders. But, for reasons still unclear, Travis suddenly changed his mind and moved hastily to Béxar ahead of his small force, arriving on February 3, while his men, under Forsyth's command, arrived days later. Whatever Travis's reason for suddenly racing to Bèxar, he found the situation there desperate. He would soon add his voice to the litany of urgent appeals from Neill and Bowie to Governor Smith, Houston, the council, the colonies, and anyone who might listen. Béxar needed help—a lot of it—and now.[39]

It was into this chaotic political and military landscape that Crockett rode after leaving Tennessee for the last time. He had read about events in Texas for years, discussed it with friends who had been there, and was aware of the fighting, but it is unlikely that he knew of the turmoil roiling the revolt. However, it is equally unlikely that he would have changed his plans even if he had known. He would learn of it soon enough, but his mind was made up and his plans set. As he had done most of his life, he would "go ahead," come what may.

CHAPTER 3
The Journey

Long before he left home Crockett was aware of events in Texas. Now that war had come, Crockett was not rushing to the front. He was determined "to explore the Texes well before I return," as he wrote to his brother-in-law one day before leaving Tennessee, making no mention of the war. Nor did he hint to his family that he had any interest in it. It's not likely that he did since he originally planned to take his family with him.[1]

Crockett's company included his brother-in-law, Abner Burgin; Elizabeth's nephew, William Patton; and Lindsey K. Tinkle, who was married to Elizabeth's niece, Rebecca McWhorter. Mounted on a fine bay horse, he led the little group to Jackson, about forty miles south of his home, where he visited Atlas Jones, a lawyer who later observed that "Col. Crockett went on some time ago at the head of 30 men well armed and equipped." There's no telling how many of those fellow travelers were bound for Texas and how many simply wanted the thrill of riding along with the celebrated Colonel Crockett for a while before returning home. A few days later he arrived in Bolivar, Tennessee, where he stayed with Atlas's brother, Calvin Jones, a doctor and land speculator who had once offered to lease Crockett some land. He was not enthusiastic about the Texas cause and regarded the men he saw heading that way as intruders and troublemakers. He later wrote to a friend that "emigrants are passing to Mississippi and Texas—some few stop here. . . . Armed men are passing to . . . take part in the domestic dissensions of another country and it seems generally to be regarded as an act of patriotism." But Jones thought these interlopers no better than men who Andrew Jackson had once hung in Florida. And although he rolled his eyes at the outsized "Davy" image identified with Crockett, he now saw the Colonel in a more flattering light and admired his commitment to his Texas venture. "Crockett, who cannot blow his nose without acquiring remark or observation, was regarded as a passing comet, not to be seen again," Jones wrote, observing that "every eye was . . . bent upon him, and every hand extended either in curiosity or regard. This occasion proved him to be more of a Lion than I had supposed." Jones's reference to a comet may have reflected the nightly appearance of Halley's Comet, which reached a point of brilliance around the time that Crockett left home.[2]

From Bolivar, Crockett turned west for Memphis and the Mississippi River, about a three-day ride, arriving there around November 7. He had often campaigned in Memphis and had many friends there, notably Marcus Winchester, who had rescued Crockett from his hare-brained barrel stave venture and later bankrolled his political campaigns. Crockett stayed at the City Hotel and spent much of the day looking up old friends. Still very much a celebrity, he drew more than his share of gawkers and followers as he made his way around town. They gathered at taverns that evening to celebrate the Colonel's visit, but the tales of drunken carousing during that evening later recounted by James D. Davis in his 1873 book, *The History of the City of Memphis*, seem embellished or completely apocryphal. Rather than carousing, fighting, boozing, and arguing over the tab, as Davis's yarn would have it, Crockett and his friends more likely enjoyed a good time that might have gotten a bit loud now and then. It is likely that Crockett addressed the crowd during the evening with one of his entertaining speeches as he did nearly everywhere throughout his journey. In contrast to Davis's account, a traveler from Cincinnati who was in Memphis at the time later wrote that "Davy Crockett passed through this place on his way to Texas. He was dressed appropriately in a full suit of 'coon skins, and had a leash of hunting dogs and his rifle, accompanied by some of his neighbors. Davy at a supper given him by some young men in Memphis declared that he meant to have Santana's head and wear it for a watch seal!" Although somewhat embellished, the description makes no mention of rowdy behavior by Crockett and his companions.[3]

It is possible that Crockett's speeches that night included his oft-quoted declaration that, having voted him out of office, his constituents might "go to hell and I will go to Texas." Davis has the Colonel saying, "My friends, I suppose you are all aware that I was recently a candidate for Congress in an adjoining District. I told the voters that if they would elect me I would serve them to the best of my ability; but if they did not, they might go to hell, and I would go to Texas. I am on my way now." Crockett had made it clear that he intended to leave the United States in anticipation of Martin Van Buren winning the presidency, but it is not likely that he would have issued such an insulting statement to his constituents during the campaign. News reports quoted Crockett making this or a similar statement all along his route to Texas, but that was after his defeat, and he was clearly playing to the crowd. Another version of the statement's origins places it much earlier in 1835, during Crockett's campaign against Adam Huntsman. That account has Crockett assuring Huntsman that he never made the statement. "Now, Huntsman, I never said that," Crockett allegedly told his opponent, "I said you may go to Congress and I will go to Texas." Crockett appears to have used the harsher, more familiar version during his Texas journey since he always told the crowd what it wanted to hear. Crockett may have decided to put the United States behind him, but "Davy" was along for the ride.[4]

The next morning, Crockett, reportedly wearing a coonskin cap and hunting shirt and shouldering his rifle, left the City Hotel and together with a small group of men, including Marcus Winchester, went down to the Catfish Bay landing. There, he and his companions boarded the ferry operated by a Black man named Limus, who ferried them down the Wolf River and then across the Mississippi to the Arkansas side, "bearing that remarkable man away from his State and his kindred forever," as Davis later recalled. Once across the mighty river that the Algonkian-speaking people called the "Father of Waters," the little group mounted up and made its way along the Military Road to Little Rock—the Arkansas territorial capital and a major crossroads on the way to Texas—where large numbers of Americans passed on their way to the Red River country, "many of them with large droves of negroes," according to the *Arkansas Gazette*. Crockett arrived there on November 12.[5]

Shortly before his arrival, Crockett shot a deer and brought it into town tied to a pack horse. After checking into Jeffries City Hotel, he set about dressing the deer behind the building when he was approached by Col. Robertson Childers, whom Crockett immediately recognized as an old Tennessee friend and exclaimed, "Robertson Childers, as I'm alive." Childers led a hastily formed committee that organized a dinner in Crockett's honor in the hotel. In recounting this incident sixty years later, Judge William F. Pope also leapt to the inescapable conclusion that Crockett was making a beeline for battle in Texas, "to assist the patriots in their struggle to free themselves from the Mexican yoke." Throughout his journey newspapers reported that Crockett was on his way to join the war in Texas and, apparently, Crockett said nothing to disabuse them of the idea. Little Rock newspapers covered the Colonel's appearance, and their stories spread to papers throughout the country with the usual degree of embellishment that painted Crockett as a warrior on his way to finish off Santa Anna.[6]

The anti-Jacksonian *Arkansas Advocate* had time to print only a brief mention of Crockett's arrival in its November 13 edition. "We shall die contented," the editor gushed. "We have seen the Hon. David Crockett who arrived in this place last evening, on his way to Texas, where he contemplates ending his days. A supper was given him at Jeffries' Hotel, of which many citizens partook." The anti-Whig *Arkansas Gazette* was kinder to Crockett than it had been when it gleefully announced Huntsman's defeat of "the buffoon, Davy Crockett" in August. Now, the *Gazette* called Crockett's visit a "rare treat" and reported that "among the distinguished characters who have honored our City with their presence within the last week was no less a personage than Col. David Crockett—better known as Davy Crockett—the *real critter* himself—who arrived on Thursday evening last, with some 6 or 8 followers." Aware of the popularity of the Texas cause, the *Gazette* felt compelled to compliment the Colonel on his mission "to join the patriots of that country in freeing it from the shackles of the Mexican government. The news of his arrival rapidly spread, and we believe we speak within bounds, when we say, that hundreds flocked to see the wonderful man, who, it is said, can whip his weight in wildcats, or grin the largest panther out of the highest tree." Still, the *Gazette* couldn't resist taking a swipe at the Whigs and the anti-Jackson *Advocate* in its report of the supper given in Crockett's honor that evening "by several *Anti-Jackson-men*, merely for the sport of hearing him abuse the Administration, in his outlandish style, and we understand they enjoyed a most delectable treat, in a speech of some length with which he amused them. Having no curiosity that way ourselves, we did not attend the *show*. But our neighbor of the Advocate was there, and so delighted was he, that he says he can now '*die contented*.' Happy man! The Colonel and his party, all completely armed and well mounted, took their departure on Friday morning, for Texas, in which country, we understand, they intend establishing their future abode, and in the defence of which, we hope they may cover themselves with glory."[7]

The *Advocate* took exception a few days later and proclaimed, "We have a single word to say for Colonel Crockett. He was honored and hospitably received here—not because 'he can whip his weight in wild cats, or grin a panther out of the highest tree'—(as the Gazette says)—because there are plenty of Arkansas *boys* who can do the same—but because he is an honest man, and a true friend to Hugh L. White. Neither was the supper given by several *anti-Jackson* men. As well men of one party as of another joined in it. Neither did he *abuse* the Administration in an outlandish style. His remarks were few, plain, moderate and unaffected—without violence or acrimony. He spoke against the Administration and against the *heir apparent*—but he did it by quietly detailing facts. His remarks were far from outlandish. He neither aimed at display of eloquence—and was simply rough, natural, and pleasant. We have lost our partner. He has shouldered his rifle and taken up the line of March for Texas, in company with five or six young men, desirous 'to stain with hostile blood their maiden arms.' Success to them all, and him in particular."[8]

Like the *Gazette*, the *Little Rock Times* chose not to attend the Crockett dinner but claimed to have sought out the Colonel the following morning. The paper reported finding him "not in the hall of legislation, not in the bar room of a tavern, neither was it in a lady's chamber—but in a carpenter's shop *grinding an axe*. Oh! 'what a falling off there was there.' His Honor grinding an axe." This might have been a political pun rather than an observation of Crockett. The pro-Jackson *Times* would not have hesitated to poke fun at Crockett and, like the *Gazette*, reported that the Colonel had taken aim at Jackson during his dinner speech. "We are told that he 'used up' the Administration 'head and tail,'" it said, thus portraying Crockett as grinding his political axe before the crowd.[9]

Judge Pope heard Crockett's speech and was impressed by the frontier politician. He recalled that most of Crockett's speech was devoted to the subject of Texas independence but that the Colonel also "dwelt at some length upon the causes that had brought about his recent defeat for re-election to Congress." Pope later recalled that he "was very agreeably surprised in Colonel Crockett, both as to his manners and personal appearance. I had always been of the impression that the clown was one of his leading characteristics. His manner was dignified and gentlemanly and, while he showed some lack of a thorough education, he displayed a wide range of information upon the leading topics of the day. While his speech abounded in flashes of wit and humor, it never descended to the clownish or vulgar." Although these recollections were published sixty years after the fact, when Pope was eighty years old, they comport with those of Albert Pike, editor of the *Advocate*, which published his account of Crockett's visit only days after it occurred. They are consistent with other descriptions of Crockett by people who met him and found him civil, well informed, and amusing. Benjamin Perley Poore, clerk of the Senate Printing Records and editor of the *Congressional Directory*, recalled Crockett much the same way and described him as a "true frontiersman, with a small dash of civilization and a great deal of shrewdness transplanted in political life. He was neither grammatical nor graceful, but no rudeness of language can disguise strong sense and shrewdness, and a 'demonstration,' as Bulwer says, 'will force its way through all perversions of grammar.'"[10]

Many news stories mentioned Crockett's open vow to leave the United States if Van Buren were elected president and cited his journey as proof that he was making good on his promise since Van Buren's election was all but assured. "*Davy Crockett* has actually gone to Texas with his rifle and a hundred rounds," the *New York Sunday Morning News* told its readers. "His farewell letter to his quondam constituents, states that he left his native state and country in consequence of a determination long ago formed and expressed, of expatriating himself in case Martin Van Buren should be elected president—strong *premonitories* [*sic*] of which event he now begins to see. Davy also has discovered, he says, that our politicians are inconsistent, selfish, and insincere. . . . Perhaps he will find more sincerity amongst the Texians, and less of party intrigue; and we are quite certain he will find there fewer political mountebanks." Referring to Crockett's fondness for gambling, the editor added the caution that if "there be, however, such a thing as a faro-bank to be found in Texas, we fear Davy will forget all his prudential maxims."[11]

The Philadelphia *Public Ledger* envied Texas for luring Crockett away and regretted his departure. "Davy Crockett, it seems, is exacting wonders in Texas. It does not appear that he makes long speeches on political subjects . . . but he makes the woods of Texas resound with his alligator voice and the conversation of his rifle. Texas can certainly boast now, of possessing in her midst several distinguished men. . . . The course of this last 'stupendous man,' is somewhat more eccentric than that of his crusading compeers. We heard him say once, as he stood before the humming crowd under the semicircular row of pillars at the Exchange—'I love my country—if I don't I wish I may be shot!' but he has left her, and gone to Texas. What can be done without him?"[12]

Like most newspapers, the *Jackson Truth Teller* said he was on his way to Texas to join the army, but that was far from Crockett's mind. His destination was Texas's lush Red River country, not the battlefield, as he had clearly told his family. But Crockett quickly realized that wherever he went crowds assumed that he was heading for the war. It was a natural assumption. Many men were passing through the same towns daily, rifles in hand, answering Sam Houston's call to arms. Surely the legendary "Davy," who came well-armed with other men heading for Texas, was equally bent on joining the fight. Crockett knew it wasn't true, but he always played to the crowd, and it was easier to go along with the news stories that cheered him on to war than spend time explaining why he wasn't doing that at all. Crockett was always able to read a crowd and sense what it wanted to hear, so he said nothing to contradict these assumptions. Newspapers along his route marked his passing and emphasized that he and his followers were armed head to foot on their way to do battle in Texas. Crockett "was honored with a public dinner at Little Rock, Arkansas," the *New York Sun* proclaimed, "where there were many fine things said to the western coon hunter, and as many returned." Others anticipated the damage that Crockett's legendary marksmanship would wreak on the Mexican army. "Two such men as Ex-Governor Houston and David Crockett will probably handle the Mexicans rather roughly," the *Sun* boasted. The *Albany Journal*, a New York tabloid, poked a bit of bearish fun at Crockett, reporting that he "is probably one of the best shots in the world. One hundred men like Crockett would be of immense service to the Texians at this time—if you could only make them believe that their enemies were *bears*, instead of men." The story ended with the outrageous suggestion that "Crockett has been known to send a rifle ball through the same hole nine times in successive fire." Such was the "Davy" baggage that followed Crockett everywhere.[13]

Crockett kept up with reports from Texas. Word of Santa Anna smashing the Zacatecas rebellion reached Little Rock more than a week before his arrival there along with speculation the dictator planned to march on Texas. The *Arkansas Gazette* reported the Texian capture of Goliad and printed Houston's October 5 recruiting broadside. The November 3 edition of the *Gazette* carried Austin's letters of October 4 and 5 regarding formation of the "Army of the People." Crockett learned of these events, but they did not change his plans. He intended to explore Texas, not fight the Mexican army. He was bound for the Red River country, a common destination for many Tennessee migrants on their way to Texas. Crockett's friend and fellow congressman, Samuel Carson, had purchased more than one thousand acres of Red River land earlier in the year and was in the process of moving there at the same time as Crockett. Carson was anxious to close a deal with James A. Bass for the sale of several hundred acres of land and eighty-four slaves that would bring Carson $107,000. Carson left his home in North Carolina on September 22 with his entire family, headed for his Red River plantation, and arrived in Little Rock one day after Crockett left the city. Traveling by wagon, Carson made slower time than Crockett on horseback, and the two may have even run into each other on the road to Little Rock. It had been eight years since Crockett witnessed Carson kill Robert Vance in a duel while both were in North Carolina. Then, they were on their way to Washington to serve in Congress. Now both were headed for Texas; Carson to settle on his plantation, Crockett to explore the same territory. It was likely Carson who marked out the route that Crockett followed long before either left home, and Crockett had enough confidence in Carson's familiarity with the territory to travel without a guide.[14]

Although the *Gazette* accurately reported Carson's arrival in Little Rock, noting he was on his way to the Red River country, it also insisted that Crockett and his companions were on their way to Texas to battle the Mexican army. But Crockett and Carson had the same destination, and neither was on his way to war. Crockett, of course, did nothing to correct the error and was resigned to being seen as the mythical "Davy: the wild man."[15]

Crockett and Carson were not unique. Americans flocked to the fertile soil of the Red River. The land was perfect for the cultivation of cotton and most immigrants planned to grow the lucrative crop, which required large numbers of slaves. Thus, Mexico's opposition to slavery created friction with American immigrants who feared the government would cease recognizing their slave "property." This did not stop American slave owners and land speculators from embarking for the Red River country.

Samuel Swartwout was one of several New York investors who founded the New Washington Association in 1834 to speculate in Texas lands and was pressing to get its agents to the Red River country as fast as possible. Several prominent Tennesseans were part of this group, including Crockett's one-time associate John C. McLemore and George C. Childress from Nashville. Childress was a major booster of the Texas cause and raised funds and recruited volunteers in Tennessee for the effort, but he was just as interested in speculating in Red River land. He was dispatched to the

Red River country by the syndicate to spur land purchases in the region and was on his way there in early December 1835. Swartwout wrote to McLemore from New York on December 7 urging him to get Childress on his way quickly "as every day's delay diminishes his prospects of procuring the lands—Companies are forming here to proceed direct to the Red River & take up the lands . . . and I am invited to become interested. It would be most distressing & mortifying to have others reap the benefit of our planning entered into by them two months after the departure of Mr. Childress." Swartwout was aware many Red River colonists were sitting out the war in Texas and might be interested in selling their land. He told McLemore, "I am now more than ever satisfied that [Childress] can get the best lands and make the best bargains on *Red River* above the raft. There are two or 300 families settled there and they, being so far from the seat of war, will be found at home, ready for him. Let him go there *first*, by all means . . . for God's sake, send him off & let his first landing be on Red River." Swartwout needn't have feared, for Childress was already on his way to Texas and arrived in the Red River country on December 13, 1835. He was exploring the area at the same time as Crockett and there was no need for McLemore to spur him on. However, like Crockett, Childress's efforts at land dealing were stymied when the provisional Texas government closed all land offices and barred land transactions until the end of the war. Nonetheless, land transactions continued throughout the period but ran the risk of being nullified later by a future Texas government, as some were. As with most issues, controlling the land situation in Texas proved elusive for the provisional government.[16]

Crockett's company, which may have added a few more men along the way, departed Little Rock on November 13 and took the Southwest Trail to Washington, Arkansas. Armstead Blevins later recalled that Crockett stayed there with his family for a week and hunted deer with his father. It seems unlikely that Crockett would delay his journey a full week, but he may have been enticed to spend a few days hunting. If so, assuming he arrived around November 18, he would have left two or three days later, or by November 21. From that point on there is no certainty regarding the path Crockett followed, but he most likely travelled from Washington to Fulton, Arkansas, and then south to Dooley's Ferry where he crossed the Red River. From there it was only a few miles west to the plantation of Dr. Isaac N. Jones, near Lost Prairie, where we know Crockett spent at least a day. It is one of the few places that we know for sure he visited after leaving

Washington because Dr. Jones later wrote to Crockett's widow about the visit.

Travelers could reach the Red River country by boat from the Mississippi River to the Red River, or by the more desirable Southwest Trail that ran from Little Rock to Washington, Arkansas, and then split at Fulton into two separate paths, one of which went to the Dooley's Ferry crossing, about twelve miles below Fulton and within a few miles of Lost Prairie. George Dooley's ferry was the quickest and most comfortable route across the Red River and into Texas. It was so attractive to travelers that Dooley found himself the target of competing ferry operators who spread false rumors that the road to Dooley's was in poor condition.

Crockett may have thought he entered Texas when he crossed the Red River and visited Lost Prairie, although the area now lies in Arkansas. Although the Adams-Onis Treaty of 1819 between Spain and the United States established boundaries between the two countries, and the borders were later confirmed in a treaty between the United States and Mexico, those borders remained unclear. The loyalty of settlers often vacillated depending upon policies of the countries involved, such as taxes, tolerance of slavery, objections to settlers' antagonism toward Native Americans, and other issues. People living in the Pecan Point and Jonesboro area might claim to be part of New Spain one day and the United States the next. It was not clear if Sam Carson's Red River property lay in Texas or Arkansas Territory, but Carson was one of five delegates who represented Pecan Point at the Texas Convention in March 1836, where he was elected secretary of state. Lost Prairie was located directly within disputed territory. In any case, as far as Crockett was concerned, he had crossed the Red River and begun to "explore the Texes," as he had set out to do.[17]

Significantly, neither this route nor an alternative one via Fort Towson took Crockett anywhere near the war, particularly the siege and Battle of Béxar, which began in October and continued into the first week of December. If Crockett had come to Texas to join the fight, he could have made his way to Nacogdoches by Trammel's Trace, which lay about forty-five miles west of Lost Prairie, and enlisted there, or he could have gone directly to Béxar and joined the fight. But Crockett instead took the road that ran along the south bank of the Red River to Pecan Point, clearly away from Béxar. Micajah Autry left Jackson, Tennessee, nearly a month after Crockett's departure and reached Nacogdoches in mid-January, around the same time Crockett did, where they both enlisted at the same time.

Clearly, Crockett could have reached Nacogdoches weeks earlier, way ahead of Autry, if that was his destination. Autry and his companions were bound for the war from the time they left home, but Crockett was not. He was off to explore land, which he did for most of December.

Late on November 23, Isaac Jones saw Crockett and his companions approaching his house, where they introduced themselves and asked for accommodations for the night. Jones was forced to turn them away because his wife was ill, but he directed them to a neighbor who was able to put them up. Crockett returned to Jones's plantation the next day and the two spent much of it talking. They developed an easy rapport, and Crockett felt comfortable enough to ask a favor of Jones. The Colonel had used up much of his ready cash paying for lodgings and provisions at various hotels, inns, and taverns along his route, which typically charged exorbitant rates. He proposed exchanging watches with Jones and estimated that his watch was worth thirty dollars more than Jones's. His host agreed to the exchange and gave Crockett thirty dollars and his watch in exchange for Crockett's timepiece. The Colonel was glad to have the cash, as he still faced a long journey.[18]

The Dooley's Ferry route wasn't merely convenient for Crockett but also marked the start of his land exploration, for there was land in the area well worth looking at. When he crossed by Dooley's Ferry and visited Isaac Jones's plantation a year earlier, George William Featherstonhaugh (pronounced *Fanshaw*), a British geologist and geographer, remarked, "It is impossible to exaggerate the extraordinary fertility of the soil of Lost Prairie," and concluded that "it would seem impossible to exhaust a soil of this kind. In favourable seasons they gather from 1500 to 2500 lbs. of cotton in the seed to the acre, which, when the seed is taken out by the cotton gin, leaves from twenty-five to thirty per cent, in weight of marketable raw cotton. . . . Some of the plants were near six feet high, and sent forth branches in great profusion, covered with large white bolls resembling the Guelder Rose when in full perfection. I counted 300 bolls on one stem, but Dr. Jones's overseer told me that he had counted as many as 360 on one stem this season." This was just the sort of land that interested Crockett.[19]

The need for slaves to cultivate cotton was inescapable, and from the start, Texas meant to make its territory safe for slavery. As early as January 5, 1836, the General Council passed an ordinance making it illegal for any free negro or mulatto to enter or reside in Texas, stipulating that any free person of color found in Texas could be arrested and, if found guilty, sold into slavery. Emigration from the United States to Texas surged in the early 1830s when the price of cotton soared, and the Americans brought hundreds of slaves into Texas, leading to apprehension about the possible abolition of slavery in Mexico.

While he was impressed with Jones's bumper crops, Featherstonhaugh lamented their price in human suffering and clearly saw the unbreakable bond between slavery and the cultivation of cotton. In his memoir, he wrote that the Texians were superior to the Mexicans "in industry and enterprise":

> Yet the Mexicans stand at a proud moral distance from them in regard to slavery, which is abolished in their republic. What can be more abominable than the hypocritical cant with which these people intrude into a country which does not belong to them? To believe them, they have no motive but to establish 'free institutions, civil and religious.' Yet in defiance of human freedom, just laws, and true religion, they proceed to consummate their real purpose, which is to people the country with slaves in order to cover it with cotton crops. The poor slaves I saw here did not appear to me to stand any higher in the scale of animal existence than the horse. . . . This is the history of the slave in Texas, differing in nothing from that of the horse, except that instead of maize and straw he is supplied with a little salt pork to his maize, day after day, without any change, until death relieves him from his wearisome existence. The occupation of Texas by the Americans, where there are so many millions of acres of the most fertile cotton lands, will convert the old slave-holding part of the United States into a disgusting nursery for young slaves, because the black crop will produce more money to the proprietors than any other crop they can cultivate. For this reason the insufficiency of the Mexican Government for the protection of their own territory appears to me to be one of the greatest misfortunes that could have happened to the human family in our times, when the minds of men, especially in North America, were gradually inclining to the universal abolition of slavery.[20]

Crockett was not bothered by the number of slaves on Isaac Jones's plantation, nor the ill treatment of many of those slaves by Jones's overseer. During his more prosperous years in Tennessee, Crockett bought and sold a few slaves but was never financially able to operate a large plantation that would require many slaves. He never showed any interest in undertaking such an enterprise, but neither did he ever express misgivings about slavery, and he was somewhat ambivalent about the institution. In 1821, during his first term in the Tennessee legislature, he opposed repealing a law that allowed freeing slaves from bondage, and he voted for the relief of a free Black man named Mathias. But a decade later, finding himself strapped for cash, he sold a young slave girl named Adeline to his stepson for $300. In 1827, Crockett's father-in-law, Robert Patton, gave Crockett's wife three young slaves as a gift, and they were put to work on the Crockett homestead. In 1828, Crockett wrote of turning down an offer from a relative who offered to exchange a ten-year-old "negro boy" to be delivered to Crockett in one year in exchange for a colt, a mare, and $150 cash. Crockett turned him down because he lacked the cash, was in serious debt, and in any case, as Crockett put it, "I can get a negro here of that discription [*sic*] for less than $150." Referring to the mill disaster in his 1834 autobiography, Crockett mentioned that he retained some property, including "some likely negroes," further evidence that he engaged in slavery. However, James Strange French, author of *Sketches & Eccentricities of Col. Crockett*, visited Crockett's Tennessee home in 1833 and observed the "colonel has no slaves."

Crockett shared the common prejudices of his time and place. He engaged in what would today be regarded as racist or bigoted language, but which would have been commonplace in his world. He freely used such language in his autobiography, at one point saying that, prior to a hunting trip, he dreamed of "having a hard fight with a big black nigger" and saw it as a "sign that I was to have a battle with a bear." Elsewhere in the book he tells of giving a hunting companion "a thousand weight of fine fat bear-meat, which pleased him mightily, and made him feel as rich as a Jew," thus repeating a negative, antisemitic stereotype common at the time and still in use today. Crockett never raised objections to slavery and, typical of white men of his time and place, never questioned it. Its role in the Texas Revolution would not have mattered to him or affected his plans. Indeed, his friend Sam Carson was already operating a plantation in Texas with at least one hundred slaves.[21]

After spending the night as Dr. Jones's guest, Crockett bid his host farewell and headed up the Ridge Road along the Red River, bound for Pecan Point and the land he had come to explore. In Tennessee, Crockett repeatedly moved to new country, always further west, and he always seemed to know where best to explore. In Texas he chose the Red River country, no doubt being directed there by Carson or John C. McLemore, one of Crockett's Tennessee business associates, who was part of the consortium of Texas land speculators. He reached Pecan Point in two or three days and then, by the end of November, covered the twenty miles from there to the Clarksville area and the home of John Stiles, where he spent the night. The next day, at Crockett's request, Stiles directed him to the home of William Becknell, about nine miles further west. There is no evidence Crockett knew either Stiles, a longtime Red River resident, or Becknell, who had only recently moved to Texas. But he could have been referred to them as guides who could provide him with information about the local country and, perhaps, the status of the war. Although he had come this far without a guide, Crockett would have sought local guides to show him the way to specific locations in the area. He may have looked forward to meeting Becknell who was celebrated for pioneering the Santa Fe Trail in the 1820s. Like Crockett and Carson, none of the men he met in the area had rushed off to war either, although Becknell led a company of mounted volunteers later in 1836 and Stiles joined his unit.[22]

Crockett spent a month exploring the Red River country, but there is little certainty about exactly where he travelled or when. He visited places in present-day Grayson, Fannin, Lamar, Red River, and Bowie counties and wrote about several of them in his only letter home from Texas. His path followed an east-west direction between the Red River to the north and the Sulphur River to the south. It cut a path of about one hundred miles extending roughly from present-day Whitewright to Clarksville and came near to present-day Honey Grove and Paris. He focused primarily on the land between Choctaw Creek and Bois d'Arc Creek. Crockett's letter referred to several specific locations in the area, including a pass where bison migrated twice each year—a reference to the Blackland Prairie that ran from the Red River as far south as San Antonio and extended across the area bounded by Choctaw Creek and Bois d'Arc Creek. He reported that game was plentiful and fertile lands extended for miles across the area.[23]

Crockett did not pass up the opportunity to join a hunting party in search of bison, and he must have relished his first stab at hunting the majestic beasts. He was accompanied by a group that included Becknell, Stiles, and Henry Stout, who served as their guide. The group may have travelled as far as one hundred miles west of Clarksville.

Word of the buffalo hunt filtered back to the United States where newspapers reported that "Davy Crockett started for Texas some months ago, to try his hand in a 'skirmmage' with the Mexicans" but that "on his way, he took a new scent, on reaching Red river, and scampered off on a Buffalo hunt." Edward Warren, who was traveling through Texas at the time, heard about it too and wrote to his uncle, "You may have heard that

David Crockett set out for this country with a company of men to join the army. He has forgotten or waved his original intention & stopped some 80 or 100 miles to the north of this place to hunt Buffalo for the winter! For a long time, it was feared that he & his party had been destroyed by the tribes of wild Indians through which he intended to pass. But, at last, it is ascertained that he is at his favorite amusement." Warren's report appeared in newspapers back in Maine, and word of Crockett's activities spread southward as well, suggesting that, by the same token, Crockett received news from there about the war.[24]

By the time the story reached US newspapers a month later it had been distorted with added reports that Crockett had been killed. These stories may have been seen by Crockett's family. "Death of Colonel David Crockett," headlined one report. "The Washington correspondent of the Journal of Commerce under date of 17th instant says—A letter was read to-day by a member of Congress from Brownsville, Tennessee, in which it was stated that intelligence had been received there of the death of Col. David Crockett, in Texas, soon after his arrival in that country." Another paper reported that "David Crockett is no more! He died on his way to Texas. Alas, poor Yorick!" But the stories were quickly extinguished: "Davy Crockett not Dead," read one headline weeks later. "We are happy to state, on the authority of a letter from Tennessee, that the report of the death of the eccentric Davy Crockett, is not true. 'He started (says the letter) on a hunting expedition to the Rocky Mountains, and then dropped down to Texas; but we expect him home early in Spring.'" The newspapers, having created the illusion that Crockett was on his way to war from the start, now wondered why he had detoured into a hunting adventure, thus basing one story on earlier false ones about the Colonel's destination. Of course, Crockett shared some of the blame for this inaccuracy by failing to correct the media's assumptions regarding his itinerary. He knew that, to most people, he was "Davy" and doubtless on his way to war, so why spoil the illusion? [25]

While out hunting, Crockett ran into a man named William Brinton, who later told Mrs. Isabella Clark of their meeting. According to Isabella's grandson, the report alarmed Mrs. Clark as she had learned of Comanche raiding parties operating south of where Brinton had seen Crockett. According to this story, Mrs. Clark's husband, James Clark, had organized a company of armed men to drive the Comanche out of the area. She took out after Crockett to warn him of the Comanche and was later joined by Jane Latimer, a neighbor. They tracked Crockett to Becknell's home, where she and Becknell told Crockett to avoid the Comanche by taking the Choctaw Trail south to the Spanish Trail "into San Antonio at Nacogdoches," which was more likely a reference to taking Trammel's Trace to Nacogdoches and then the old El Camino Real to San Antonio from there. The story is another one that originated with Isabella's grandson, Judge Pat B. Clark, who published recollections of his grandmother's tales decades after hearing them and more than a century after the described events took place. Mrs. Clark gave her own version of the events in an 1894 interview published in *The Dallas Morning News*, nearly sixty years after the fact when she was nearly ninety years old, quite different from her grandson's account, which was not published until 1937. There are no dangerous Indians in her version, and she says that she, along with Jane and Betsy Latimer, rode out to meet Crockett simply because they heard he was in the area and wanted to see the famous man for themselves. "Fearing that he might not come through Clarksville, but keep on the old Trammell trace," she recalled, "we intended to meet him" and they encountered Crockett's party at the home of Edward Deen, not at Becknell's, about four miles from Clarksville, where a friend who knew Crockett in Tennessee introduced the young women to the Colonel. Her recollection of Crockett's appearance may have been fogged by the passing of decades, but it comports with portraits and other descriptions of Crockett. He was, she remembered, "dressed like a gentleman, and not as a backwoodsman" but added that he wore a coonskin cap. Whether or not he did, the head gear appears in many later recollections of Crockett's Texas journey, including those of his daughter, Matilda. By the late nineteenth century, popular images of Crockett in theaters, on sheet music, in pulp fiction, and the notorious *Crockett Almanacks* typically placed him in a fur cap of some kind. Mrs. Clark said it "disgusted me to read these accounts of Crockett that characterize him as an ignorant backwoodsman. Neither in dress, conversation nor bearing could he have created the impression that he was ignorant or uncouth. He was a man of wide practical information, and was dignified and entertaining. His language was about as good as any we hear nowadays. He was a gentleman all over. Crockett was a handsome fellow, tall, straight and clean-shaven." She even recalled the "fine horse" that he rode. After finishing their breakfast, "Crockett and his men . . . prepared to resume their journey to the south." This could mean the event occurred late in Crockett's sojourn, after he had finished his Red River exploration and was about to head south to Nacogdoches. Or, it might just have been a ninety-year-old woman coloring her Crockett memories with sixty years of his name being linked to the Alamo.

Like many recollections of Crockett in Texas, Judge Clark's appears to conflate the Colonel's exploration of the Red River with his later travel to Nacogdoches, San Antonio, and the Alamo. He claims that Crockett "was very anxious to reach Col. Travis, who was at that time near San Antonio," although Crockett had no idea who Travis was, and at the same time Clark says Crockett was "desirous to see another Red River County citizen" and asked for directions to Becknell's home, not to Béxar. Clark seems to go off the deep end in saying Isabella convinced Crockett to remain at Becknell's house "for a few days waiting for recruits to escort them on to join Houston's Army." This is as unfounded as his claim that Crockett was looking for Travis. Why would Crockett be chosen to guide anyone through Texas when he was a newcomer there? And where were these recruits? By this time, with the Battle of Béxar in full swing, most volunteers were already there. Many recollections of Crockett in Texas conflate his travels with a determination to get to Béxar as fast as possible, while ignoring the incongruity of his weeks of leisurely exploring and hunting far from the war. Mrs. Clark's account, or her grandson's version of it, may have been similarly influenced.[26]

Crockett was smitten with the Red River country, where he found the promised land he was searching for when he set out for Texas. It offered fertile soil for rich farmland and produced bumper crops of cotton and corn. There were vast timber tracts and abundant wild game—particularly bison—abundant rainfall, and countless streams. The region's rich soil quickly drew colonists, and by the time Crockett arrived, eighty-eight first-class land certificates had been granted in the area. Judge John Forbes thought the population large enough to merit creation of three municipalities and the election of six representatives to the Convention of 1836. By mid-December, James Clark was on his way to Nacogdoches to pick up a letter of introduction from Forbes to Lieutenant Governor James W. Robinson and he arrived there on December 23. It is likely Clark fully informed Crockett about the precarious state of political affairs in Texas. That did not deter Crockett, who was so taken with this land that he determined to relocate his family there, whatever the cost.[27]

The Texas journey Crockett planned was over, and at this point he could have headed home, probably the same way he came, through Arkansas and Memphis. But something changed Crockett's mind during his Red River travels and altered his plans. Along the way he learned that the provisional government had closed all land offices in November and suspended all land transactions and surveys for the duration of the war. That closed any opportunity Crockett might have had to legally buy or claim land. He may have learned that the shady Monclova land deals that took place the previous spring were partly responsible for his predicament. These land deals were ultimately nullified by the Mexican Congress and by the Texas provisional government, which closed the land offices.[28]

But Crockett also learned of the fighting in Béxar, and he got wind of the land bounties being offered to volunteers. The provisional government had created an Auxiliary Volunteer Corps on December 5, 1835, which promised 640 acres, or one square mile of land, to all volunteers or their heirs if they were killed. Married volunteers who permanently moved their families to Texas would also receive the same amount of land that the original Mexican colonization laws provided—a league and labor, or 4,605.5 acres. So, Crockett stood to gain more than five thousand acres of land for volunteering and moving his family to Texas, which he planned to do anyway. It was more land than he could have dreamed of in Tennessee.[29]

This created a serious dilemma for Crockett. Although he promised his family that he would return home after exploring Texas, he realized it would take considerable time to reach Tennessee, prepare his family for the move west, and embark on the long journey by wagon, which was much slower than horseback and could take more than a month. By that time the war might have ended along with the opportunity to secure all that land as a volunteer. The consensus in Texas was the war was practically over already and that if Santa Anna marched north, he would be repelled as easily as General Cós was in December. In fact, all Mexican troops had been driven out of Texas with seeming ease, and should Santa Anna return, Texians would doubtless rally by the hundreds to repulse him. It may not have seemed like much of a risk at all and one worth taking with so much land at stake. Although he had shown no interest in the war during his exploration of Texas, he now saw the promise of a bright future there, one worth fighting for. After mulling this over in his mind, Crockett reconsidered his promise to return home.

Crockett may have learned that, despite the closing of land offices and the moratorium on land sales, a brisk, if illegal, land business continued among speculators, land agents, and colonists. But if the decree was ignored by some, it was also effective enough to raise a chorus of cries to lift the moratorium on sales. After all, legal title to any land exchanged during this period could not be secured until the land offices reopened. This unstable situation would have discouraged Crockett from engaging in land deals that might be ruled invalid by a future Texas government, as the Monclova transactions were, since they would have taken place illegally under the moratorium. He had seen land deals nullified in Tennessee for various reasons and claims tied up in court for years. Given the volatile Texas environment, he knew it could happen here too. But should Texas prevail in its war for independence, the military land grants that were promised to soldiers would be solid, backed by the government, and could not be questioned. Indeed, one reason for the moratorium was the fear that continued unchecked land speculation would rob soldiers of land they intended to claim for their service. Also, the military bounty lands were free, doubtless a more attractive alternative to Crockett than paying for the land himself. Holding true to form, Crockett made up his mind to join the army and secure his land grants, and once he made up his mind, he never reconsidered. Sticking to his decisions had long been his unwavering pattern and there is no reason to think it would have changed in this case. Once he made a decision, he really did "go ahead."

There was nothing mercenary in Crockett's decision, nor did it differ from that of many volunteers arriving in Texas at the time. Autry expressed the same thoughts and wrote to his wife that he would be "entitled to 640 acres of land for my services in the army and 4444 acres upon condition of settling my family here. Whether I shall be able to move you here next fall or not will depend upon the termination of the present contest." Daniel William Cloud, also on his way to Texas, expressed similar sentiments in a letter to his brother: "If we succeed, the Country is ours. It is immense in extent, and fertile in its soil, and will amply reward all our toils. If we fail, death in the cause of Liberty and humanity is not cause for shuddering. Our rifles are by our sides, and choice guns they are. We know what awaits us and are prepared to meet it." Crockett's thinking was much the same. He wanted the land, and he was willing to fight for it. Perhaps he recalled his speech in Congress proclaiming that land ownership bound men to their country.[30]

The decision could not have been too difficult for Crockett, considering he had decided to leave the United States for good long before his departure for Texas. His disgust with Jackson and Van Buren and the sale of his Tennessee land proclaimed his clear intention to abandon the United States. Long before, he had told his family that he wanted to move to Texas and urged them to go with him because he had no intention of returning to the United States. Now, he was determined to grasp what might be his last chance to realize his dream of a land empire, and joining the Texas army was the price of that dream. Sure, it was a gamble. Joining any army posed the risk of moving into harm's way and possibly perishing. But Crockett was a gambler who had repeatedly taken big chances to achieve his goals. As a volunteer during the Creek War, he saw the carnage of warfare. He remembered what war was, what it looked and smelled like— even two decades after witnessing it—and he understood the risks. But when he later wrote to his family explaining his decision to remain in Texas, he emphasized the promising future offered by the land bounties and played down his enlistment and any danger it might bring.

Crockett may have seen the chance to revive his political career as well. Although he had soured on politics back home, all those honorary dinners and hero's greetings he received along his route and the crowds that gathered around and cheered him wherever he went might have re-awakened his taste for the campaign stump. All amounted to the promise of a bright future, one well worth the risk of doing battle with Santa Anna. Uninterested in the war or land bounties, Lindsey K. Tinkle and Abner Burgin, who had been with him from the beginning, headed for home, but William Patton, Crockett's nephew, remained with him.

Throughout his journey observers and newspapers reported that Crockett was going to Texas to join the fight for independence. Now, for the first time, he was able to confirm those reports openly and ingenuously. Years later someone who watched him depart the Red River country recalled the "last words we ever heard from Davy Crockett . . . were memorable and characteristic: 'I'm as good for Santa Anna's scalp, as a ninepence is for a dram.'" During the last week of December, he bid his new friends farewell and, rather than heading east toward home, turned south down Trammel's Trace toward Nacogdoches where he planned to join the Texas army. Crockett was going to fight for Texas independence after all.[31]

* * * * *

On December 30, 1835, in the wake of Cós's defeat in Béxar, the Mexican government adopted the Tornel Decree, which required the execution of armed foreigners found in Mexican territory. Santa Anna was a staunch defender of the decree and adamant about enforcing it. Crockett could not have known that.[32]

CHAPTER 4
Staying

Crockett found Nacogdoches a dreary, cold place. Mornings were frosty with temperatures as low as fourteen to twenty-eight degrees, and it rained every few days. William Fairfax Gray, a recent traveler from Virginia, described the area as "a diversified country, much sand, and pine growth, some strips of red land and some black land on the bayous" and found the general appearance of the land "not promising." Although he thought Nacogdoches "prettily situated on a sandy plain, between two fine, clear streams," he also described it as "old," having "once contained four or five thousand souls, now scarce as many hundreds; the buildings, with one or two exceptions, miserable, shabby, old Mexican *jacales*, or small wooden houses. The appearance is shabby in the extreme; not a decent tavern in the place. But there is a tolerably good society in a few families of *Anglo-Americans*. There is no social intercourse between them and the Mexicans. The latter much resemble our mulattos in appearance and manners. Yet there are among them some intelligent and respectable people, and their character generally is that of a quiet, orderly, cheerful people, fond of dancing and gambling, unthrifty and unambitious." Gray was accompanied by Col. Henry Millard of the Texas Infantry's 1st Regiment, who made it clear to him that if the upcoming convention did not declare independence from Mexico, the army would.[1]

Millard's remark highlighted a major issue among Texas colonists that Crockett eventually became aware of. Competing factions argued over whether to remain part of Mexico under a restored 1824 Constitution or break away completely from the mother country. On December 20 the garrison at Goliad issued its own declaration of independence, stirring up deep differences among Texians regarding the movement's objectives. While the war hawks favored independence, with some seeking eventual annexation to the United States, others, particularly Tejanos, only sought to remove

Santa Anna from power and restore the 1824 Constitution. A movement for independence could cost the revolt much of its Tejano support.

Just as news about Crockett had drifted south from the Red River country, so did news of the war reach him during his exploration. He learned that Béxar had been taken early in December and that all Mexican troops had been driven out of Texas. He was aware that the Consultation had created the Organic Law and a provisional government, although he may not have known about the squabbling between Governor Henry Smith and the General Council led by Lieutenant Governor James Robinson. News that the rebels had won their early battles with seeming ease fed Texian hubris and the belief that they would prevail against any Mexican army. In fact, some Texians thought that an invasion of Mexico was the next logical step in keeping Santa Anna on the defensive and the war outside of Texas, while also keeping men from drifting home out of boredom. This thinking gave rise to the doomed Matamoros expedition, which was still underway when Crockett arrived in Nacogdoches but fizzled a few weeks later. Focus then returned to shoring up Béxar, although little was done to achieve that.

Although Houston placed Col. J. C. Neill in command of the post in December and later sent James Bowie there to assess the situation, he thought it more important to secure port cities, especially Copano, which were crucial to supply lines and would facilitate transport of men and supplies from the United States by sea. Indeed, reports of the dire conditions in Béxar led Houston to consider abandoning the place altogether, moving its troops east, and building a credible force there. But there was general agreement that Béxar should be held, and Houston deferred to Governor Smith and the council, which ordered troops to be sent there in adequate numbers, but efforts to recruit enough soldiers proved futile. At the start of the year Houston told a traveling companion of his plan to raise five thousand troops and invade Mexico where he would dictate terms to Santa Anna. Now the reality of dwindling numbers of soldiers made it impractical to defend the frontier at Béxar while also defending coastal ports. Houston continued to lean toward abandoning Béxar, but after the government collapsed and Houston dissolved the Matamoros expedition, he played no official role until the Convention of 1836 convened on March 1.[2]

This perplexing news was in the air when Crockett and his nephew William Patton arrived in Nacogdoches on January 5 with a few other men who had joined them along Trammel's Trace. The timing of Crockett's arrival was a bit awkward. On the same evening town officials were hosting a dinner for Don Agustín Viesca, the recently deposed governor of Coahuila and Texas, when word came of Crockett's unanticipated arrival. According to one account, "A sumptuous table was spread for them in the large hall of Major Nixon, and they had sat down, with the citizens . . . to partake of it. It was then announced that David Crockett had arrived in town, on his way to the Texan army. A committee was forthwith despatched to wait on him and bring him to the feast. His appearance in the hall was greeted with three hearty cheers. He added to the pleasure of the company by his numerous and quaint stories." *Niles' Weekly Register* reported that a "gentleman from Nacogdoches, in Texas, informs us, that, whilst there, he dined in public with Col. Crockett, who had just arrived from Tennessee. The old bear-hunter, on being toasted, made a speech to the Texians, replete with his usual dry humor. He began nearly in this style: 'I am told, gentlemen, that when a stranger, like myself, arrives among you, the first inquiry is—what brought you here? To satisfy your curiosity at once as to myself, I will tell you all about it. I was, for some years, a member of Congress. In my last canvass, I told the people in my district, that, if they saw fit to reelect me, I would serve them faithfully as I had done; but, if not, they might go to h—-, and I would go to Texas. I was beaten, gentlemen, and here I am.' The roar of applause was like a thunder-burst." He had likely used some version of this speech in Memphis and Little Rock and would continue to recycle it throughout Texas, always omitting mention of the search for land, not war, that had really brought him to Texas.[3]

In Nacogdoches, Crockett met other volunteers from the United States, including Micajah Autry, Peter James Bailey, B. Archer Thomas, William Irvine Lewis, Joseph G. Washington, Peter Harper, Joseph Kerr, Herbert S. Kimble, and a twenty-five-year-old captain from Ohio named William B. Harrison. Autry had come from Jackson, Tennessee, not far from Crockett's home, but his journey was far more arduous than Crockett's leisurely investigation of the Red River country. In Memphis, Autry boarded the steamboat *Pacific* where he ran into George C. Childress and his brother who were among a group of twenty men bound for Texas. Childress was working for the New Washington Association, the New York-based consortium of Texas land speculators, which had dispatched him to the Red River country. Autry wrote his wife that Childress had assured him that "the fighting will be over before we get there, and [he] speaks cheeringly of the prospects." Autry reached Natchitoches, Louisiana, on December

13, less than two weeks after leaving Jackson, putting him only about 120 miles from Nacogdoches, but he was delayed at a number of points during his journey. Unlike Crockett, Autry had no horse and travelled by foot until he joined with others in purchasing a wagon. His itinerary included a detour from Memphis to New Orleans with several other men "for the purpose of learning the true state of things in Texas as well as which would be the best probable rout." He was delayed in Natchitoches through Christmas, by which time Daniel Cloud, the twenty-four-year-old lawyer from Kentucky, arrived with another group of volunteers. A smallpox epidemic prevented them from entering the town itself, but Autry fretted more over his anticipated tavern bill than the risk of disease. Like Crockett, the forty-two-year-old Autry was enthralled by the Texas land, although he saw far less of it than Crockett did, and he wrote his wife, "I have had many glowing descriptions of the country by those who have been there."

The road to Nacogdoches proved a hard one—it took Autry a month to complete the journey. In San Augustine he wrote his wife, "I walked from Natchitoches whence I wrote you last to this place 115 miles through torrents of rain, mud and water." He noted the volunteers did not know where they would be assigned but that "we expect to march to head quarters (Washington) 125 miles from here, where we shall join Houston the commander in chief and receive our destination." But, by the middle of January, the Texas government was spiraling into paralysis. The volunteers could be sent to join the misguided Matamoros expedition, still a priority for the General Council, or perhaps to Béxar in response to Colonel Neill's increasingly desperate appeals for help, coupled with dire warnings of an imminent Mexican invasion. None of it seemed to trouble Autry, whose thoughts were already drifting toward settling his family in Texas, reflecting the notion that defeating Santa Anna would not be very difficult.[4]

Crockett heard the same news, including word of the Matamoros expedition, and drew the same conclusions regarding Texian chances against Santa Anna. He shared the belief that volunteers would rush to the front in large numbers as soon as a threat emerged. Seeing the number of volunteers passing through Nacogdoches added to his confidence, but the dysfunction in the army was as bad as that in the government.

Early on January 8 Crockett stood before Judge John Forbes, raised his right hand, swore allegiance to the Texas government, signed his name to the oath, and enlisted for six months in the Auxiliary Volunteer Corps, which ultimately entitled him to thousands of acres of Texas land.

Judge Forbes issued the oath to dozens of volunteers in Nacogdoches, but Crockett found a flaw in a section that read, "I do solemnly swear that I will bear true allegiance to the provisional government of Texas or any future government that may be hereafter declared." Crockett insisted that it be rephrased to read "any future *republican* government that may be hereafter declared." It is possible that Crockett was merely grandstanding for the crowd, but his demand also might have been motivated by his misgivings about the degree of power Andrew Jackson had acquired and the ease with which Santa Anna had scrapped the Constitution of 1824. In resisting Jackson at the cost of his political career, Crockett showed that he did not take such things lightly.

After Autry took the oath, he wrote to his wife and urged her to "be of good cheer" and promised to provide her "a sweet home," but his assessment of the military situation was equivocal. "Some say that Santa Ana is in the field with an immense army and near the confines of Texas, others say since the conquest of St. Antonio by the Texians and the imprisonment of Genl. Cos and 1100 men of which you have no doubt heard, that Santa Ana has become intimidated for fear that the Texians will drive the war into his dominions and is now holding himself in readiness to fly to Europe which latter report I am inclined to discredit. What is the truth of the matter no one here knows or pretends to know." That was Crockett's dilemma as well—no one knew or pretended to know, but they seemed to adhere to Crockett's oft-quoted motto, "Be always sure you're right—then go ahead." Right or misguided, go ahead they did.[5]

While in Nacogdoches Crockett received an invitation from the ladies of San Augustine, thirty-five miles away, to attend a dinner in his honor. A formal welcoming committee assembled to greet him when he arrived on January 9 and even fired off a small cannon in honor of the occasion. Some time that day Crockett found an opportunity to write his only surviving letter from Texas, addressed to his family, more than two months after he'd last seen them. Since his wife, Elizabeth, was illiterate, he sent the letter to his daughter, Margaret, and her husband, Wiley Flowers, knowing they would share it with the family. He struck a decidedly upbeat tone, emphasizing the land bounties he would receive once the family moved to Texas, and he related his exploration of the Red River country, practically gushing in his description of it.

> I must say as to what I have seen of Texas it is the Garden spot of the world the best land and the best prospects for health I ever saw is here

and I do believe it is a fortune for any man to come here; there is a world of country to settle, it is not required to pay down for your league of land; every man is entitled to make his headright of 4,438 acres; they may make the money to pay for it off the land. I expect in all probility to settle on the Bodark [Bois d'Arc] or Choctaw Bayou of Red River, that I have no doubt is the richest country in the world, good land and plenty of timber and the best springs and good mill streams, good range, clear water, and every appearance of health, game plenty. It is in the pass where the Buffalo passes from North to South and back twice a year, and bees and honey plenty.

Crockett suggested that Texas land offered business opportunities too. Perhaps recalling his efforts to accumulate enough land in Tennessee to become a speculator and land agent, he wrote, "I have a great hope of getting the agency to settle that country and I would be glad to see every friend I have settle there, it would be a fortune to them all." Contemplating the potential income from brokering land deals for his friends, Crockett was already thinking about drumming up business in an independent Texas. Micajah Autry saw the same opportunities and instructed his wife, Martha, to "tell Mr. Smith not to think of remaining where he is but to be ready to come to this country at the very moment the government shall be settled, as for a trifle he may procure a possession of land that will make a fortune for himself, his children and his children's children . . . and such a cotton country is not under the sun." In a postscript he noted that "Col. Crockett has joined our company."[6]

Only toward the end of his letter, practically in passing, did Crockett mention that "I have taken the Oath of the Government and have enrolled my name as a volunteer for six months and will set out for the Rio grand in a few days with the Volunteers of the United States." Despite his effort to downplay this critical and risky decision, Elizabeth Crockett and her children greeted it with alarm. Years later his daughter Matilda recalled, "We did not know that he was going into the Texan war when he went off. We did not know that he intended going into the army until he wrote mother a letter after he got to Texas." For months they would endure the stress of not knowing his whereabouts or fate.[7]

Perhaps to take the edge off that news, Crockett hastened to add that "all volunteers is intitled to a vote for a member to the convention or to be voted for and I have but little doubt of being elected a member to form a Constitution for this province." He had reason for such optimism. On December

10, while Crockett was meandering through the Red River country, the provisional government issued a resolution calling for a convention to convene on March 1, 1836, in the Texas town of Washington. Election of delegates was set for February 1, and all free white males, Mexicans "opposed to a Central Government," and all "Citizen Volunteers in the Army" were allowed to elect delegates. This provided another inducement for Crockett to enlist. If soldiers could elect their own delegates, who better to represent them than the highly popular former Congressman Crockett? The Colonel certainly saw it as a real possibility, one that could take his political career off life support. He was welcomed as a popular celebrity throughout his journey, notably in Nacogdoches and San Augustine, where he was wined, dined, and called upon to entertain the crowd with speeches. James Gaines recorded the event in San Augustine, writing to Lieutenant Governor Robinson that "David Crockett delivered one of his Corner Speeches yesterday at San Augustine and is to Represent them in the Convention on the first of March." US newspapers reported that Crockett was to represent Nacogdoches, but they and Gaines erred in thinking Crockett could represent either town. As a nonresident visitor he did not qualify for election, but he was entitled to represent volunteer units. Unfortunately, Crockett was again on the trail when the elections were held on February 1 and missed the opportunity to offer himself as a candidate. Nonetheless, he added a glowing report of the receptions he had received in Texas. "I am hailed with a harty welcom to this country," he told his family. "A dinner and a party of ladys have honored me with an invitation to partisapate both at Nacing doches and at this place The cannon was fired here on my arivil." He ended with an optimistic flourish: "I am rejoiced at my fate I had rather be in my present situation than to be elected to a seat in congress for life I am in hopes of making a fortune yet for myself and family bad as my prospects has been."[8]

Bounties of land and political possibilities clearly danced in Crockett's head, and he was not about to pass up what might be his final chance at the brass ring. If enlisting in the cause and putting his life on the line in battle was the price exacted for such tantalizing rewards, Crockett was willing to take the risk, perhaps without reckoning on the impact his decision would have on his family, who expected him to return after exploring Texas. Instead, the family received the unwelcome news that Crockett was about to move into harm's way. Crockett's decision was not unlike his actions more than two decades earlier when he enlisted during the Creek War. Then, he left his young wife, Polly, alone to fend for herself and their children. Now, Crockett again chose to go to war without consulting his family, but he believed that his decision would enable him to provide far more for them than he had in the past. It was not a selfish decision, but his family likely saw it as ill-advised, dangerous, and completely unexpected. Crockett, however, saw enlistment as a way to establish himself in Texas by committing to fight for its independence while reaping free land and a fresh start in a new country. This was a common thread among the newly arrived volunteers from the United States. Autry and Cloud expressed the same sentiments in their letters home. "I go the whole Hog in the cause of Texas," Autry wrote to his wife. "I expect to help them gain their independence and also to form their civil government, for it is worth risking many lives for. From what I have seen and learned from others there is not so fair a portion of the earth's surface warmed by the sun." Of course, unlike Crockett's family, Autry's knew from the start that he had gone to Texas to join the war effort.[9]

Autry expounded on the war in more detail than Crockett did and told his wife that it "is still going on favourably to the Texians but it is thought that Santa Ana will make a descent with his whole forces in the Spring but there will be soldiers enough of the real grit in Texas by that time to overrun all Mexico. I have little doubt but that the army will receive ample supplies from [New] Orleans both of provisions and munitions of war as the people of Texas have formed themselves into something like a government which will give them credit in Orleans." In his letter home Crockett never mentioned the return of Santa Anna or weighed in on Texian chances, reinforcements, or the state of the Texas government and military, not wishing to upset his family and trying to keep his letter upbeat. He only mentioned joining the army in passing, as if it were a minor detail in his ambitious plan. Autry's misguided faith in the Texas government, his optimism and hubris, doubtless shared by Crockett and other volunteers, would prove fatal. There would not be "soldiers enough" in time to save them, let alone "overrun all Mexico." Yet the men in Nacogdoches seemed to have found reason for optimism.[10]

Cloud wrote much the same to his brother but added a note of foreboding: "I am in the hands of Omnipotence and rejoice in the hope of his favor and protection. May our united petitions to a throne of divine grace invoke the same bread of life and may our souls united in love, finally nestle under the protecting shield of the same all-wise and all-merciful redeemer." A day earlier he showed more zealous devotion to Texas's struggle in a letter to a friend. "We go with arms in our hands," he wrote, "determined to conquer or die; resolved to bury our all in the same ditch which ingulphs the liberties of Texas, or see it freed from this government." Cloud even repeated conspiracy theories he must have picked up along the way, such as an attempt by Santa Anna to sell Texas "to the Rothchilds, of Europe, for ten millions of dollars." Nor was Cloud warm to the idea of Texas achieving independence only as an avenue to US annexation. Instead, he saw the endgame being US recognition of Texas as a sovereign, independent nation, which he thought would end Mexican efforts to retain control of the province. "[L]et her commissioners be received at Washington as the agents, of an independent state—and in return, let Gen. Jackson send a charge d'affairs or diplomatic agent to Texas. Then the Texas question is forever settled." Cloud added a bit of hubris to his unrealistic expectations by proclaiming that "Mexico can no more conquer Texas than she can Louisiana—She may occupy the extent of soil her soldiery encamp upon—but no more. Texas can battle it for years." He also shared the illusion that legions of volunteers were rushing to the front, or soon would be. "Thousands of magnanimous youths from all quarters of this mighty nursery of freemen are pushing on to the seat of war," he wrote, "and many are destined to signalize themselves and win renown in the war of Texas. When Texas becomes free, I see in prospective a charming picture; when the genial rays of freedom's sun whose fructifying beams have so long and so gloriously illuminated their portions of America, begins to shine with undiminished effluence upon Texas also, not one quarter of a century will stand between her and opulence, security, intelligence, religious and moral excellence, and social happiness and refinement." Cloud's certainty in Texas victory was coupled with a vision of the future that far eclipsed Crockett's relatively modest hope for vast acreage, but Crockett doubtless shared some of Cloud's hopes.[11]

Cloud's convictions raise an often-neglected aspect of the Texas Revolution. The early disputes between advocates of a return to the 1824 Constitution and those who wanted complete independence from Mexico, some with the ultimate aim of annexation to the United States, had dissipated by the time real fighting broke out and increasing numbers of volunteers were arriving in Texas. The men under arms from that point on were fighting for complete independence from Mexico and would not settle for anything less than a new country of their own in Texas. Like Cloud, they were equally disinterested in annexation to the United States, which would have been at odds with the idea of an independent Texas and would, again, place Texas under another government. Although Travis, too, had once supported annexation to the United States, he abandoned the idea and expressed resentment of the colonists who rejected independence and continued to seek reconciliation with Mexico, and he repeatedly urged the government to seek complete independence. In one of his last letters from the Alamo he told the convention delegates that, unless they declared independence, he would give up the fight. Nothing short of independence was worth the risks of war. Micajah Autry also wrote to his wife that he saw a bright future in an independent Texas and that he expected "to help them gain their independence and also to form their civil government, for it is worth risking many lives for." Crockett shared this view. He had made clear his disgust with the Jackson political machine and especially Martin Van Buren's impending presidency. In a letter to a friend he again said, "I have sworn for the last four years that if Vanburen is our next President I will leave the united States I will not live under his king dom and I see no chance to beat him at present every thing apears favourable to him and I am sorry for it I have said for the last four years that I would vote for the devil against Van and any man under the Sun against Jackson and I have got no better yet."[12]

Crockett had given up on the United States, and it is difficult to imagine he would have signed up to fight for a country that did not seek complete independence or that favored US annexation, placing it under the same political system he had just abandoned. It was Texas, not the United States, that promised free land to enlistees. Crockett would have wanted any land he received to be free of US interference and free of the horrendous, convoluted land policies and legal tangles that he faced in Tennessee. Like Autry, Crockett went "the whole Hog in the cause of Texas," and that meant Texas as an independent country. Nonetheless, most American immigrants to Texas felt strong ties to their former homeland, and an independent Texas nation would adhere closely to the US model. It is significant that Travis addressed his most famous letter from the Alamo to "the people of Texas and all *Americans* in the world" (italics added), and that the garrison celebrated George Washington's birthday on the eve of the siege.

The volunteers' thirst for Texas land was neither cynical nor calculated. Crockett and his comrades saw Santa Anna's rule as oppressive and tyrannical and sufficient cause to join the fight against him. During his years in Congress, Crockett became increasingly alarmed by what he viewed as President Andrew Jackson's encroachment on constitutional government. He believed Jackson often exceeded his authority, notably by removing US funds from the Second Bank of the United States and refusing to renew the bank's charter. Alone among his Tennessee colleagues, he voted against Jackson's brutal Indian Removal Act in 1830. Crockett was particularly concerned that both Congress and a large majority of voters misguidedly cast an approving, perhaps blind eye on Jackson's policies. He saw danger in the rise of a personality cult around Old Hickory that was at odds with constitutional government, and he warned that such a cult would lead to suffering "the yoke of bondage." Crockett feared excessive power gravitating to the president and believed strongly in the constitutional separation of powers through which the three branches of government were designed to prevent any one of them from obtaining a disproportionate share of power. A man who saw Jackson as a tyrant must have considered Santa Anna an insufferable monster, even if Crockett exaggerated in making his point by suggesting that "Santa Ana's kingdom" might well be a "paradise" compared to Jackson's rule, which only emphasized how repressive he considered the Mexican dictator.[13]

Crockett was back in Nacogdoches by January 14, and he was treated to another honorary dinner, this one hosted by the ladies of the town. Doubtless the evening's highlight was another of the Colonel's stock speeches, much like those he had delivered at the Viesca dinner and in San Augustine. The next day he and the other volunteers began preparing to move south. Once again in need of cash, or perhaps to lighten his travel burden, Crockett sold two rifles to the provisional government for sixty dollars but received only $2.50 in cash. His family would receive the $57.50 balance the following December. He also procured ten dollars' worth of tent cloth for his journey, no doubt anticipating camping along the trail, and had his horse, rifle, and other equipment valued at $240 and placed into the service of Texas.[14]

As Autry told his wife, the volunteers did not receive orders in Nacogdoches but were told to go to Washington where they would be directed to their ultimate destination, presumably by Houston who was headquartered there. Crockett's letter made only a passing reference to setting "out for the Rio grand in a few days," which may indicate he had reason to think the volunteers would be sent to join the Matamoros expedition. It's not clear who directed them to Washington, but it was likely Judge Forbes, who had administered the oath to them and who still thought the Matamoros expedition was a priority. He could not have known of the government's collapse in San Felipe only a few days earlier, nor that Houston was racing to Refugio intending to talk the men out of the expedition. Apparently somewhat in the dark, the volunteers moved on to Washington, breaking into smaller groups along the way, some moving faster than others. Crockett, Captain Harrison, and five others, including Joseph Kerr, left Nacogdoches on January 16 and arrived in Washington on January 22. They found lodgings at John Lott's ramshackle hostelry, a miserable frame house with but a single, large room with a fireplace. Lott lived there with his wife and children and up to thirty lodgers, many of them described as "a blackguard, rowdy set lounging about." Lott provided boarders with a supper, which William Fairfax Gray described as "fried pork and coarse corn bread and miserable coffee."[15]

The men did not stay together for long and quickly broke into smaller groups with some ending up in Béxar with Crockett while others drifted elsewhere. At least one group was headed by Capt. William B. Harrison, the ranking officer. Crockett may have been a militia colonel and Autry referred to as a major, but they were enrolled as privates and remained privates throughout their enlistments. Still, it is likely that Crockett's reputation lent him higher regard among the men, who called him "colonel." When the eighteen-year-old B. Archer Thomas later signed a claims receipt for his lodgings in Washington, he wrote that he was "One of D Crocketts Com." It also may have been in Crockett's honor that some of the volunteers who rode with Crockett dubbed themselves the "Tennessee Mounted Volunteers," although many of the men, including Harrison, were not from Tennessee and the group didn't remain together as a single company. Crockett and Harrison arrived in Washington at the same time, both traveling on horseback with five other men, including Joseph Kerr. Others traveled on foot or by wagon and made slower time. The length of time a day's journey took also depended on the location of rest stops along the way, called "stands," which offered a place to sleep and rudimentary meals, usually corn and meat of some kind and corn for horses. Although the quality of accommodations and fare were typically minimal, these stands were preferable to the possible dangers of camping on the trail.[16]

The ride from Nacogdoches to Washington must have reinforced Crockett's love affair with Texas. Edward Warren had traversed the same route only weeks earlier and wrote of it to his uncle back in Maine. "The country we passed over the last day of our ride was by far the most beautiful," he said. "Towards evening we ascended a very high swell, from which, we could see the country some twenty miles in every direction. The sun was just going down & the sky had assumed that grandeur of appearance peculiar to the climate. The country was undulating more than usual, and the long swells with the deep green virdue [verdure] at their feet and about their base, looked not unlike the successive folds of an immense garment or drapery with evergreens woven in between. The sun was setting before, the moon rising behind, while on either hand was stretched out this beautiful landscape. The scene was beautiful beyond description." One can only imagine what thoughts came to Crockett when he viewed this same scene a short time later.[17]

In addition to maintaining his Washington inn, John Lott was a commissary operator and a recruiter for the Texas army. Many soldiers received provisions from him and paid for them with Texas government promissory vouchers that their hosts could cash later. Lott also was authorized to direct recruits to their next destination. When Crockett arrived in Washington, Lott was sending volunteers to Béxar as he had been told to do. After January 31, however, he was told to begin directing volunteers to Goliad or Copano instead to shore up the Matamoros expedition because the General Council had misguidedly deemed Béxar adequately garrisoned, despite Neill's frantic pleas for help. With only four horses among their ten men, Autry's squad lagged behind Crockett's and did not reach Washington until January 28. They lingered for days before being directed to Béxar. By then, Houston had returned to Washington with news that the Matamoros adventure had ended, meaning there was no reason to devote more recruits to that effort. Instead, volunteers were badly needed in Béxar, thus Lott continued sending them there. If there was a fear that volunteers were deserting due to idleness, then Béxar was a logical place to send them as it seemed increasingly certain that Santa Anna would soon bring his army there and break up the boredom.[18]

Crockett and Harrison spent only one night in Washington, signed payment vouchers to Lott for their accommodations, and began the trek to San Antonio on January 23. Within those few hours Crockett learned the bitter truth about the disintegration of the Texas government, the disorganization of its army, and the fact that Houston was gone. The volunteers now understood there was genuine fear that Santa Anna was on his way toward Béxar with an army of thousands, which they would very likely soon face, possibly within weeks. Nonetheless, they hastened on their way, doubtless assuming that hundreds more volunteers would soon follow when they learned of the threat. It was as if they held a kind of blind faith, based on their own experiences as citizen soldiers, that more men would quickly form armed companies and rush to San Antonio as they had during the Battle of Béxar. With that in mind, they moved on to San Antonio.

B. Archer Thomas left Washington the day after Crockett and soon joined him at the home of James Swisher, about ten miles from Washington near the village of Gay Hill. Crockett spent several days as a guest of the Swishers and was doubtless glad to enjoy the company and greater comfort than John Lott's place offered. Although Harrison and Kerr left Washington at the same time as Crockett, they did not accompany him to Gay Hill.[19]

Autry and nine other men reached Washington five days after Crockett left and found lodging with Stephen R. Roberts, "there being no possible provisions at this point for the soldiers." They arrived exhausted and would remain there until February 2. The ten men shared four horses and spent much of the trek on foot while some rode or loaded their baggage into a buggy they had procured. Autry explained that their "circumstances after a long march made it necessary for us to remain here that length of time." Roberts charged them forty-five dollars for lodging and provisions, twenty-five dollars for the men, and twenty dollars for their horses. Like Crockett and Harrison, they learned of the government's collapse, the end of the Matamoros adventure, and the desperate situation in Béxar. They may even have learned of the difficulties Texas was having recruiting volunteers or even raising local militias. Somehow, all that bad news did not dissuade them from continuing on.[20]

Crockett made himself at home with the Swishers and captivated their sixteen-year-old son, John, who was surprised to find the great man a guest in his home when he returned late one evening from a deer hunt, a fresh kill tied to his horse. Crockett helped unload the deer and complimented John, calling him his "young hunter." He engaged in daily shooting matches with the lad while keeping the family amused late into the nights with stories and jokes. Like many others who met Crockett, John noted the Colonel enjoyed talking, and the Swishers enjoyed listening to him. "During his stay at my father's it was a rare occurrence for any of us to get to bed before 12 or 1 o'clock we were so interested in hearing him talk," John later recalled. "He conversed about himself in the most unaffected manner without the slightest attempt to display any genius or even smartness. He told us a great many anecdotes, many of which were common place and amounted to nothing within themselves, but his inimitable way of telling them would convulse one with laughter." Some of these yarns were pure

"Davy" concoctions, such as swearing he had no idea why people elected him to Congress, "as it was a matter he knew precious little about at the time and had no idea what he would be called on to do when he arrived in Washington." As usual, it roused his audience to laughter, and he predictably threw in the account of telling his constituents they might "go to hell" if they chose not to reelect him. He assured the Swishers "he never intended to set foot upon Tennessee soil again and that his future life should be devoted to the cause of the Texans." His very presence on the road to San Antonio lent veracity to the claim.

The observant teenaged Swisher also recalled Crockett's appearance, judging him to be stout and muscular, about six feet tall, weighing 180–200 pounds, and about forty years old, underestimating his age by nearly a decade. "He was of florid complexion," John noticed, "with intelligent gray eyes. He had small side whiskers inclining to sandy. His countenance, although firm and determined, wore a pleasant and genial expression. Although his early education had been neglected, he had acquired such a polish from his context with good society, that few men could eclipse him in conversation. He was fond of talking and had an ease and grace about him which added to his strong natural sense and the fund of anecdotes that he had gathered, rendered him irresistible."[21]

John Swisher also picked up on the political turmoil that had driven Crockett out of the United States. Although Crockett had clearly broken with Jackson, he now spoke more favorably about the president, perhaps sensing how popular Jackson was, especially among former Tennesseans like the Swishers. Instead, he saved his vitriol for Martin Van Buren, a much safer target, and John remembered Crockett allying himself with Hugh Lawson White in opposition to Van Buren. Crockett told the Swishers that he hated Van Buren so much that he refused to even speak to the vice president. Nonetheless, even in this instance Crockett was able to turn the conversation to a humorous anecdote. He claimed that Van Buren was anxious to meet him and had been angling for an introduction. One evening he found himself seated behind Crockett in a theater and asked his companion to use the opportunity to introduce the two. Van Buren's friend tapped Crockett on the shoulder and said, "Colonel Crockett, allow me to take the liberty of introducing to you the future president of the United States." Crockett turned to acknowledge the vice president but addressed his companion instead: "Really, my friend," Crockett said, "anything in reason, but by heaven I cannot permit any one to take such a liberty with me."[22]

The young Swisher vividly remembered Crockett's departure. "We watched him as he rode at the side of his young traveling companion, B. Archer Thomas, with feelings of admiration and regret—admiration for the man and regret that he was leaving us." It is interesting that Crockett's nephew William Patton was no longer with him. Perhaps he joined with Harrison's or Autry's group or preferred not to go to Gay Hill and planned to catch up with his uncle later. If Patton ever made it to Béxar, he left there prior to the siege and battle but continued to serve in the army and was later in Galveston. He remains a somewhat mercurial figure in Crockett's Texas journey.[23]

Crockett left the Swisher home during the last week of January and made his way to the Old San Antonio Road near present-day La Grange, then through modern-day Smithville, and reached Bastrop (then known as Mina) in two days. There he met James Lester, who was serving as a recruiter. Having recently been in San Antonio, Lester was able to confirm the desperate situation there and provide Crockett and other volunteers with directions to Béxar. On January 28, Harrison's company paid fourteen dollars to William Kerr for forage near modern-day Burton, and on January 30 they bought provisions from James Gotcher while on their way to Bastrop. The following day, Harrison procured additional provisions from John Eblin and may have joined Crockett in Bastrop shortly thereafter, or the two may have linked up earlier. From Bastrop they took El Camino Real—the King's Highway—to Béxar, a distance of some ninety miles, about a three-day ride, but the trek would have involved an unknown number of rest stops along the way and time spent hunting and foraging. The trail was not without hazards. Edward Warren, who had traveled the same route two weeks earlier, found himself on constant alert and in fear of roaming Comanches and bandits. He regarded the territory west of Washington as "not safe to travel but in considerable companies or at least it is not for some 150 miles, which distance there are no settlers. I never go out doors, or move within, without my pistols close about me—they are, day and night, my constant companions. Next to these is a knife about the length of our largest carving knives & weighing about two pounds." Crockett left Bastrop at the end of January or during the first few days of February, bound for San Antonio and uncertain about what awaited him there.[24]

CHAPTER 5
Béxar

Crockett could have covered the ninety-five miles from Bastrop to Béxar in three or four days, but he did not arrive in San Antonio until February 7 and missed the February 1 election of convention delegates. Although that does not appear to have been a major objective for him, he recognized the potential for a rejuvenated political career in Texas if only from the celebrity treatment he had received throughout his journey. For now, though, that would have to wait.[1]

From a distance, San Antonio de Béxar might have appeared to Crockett as a shining oasis bordered by hills and lying between the San Antonio River and San Pedro Creek. Its central feature was San Fernando Church, which was flanked by the Plaza de Armas, or Military Plaza, and the Plaza de las Islas, or Main Plaza. Narrow, irregular streets ran in all directions, dotted with whitewashed adobe buildings, wooden homes, and mud huts. The town's surrounding fields were irrigated by a system of ditches called *acequias*. The population of less than two thousand citizens included few Anglos and most residents spoke Spanish. The Tejano residents worked hard to scratch out a living from their land and labored under continuing threats of Comanche raids. They raised mostly corn and cattle and relied on trade with the Anglo colonies. Crockett had never seen anything quite like it. Across the San Antonio River stood the Alamo, largely a ruin but once the Mission San Antonio de Valero, one of five abandoned Spanish missions in the area. It most likely acquired its name from a Mexican company once stationed there that came from the town of San Jose y Santiago del Alamo and was later called The Second Flying Company of San Carlos De Alamo de Parras.[2]

Crockett arrived in Béxar with about a dozen men in a most unlikely spot, a Mexican cemetery on San Pedro Creek. None of the men were from Autry's group, which continued to lag behind and had been reduced from ten men to eight by February 8, when they stopped at the home of Capt. Stephen Townsend near Round Top to buy bacon. Two days later they were again out of provisions and spent the night at the home of John Y. Criswell near West Point, where they were fed and lodged. They later stopped at the home of Zadock Woods to buy nine dollars' worth of corn "for their subsistence on their march toward Headquarters." They were still at West Point on February 11, nine days after leaving Washington and still more than one hundred miles from Béxar.[3]

While Crockett waited in the cemetery, word of his arrival was sent to Bowie, who went out with his friend, Antonio Menchaca, to escort him into the city. Crockett was initially quartered at the home of Erasmo Seguin but later lodged elsewhere in town. It wasn't long before a crowd gathered around him and demanded a speech. The Colonel complied and delivered what had become a well-honed performance, punctuated by his "go to hell" punchline. But here in San Antonio, he added a more serious note, telling the gathering, "I have come to your country, though not I hope, through any selfish motive whatever. I have come to aid you all that I can in your noble cause. I shall identify myself with your interests, and all the honor that I desire is that of defending, as a high private, in common with my fellow-citizens, the liberties of our common country." Whether consciously or not, Crockett's use of the term "high private" seemed to acknowledge that the volunteers saw him as something of a leader and gave him a status greater than the rank he held as an enlistee.[4]

Staging a special event was now a standard feature wherever Crockett arrived, including San Antonio, where a ball was quickly arranged in his honor. Menchaca invited all the ladies of San Antonio and found that everyone was anxious to rub shoulders with the famous frontier congressman. Even those who had lived in Texas throughout Crockett's halcyon days in Congress knew all about him—his adventures, real or imaginary, and his celebrity. Many would have read his autobiography or the 1833 unauthorized biography, *Life and Adventures of Col. David Crockett of West Tennessee*, and learned about his exploits and political battles in local newspapers.

Menchaca later recalled that, while the ball was in full swing, a messenger arrived from Camargo around 1:00 a.m. with news that Santa Anna was moving north from the Rio Grande toward San Antonio with thousands of troops. Bowie, Travis, and Crockett were all shown the message. Travis estimated it would take two weeks for such an army to reach Béxar and he returned to the ball, which continued until 7:00 a.m. Dr. John Sutherland identified the messenger as a spy named Blaz Herrera, but he says he arrived on Saturday evening, February 20, ten days after Menchaca said the ball for Crockett was held. Sutherland's account is more credible because any message arriving in Béxar prior to February 11 would have been given to Colonel Neill, who commanded until that date. Herrera told Seguin that Santa Anna was moving from the Rio Grande with five thousand men and he had seen the army crossing the river with 3,500 in the main body and 1,500 cavalry moving faster to make a surprise attack on Béxar. Seguin reported the news to Travis and vouched for Herrera, after which a council of war was held to hear Herrera's report. Following a long discussion, some in the room regarded Herrera's intelligence as the most credible received to date, but, according to Sutherland, a majority dismissed it as "only the report of a Mexican, and entitled to no more consideration than many others of a like character that were daily harangued throughout the country. The council adjourned without coming to any conclusion as to whether it was necessary to give any heed to the warning or not." Sutherland added that Herrera's report was dismissed by many as unreliable because most Tejano intelligence was merely the word of "a degraded class of 'Greasers,'" who were routinely ignored. More tellingly, he noted that many "had persuaded themselves, that Santa Anna would never attempt to conquer Texas, and the most general reply to any argument to the contrary was that he was afraid to meet us. [But] 'He [Santa Anna] knew better.' A majority believed that Cos's defeat would intimidate him and, if not, to deter him from an invasion altogether, or at least induce him to postpone it till a late day." But Herrera's report was accurate and should hardly have come as a surprise. Since January, Neill, Bowie, and even Johnson had sent urgent appeals for help along with credible intelligence that Santa Anna was leading an army of thousands toward Béxar.[5]

Not long after his arrival Crockett was involved in the court-martial of a Texian soldier named D. H. Barre, a private in Travis's Legion of Cavalry, who had been found guilty of mutiny and sentenced to prison. Crockett provided key testimony in Barre's court-martial, and Travis made a point of including it with his report to the governor.[6]

The small garrison was demoralized when Neill left suddenly on February 11 after learning of serious illness in his family, although he promised to return as soon as he could. Crockett caught up with Neill in time to have him endorse his claim for the $57.50 balance due him for the rifles he sold to the army in Nacogdoches. At the same time, Crockett befriended Horace Alsbury and trusted him enough to ask that he serve as Crockett's agent in collecting the money due him. Crockett wrote a note to the auditor asking that he validate the claim and pay Alsbury the amount due on Crockett's behalf. Crockett also met Alsbury's young wife, Juana, daughter of José Ángel Navarro, who served for a time as alcalde of Béxar and later signed the Texas Declaration of Independence. Juana was reared by her godmother and aunt, Josefa Navarro Veramendi, and Josefa's husband, Juan Martín de Veramendi. Her cousin and adopted sister was Ursula Veramendi, James Bowie's wife, who died in 1833 during a cholera epidemic that also killed her parents.[7]

Since Travis was the senior remaining officer in Béxar, Neill left him in command. Travis wasted no time in firing off a letter to Governor Smith summarizing the woeful state of the garrison. He complained that the citizens of Texas had failed to respond to the current emergency or provide reinforcements. The impotent government was partly to blame, but a sizeable number of colonists still rejected calls for independence and favored continuing efforts to reconcile with Mexico. Travis urged the government to commit to a fight for independence and rush more troops to Béxar. He felt certain he could hold the place with around two hundred men, a wildly optimistic assumption. He emphasized the garrison was "prepared to sustain it as long as there is a man left; because we consider death preferable to disgrace, which would be the result of giving up a Post which was so dearly won, and thus opening the door for the Invaders to enter the Sacred Territory of the Colonies." That, in a nutshell, was the rationale for holding Béxar and, ultimately, the Alamo. Unless Santa Anna was stopped there, he could march unimpaired into the colonies and smash the revolt, invoke martial law, and arrest and likely execute the leaders of the rebellion.

Travis's doubts about being reinforced were based on his unhappy experience with citizen soldiers and their democratically run units. He insisted that relief forces comprise only regular army soldiers, which was wishful thinking since few men were willing to enlist as regulars. Although he correctly surmised that "militia and volunteers are but ill-suited to garrison a town" and "can no longer be had or relied upon," he urged a draft of militia as "the only measure that will ever again bring the Citizens of Texas to the Frontiers." But the grim reality was that the only reinforcements he was likely to receive must come in the form of companies of volunteers and there was no guarantee that they would be forthcoming. Travis seemed to sense his precarious situation and, in the "victory or death" style he would invoke in most of his messages from the Alamo, proclaimed "should we receive no reinforcements, I am determined to defend it to the last, and should Bejar fall, your friend will be buried beneath its ruins."[8]

Travis was aware that his appointment as commander did not give him authority over volunteers, who insisted on electing their own officers. Most refused to serve under Travis, a regular army officer, although they had served harmoniously under Neill, who had worked hard to cultivate their trust. Many of them fought beside Neill in the Battle of Béxar, but they didn't know Travis very well. Travis found the situation "truly awkward & delicate—Col Neil left me in the command—but wishing to give satisfaction to the volunteers here & not wishing to assume any command over them I issued an order for the election of an officer to command them." The only candidate was Bowie. Two companies voted for him, but another was already pledged to serve under Travis and declined to vote. There is slight evidence that others asked Crockett to run against Bowie or that Travis asked him to do so. If true, Crockett wisely declined, preferring to maintain his "high private" status. He also knew he was an outsider, no matter how well-liked, and a run for command might appear presumptuous. In any case, he had enlisted in the Auxiliary Volunteer Corps, which operated in conjunction with the regular army. Although these units elected their own officers, they were bound to serve under Travis, thus Crockett would not have taken part in the election of a volunteer commander either as a voter or candidate.[9]

Bowie broke out the corn liquor to celebrate his election, but matters quickly got out of hand when the intoxicated Bowie tried to leverage his small victory into full command of the entire garrison and remove Travis altogether. Travis complained to Governor Smith that Bowie "has been roaring drunk all the time; has assumed all command—& is proceeding in a most disorderly & irregular manner—interfering with private property, releasing prisoners sentenced by court martial & the Civil Court & turning everything topsy turvey." On the same day John J. Baugh, Béxar adjutant, also wrote to Smith noting that Bowie was elected "without opposition none but the volunteers voted & in Fact, not all of them—The Consequence was, a split in the Garrison. Col. Travis, as a matter of course, would not submit to the control of Bowie, and he (Bowie) availing himself of his popularity among the volunteers seemed anxious to arrogate to himself the entire control." Travis added that he would pull his troops out of Béxar if "I did not feel my honor & that of my country compromitted . . . as I am unwilling to be responsible for the drunken irregularities of any man." Baugh told Smith that Bowie had prevented people from leaving town and ordered the release of prisoners, including D. H. Barre, the court-martialed private against whom Crockett had testified, and robbers who had been convicted by juries that actually included Travis and Bowie. When a judge ordered one man returned to prison, an infuriated Bowie sent for men from the Alamo and led them as they "paraded in the Square, under arms, in a tumultuously and disorderly manner. Bowie, himself, and many of his men, being drunk—which has been the case [since] he has been in command." Travis became so frustrated that he withdrew his own troops some twenty miles to the Medina River, where, Baugh opined, "he believes he may be as useful as in the Garrison, [and] at all events, save himself implication in this disgraceful business." Nonetheless, Travis did not lose sight of his purpose and reminded Smith that "it is more important to occupy this Post than I imagined when I last saw you—It is the key to Texas from the Interior; without a footing here the enemy can do nothing against us in the Colonies." He again urged Smith to "immediately order some regular troops to this place." There is no indication that Crockett joined Travis on the Medina, despite his attachment to his command, but he could not have been encouraged by the chaos and breakdown of order among the garrison, especially given reports of Santa Anna's approach. This was not the sort of military Crockett had served in during the Creek War or as a militia officer.[10]

Bowie shared Travis's commitment to holding Béxar and he soon sobered up, no doubt embarrassed by his behavior, especially his rashness in releasing prisoners and possibly dividing and demoralizing the garrison. The two quickly agreed to share command and before Smith could even respond to the discouraging reports from Travis and Baugh, he received a follow-up communication signed by both Travis and Bowie telling him that they had patched up their differences. Bowie would command the volunteers and Travis the regulars and volunteer cavalry until Neill returned. Then they resumed writing appeals for help as they believed Santa Anna would soon arrive. Spies reported seeing a thousand Mexican troops assembled on the Rio Grande, and Travis expected an invasion by March 15.[11]

Crockett did his best to steer a neutral course and remained on good terms with both co-commanders. Travis admired him and made a point of transmitting his testimony in the Barre court-martial to Smith, so it is doubtful that Crockett joined in Bowie's drunken revelry, which more likely alarmed him. Popular accounts of the Alamo often portray Bowie and Crockett as kindred spirits and fellow frontier adventurers, but the two were quite different from one another and the nature of their relationship remains unclear. Although both were driven by the desire to acquire land, Crockett always pursued it legally while Bowie engaged in several dodgy land scams in Texas, Louisiana, and Arkansas, and was involved in the discredited Monclova land deals.[12]

The instability of command and desperate situation in San Antonio reinforced the sobering news Crockett had received earlier in Washington about the collapse of the government. Not only had the provisional government's squabbling spread to the garrison's co-commanders, but the lack of men and provisions sufficient to defend the place was painfully obvious. Crockett was outraged by the damage Grant and Johnson had done, especially their removal of two hundred men who were badly needed now. Like the rest of the garrison, Crockett counted on reinforcements arriving before Santa Anna did and somehow clung to the hope that large numbers of colonists and volunteers from the United States would soon arrive. The garrison relied heavily on the upcoming convention acting swiftly to recruit an army that would provide relief to Béxar before it was too late. But the convention would not convene until March 1 and on February 16 Santa Anna's army began crossing the Rio Grande following a grueling march. By February 20 his main army was camped just forty miles and a few days march from San Antonio. In fact, Gen. Joaquín Ramírez y Sesma's cavalry had already crossed by the sixteenth and was on its way to San Antonio.[13]

Crockett may have called himself a "high private," but he assumed a leadership role from the beginning and sometimes took matters into his own hands. One morning he was tending horses with David Harman, Payton Bland, and Robert Evans when they were approached by two soldiers as they arrived in Béxar. They asked Crockett if there was any chance of a fight and, if there was none, said they would sooner go home than endure the boredom of camp idleness. Crockett took the opportunity to vent his anger over the abandonment of San Antonio by Grant and Johnson, as well as the departure of men who hadn't been paid, as promised, and who lacked even adequate clothing. According to Harman, Crockett told the two that "there had been plenty of men there to take the town" during the earlier Battle of Béxar, "but that the men were going away as fast as they came, and remarked that if he (Crockett) was in command he would have given them 'sheet' [shit] long ago, meaning that he would whip them out." Crockett emphasized the need to send out messengers in search of reinforcements and Harman offered to go, but Crockett expressed doubts about his ability to serve as a courier. Harman told him he was a soldier in Capt. David Garner's company and capable of taking on the assignment. Crockett took Harman to see Bowie and introduced him as "a man who would undertake to go back for reinforcements," Harman recalled, but "Col. Bowie remarked that I looked very young to be a soldier." Bowie asked him if he really thought he could make it through, and Harman told him that "as I came, I could certainly go back." Bowie gave the lad written orders to the enrolling officers at San Felipe, Liberty, and Jefferson, to send all enrolled men to San Antonio at once and Harman soon departed. Although he later claimed to have raised seventy-five or one hundred men during his mission, he never made it back to Béxar.[14]

The Béxar garrison numbered a mere one hundred or so after Grant and Johnson departed, including recent arrivals from the United States. Most could handle a rifle but few had received formal training, although some, like Crockett, were members of militias back home. The soldiers wore their own clothing and brought their own weapons. Only a small group of volunteers from Louisiana, the New Orleans Greys, wore uniforms, which were put together using US Army-issued clothing. The Alamo's arsenal included many British smoothbore "Brown Bess" muskets taken from Cós's force as well as more accurate rifles brought by volunteers, augmented by a variety of knives, flintlock pistols, and even tomahawks.[15]

The Alamo itself was built as a mission and secure enough to stave off Native American attacks but never a real fort. It's three-acre plaza comprised several small rooms and houses encircled by a protective outer wall. Begun in 1724, it was closed in 1793 and may never have been completed. Most of the eastern side of the compound featured a large, partly two-story building used as a convent and a granary while the smaller buildings along the west side housed the native converts. The mission's first church collapsed before it was completed, and construction began on a new one in 1756 but was never finished. The church walls were formidable, measuring four feet thick in some places and more than twenty feet high. The church was distinguished by an ornamental facade with columns flanking its large doorway and four niches between the columns, each housing the figure of a saint. The church was joined to the convent by a large wall. Both the Spanish and Mexican governments had sought to fortify the Alamo after 1800 by strengthening the gatehouse, a low building comprising most of the south wall of the compound—later called the Low Barrack—which also served as a guard house or jail. General Cós made improvements during the 1835 siege and constructed earthen platforms that were used to mount artillery, including one at the rear of the roofless church, enabling artillery to fire on foes coming from three directions. The two-story convent and attached, one-story, granary—collectively called the Long Barrack—housed troops during several eras, while the smaller buildings became officers' quarters and served other purposes. A glaring gap between the church and the Low Barrack was blocked by a stockade palisade. An abattis of felled trees was placed outside the palisade with sharpened ends facing attacking forces. The main entry gate in the center of the Low Barrack was protected by a tambour built of earth and stockade, also referred to as a lunette. The walls that encircled most of the compound were only a foot thick at most and no more than eight or nine feet high. A sizeable attack force facing the relatively small Alamo garrison would have little difficulty in scaling those walls. The partly deteriorated north wall was particularly problematic. Two of the large cannon platforms stood behind it, but its weak condition required that Cós reinforce it with wooden planks five or six inches thick placed horizontally and supported by additional wood props.[16]

Houston dispatched Green B. Jameson to Béxar in January 1836 to direct fortification of the Alamo, although Jameson was a lawyer by trade. Jameson drew up ambitious plans but most of his proposed improvements were never completed. He lacked money and other resources and found the garrison generally averse to work. He did what he could using Cós's improvements and mounted most of the Alamo's twenty cannons on the existing platforms, making them effective when firing at a distant enemy but virtually useless once the enemy reached the walls and was in position to climb them. The soldiers themselves were exposed when firing from the walls as there were no firing steps or shelter for them, although some could fire through loopholes cut into the outer walls and earthen embankments thrown up against the walls. Regardless of the state of its fortifications, the Alamo was clearly too large to be held by such a small force.

In a January report to Houston, Jameson boasted that the fort's cannons alone would enable the garrison to overcome a force ten times its size, but by February he scaled back his optimism and suggested that it was impractical to maintain a strong garrison in Béxar at all. Instead, he proposed "to square the Alamo and erect a large redoubt at each corner Supported by Bastions & have a ditch all around full of water." He thought that cannons placed at the corners would be most effective. Jameson's plans remained just that, and the only tangible improvements he reported were "exacting redoubts, digging wells & mounting cannon." Gunpowder was stored in a small room in the church covered by a stone roof and safe from being set off by sparks.[17]

Not long after making peace with Travis, Bowie began to feel ill and his role as an Alamo commander diminished rapidly. Nearing his fortieth birthday, Bowie was deteriorating physically, possibly suffering effects of the grueling "sandbar brawl" in 1827 near Natchez, Mississippi, where his lung was punctured by a pistol ball and he was stabbed several times. Those injuries combined with his drunken binge may have exacerbated whatever illness was already infecting him, most likely typhoid pneumonia, which soon rendered him bedridden. Within days of Bowie co-signing a letter to Governor Smith on February 14, sole command effectively passed to Travis, who signed all communications afterward, save one.[18]

Now in sole command, Travis continued sending pleas for reinforcements. He transmitted Jameson's ambitious plans for the Alamo to Governor Smith, praised Jameson's industriousness and dedication, and reiterated yet again that "this point is the key of Texas & should not be neglected by the Government. Men, money and provisions are needed—with them this post can & shall be maintained & Texas (that is) the colonies, will be saved from the fatal effects of an Invasion." Travis took action to stir up more recruits on February 19 by dispatching Capt. J. L. Vaughan to twelve municipalities where he was to recruit volunteers. Speed was of the essence, and he reminded Vaughan, "The situation of [the] enemy must not be lost sight of, you must report weekly in relation to him."[19]

Travis's increasingly desperate appeals for help fell on deaf ears in San Felipe, where the remnants of the provisional government remained paralyzed. Lieutenant Governor Robinson misguidedly wrote to Col. James Fannin, commandant of Goliad, confidently expressing doubt that Santa Anna would attack either Béxar or Goliad and would, instead, "throw reinforcements into Matamoros." The Advisory Council added to the chorus by telling Robinson that "every effort should be made to sustain the expedition to Matamoros under command of Col Fannin," apparently unaware that Houston had derailed the Matamoros expedition a month earlier or that Fannin had broken off from it and moved back to Goliad. Echoing Neill, Fannin responded to Robinson with more sobering reports that his men were without pay, clothing, or adequate food. There was a general fear among commanders that men would desert unless they were paid. Commanders were also frustrated with the lack of interest in the war on the part of Texas colonists, most of whom misguidedly believed that it was over or simply did not support it. Fannin estimated that most of his force comprised recent arrivals from the United States with a mere half dozen coming from the colonies. Robinson quickly issued a new recruiting broadside that took Texas colonists to task for their sluggishness. "Our brethren from the United States are, by hundreds in the field, leading the van guard for our defence; and shall we look to others alone, for that protection from dangers so alarming? No Texians! shoulder your rifles, join our Patriotic Friends." This fell short of the recommendation by Fannin and Travis that the militia be called out and relied instead on shaming Texians into action.[20]

The breakdown of government added to the Alamo's peril. Governor Smith and the council, led by Robinson, weren't speaking to each other. Travis and Bowie directed their communications to Smith, while Fannin corresponded almost exclusively with Robinson. Smith and Robinson gave conflicting orders, most of which could not be carried out in any case due to a lack of resources. After putting Houston on furlough, Smith failed to replace him. Robinson attempted to place Fannin in command and must have been stunned by the Colonel's response. "I do not desire any command, and particularly that of chief," Fannin proclaimed. "I feel, I *know*, if you and the council do not, that I am incompetent." He begged Robinson to relieve him and recommended Houston be returned to leadership. It was a candid and accurate self-appraisal, yet Travis would come to rely on Fannin more than anyone else to relieve the Alamo. On February 16, Travis sent James Butler Bonham to Goliad with an appeal to Fannin for help. Bonham arrived two days later, but Fannin declined to send relief to Béxar since no Mexican troops had arrived there and he was concerned that Mexican forces might be heading his way.[21]

Small groups of volunteers continued arriving in Béxar, including Cloud and Bailey, who got in by mid-February and were assigned to Capt. William H. Patton. On February 21 the rest of the Autry group straggled in, several still on foot, a few on horseback, with a buggy they had acquired to carry their baggage. Along the way they passed Crockett's friend Horace Alsbury who was headed for Nacogdoches via Washington in search of shelter for his wife, Juana, and her family in East Texas, hoping to get them out of Béxar before Santa Anna arrived. These few new arrivals brought the Alamo garrison's effective strength to a mere 150 men with as many as forty more on the sick list.[22]

The men took a break from their labors on February 22 to celebrate George Washington's birthday at a fandango in town. The party went on well into the wee hours of February 23 when the revelers, doubtless including Crockett, wandered to their beds. They were completely unaware that Mexican forces under General Ramírez y Sesma had reached the Medina River, a mere twenty miles from Béxar, and had only been prevented from seizing the town and the Texians by a heavy rain that rendered the river impassable.[23]

Around eight the next morning, the Texians were roused from their stupor by a frantic clamor in town that arose when word spread that the Mexican army was nearby. Ramírez y Sesma's troops were seen on Leon Creek by Tejanos who reported the news to Travis. That placed the Mexican cavalry less than ten miles from Béxar, confirming Herrera's earlier report that had been ignored. Word of their approach reached residents first, who hastily packed up and left town on foot or with carts, but without explanation. Travis attempted to find out why so many people were suddenly leaving and eventually learned how close the Mexicans were. The Texians had been taken completely by surprise.

Travis ordered a man posted in the bell tower of San Fernando Church and instructed him to ring the bell if he spotted Mexican troops. Around 3:00 p.m. the lookout sounded the alarm and shouted that the Mexicans were within view. Others ran up the tower to have a look, but saw no troops, although the sentinel swore he had seen them. As they had with Herrera, the Texians were too willing to dismiss the sentinel's alarm as a false one. Sutherland volunteered to ride out and investigate, and Travis sent him and John W. Smith, a man familiar with the area, to check the sentinel's report. The scouts had gone only a mile-and-a-half when they suddenly found themselves a mere 150 yards from an estimated 1,500 Mexican soldiers, mounted and well-equipped, behind chaparral and mesquite bushes, just as the sentinel had described. The two riders quickly raced back toward town, but the muddy ground that had stifled the Mexicans now caused Sutherland's horse to slide and tumble over, landing across his knees and smashing his rifle. Smith helped him back onto the horse and they made it to town.

On reaching the civil plaza they ran into Crockett, who told them that Travis had already moved the garrison into the Alamo since it was impossible for the small force to hold the town. Crockett, Sutherland, and Smith made their way across a small footbridge and into the Alamo where they reported to Travis. Sutherland's injured knee gave out, and Crockett helped him into Travis's room where they found the commander scribbling messages. Crockett told Travis, "Colonel, here am I, assign me a position, and I and my twelve boys will try to defend it." Travis replied that he wanted him to defend the wooden palisade that extended from the end of the Low Barrack on the south side of the compound to the southwest corner of the church. Although Crockett lacked a formal command, Travis understood that many of the men recognized him as a leader. Travis did not hesitate to place him in a command position, and Crockett would play a leadership role in the coming weeks when it would be sorely needed.[24]

The Texians scrambled to gather what they could before taking refuge in the Alamo. Almaron Dickinson, a Texian artilleryman, his wife, Susanna, and their infant daughter, Angelina, hastily made their way to the fort from the Ramón Músquiz house on the southeast corner of the intersection of Potrero Street and the Main Plaza, where they and Crockett were staying. Gregorio Esparza, a Tejano member of the garrison, brought his wife, Anita, a daughter and four sons, including eight-year-old Enrique, into the fort. With Alsbury away, Crockett and others helped Alsbury's wife, Juana, and her family into the relative safety of the Alamo. Bowie was placed in a room near the main gate in the Low Barrack, while Juana, her infant son, Alejo, and younger sister, Gertrudis Navarro, remained in Bowie's former quarters along the west wall, not far from the cannon platform that stood in the northwest corner of the compound. Bowie reassured Juana that she would be safe. "Sister, do not be afraid," he told her. "I leave you with Col. Travis, Col. Crockett, and other friends. They are gentlemen, and will treat you kindly."[25]

The surprised Texians failed to supply the Alamo with sufficient food to sustain themselves prior to the arrival of the Mexicans. By sheer luck they found a few dozen cattle belonging to Ignacio Pérez wandering the streets near the Alamo and herded them into the compound. They were also out of corn and had no money to buy any but confiscated some eighty or ninety bushels of it from abandoned houses near the fort. The little coffee, salt, and sugar that Grant and Johnson left behind was already consumed. Apart from their supply of corn and beef, the garrison had little to eat.[26]

The approaching Mexicans saw a Texian flag atop San Fernando Church. It was a modified Mexican flag that replaced the eagle and serpent in the center white stripe with two distinct stars, symbolizing Texian demands for separate statehood from Coahuila. However, by that time few Texians were willing to settle for anything short of complete independence from Mexico. In any case, the Texians hastily removed the flag from the church and hoisted it over the Alamo in the absence of a more up-to-date banner. The New Orleans Greys brought their own flag and that, too, was raised.

Shortly afterward, Santa Anna ordered a red banner raised atop the church tower, clearly visible from the Alamo. The banner made it clear that no quarter would be given to the garrison. Travis got the message and impulsively fired a cannon shot squarely at a group of soldiers assembled in Main Plaza. The Mexicans responded by lobbing four grenades into the fort, which caused no damage or injury. The bedridden Bowie was angered by Travis's impulsiveness and, responding to what he thought was a Mexican signal to parley, dispatched Jameson with a note asking if the Mexicans had requested one. Bowie was so weak that he asked Juan Seguin to write the note, which he signed in a shaky hand after crossing out the closing "God and The Mexican Federation" and replacing it with "God and Texas," which Santa Anna found particularly insulting. Jameson was met at the footbridge by Col. Juan Nepomuceno Almonte, who sent Bowie's note to Santa Anna. A reply from Santa Anna's aide de camp, José Batres, arrived a short time later and bluntly informed the rebels that "the Mexican army cannot come to terms under any conditions with rebellious foreigners to whom there is no other recourse left, if they wish to save their lives, than to place themselves immediately at the disposal of the Supreme Government from whom alone they may expect clemency after some considerations are taken up. God and Liberty!" The "considerations" were likely a veiled threat to execute the Alamo leaders, but the red flag and the reference to "rebellious foreigners" left little hope that any of the garrison would be spared if they surrendered. Travis, doubtless miffed at Bowie's unilateral action, dispatched his own messenger, Albert Martin, to the footbridge with an offer to meet with Almonte, who responded that he was not authorized to hear such proposals from "rebels."[27]

Bowie and Travis quickly drafted a message to Fannin in Goliad notifying him of the enemy's arrival and urging him to hasten to their aid. The message was carried by John Johnson and was more urgent than the one taken out by Bonham a week earlier. With the wolf clearly at the door, the commanders sounded more desperate. "We have removed all the men to the Alamo where we make such resistance as is due our honor, and that of the country, until we can get assistance from you, which we expect you to forward immediately," they wrote, adding, "We have one hundred and forty six men, who are determined never to retreat. We have but little provisions, but enough to serve us till you and your men arrive." These were not words that suggested options for Fannin; the Alamo commanders expected him to march to their aid forthwith. For good measure they reminded him: "We deem it unnecessary to repeat to a brave officer, who knows his duty, that we call on him for assistance," suggesting that they did, in fact, deem it necessary. The Alamo commanders remained apprehensive about Fannin since he had not responded to their earlier appeal.[28]

Bowie's illness worsened; his message to Santa Anna was the last command document he signed. Travis then took sole command and all future communications bore his signature alone. His pen was his most potent weapon, and he began wielding it immediately. Shortly after dispatching Johnson to Goliad, Travis wrote hastily to Judge Andrew Ponton in Gonzales: "The enemy in large force is in sight—We want men & provisions—Send them to us—We have 150 men & are determined to defend the Alamo to the last—P. S. Send an express to San Felipe with the news—night & day." He tasked Sutherland, who was still nursing his injured leg, with carrying the message to Gonzales along with John W. Smith who was on his way there to see to his family.

There was no more firing that day, and as night fell, the sobered garrison realized that they were under siege, hopelessly outnumbered, and that the Alamo was more a lifeboat than a fortress. Their only hope lay in the timely arrival of a large reinforcement, and in the days to come Travis sent many variations of his first appeals throughout Texas. There was little else he could do, but that night he sent men out to dismantle some *jacales* that stood just outside the Alamo walls to provide firewood to fend off the cold nights to come.[29]

CHAPTER 6
The Alamo

The next morning, even as Travis's message arrived in Gonzales, the defenders woke to see a new Mexican battery only 350 yards from the Alamo. By afternoon it was pounding the walls so heavily that it dismounted two of the Alamo cannons, including the eighteen-pounder. Despite the noise, Travis found more time to compose his thoughts than he could on the previous, more hectic day, and he wrote another appeal for help, addressed to "The People of Texas and All Americans in the World," which was directed to San Felipe:

Send this to San Felipe by Express night & day

To the People of Texas & All Americans in the World:

Fellow citizens & compatriots—I am besieged, by a thousand or more of the Mexicans under Santa Anna—I have sustained a continual Bombardment & cannonade for 24 hours & have not lost a man. The enemy has demanded a surrender at discretion, otherwise, the garrison are to be put to the sword, if the fort is taken—I have answered the demand with a cannon shot, & our flag still waves proudly from the walls. I shall never surrender or retreat. Then, I call on you in the name of Liberty, of patriotism & everything dear to the American character, to come to our aid, with all dispatch—The enemy is receiving reinforcements daily & will no doubt increase to three or four thousand in four or five days. If this call is neglected, I am determined to sustain myself as long as possible & die like a soldier who never forgets what is due to his own honor & that of his country—Victory or Death.

William Barret Travis
Lt. Col. comdt

P. S. The Lord is on our side—When the enemy appeared in sight we had
not three bushels of corn—We have since found in deserted houses 80 or
90 bushels & got into the walls 20 or 30 head of Beeves. Travis[1]

Albert Martin carried the letter to Gonzales and added his own postscript:
"Since the above was writen I heard very heavy Canonade during the whole
day [I] think there must have been an attack made upon the alamo[.] We
were short of Amunition when I left Hurry on all the men you can in
haste—Albert Martin."

Martin passed the letter to Launcelot Smither, who carried it to San
Felipe and added his own urgent postscript: "When I left there was but
150 determined to do or die[;] tomorrow I leave for Bejar with what men
I can raise . . . Col Almonte is there[;] the troops are under the Command
of Gen Seisman. I hope Every one will Randeves at gonzales as soon as
poseble as the Brave Soldiers are suffering[;] do not neglect the powder is
very scarce and should not be delad one moment. L. Smither."

Earlier, Smither penned his own appeal from Gonzales: "To All the
Inhabitants of Texas: In a few words there is 2000 Mexican soldiers in
Béxar, and 150 Americans in the Alamo. Sesma is at the head of them,
and from the best accounts that can be obtained, they intend to show no
quarter. If every man cannot turn out to a man every man in the Alamo
will be murdered. They have not more than 8 or 10 days provisions. They
say they will defend it or die on the ground. Provisions, ammunition and
Men, or you suffer your men to be murdered in the Fort. If you do not turn
out Texas is gone. I left Bexar on the 23rd at 4 p.m." Smither signed the
document, "By Order of W. V. [*sic*] Travis; L. Smither." As evening came,
the music of the Mexican band could be heard in the Alamo and several
grenades were lobbed into the fort.[2]

It is interesting that Travis addressed his February 24 letter to both the
people of Texas *and* to all *Americans* in the world, as if this was not the
Texians' fight alone. The reference also reflected his growing frustration
over the failure of longtime Texas colonists to join the fight. In his own
message, Smither refers to the Alamo defenders as "Americans," as if the
term is synonymous with the Texas revolt and those who were fighting in
it. This was, perhaps, a subconscious association that revealed a belief that
this was not a domestic dispute among Mexican citizens, but a struggle by
Americans who felt alien from Mexico, rather than part of it. The reference

reveals a significant factor that contributed to the outbreak of violent revolt by the Texas colonists, and which was now being carried out mostly by new arrivals from the United States.

Although the nights remained relatively quiet, each morning brought renewed bombardment by the Mexican guns. On February 25 Santa Anna sent soldiers across the river, and they took shelter about one hundred yards from the Alamo in small houses the Texians had partly dismantled earlier for firewood. Travis sent a squad of men to drive them out. Crockett was among the leaders of the operation, along with Charles Despallier and Robert Brown, who burned the houses while under fire. The Texians opened fire on the Mexicans at point-blank range with grape and cannister charges and small-arms fire, while the Mexicans kept up cannon fire during the engagement. Crockett fired on the enemy and directed the men. James Rose narrowly escaped fire from a Mexican officer. The fighting lasted about two hours and broke off in the afternoon when the Mexicans retreated across the river after suffering one killed and a half dozen wounded. Texian casualties were limited to minor scratches from flying stones. In his letter that day to Houston, Travis mentioned Despallier and Brown and singled out Crockett for praise, noting, "The Hon. David Crockett was seen at all points, animating the men to do their duty," an indication of the leadership role Crockett either assumed or was given at the Alamo and a way for Travis to remind Texian leaders that one of the most celebrated Americans was in the Alamo. That night the Texians returned to the area and burned the remaining houses. The day's success bolstered garrison spirits but did not alter their situation. The Mexicans continued to pound the fort, erected two more batteries in the Alameda southeast of the fort, and posted Ramírez y Sesma's cavalry to the east and on the Gonzales road. In a letter to Houston, Travis again emphasized that he was vastly outnumbered and in need of help. As in many of his messages Travis waxed apocalyptic, vowing again to go down fighting if he was abandoned "as a sacrifice at the shrine of our country."[3]

Crockett's action that day showed he was prepared to lead men into battle and that Travis was willing to send him on such missions. Although he lacked formal rank or command, Crockett was clearly seen as a leader among the garrison and someone whom Travis relied on, perhaps as a man the volunteers could relate to as their unofficial leader now that Bowie was sidelined. Crockett was of great value as an inspirational leader as well, making his way around the compound each day as the bombardment continued. He engaged defenders and civilians alike by their fires each night with the kind of stories and jokes that had recently entertained the Swisher family in Gay Hill and had always amused crowds during his political campaigns. As John Swisher mentioned, Crockett liked to talk, and people enjoyed listening to him.[4]

The following day another detachment of Texians ventured out on the east side of the fort to collect firewood and unblock an irrigation ditch, or *acequia*, that provided water to the garrison. They came under fire from some of Ramírez y Sesma's men, skirmished with them, and withdrew into the fort, where the garrison was forced to rely on well water. The Mexican cannon fire continued throughout the day with little response from the Alamo. That night a squad burned more houses near the fort. The Mexicans began bombarding the fort each morning and continued the cannonade all day. The Texians needed to conserve powder and shot and responded only sporadically with little effect. There were no casualties from the Mexican cannon fire, but it took a steady toll on the ancient Alamo, particularly the north wall, which had been weak to start with, keeping Texians busy at night trying to repair each day's damage.[5]

Johnson arrived in Goliad on February 25 to deliver the appeal written by Travis and Bowie two days earlier. The message prompted Fannin to plan a march to the Alamo the following day with 320 men, about three-fourths of his garrison, and four pieces of artillery. Like Travis, Fannin and his men were frustrated by the lack of volunteers coming forward and militias failing to muster. John Sowers Brooks, a soldier in Goliad, estimated that the entire Texas army numbered a paltry eight hundred men. Burr H. Duval, also in Goliad, recalled that the Texians were completely unprepared for Santa Anna's arrival and wrote his father that "not a Texian was in the field, nor has even *one* yet made his appearance at this post." And, like Travis, Fannin's men were desperately in need of provisions, including clothing, shoes, and food. He was reluctant to remove his men under those conditions, unable to bring even enough provisions for them, let alone for the Alamo. In any case, loading several ox-drawn wagons and hauling artillery would make for a slow journey to Béxar, possibly rendering it impossible to reach Travis before a Mexican assault on the Alamo took place and possibly leaving Fannin's own relief force exposed. At best, Fannin thought, his men might help the Alamo hold out a bit longer, but they would ultimately make little difference unless a large reinforcement was raised elsewhere in Texas, and that did not appear likely. Brooks was certain that "without the interposition of Providence, we can not rationally anticipate any other result to our Quixotic expedition than total defeat." He expected the relief force to be intercepted by Mexican cavalry. Fannin wrote to Lieutenant Governor Robinson notifying him of his relief effort but cautioned that he would return to Goliad if he learned that Béxar had fallen, something he considered quite possible. He thought the move unsound militarily but could not ignore the appeals of Travis and Bowie. In fact, Fannin had contemplated moving his headquarters to Béxar earlier but, as he often did, hesitated. Now it was too late.[6]

Nonetheless, Fannin began moving his relief force out on February 26. After progressing only two miles, three of his wagons broke down while crossing the San Antonio River, and it was only with difficulty that the four cannons made it across. There Fannin halted for the night, during which some of the oxen wandered off and were not to be found the next morning, when the men decided to rethink the entire effort. Moving on could mean starvation, and without the wagons or oxen they would have to leave their luggage and artillery behind. They anticipated finding no provisions along their barren route and had brought a mere twelve rounds of ammunition per man. Brooks expressed the men's dilemma in a letter to his mother. "Everyone felt an anxiety to relieve our friends, who we had been informed, had retired to the Alamo . . . resolved to hold out, until our arrival," he told her. "Yet every one saw the impropriety, if not the impossibility of our proceeding under existing circumstances and it was equally apparent to all that our evacuation of Goliad, would leave the whole frontier from Bexar to the coast open to the incursions of the enemy." Word had reached Goliad that Mexican General José de Urrea was only sixty miles away in San Patricio with a sizeable force.

Fannin received a note from his commander of volunteers requesting a council of war, which he had no choice but to grant, and where it was unanimously decided to return to Fort Defiance, as Fannin had dubbed the Goliad presidio. The next morning, he dashed off a letter to Robinson notifying him of his decision and separately sent an express to the Gonzales committee of safety with the same news. Within hours he learned that Johnson's small force was nearly wiped out by General Urrea at San Patricio. Only Johnson and two others escaped, and Fannin saw this as vindication of his decision to remain in Goliad. He echoed Travis in rebuking Texian colonists for failing to come forward. "Should the worst happen—on whose head should the burthen of censure fall—not on the heads of those brave men who have left their homes in the United States to aid us in our struggle for Liberty—but on those whose all is in Texas & who notwithstanding the repeated calls have remained at home without raising a finger to keep the Enemy from their thresholds," Fannin said. "What must be the feelings of the volunteers now shut in Bexar—& what will be those of this command if a sufficient force of the enemy should appear to besiege us here without provisions—Will not curses be heaped upon the heads of the sluggards who remained at home with a knowledge of our situation." Thus did the frustrated and angry Fannin capture the deplorable state of the revolution, joining Travis and others in his bitter condemnation of the colonists whose homes were at stake in the war, but who failed to come forward to defend them. Brooks's fear that the expedition would be intercepted by Santa Anna's cavalry was vindicated when word of Fannin's movements reached Béxar and Ramírez y Sesma was dispatched to intercept him. However, the Mexican general found no trace of Fannin, who had returned to Goliad by then, unable to help the Alamo and in a position little better than Travis's.[7]

Brooks held out hope that Fannin might make a second attempt to reach the Alamo, but as Fannin had already surmised, such a reinforcement could, at best, enable the Alamo to hold out only until a much larger force arrived. "We will probably march tomorrow or the next day, if we can procure fresh oxen enough to transport our baggage and two six pounders," Brooks wrote, clinging to the hope that the "people in the settlements are all arming themselves." But he added that it was clearly a case of "Now or never." More realistically, he noted, "We are all nearly naked—and there are but few of us who have a pair of shoes. We have nothing but fresh beef without salt—no bread for several days."[8]

Launcelot Smither arrived in San Felipe on February 25 with Travis's message, which raised alarm in the town. Gail Borden, publisher of the *Telegraph and Texas Register,* packed up land office papers in preparation for evacuating to the east should Santa Anna's army arrive. William Fairfax Gray left San Felipe and arrived in Washington on February 27, where he observed a "considerable excitement prevailing . . . owing to the news from Bexar." But he also noted that no effort was underway to raise troops for Travis. Maj. Robert. M. Williamson was a lawyer and friend of Travis's from his days in Anahuac, sometimes called "Three-legged Willie" because of a wooden leg he used to compensate for a limb that was permanently bent. He was genuinely alarmed when he received Travis's message in Gonzales and wrote to the governor and council urging them to undertake a strong recruitment effort. Williamson ordered Capt. J. J. Tomlinson to Bastrop where he was to await further orders from him. He emphasized that Travis was relying on the willingness of fellow Texians to come forward and vowed that "no exertions on my part will be wanting to give the earliest aid practical to your fellow soldiers in liberties all must act and act in unison."[9]

In the coming weeks Travis would send out a stream of couriers to Fannin, to Gonzales, to Houston, to the provisional government, all with essentially the same desperate appeal for help, somber news about the size of Santa Anna's army, the Alamo's limited provisions, and his determination to hold the place at all cost in the near certainty that, without help, the Alamo would be overwhelmed. Juan Seguin, leader of a Tejano company, was among those who served as Alamo couriers. Crockett watched as each of them left and, like everyone else in the fort, was aware that none were returning with any help. Crockett did his best to keep defenders' minds off that by doing what he could to amuse, entertain, and reassure them.[10]

Word from the Alamo finally stirred the interim government to action. As Fannin hastily scrambled to move a relief force to Béxar, Lieutenant Governor Robinson wrote to Houston with news of Travis's appeals. He ordered Houston to "come quickly and organize our countrymen for battle. Call the militia out en masse, send your order East by the express for that purpose. Say it is done by the order of the Gov. & Council & by your own order, and by the unanimous call of Texas." He ordered it sent by express "night & day." Houston, of course, had been taking orders from Governor Smith, who had furloughed him to negotiate with the Cherokee and was not to be found. Not to be outdone by Robinson, Governor Smith issued his own recruitment broadside after receiving Travis's appeal, scolding that an enemy of "mercenary troops of the Dictator, who are daily receiving reinforcements, should be a sufficient call upon you without saying more." Noting the garrison's provisions were sufficient for a thirty-day siege at most, and addressing no one in particular, Smith wrote, "I call upon you as an officer, I implore you as a man, to fly to the aid of your besieged countrymen and not permit them to be massacred by a mercenary foe. The call is to ALL who are able to bear arms to rally without a moment's delay, or in fifteen days the heart of Texas will be the seat of war. This is not imaginary. The enemy from 6,000 to 8,000 strong are on our border and rapidly moving by forced marches for the colonies." The advisory committee, which had been acting in the absence of a General Council quorum, recommended that Tomlinson's ranger company be sent to Béxar, that Capt. Amasa Turner be ordered there with all the troops he could raise, and that the militia be called out as a check on Indian attacks. Alas, the recruitment effort failed to coax many colonists toward the battlefield.

As soon as Sutherland and John W. Smith arrived in Gonzales on February 24, they set about organizing a relief force for the Alamo, but they could gather only a mere twenty-five volunteers. They were led by Albert Martin, who had carried Travis's stirring February 24 letter from the Alamo, and Smith guided the group, which left Gonzales on February 27, headed for Béxar. Along the way they picked up a few more men until there were thirty-two in all. These longtime residents of Gonzales were among the minority of colonists who took up arms alongside recently arrived volunteers from the United States.

Back in Fort Defiance, Fannin again warned Lieutenant Governor Robinson that "unless the people of Texas, forthwith, turn out in mass . . . those now in the field will be sacrificed," adding that "if we should fail in the effort, and fall a sacrifice to the criminal indifference, cold and unpardonable apathy and neglect . . . there are people . . . who will bestow censure where it is due, and, peradventure, drop a tear over our memory." In Gonzales and elsewhere efforts to raise volunteers continued with little effect and no credible relief force for the Alamo was ever raised. The companies that were formed included a few dozen men at most and never coalesced in time to reach the Alamo, nor would they likely have made any significant difference in the outcome there other than adding to the number of casualties.[11]

All of Travis's letters, along with the panicky appeals issued by what remained of the interim government, sank into a black hole of indifference. Things had not changed in the months since Travis first warned that the war could not be sustained by "a mob" but required a regular army of trained, disciplined soldiers under a unified command. The men in the Alamo clung to the hope that Texians would spontaneously form up and rush to Béxar in large numbers. They had been living under that illusion since Neill commanded them. But very few longtime Texas colonists came forward, and most volunteers were recent arrivals from the United States, like Crockett, Autry, Cloud, and other Alamo defenders. Fannin, who has often been demonized for his failure to relieve the Alamo, made a sound decision when he turned back from his mission to the Alamo and accurately pointed out that it was Texas that had abandoned both him and Travis. He was also probably right in estimating that his three hundred men would make little difference to the Alamo's defense unless a much larger relief force was formed and mobilized. The Texas government and military were no more prepared to do that than they had been all winter. When Travis's letter of February 24 reached Washington on February 28, William Fairfax Gray observed that a few men were preparing to go to the Alamo "but the *vile rabble* here cannot be moved."[12]

Crockett was highly visible throughout the siege. Enrique Esparza recalled the Colonel "made everybody laugh and forget their worries. He had a gun he called 'Betsey.' They told me that he had killed many bears. I knew he would kill many of Santa Anna's soldiers. Señor Crockett seemed everywhere. He would shoot from the wall or through the portholes. Then he would run back and say something funny. He tried to speak Spanish sometimes. Now and then he would run to the fire we had in the courtyard where we were to make us laugh."

As the siege wore on, Crockett did his best to raise spirits and morale; it is hard to imagine Crockett doing otherwise. According to Susanna Dickinson, he often hacked away at a violin he'd found to amusing effect and was sometimes joined by twenty-eight-year-old John McGregor from Scotland, who brought his bagpipes into the Alamo. Years later, Dickinson recalled that the two engaged in comical duels as each tried to make the most noise with their respective instruments. The cacophony of Crockett's "fiddling" and McGregor's piping amused the garrison, broke the monotony, and distracted momentarily from the reality of the Mexican army beyond the Alamo's walls. Contrary to legend, there is no evidence Crockett ever played the fiddle, but Micajah Autry did play the violin quite well and soothed the defenders' ears with his own playing when Crockett and McGregor ran out of steam. Although no other Alamo survivor mentioned these musical duels, Susanna repeated the story many times over the years.[13]

Bowie had himself brought out from his room a few times to encourage the men and check on Juana and Gertrudis. Mornings were cold with temperatures in the mid- to high-thirties and rising no higher than the mid-sixties during the day, often punctuated by dreaded "northers," strong north winds that intensified the cold. Those who stood picket or remained on the walls suffered most, especially at night. Others, including civilians, huddled around fires. The lack of coffee added to their debilitation while their diet consisted almost entirely of beef and cornbread. They lived in close quarters within the dreary compound and shared common toilets, or "sinks," as they were called by the US military. There is no way of knowing how much privacy they afforded the women, children, and soldiers. There were likely few beds or cots, and many would have slept on straw ticks—makeshift mattresses that had to frequently be refilled with straw. In addition to keeping up with repairs to the walls after each day's cannon pounding, soldiers would have shared the chore of filling the latrine pits with fresh dirt to suppress the odors. The cold weather, poor diet, poor hygiene, and bad sleeping conditions would wear men down quickly.[14]

The garrison enjoyed slightly warmer weather on February 29 and fired off two twelve-pound cannon shots toward the house where Santa Anna may have been quartered, one of which hit its mark. But the president was out at the time reconnoitering near a mill site northwest of the Alamo. It is unlikely they were aiming for him anyway since Travis believed Santa Anna had not yet arrived in Béxar. Late that evening, the wind shifted to the north and again chilled the night air. Texians sometimes spotted Mexican soldiers who came within range of their long rifles, and someone picked off one of the soldiers during the night.

Near midnight on February 29, Ramírez y Sesma's cavalry started toward Goliad to intercept Fannin's column, which had already turned back to Fort Defiance. An hour later the thirty-two men from Gonzales approached the Alamo, led by John W. Smith. The men worked their way toward the gate at the southern end of the compound but were detected and fired upon by Mexican sentries. One man was hit in the foot, but the company made it into the Alamo without further injury. The sight of these reinforcements lifted the garrison's spirits for the first time in a week. True, it was a small company that made little difference in the Alamo's situation, but it confirmed that Travis's messages were getting through and Texians were responding to them. The Gonzales men made their way to warming fires, and Crockett doubtless welcomed them, recognizing both John W. Smith and Martin. Enrique Esparza recalled decades later that "there was great shouting. The Texans beat drums and played on a flute." Crockett may have warmed the men a bit more with another comical attack on his fiddle, after which Autry relieved their ears by serenading them with his own playing. It was the happiest moment the men would enjoy, one that gave them cause for hope. During the night the temperature again plunged to thirty-four degrees.[15]

Travis was encouraged by their arrival but concerned that so few men had gotten through. Martin and Smith reported that efforts were continuing in Gonzales and elsewhere to raise more relief forces, and that as far as they knew, Fannin was still thought to be on the march to the Alamo with as many as three hundred men. But things had, in fact, moved in a different direction. Shortly after Smith led these thirty-two men out of Gonzales, Fannin's express arrived there with word that he had turned back, while efforts to raise additional relief companies floundered. Meanwhile, Bonham, who left the Alamo on February 16 with an early appeal to Fannin, had been roaming far and wide in search of volunteers but with little luck. By late February he arrived in Gonzales where he learned that only thirty-two men had been raised there and saw for himself that significant numbers of volunteers were not forthcoming. He was there when Fannin's February 27 express arrived with the news that he had given up his efforts to relieve the Alamo—all bad news for Travis.

Although Travis's friend Williamson was seriously concerned for the fate of his friend in the Alamo, he was eager to put a brave face on things for Travis, despite the dour situation in Gonzales and the crushing news from Fannin. On March 1 he penned a letter to Travis filled with optimism. "Sixty men have set out from this municipality and in all human probability they are with you at this date. Colonel Fannin, with three hundred men and four pieces of artillery, has been on the march toward Béjar for three days. Tonight we expect some three hundred reinforcements from Washington, Bastro [sic], Brazoria, and San Felipe, and no time will be wasted in seeking their help for you." In a postscript he added, "For God's sake, hold out until we can help you.—I am sending to you with Major Bonham a message from the interior government.—A thousand greetings to all of your people, and tell them to hold firm 'for Willie' until I get there." Since both Bonham and Williamson knew by March 1 that Fannin had turned back on February 27, it is to be wondered why Williamson told Travis that Fannin was marching to Béxar. It's possible that, like John Sowers Brooks, he held out hope that Fannin would make another try. Fannin himself wrote on March 1 that he was contemplating sending two hundred men to rendezvous with other companies in Gonzales if he could procure sufficient provisions for them. Fannin was under the misguided notion that William H. Wharton was on his way to Béxar with provisions and 270 men, but Wharton was in Matagorda awaiting orders from Houston and not going anywhere. Williamson seemed to be engaging in wishful thinking when he estimated that as many as three hundred more volunteers were on their way from other places, but it is possible that in his

February 27 express Fannin mentioned his assumptions about Wharton and Williamson took him seriously, possibly including them in his inflated estimate of reinforcements. His reference to sixty men having already left clearly combines the group of thirty-two who reached the Alamo with Martin and Smith, and thirty or forty men that Sutherland, Seguin, and Alsbury had assembled on Cibolo Creek to wait for Fannin. They did not return to Gonzales until March 3, so Williamson likely thought they were on their way to the Alamo when he wrote to Travis on March 1. If these were Williamson's assumptions, Bonham likely shared them.

Williamson said he was enclosing a message from the interior government, but it has been lost along with another enclosure he mentioned: "With regards to *the other letter of the same date, let it pass*; today you will know what it means. If the multitude gets hold of it, let them figure it out." These references are unclear since no letters other than Williamson's have survived. It is possible that Governor Smith or Lieutenant Governor Robinson sent a message to Travis, possibly with more empty promises of help for the Alamo. Williamson's reference to "*the other letter*" is more problematic, and we can only guess who wrote it or what message it conveyed. We have only Williamson's word that Travis should ignore it, suggesting it contained a negative message of some kind that might have discouraged him in some way. Travis never mentioned it in subsequent communications.[16]

On March 1 Travis's message of February 25 reached Washington, where it was still believed that Fannin was on his way to Béxar and that other forces were heading there too. William Fairfax Gray heard the news and estimated the combined forces would bring the Alamo's strength to "some six or seven hundred. It is believed the Alamo is safe." This sounds very similar to the information in Williamson's letter of the same date. No doubt rumors were circulating through the colonies about such reinforcements, which never materialized beyond the Gonzales thirty-two.[17]

Bonham left Gonzales on March 1 and arrived at the Alamo around 11:00 a.m. on March 3. Handing Williamson's optimistic letter to Travis, Bonham tempered its sentiments with the more sobering news that Fannin had turned back to Goliad. Although it was possible that he might make another try, it was clear that it would take him many days to reach the Alamo with a sizeable force, which would likely be too late. In any case, Travis knew that if Fannin had left Goliad by February 27, he should have gotten to Béxar by now. Bonham also confirmed Williamson's claim that recruiting efforts were continuing in Gonzales and that a second small group of reinforcements was likely on its way, although it was puzzling that they hadn't arrived yet. The courier may also have repeated William-son's claim that another three hundred men were on their way, possibly the Wharton men that Fannin mentioned. Thus, Bonham's report mixed promising news with discouraging possibilities. Some hope was offered in the chance that another three hundred to four hundred men were on their way to the Alamo but, again, gave Travis reason to wonder why none had arrived yet.

Travis barely had time to process Bonham's report before more bad news arrived in the form of three battalions of Mexican reinforcements entering the city to cries of "Santa Anna! Santa Anna!" The defenders mistakenly thought this signaled the president's arrival in the city with the new troops, unaware that he had been there since the first day of the siege. The soldiers were cheering the new arrivals and the news that General Urrea had smashed Johnson's company at San Patricio on February 27, killing sixteen and taking twenty-one men prisoner. The soldiers would have celebrated even more had they known that a day earlier Urrea caught up with James Grant and nearly wiped out his small company at Agua Dulce Creek, where Grant was among those killed. Urrea was then free to move on Goliad, vindicating Fannin and justifying his return to Fort Defiance. Travis attempted to still the Mexican cheering by firing a few cannon shots and some musket fire at the city to no effect. Meanwhile, the Mexicans erected a new battery aimed at the north wall, within musket range of the fort.[18]

Even the most optimistic view of Bonham's news could not have en-couraged Travis much as he watched the Mexican columns march into town, including the Toluca Battalion sporting their dress uniforms. It was a chilling sight that badly offset any optimism the men from Gonzales had raised. If Fannin was on his way he would have to hurry, as would those companies Williamson mentioned. Travis weighed the Alamo's declining chances in the face of the sheer size of Santa Anna's reinforced army and the deteriorating state of his own small garrison, which now saw the Mex-icans constructing scaling ladders, signaling that an assault would come soon. In fact, Santa Anna wrote to Urrea the same day and told him that "I am currently readying the assault on the Alamo, the place to which the enemy has fallen back, and very soon they will experience the punishment that is duly merited to them." Meanwhile, Travis wrote another appeal to his fellow Texians, this one addressed to the convention that was meeting in Washington and had, unknown to him, declared Texas independence the previous day.[19]

In his March 3, 1836, letter to the convention, Travis referred to the government's state of near paralysis, or as he put it "the confusion of the political authorities of the country," as well as "the absence of the commander in chief," a reference to the sorry state of the army. He reported the state of things at the Alamo, noting that the Mexicans had kept up daily bombardment with howitzers and heavy cannonade from batteries as close as four hundred yards and that the enemy had steadily advanced their entrenchments on all sides of the fort. He mentioned the earlier arrival of the Gonzales men and Bonham's return to the Alamo that morning. Meanwhile, he said, the fort had held up well thus far and he was continuing to strengthen the walls with earthworks. He had not yet lost a man and the garrison's spirits remained high, but hope began to fade with the arrival of at least a thousand fresh Mexican troops.

"Fannin is said to be on the march to this place with reinforcements," Travis told the convention, "but I fear it is not true, as I have repeatedly sent to him for aid without receiving any." He noted that he sent Bonham to Goliad with a plea for help prior to the siege, that Bonham met with Fannin on February 18, and that he dispatched Johnson there on February 23 with a more urgent appeal for reinforcements. Johnson arrived there the next day, he noted, but emphasized, *none have yet arrived.* With no army in Texas and Fannin unresponsive, Travis was forced to "look to the *colonies alone* for aid: unless it arrives soon, I shall have to fight the enemy on his own terms." By "the colonies," Travis meant the longtime colonists, the citizen soldiers, who were expected to rise up and join the fight, something they had failed to do in significant numbers thus far. Volunteers from the United States, like Crockett, had not arrived in sufficient numbers either.

Travis seemed not to believe help would come and he turned fatalistic. He expressed admiration for the courage his hopelessly outnumbered men had shown throughout the siege and was certain their determination "will not fail them in the last struggle; and although they may be sacrificed to the vengeance of a gothic enemy, the victory will cost the enemy so dear, that it will be worse for him than a defeat." He had not abandoned all hope, however, and asked the government to hasten reinforcements, provisions, and badly needed ammunition. He even included an itemized list of how much powder, cannon balls, and lead should be rushed to the Alamo. "If these things are promptly sent and large reinforcements are hastened to this frontier," he promised, "this neighborhood will be the great and decisive battle ground." He was addressing the very colonies he was protecting at the Alamo, emphasizing that it was those colonies who held the power to stop Santa Anna before he destroyed them. "The power of Santa Ana is to be met here, or in the colonies," he warned, and "we had better meet them here, than to suffer a war of desolation to rage in our settlements."

He was angry with the Tejanos and said that all but three had deserted. He wanted those who had refused to join the fight to be "declared public enemies, and their property should aid in paying the expenses of the war." As he closed his letter to the convention, Travis observed that more Mexican reinforcements were still streaming into town, bringing the total to two thousand or three thousand.

Travis quickly penned two more letters, one was private and has been lost, while the other one was addressed to his friend Jesse Grimes, who was a delegate to the convention in Washington. He asked Grimes to transmit the private letter to its destination and told him he was "still here, in fine spirits, and well to do. With 140 men I have held this place 10 days against a force variously estimated from 1500 to 6000, and I will continue to hold it till I get relief from my countrymen, or I will perish in its defence." He told his friend that the convention delegates must declare independence so Texas and the world would know what they were fighting for. Short of that, neither he nor his men would remain under arms, although he realized that surrender was not really an option. Then he showed some bitterness and warned that "if my countrymen do not rally to my relief, I am determined to perish in the defence of this place, and my bones shall reproach my country for her neglect." The old braggadocio returned briefly as he swore that "with 500 men more, I will drive Sesma beyond the Rio Grande," and he promised to vanquish all enemies of Texas "whether invaders or resident Mexican enemies"—another dig at the Tejanos he regarded as disloyal. "All the citizens that have not joined us," he swore, "are with the enemy fighting against us." Curiously, Travis did not mention the Williamson letter, nor the news that Fannin had turned back to Goliad, which Bonham must have given him, saying only that he feared Fannin was not coming, despite word that he was on the march to Béxar. Perhaps he placed hope in the hundreds of volunteers Williamson said were on their way.[20]

Travis felt it was vital for his letters to go out that night and reach Washington as quickly as possible. He chose John W. Smith to carry them, and perhaps sensing the end might be near, many in the garrison handed Smith letters of their own, likely including Crockett who had last written to his family on January 9. He had been gone for four months and his wife,

Elizabeth, and their children had no idea where he was, only that he had not returned with Burgin and Tinkle. By now, they would have received his letter, which gave them the shocking news that he had joined the army, and Burgin or Tinkle could have passed on whatever Crockett may have told them before they departed for Tennessee, perhaps that he was on his way to Nacogdoches to enlist. They may have described the Red River country and tried to explain to the family how Crockett had fallen in love with it and was determined to win some of it for them.

As Smith prepared to leave, Travis hastily scribbled one more message, this one to David Ayers, who was caring for Travis's son, Charles. He could find only a scrap of yellow paper to write on, and he asked Ayers to "take care of my little boy. If the country should be saved I may make him a splendid fortune. But if the country should be lost, and I should perish, he will have nothing but the proud recollection that he is the son of a man who died for his country." It was a far cry from the bombastic "victory or death" messages Travis had been sending out for more than a week and reflected the general tone of ambivalence in all his March 3 letters.[21]

Smith packed up the letters and mounted his horse, but the Mexicans now encircled the Alamo and getting through would be more difficult. Around midnight, Travis assembled a company of men, including Crockett, and sent them out to stage a diversionary attack on Mexican troops at one of the sugar mills north of the Alamo. The attack was convincing and drew Mexican attention away from the fort, allowing Smith to dash from the Alamo through enemy lines and onto the Gonzales road, carrying with him the garrison's last words and sinking hopes. Crockett and the others exchanged fire with the Mexicans, but hastened back to the Alamo once Smith was on his way.[22]

Crockett continued to circulate through the fort trying to keep up sagging spirits, but he understood the perilous situation the garrison faced. The walls were weakening, the Mexican army growing, and their cannons drawing ever closer. Like the others, he saw the Mexicans constructing scaling ladders and knew it would not be long before thousands of them charged the fort and very likely overwhelmed it. Travis's letters were eloquent and passionate, but they had not brought any help to the Alamo. Crockett reflected on what seemed to lie ahead and told Susanna Dickinson that "I think we had better march out and die in the open air. I don't like to be hemmed up."[23]

By March 4 there were still no reinforcements and a sense of foreboding settled over the defenders. The morning dawned windy and cold again, and the Mexicans resumed their cannonade early. During the night, the Mexicans moved their northeastern battery within two hundred yards of the already weakened north wall, and cannonballs now punched through the crumbling barrier. Conserving powder, Travis did not respond until the afternoon by firing a couple of harmless shots. By night, the Texians worked feverishly to repair the damaged walls, the Mexican soldiers close enough to hear them hammering. Meanwhile, the Texians were suffering the expected impact of a siege, finding themselves nearly out of beef, lacking medical supplies, and experiencing the unpleasantness associated with people living near latrines and livestock. That night Santa Anna met with his officers to discuss options for attacking the Alamo. Some, including Almonte, recommended attacking immediately, while others advised waiting a few days until twelve-pound guns arrived and the Alamo's walls could be breached.[24]

March 5 dawned clear and a bit warmer, the temperature reaching sixty-eight degrees by midday. The Mexicans resumed brisk fire from their northern battery with little return fire from the Alamo. Unknown to the weary defenders, Santa Anna rendered his decision and decided that the Alamo would be assaulted the following morning before dawn, but that hardly could have come as much of a surprise to the defenders, who sensed an attack would come at any time. As pointless as it may have been, Travis sent out one last messenger, thought to be James Allen, a twenty-one-year-old college student from Kentucky. No letter has survived, and it may be that Travis gave Allen only a verbal message. He may not have had time for more as he sensed an attack was imminent and he needed time to address his men. The Mexican battery north of the fort, having been moved ever closer, was tearing through the walls. When Allen reached Goliad, he told Fannin the fort had been holding up but that now, "every shot goes through the walls," which he described as "weak."[25]

Travis called the men together and bluntly told them what they already suspected. No help was coming, and "Three-Legged Willie's" soothing words had proven empty. Escape seemed impossible since the Mexican army had swelled to several thousand and tightened its ring around the Alamo. Still, it was always possible that some of them might escape, and he gave them leave to try. He owed them that much. They had stuck with him through nothing but bad news and sinking hopes, lousy food, and frigid temperatures. Many of them had been among the few who remained in Béxar when most of the garrison galloped off with Grant and Johnson for Matamoros. This was the way of the volunteer citizen-soldier armies that had done most of the Texian fighting and who might want to exercise their right to leave. Back in December, many companies refused to follow orders from Austin and Burleson to attack Cós's army in Béxar. That impasse was broken only when Ben Milam told the men to "vote" in a sense by asking which of them would follow him in an attack on the city. Some chose to join him while others refused. Officers, including Travis and Fannin, had complained about the handicap of trying to command such an army, which Travis once called "a mob." Now he found himself in command of a garrison largely made up of such volunteers, and it would not be at all surprising if he gave them a chance to vote on the question of leaving or staying. Travis and his regulars didn't have that choice, nor did Crockett and the others who had sworn an oath and enlisted in the Auxiliary Volunteer Corps, whose mission was to support the regulars. But none of that mattered now. Travis gave them all permission to go without censure. That night, several Alamo defenders appear to have made their way out of the fort, perhaps some of the Tejanos who were said to have deserted, as well as a man named Louis Rose, a fifty-year-old Frenchman. Some may have deserted before this and at least one was killed in the effort. Some survivors later told the Mexicans that, once it was clear no help was coming, Travis promised to either surrender or attempt escape under cover of darkness. In any case, most of them stayed.[26]

The image of the men crossing a line that Travis drew in the dirt, signifying that they would remain by his side, is powerfully seared into Alamo mythology. It has also been suggested that, even if the event never took place, the Alamo garrison crossed a figurative "line" simply by staying when the men must have known they would not survive and could have attempted escape.[27]

Ramírez y Sesma and Almonte agreed with Santa Anna's plan to attack, but other officers thought it unnecessary since the Alamo's walls were crumbling and the twelve-pound guns that were expected within a few days were sure to breach the walls. No Texian relief column had appeared, and Urrea had eliminated Johnson and Grant and was on his way to Goliad. When the Alamo's provisions ran out, surrender would remain the rebels' only option. There seemed no valid military justification for a costly attack on a stronghold bristling with cannons. But Santa Anna insisted on storming the Alamo in a show of force that would end the siege brutally and terrify other rebels in Texas and elsewhere in Mexico. A bloody victory, regardless of cost, should make that point quite well.[28]

Bowie, who had been among the enthusiastic leaders determined to hold Béxar, continued to deteriorate physically throughout the siege and was wracked with fever, struggling to breath between fits of coughing, and drifting in and out of consciousness. Bonham, who had dashed back into the Alamo two days earlier, now shared tea with the Dickinsons. The other defenders tried to come to grips with their reality, collected their thoughts, and probably conjured their fondest memories. Daniel Cloud might have recalled writing to his brother in December that "death in the cause of Liberty and humanity is not cause for shuddering." At that time, Autry had been certain that, if Santa Anna arrived "with his whole forces in the Spring . . . there will be soldiers enough of the real grit in Texas by that time to overrun all Mexico." Now he may have wondered if his wife and children would ever learn of his fate. Meanwhile, the tired work crews under Jameson continued making repairs to the north wall throughout the night. Perhaps Jameson was haunted by his optimistic estimate of the Alamo's capabilities only weeks earlier. Once Santa Anna silenced his cannons and the brass bands that had played during most nights, the Texians found sleep irresistible, and it must have fallen over the pickets posted outside the fort, for they were never heard from again.

Crockett recognized that, official or not, he occupied a position of leadership in the Alamo. Although he lacked official rank, he was still "Colonel Crockett" to the men. He was made a sergeant during the Creek War, had been a militia colonel for years, and at one time was commandant of his unit. Although it had been more than twenty years since he faced an enemy, Crockett understood what command and leadership meant. Like Rose, he could have abandoned the garrison, but that would have been out of character for him, a man who typically stuck to his decisions. He understood the danger he faced when he enlisted, although, like many others, he may have mistakenly believed the toughest fighting was over. Despite reports that Santa Anna was returning with a huge army, he shared the belief that a large enough Texian relief force would be raised before the Mexicans arrived and, like the others who clung to that belief, was disappointed. Nevertheless, he stayed. It can only be wondered what thoughts crossed his mind in those final days and hours. Had he let his family down by failing to provide them the home he promised them? He knew that they would be entitled to whatever land his service earned, but would they ever see it? Would Texas ever really exist as a republic, or would Santa Anna quickly reestablish his control over the country, smash the rebellion, and put its leaders to death? Now, that seemed the more likely outcome.

Crockett was typically single-minded and his vision often myopic. As a three-term congressman he focused on a single issue, his land reform bill, to the near exclusion of all others. He tried to cut deals with other legislators, but only related to tradeoffs that would help get his land bill through. He didn't hesitate to alienate the entire Tennessee delegation and Jackson, a popular president from his own state who held a tight grip on that delegation. In the end, Crockett isolated himself and was left with little maneuvering room, his bill failed, and he lost his congressional seat. Land was at the heart of his journey to Texas and determined the course he followed there. Unable to buy land, his only remaining option was to enlist and qualify for the land bounties offered to volunteers. Once he chose that course, he was bound to take his chances in the field. Or was he? His fate might have been different if, like Herbert S. Kimble, who enlisted with him in Nacogdoches, he had dawdled along the trail to Washington and then simply remained there to see how events unfolded. That's what Kimble did, and he became secretary of the Convention of 1836 while Crockett ended up in the Alamo. To some degree, his fate was the kind of bad luck that often dashed his fondest hopes, including his failed mill enterprise, his harebrained barrel stave fiasco, and his narrow campaign losses. It was also another manifestation of Crockett's inability or unwillingness to stray from a course of action once he decided upon it. In a sense, he lived up to his motto, "Be always sure you're right, then go ahead." Once set upon a course that he believed was right, there was no dissuading him, whether it was his mission to retrieve gunpowder during a winter storm or his decision to remain in Texas and join the fight. Perhaps it was another decision made too hastily, or simply one more run of bad luck.

Looking over the Alamo walls at the army that was sure to crush them and realizing how Texas had failed to raise even a minimal relief force for the Alamo, Crockett saw what was coming. Once, when his land bill was stalled in Congress by his own Tennessee delegation, he was not deterred and swore that, "If I am whipped, I will not stay whipped," and vowed to "keep a kicking with a hope of success." He fought tenaciously for the bill and surely some of that stubborn spirit remained with him in his last hours. He called for a clean suit of clothes that had been washed for him. He said he expected to be killed and wished to meet his end in clean clothes "that they might give him a decent burial." Gone were his dreams of a land empire, and it was too late to worry about his family back in Tennessee.[29]

The Mexicans ceased firing their cannons at 10:00 p.m. on March 5. While most of the garrison fell into a welcome sleep that night, the Mexican senior staff were wide awake and actively planning a dawn assault on the Alamo. Santa Anna ordered his cook, Ben, a free Black man, to have coffee on hand all night. Neither the president nor Almonte went to bed, and they conversed throughout the night. They went out around midnight and returned between two and three in the morning. Santa Anna again ordered coffee and threatened to run Ben through if it was not brought immediately. Santa Anna was noticeably agitated and Almonte warned him that the assault "would cost them much," but Santa Anna replied, "It is of no importance what the cost was, that it must be done."[30]

By 3:00 a.m. Mexican troops moved toward the river, walked two abreast across narrow wooden bridges, and were in place within an hour. Although the moon was full, dense clouds obscured its light. The soldiers lay on the cold ground awaiting the order to attack while the cavalry moved into position east and south of the fort. Santa Anna and Almonte observed from the northeast battery so they might view the progress of the main assault at the north wall. The Mexican reserves were positioned nearby. At 5:30 a.m. a bugle sounded the signal to attack, although some soldiers broke the silence before that with cries of "long live the Republic!" and bands near Santa Anna also sounded the charge. Some one thousand Mexican soldiers comprised the force that attacked the northern end of the fort, seven hundred under Cós, who assaulted the northern end of the west wall. Col. Francisco Duque's Toluca Battalion hit the north wall, while José María Romero's column of about three hundred men attacked the east side of the compound. Ben later described seeing Mexican rockets ascending in different directions, lighting the Alamo, then heard musketry and cannons. By the flashes of light, he saw large bodies of Mexican troops under the Alamo walls. The troops charged the fort as fast as they could and were greeted by heavy fire from Texian rifles and cannons on the north wall. Some Mexican units suffered heavy casualties, including the Toluca Battalion, which lost half its company of chasseurs from a single blast of cannon fire. Duque, the battalion commander, was badly wounded in the thigh, trampled by his own men, and quickly replaced by Gen. Manuel

Fernández Castrillón. Many soldiers fired rifles wildly as they charged, some killing their own comrades. Most of the flimsy scaling ladders were quickly lost. To the east, Romero's column soon swung to the north as it was battered by cannon fire from the batteries at the rear of the Alamo church and the cattle pen, and rifle fire from the roof of the two-story barrack. At the same time, some of Cós's soldiers drifted down the west wall, while others moved further toward the northwest corner of the compound. Soon, all three columns mingled and foundered in a confused mass at the north end of the compound and attempted to find a way over the wall. Ironically, the way in was provided by the lumber the defenders used to shore up the battered and weakened north wall, which the soldiers climbed, some scrambling over the backs of their comrades. Order quickly broke down and officers either couldn't be heard or were ignored. Many soldiers continued to mill around the wall, going nowhere and obstructing those behind them. Although those close to the wall were sheltered from the Texian rifle and cannon fire, those in the rear were battered by them.[31]

Texians rushed to meet the Mexican troops at the north wall, possibly hearing strains of Mexican bugles blaring "El Degüello"—a signal that no prisoners were to be taken—while Mexican rockets lit the area. Crockett quickly realized the north wall was enduring the brunt of the attack, and he rushed to the cannon platform in the northwest corner of the compound. Before he left the Alamo on the first day of the siege, Sutherland saw Crockett stationed at the palisade and most accounts assume he remained there, but much had changed over the following two weeks as Crockett took on a more prominent leadership role and moved throughout the compound. The palisade was not particularly vulnerable as it was protected by a stockade and an abattis of felled trees, and the Mexicans did not attack it, opting instead to secure the southwest corner of the compound. We don't know where Crockett was quartered, but it might have been in one of the rooms that lined the west wall, near both Travis's room and the one originally occupied by Bowie, where the Navarro sisters now sheltered, and near the main attack at the north wall. On the other hand, with an imminent attack expected, he may have been sleeping outside, perhaps on a straw tick. Regardless of where Crockett was that morning, like most of the defenders, he would have rushed to meet the main assault at the north wall.

Travis was awakened almost immediately. He grabbed his shotgun and rushed with his slave, Joe, to the cannon platform near the center of the north wall, where he encouraged his men to "give them hell!" He was killed almost immediately by a bullet through the head, having made the mistake of exposing himself at the top of the wall while firing down into the oncoming *soldados*. Joe quickly retreated into Travis's quarters where he saw little more of the battle but heard its ghastly sounds and feared for his life.[32]

Texians raked the Mexicans with cannon and rifle fire that staggered the assault troops, who momentarily halted, reformed, and again drove forward. But once the attackers were at the wall, the Texian cannons became nearly useless, and it was equally difficult for the Texians to fire their rifles downward from the top of the walls without being exposed. In Duque's column, Lt. Col. José Enrique de la Peña recalled that "a horrible carnage took place, and some were trampled to death. The tumult was great, the disorder frightful; it seemed as if the furies had descended upon us; different groups of soldiers were firing in all directions, on their comrades and on their officers, so that one was as likely to die by a friendly hand as by an enemy's." Men on both sides screamed, cursed, and shouted in languages that their opponents did not understand. The confusion and apparent stagnation at the north wall alarmed Santa Anna enough for him to send in his reserves, which only added to the confused mass there. Nonetheless, slowly but inevitably, soldiers reached the top of the wall, streamed over in ever larger numbers, and quickly overwhelmed the defenders, who were either killed or retreated without time to spike their cannons.[33]

Crockett did not fall back but remained on the northwest cannon platform. No longer able to reload his rifle, he was killed in the onslaught, battling the Mexicans hand-to-hand as they overwhelmed his position. The Mexican soldiers stormed over the platform, trampling his body, which was already bloodied by bullets and bayonets. On that cannon platform, within the cold, crumbling walls of a decaying ruin, in a place that must have seemed strange to him, David Crockett reached his journey's end.

At the south, Col. Juan Morales's 120 men avoided the palisade, its daunting abatis, and the entrenched tambor that guarded the gate. They found cover among small houses near the walls, then rushed the southwest corner, overwhelmed the small force that remained there, and captured their cannons. They quickly secured the main gate and wiped out the defenders in the tambor, thus securing the south end of the compound. In one of the rooms near the main gate they found Bowie in his sick bed. He may have put up what little fight his weakened body permitted before the *soldados* shot and bayonetted him. Some Mexicans mistakenly thought he was hiding and died a coward, unaware that he was deathly ill and barely conscious.

Mexican forces flooded into the Alamo from north and south, fired wildly, and continued to die in their own crossfire. Some of Cós's men may have battered their way into the fort through openings along the west wall. Once soldiers were inside the fort it was only a matter of time before Texian resistance ended. Defenders evacuating the walls found themselves caught between soldiers pouring over the north wall and soldiers coming up from the south. Some defenders stood their ground and were quickly overwhelmed. Others fell back into the rooms that lined the compound, which they had prepared with trenches and earthworks intended to block or slow the Mexicans. But the Mexican soldiers rolled Texian cannons down from their platforms, moved them onto the plaza, and used them to blast through the doors of the rooms where defenders took cover. Santa Anna later grudgingly conceded that the defenders "were very courageous and caused much damage to Béxar." De la Peña described the defenders as fighting courageously and thought their courage merited them mercy, for which some pleaded toward the end of the battle. He saw some calling out for quarter or waving white cloth or socks, attempting to surrender. When some soldiers responded by entering these rooms, they were set upon by other Texians who had no interest in surrendering and met the Mexicans with pistol fire and Bowie knives. This enraged the soldiers who furiously attacked the defenders and quickly dispatched them. Another Mexican soldier recalled that "the tenacious resistance of our enemies was amazing."[34]

Many Texians attempted to escape the fort in small breakout groups but were quickly cut down by Ramírez y Sesma's mounted lancers, who were positioned precisely for that purpose. As many as seventy Texians, about one-third of the garrison, died this way outside the Alamo. The carnage raged for at least an hour as the soldiers went on firing, even shooting the dead and stripping the bodies of what few valuables they could find. Cós tried to halt the firing but his bugler could not be heard, and the soldiers continued their killing frenzy. Even the sick and wounded in the hospital were shot. Within ninety minutes of the initial attack, at around 6:30 a.m., it was over, and the Mexicans held the Alamo.[35]

Sheltered in rooms inside the church, most of the terrified noncombatants saw nothing of the battle and only heard the firing, the screams, the cursing, and the groans. A few Texians may have sought shelter in the church but were found and killed there. Three unarmed Texians were shot down there near Susanna Dickinson, who claimed she also saw the murder of two boys, ages eleven and twelve. A Mexican officer, possibly Almonte, came into Susanna's room and asked her in English, "Are you Mrs. Dickinson?" Susanna answered that she was, and the officer responded, "If you wish to save your life, follow me." The soldiers were still firing as she left the fort and a stray bullet hit her in the calf. Almonte himself was robbed by some of his own soldiers before he put Susanna and her child into a buggy and sent them to the Ramón Músquiz house, where she and her husband stayed prior to the siege, and where her wound was dressed.[36]

Far from the church, Juana Alsbury, her infant son, Alejo, and her nineteen-year-old sister, Gertrudis Navarro, huddled in their room along the west wall, not far from where Crockett was killed. Frightened for their lives, they too heard the mind-numbing sounds of battle. Hearing heavy firing nearby and clinging to Alejo, Juana told her sister to open the door and ask the soldiers not to fire into their room. For her trouble, Gertrudis was cursed at, and her shawl was ripped from her shoulders before she hurried back into the room. Soldiers followed her and demanded "your money and your husband!" When she assured them that she had neither, the soldiers broke open Juana's trunk and took her money and clothes, and the watches of Colonel Travis and other men who had entrusted them to her when they anticipated the attack was coming. A Texian soldier attempted to protect the women but was instantly bayoneted at Juana's side. A young Texian who was being chased by soldiers tried to use her as a shield but was repeatedly bayonetted and shot. The women were saved by a Mexican officer, who was shocked that they had been left there. He took them from the room and told them to remain by a cannon while he arranged for them to be taken to Santa Anna. Another officer soon approached them and warned them that the cannon was about to be fired, no doubt aimed at the entrances to rooms where Texians had taken shelter, and he ordered them to leave. Eventually, Juana's brother-in-law, Don Manuel Pérez, arrived on the scene and sent them to Don Ángel Navarro's house and safety.[37]

Joe sought shelter in Travis's room after he saw his master killed. As the fighting waned, Mexican soldiers searched the rooms and an officer asked in English, "Are there any negroes here?" Joe replied, "Yes, here's one." As he emerged from hiding, two soldiers immediately tried to shoot and bayonet him, but he received only minor injuries. A Mexican officer quickly drove off the soldiers with his sword. As he was led out, Joe noticed a Black woman who had been killed, her body lying between two guns.

Ben, Santa Anna's cook, could see the Alamo from a window about five hundred yards away and later remembered the loud crescendo of rifles and cannons. The noise "shortly died away, day broke upon the scene, and Santa Anna and Almonte returned, when the latter remarked, that 'another such victory would ruin them.'" When Santa Anna and Almonte entered the fort to view the carnage, the president ordered Francisco Ruiz, the alcalde of Béxar, to show him the bodies of Crockett, Bowie, and Travis. Ruiz found Travis's body on the cannon emplacement along the north wall and located Crockett's body on the nearby cannon platform in the northwest corner of the compound. Bowie's body was found in his sick room in the low barrack. Santa Anna also took Ben with him to identify Travis and Bowie. Ben said that he had known both men and recalled that "the sight was most horrid." Santa Anna also told Joe to add his own identification of Travis, which he did. Having satisfied himself that the "ringleaders" had been slain, Santa Anna ordered Ruiz to collect the Texian dead in carts, stack them in piles with kindling wood, and burn them. The funeral pyres burned long into the night; Crockett's remains among them.

After being interviewed by Santa Anna with all the other survivors, Susanna Dickinson, Angelina, and Joe were released and made their way to Gonzales, along with Ben, who had served as Santa Anna and Almonte's cook. They carried a message from Santa Anna to colonists promising punishment for those who rebelled and urging loyal citizens to return to their homes and the protection of the government. In Gonzales, the survivors met with Houston and confirmed earlier reports he had received of the Alamo's fall.[38]

* * * * *

William Fairfax Gray was enjoying breakfast in Washington on the morning of March 6 when John W. Smith arrived with Travis's March 3 letter. It was read to all members of the convention, after which Robert Potter, a delegate from Nacogdoches, moved that the convention form a provisional government and then adjourn to take the field. According to Gray, "An interesting debate arose . . . but they adjourned without any action, the motion being lost." The convention did order one thousand copies of Travis's March 3 letter printed as handbills, and Gray did see some welcome movement at last by the Texian leadership, observing, "A great many persons are starting and preparing to start to the seat of war." The convention at last gave Houston full command of *all* soldiers, including regulars, militia, and volunteers, finally making him true commander of the army with full authority over all Texian soldiers. In the afternoon, Gray watched Houston ride off toward Gonzales accompanied by Capt. William G. Cooke, Capt. James Tarleton, and others. Gray wrote in his diary that the "town has been all day in a bustle, but is quiet now." He observed that despite the presence of Santa Anna's army, possible threats from Indians, and facing the task of organizing a new government and writing a constitution, "the Convention would seem to have enough on their hands to do. Yet they get on slowly. The evil spirit of electioneering is among them for the *high offices* in prospect. And the land quest also requires much *log rolling*, to make it suit the existing interests or selfish views of members. The Constitution gets on slowly."[39]

Martin Parmer, a delegate from San Augustine, wrote somberly to his wife that "unless we have a general turn out and every man lay his helping hand too, we are lost. Santa Anna and his vassals are now on our borders, and the declaration of our freedom, unless it is sealed with blood, is of no force." It was but one more voice added to the chorus that had been echoing through Texas since Béxar was taken from Cós in December. On the same day, Robinson, signing himself "Acting Governor," responded to Fannin's March 1 appeal for help with the bad news that the ongoing chaos and squabbling within the government precluded rendering him "that effectual aid you so much need."[40]

On March 9, word of the Alamo's fall had not yet reached Goliad, but John Sowers Brooks, still stationed there, sensed the outcome. "As soon as Bexar falls, we will be surrounded by 6000 infernal Mexicans," he wrote. "But we are resolved to die under the walls rather than surrender." Brooks was later wounded in the Battle of Coleto and executed with the other Goliad prisoners on March 27, 1836.[41]

In Gonzales, Col. J. C. Neill paid ninety dollars for medicines he planned to take to the Alamo and signed himself "Col. Comdt. of the post of Bexar." He still considered himself garrison commander and, as he promised, planned to return to the Alamo.

Joe, Travis's slave and the only man who fought in the Alamo and survived, made his way to Bailey's Prairie, Texas, where he was again enslaved by Travis's heirs. He escaped with an unidentified Mexican on April 21, 1837, the first anniversary of the Battle of San Jacinto, taking two horses with them. John R. Jones, executor of Travis's estate, offered a forty-dollar reward for the return of Joe and one of the horses, and ten dollars for the Mexican and the other horse.

On March 5, Gray was still looking for land opportunities and learned that Ramón Músquiz, who lived in Béxar, was selling five-and-a-half leagues of land for $10,000. Another man offered ten leagues for $15,000 ($318,576 and $477,865 respectively in 2022 dollars). They were just the sort of deals Crockett had hoped to make one day.[42]

1. As a sixteen-year-old, John Swisher was thrilled when his father hosted Crockett for several days at Gay Hill. The young Swisher enjoyed shooting matches with Crockett and listened to the Colonel's stories far into the nights. Portrait used by permission of owner.

2. George William Featherstonhaugh (pronounced Fanshaw), a British geologist and geographer, travelled much the same path as Crockett, but he made the trip one year earlier. Unlike Crockett, he made detailed notes and descriptions of what he saw, including Isaac Jones's plantation near Lost Prairie, Arkansas. Library of Congress.

3. William Fairfax Gray traveled through Texas during the revolution and kept a journal with his observations. Like Crockett, he was interested in Texas land. Photo of a nineteenth century painting. Courtesy of Christ Church Cathedral, Houston. Unsigned and undated.

4. Samuel Price Carson and Crockett served together in Congress and became friends through Crockett's in-laws. Crockett witnessed Carson's duel with Robert B. Vance in 1827. Carson owned land in the Red River country and likely laid out the route that Crockett followed to Texas. Photo of Portrait. Prints and Photographs Collection, camh-dob-013524, The Dolph Briscoe Center for American History, The University of Texas at Austin.

5. Col. Juan Nepomuceno Almonte was Santa Anna's right-hand man throughout the Texas Revolution and was imprisoned with him after the Battle of San Jacinto. Some sources claim he witnessed Crockett's alleged execution at the Alamo. Photo, circa 1850s, taken in Paris by Sergei Lvovich Levitsky (1819–1898). Used with permission of Lawrence T. Jones.

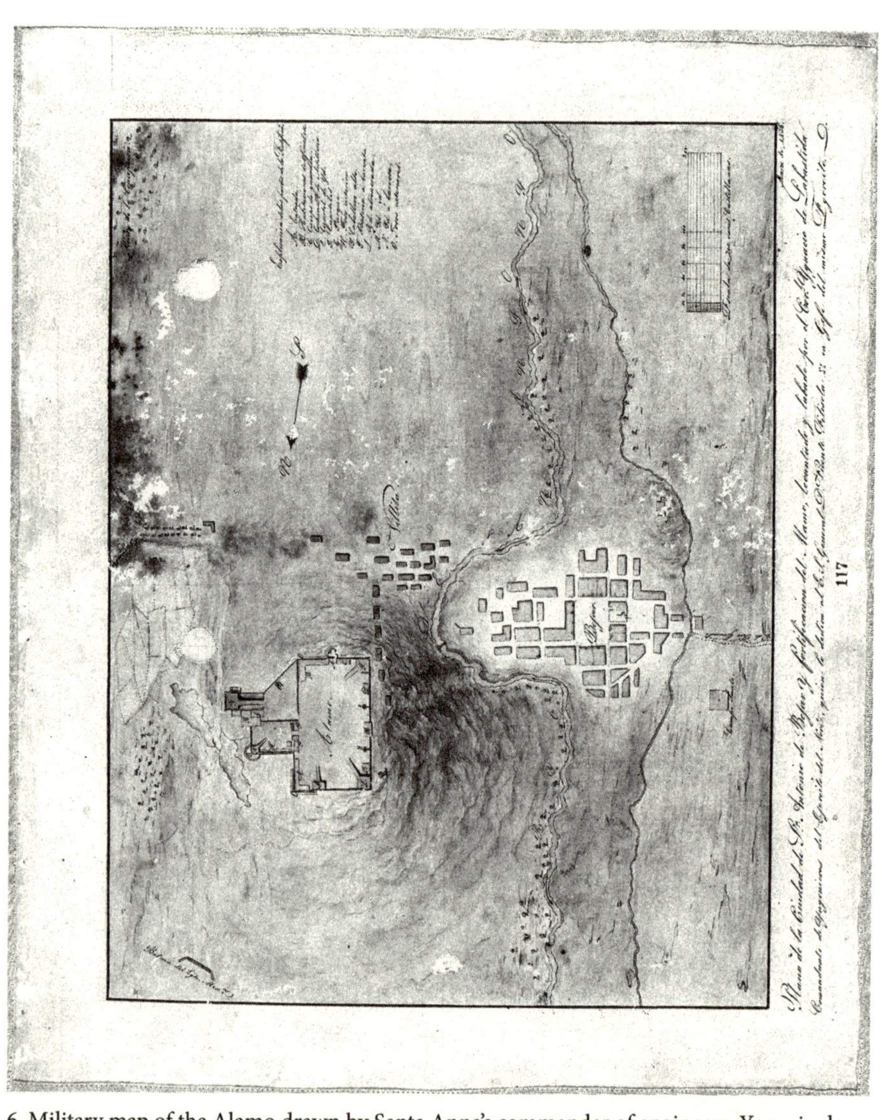

6. Military map of the Alamo drawn by Santa Anna's commander of engineers, Ygnacio de Labastida, including the town of San Antonio de Béxar and surrounding area. Prints and Photographs Collection, Dolph Briscoe Center for American History, The University of Texas at Austin.

7. *Fall of the Alamo—Death of Crockett*, from *Davy Crockett's Almanack of Wild Sports in the West*, published in 1837. The artist clearly had no idea what the Alamo looked like. National Portrait Gallery, Smithsonian Institution.

8. *Death of Colonel Crockett.* An early representation of Crockett's alleged execution after the Battle of the Alamo, from *Life of Colonel David Crockett*, circa 1860s. The book includes fictional material about Crockett's time in Texas. Author's Collection.

9. An 1859 map of Texas by Heinrich Berghaus (1797–1884), showing points where Crockett travelled after leaving Little Rock, Arkansas. David Rumsey Map Collection, David Rumsey Map Center, Stanford Libraries.

Fifty Dollars

WILL be given for delivering to me on Bailey's Prairie, seven miles from Columbia, a negro man named Joe, belonging to the succession of the late Wm. Barret Travis, who took off with him a Mexican and two horses, saddles and bridles. This negro was in the Alamo with his master when it was taken; and was the only man from the colonies who was not put to death: he is about twenty-five years of age, five feet ten or eleven inches high, very black and good countenance: had on when he left, on the night of the 21st April ult. a dark mixed sattinet round jacket and new white cotton pantaloons. One of the horses taken is a bay, about 14½ hands high very heavy built, with a blaze in his face, a bushy mane and tail, and a sore back; also the property of said succession, the other horse is a chesnut sorrel, above 16 hands high. The saddles are of the Spanish form, but of American manufacture, and one of them covered with blue cloth. Forty dollars will be given for Joe and the small bay horse, (Shannon,) and ten dollars for the Mexican other horse and saddles and bridles.

If the runaways are taken more than one hundred miles from my residence, I will pay all reasonable travelling expenses, in addition to the above reward,

JOHN R. JONES, Ex'r of W. B. Travis,

Bailey's Prairie, May 21st, 1837.   70-3m tf

10. William Travis's slave, Joe, was the only man who fought in the Alamo and survived. He was returned to slavery after the battle but escaped on the first anniversary of the Battle of San Jacinto. Travis's heirs then posted this reward notice for Joe's capture and return. *Telegraph and Texas Register*, August 24, 1837; author's collection.

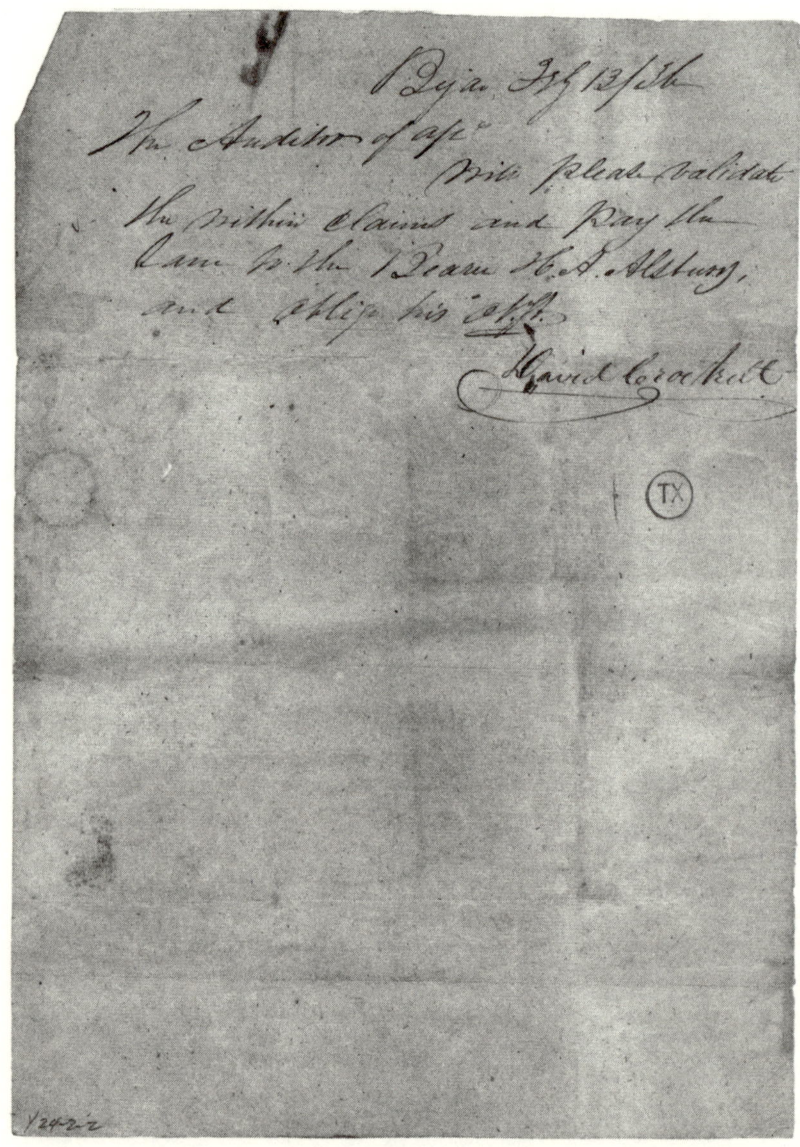

11. The February 13, 1836, authorization from Crockett for H. A. Alsbury to act as his agent in collecting $57.50 due Crockett for two rifles he sold to the army on January 15, 1836, in Nacogdoches. Texas Republic claim number 1358 is the last surviving document signed by Crockett. Courtesy of Texas State Library and Archives Commission.

12. *Colonel Crockett*, an 1839 engraving by Charles Gilbert Stuart based on the 1834 full-length portrait of Crockett by John Gadsby Chapman. National Portrait Gallery, Smithsonian Institution.

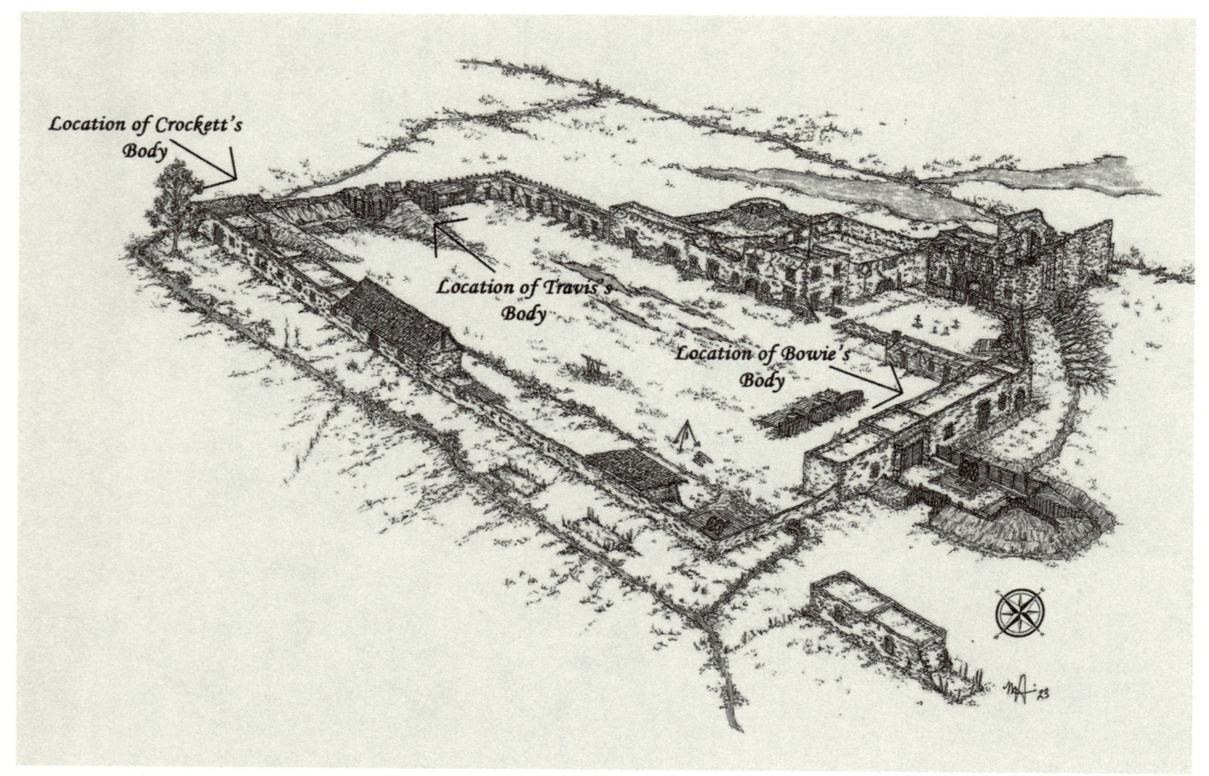

13. The Alamo as it appeared during the 1836 siege and battle, with the locations of the bodies of Crockett, Travis, and Bowie. Drawing by Mike Harris; labeling by Mike Boldt.

CHAPTER 7

In Death

It was not long after the Alamo guns were silenced and its defenders' bodies burned that accounts of the battle appeared in the press and elsewhere, most of them of dubious factual or historic value. Some of the earliest accounts mentioned Crockett and speculated about the manner and location of his death in the Alamo. Nearly a century-and-a-half after the Alamo battle, historians took up a prolonged and heated debate over the idea that Crockett somehow survived the battle only to be executed immediately thereafter on Santa Anna's personal order, which was carried out despite objections from some Mexican officers who allegedly witnessed the event.

The debate over Crockett's death centered largely on the authenticity of *With Santa Anna in Texas: A Personal Narrative of the Revolution*, the memoir of Lt. Col. José Enrique de la Peña, a Mexican officer who fought at the Alamo. The memoir claims that Crockett was captured at the end of the battle and then executed. Although published in Mexico in 1955, it did not appear in English until 1975. In 1978, Dan Kilgore was the first to evaluate this and other Mexican accounts that repeated the execution scenario in his monograph, *How Did Davy Die?* A subsequent debate took place in a series of articles by James E. Crisp, Thomas Ricks Lindley, and William Groneman, which are included in the bibliography. Although the documents were ultimately found to be authentic by David B. Gracy II, that alone does not mean they are reliable accounts, and the various reports of Crockett's death deserve a fresh look.[1]

It is significant that no Mexican post-battle reports mention Crockett's death or anything more than his being among those killed. Santa Anna's official report, written within hours of the battle, merely noted that Bowie and Travis—"who styled themselves Colonels"—and "Crocket" were among those slain. Colonel Almonte, an English-speaking special adviser to Santa Anna, did not participate in the attack but entered the fort afterward. In his diary entry that day he did not mention executions, nor did he record many details about the battle, although he did say he was robbed by his own men. Capt. José Juan Sánchez Navarro y Estrada noted in his journal that "some cruelties horrified me among others the death of an old man who they called *Cocran*," which some authors have speculated indicates Crockett, "and a boy of about fourteen." The journal of the San Luis Potosí Battalion names Bowie, Travis, and Crockett as "the ringleaders" and curiously says that Crockett "succeeded in entering [the fort] three nights ago." That information could have come from post-battle interviews with Susanna Dickinson, who, in 1874, nearly forty years after the battle, said Crockett was "one of 3 men who came into the Fort during the siege & before the assault." In an 1876 interview she said that "3 of our spys entered 3 days before the assault." She might have told her Mexican captors the same thing shortly after the battle. None of these accounts shed any light on how Crockett died.[2]

The first report of the Alamo's fall was carried from Béxar to Sam Houston in Gonzales by Andres Barsena and Anselmo Bergara (sometimes spelled Barcena and Vergara), two of Juan Seguin's men, who had remained in the San Antonio area throughout the siege. They claimed that Travis had killed himself, that Bowie was killed in his sick bed, and that seven "were killed by order of Santa Anna when in the act of giving up their arms," but they did not mention Crockett. Bergara was not a witness himself but got the story from Antonio Pérez, who said he was in San Antonio during the battle and saw scores of dead Mexican solders. In another account, Pérez said he took part in the battle but doesn't specify which side he was on. Thus, the story is, at best, thirdhand. Nonetheless, Houston sensed that the Alamo had fallen, and he wrote the same day to Fannin in Goliad relaying Bergara's account, including the report that "seven men surrendered and called for Genl. St. Anna and for quarter= [*sic*] They were murdered by his order. Col. Bowie Was Sick in his bed and also murdered." Houston did not mention Crockett in his report a few days later, which suggests the Alamo survivors did not mention him either. Houston wrote to Henry Raguet, saying, "Our friend Bowie, as is now understood, unable to get out of bed, shot himself, as the soldiers approached [his bed]. . . . Travis, tis said, rather than fall into the hands of the enemy, stabbed himself." Again, he did not mention Crockett, although some authors have claimed that the two men were good friends. Thomas Lindley suggested that the source of the Bergara-Perez account may have been María de Jesus Buquor, who was ten years old at the time of the battle. In a 1907 interview published in the *San Antonio Daily Express*, she said she witnessed the death of seven Texians who tried to escape from the Alamo and were killed on the riverbank near her house, some of whom may have tried to surrender. Some early reports claimed that only a man named Warner survived to ask for quarter before being killed, likely a reference to Henry Warnell, who may have survived the battle only to be executed. No one named Warner is listed among the Alamo dead.[3]

Reports of the Alamo's fall reached New Orleans within weeks of the battle, conveyed by passengers arriving by ship from Texas. Their word-of-mouth accounts, some of them derived from Houston's March 11 report, were quickly published in the city's newspapers. One of the earliest reports, written by Jonathan M. Shreve in Brazoria on March 17 and reprinted in many US newspapers, mentioned that seven Texians "who on asking for quarters, and being told none could be given, again commenced the work of death, and the last died as did the first, without yielding an inch of ground." Shreve said that the "celebrated Col. David Crockett of Tennessee was among the slain" and described his death as "most heroic; [Crockett] having used his rifle as long as possible by loading and discharging, and the enemy crowding upon the walls he turned the britch [breech] of his gun, and demolished more than twenty of the enemy before he fell." A letter written by Andrew Briscoe, who arrived in New Orleans aboard the steamer *Levant*, was published on March 28 and had Crockett "fighting like a tiger" to the death. An early, fanciful account practically cast Crockett in marble and described his countenance in death as exhibiting "that freshness of hue, which his exercise of pursuing the beasts of the forest and the prairie had imparted to him." Several newspapers reported that seven Texians "were found alive who cried for quarters, but were told that there was no mercy for them; they then continued fighting until the whole were butchered." The report also noted: "We regret to say that Col. David Crockett, his companion Mr. [Jesse] Benton, and Col. Bonham of South Carolina, were among the number slain," even though Benton was not in the Alamo. Almost immediately several newspapers conflated the two reports and placed Crockett, Bonham, and Benton among those who tried to surrender: "We regret to say, that Col. David Crockett and his companion, Mr. Benton, also the gallant Col. Bonham of South Carolina, were of the number who cried for quarter, but were told there was no mercy for them. They then continued fighting until the whole were butchered."

The seed of the idea that Crockett was executed, or killed after trying to surrender, was first planted in these early conflated reports, which quickly spread to newspapers throughout the United States. Within weeks some newspapers printed corrections. On March 31, the *Natchez Courier* reported that Travis's slave, Joe, told interviewers that "all the Texians fell valiantly fighting, except Colonel Bowie, who was killed in his bed" and that he said "nothing about any call for quarter by Colonel Crockett and others; and it is not true that Colonel Travis shot himself; they all fought and killed as many Mexican as they could, and were slain at last, in fair, though unequal, conflict."[4]

Ironically, it was the battles after the Alamo that gave rise to more dramatic accounts of Crockett's death. Mexican Gen. José Urrea and his troops defeated the Goliad garrison at Coleto Creek on March 19 and 20, and although Urrea favored sparing the Texians from the Mexican no quarter policy, Santa Anna angrily reprimanded him and sent no less than three orders to execute the Goliad prisoners. At sunrise on Palm Sunday, March 27, 1836, the Texians were marched out in three groups and shot at close range. Those not killed outright were run down and shot or bayoneted. Fannin and the rest of the wounded were shot inside the compound. Some twenty-eight men managed to escape, avoiding the fate of the estimated 342 who died, far more than those killed at the Alamo. Santa Anna was adamant about enforcing the decree as a deterrent against further immigration of fighters from the United States, whom he suspected of supporting the Texas revolt if not instigating it. Despite his later attempts to deny it, Santa Anna was directly responsible for the deaths of the Goliad prisoners.[5]

Less than four weeks after the Goliad massacre, Texian forces under Sam Houston soundly defeated a force of about 1,600 Mexican soldiers under Santa Anna at San Jacinto. *El presidente* himself was taken prisoner along with Almonte, Cós, Santa Anna's secretary, Ramón Martínez Caro, and other high-ranking officers. Texians remained furious over the slaughters at the Alamo and especially Goliad and were determined to see Santa Anna tried and executed as a criminal. Houston and interim Texas President David G. Burnet, however, were determined to keep Santa Anna alive to conclude a treaty with him that would recognize Texas independence and remove Mexican troops. Santa Anna, Almonte, Caro, and Col. Gabriel Nuñez Ortega were imprisoned aboard the armed schooner *Independence*. The other Mexican prisoners, including Cós, were first taken to the ranch of George M. Patrick and a week later moved to Camp Travis, a makeshift prison on Galveston Island commanded by Col. James Morgan, where the prisoners were roughly treated and often threatened. Two attempts were made to assassinate Santa Anna, and he and his entourage were moved several times to ensure their safety.

In May 1836 Santa Anna's party was moved to Velasco aboard the steamboat *Laura*, and on May 14, Santa Anna and Burnet signed two peace treaties, known as the Treaties of Velasco, one public and the other "secret." They provided that hostilities would cease, Mexican forces would withdraw below the Rio Grande and not attack Texas again, confiscated property would be restored, and prisoners would be exchanged on a one-for-one basis. The secret treaty stipulated that Santa Anna be immediately released in exchange for his pledge to advocate for Mexican recognition of Texas independence. It also stipulated that the Texas border would not extend beyond the Rio Grande.[6]

Santa Anna was about to be released on June 2 and sail to Veracruz aboard the Texas schooner of war *Invincible*, but the plan was derailed by the arrival on the same day of the steamboat *Ocean* with Gen. Thomas Jefferson Green and 230 volunteers from New Orleans, some of whom had lost friends at Goliad. The new arrivals joined local dissidents who opposed releasing Santa Anna and wanted to pull him off the *Invincible*, resulting in a few frightening hours for the Mexicans. Burnet quickly backed down, cancelled Santa Anna's release, and ordered that he be returned to Velasco. The Mexican dictator was terrified when he learned that he was not being released after all and was instead being removed from the *Invincible* and taken ashore. George Henry Tobin, who served on the *Invincible* while Santa Anna was being held prisoner there, recalled the "soldiers were so enraged against him that it was feared they might shoot him in cold blood. . . . Orders came to send him ashore next morning, at which he was excessively alarmed, fearing he should be murdered by the soldiers. He begged the sailors to shoot him, and swallowed an immense quantity of brandy and opium. In the morning he became delirious, jumped on deck, seized a bayonet from a marine and attempted to stab himself." Green also described finding Santa Anna "alternately raving like a madman and crying like a child, denying that he had any agency in the massacre at Goliad . . . threatening to take away his own life sooner than go ashore. . . . The prisoner continued to act this strange part for about two hours; stating, meanwhile, that he had taken largely of opium, and would soon die."[7]

Despite Burnet's action, most Texians remained livid and condemned the interim government's agreement to release Santa Anna, believing that he was under no obligation to fulfill a treaty signed under duress. Indeed, the Mexican Congress ultimately refused to ratify the treaty. Denunciations and violent threats were leveled at the Mexican dictator throughout his lengthy imprisonment. Green reported that violent speeches against the treaty were made at public meetings and warned that this was the prevailing mood among soldiers in Velasco. Gen. Thomas J. Rusk, commander in chief of the Texas Army, told Morgan the treaty was "a disgraceful armistice" brought about by a "wretchedly weak policy." Gen. Mirabeau Lamar warned Burnet that Green led an effort to seize Santa Anna, supported by a vast majority of the troops, who were on the move. Lamar planned to stop them, although he too thought Santa Anna should be executed but wanted him tried legally rather than by "a rebellious mob of strangers who have been made such by an arbitrary and weak General [Green]." Interim Texas Vice President Lorenzo de Zavala, an active participant in the treaty negotiations who also served as an interpreter, was so disgusted by Burnet's caving to Green's mob that he resigned on June 3, angrily stating "a government that takes orders from armed masses is no longer a body politic." He further extended his protest by helping Santa Anna compose a letter to Burnet denouncing his treatment at the hands of the mob. The Mexican prisoners had every reason to fear for their lives.[8]

Santa Anna's June 9 protest letter to Burnet condemned his treatment, his accommodations, and the failure of the Texians to release him. Burnet responded on June 10 explaining that the anger of the Texians was understandable, particularly considering the brutal execution of the Goliad prisoners, noting that Texians "feel a deep, intense and righteous indignation at the many atrocities which have been perpetrated by the troops lately under your Excellency's command, and especially at the barbarous massacre of the brave Colonel Fannin and his gallant companions. How far your Excellency participated in that abominable and inglorious slaughter I am not disposed to conjecture, but it is both natural and true, that the people of Texas impute it to your Excellency's special command." Indeed, Santa Anna feared his repeated orders to execute the Goliad prisoners would be discovered and cost him his life. Nonetheless, Burnet promised to abide by the treaty and release Santa Anna as soon as it was practicable, meaning when tempers cooled and it was safe to let him go. Burnett added a complaint of his own, reporting that "the walls of the

Alamo at Bexar, have been prostrated and that the valuable brass artillery attached to that fortress, have been melted down and destroyed. There were many painful and pleasing and glorious reminiscences connected with that Alamo, which render its wanton dilapidation particularly odious to every Texian spirit; and your Excellency needs not to be informed that the destruction of it was an infraction of the Armistice & a violation of the Treaty." Although Burnet suggested that Santa Anna was responsible for the Goliad massacre, he mentioned no executions or atrocities at the Alamo. On June 14 Burnet wrote a long appeal to all citizen soldiers asking that they abide by the agreement to release Santa Anna rather than risk a renewal of war and further incarceration of Texian prisoners.[9]

Anger against Burnet reached a fever pitch on July 14, 1836, when Eleazar Louis Ripley Wheelock, captain of a company of Texas Rangers, drew up formal charges against him for usurpation, sedition, and treason, including the specific charge that he attempted to release Santa Anna. The charges were witnessed by Green, Gen. Felix Houston, thirteen other officers, and three enlisted men. Apparently, nothing ever came of the charges and Burnet remained in office until October 22, 1836, but they show the degree of opposition to releasing Santa Anna.[10]

There also was widespread fear in Texas of a new Mexican offensive. Rusk warned that the victory at San Jacinto would not end the war, that a large Mexican force remained in Texas, and that numbers in the Texian army had dwindled to a few hundred men. Rusk also warned Morgan that "it is all important, my dear Colonel, that a force should be concentrated here . . . as no doubt remains we shall have another campaign against us before we wake up again." Indeed, thousands of Mexican troops remained in Texas under Gen. Vicente Filisola's command, and the Texians feared they could renew their attack at any time. Squabbling among Texas leaders, its dwindling army, and Filisola's presence conjured memories of the dysfunctional provisional Texas government of 1835. By June 20, Burnet fell in line and warned, "We have just heard that the Mexicans are returning to us" and alerted the Texas Navy.[11]

The presence of Filisola's army showed that fears of a renewed Mexican invasion were not unfounded, but after being cowed by Green's mob, Burnet was concerned that more newcomers from the United States might add to their ranks. He took the precaution of notifying Texas agents in New Orleans that no more volunteers were needed from the United States. However, he was challenged by Rusk, whose troops were gathering the remains of the men massacred at Goliad for burial, further fueling Texian determination to hang Santa Anna. When Burnet heard rumors that Urrea was on the march back to Texas, he panicked and warned that the Mexicans were "on the march 8–10,000 strong," thus spreading the Urrea invasion rumor without checking it, and he also rescinded his order blocking entry of more volunteers. But there was nothing to fear from Filisola, who was located near Fort Bend and already following Santa Anna's order to withdraw all Mexican forces from Texas. He also had begun carrying out the transfer of Texian prisoners to Matamoros for repatriation. But Urrea overruled him, ordered that the Texian prisoners remain in custody, took command from Filisola, and scrambled to organize a reinvasion of Texas, which proved impossible due to the devastated condition of the Mexican army. During Filisola's retreat, the army became stalled and mired in a large, boggy area in present Wharton County and was forced to abandon equipment while its soldiers were starved and exhausted. The feared Mexican invasion never occurred, but rumors continued spreading through Texas that Urrea was on the march with thousands of troops.[12]

It was in this atmosphere of fear and suspicion on both sides—Mexican prisoners afraid for their lives, and Texians angrily seeking revenge while fearing a new Mexican invasion—that stories emerged from Galveston describing Crockett's death by execution. They varied in some details, such as the number of prisoners taken (five, six, or seven) and the manner of their execution (shot or run through by sabers), but they all reported essentially the same scenario and they began filtering out of Galveston by early June. Several of them claim that Mexican General Castrillón, who led part of the attack on the Alamo's north wall, tried to spare Crockett.

On June 9, 1836, while Santa Anna was writing his irate protest letter to Burnet, an unknown author in Galveston wrote a news dispatch, which was published in New York on July 9. There is some evidence the author was William H. Attree, a New York correspondent and zealous supporter of the Texas Revolution, who also served in one of Green's companies. The author said he got the story from an unidentified "gentleman" who had talked to Mexican prisoners in Galveston, the key part of which reads:

> I will relate one circumstance, detailed by an eye-witness, not before known, that will at once establish (if not before established) the blood thirsty cruelty of the tyrant, Santa Anna. After the Mexicans had got possession of the Alamo the fighting had ceased, and it was clear day light, *six* Americans were discovered near the wall yet unconquered, and who were instantly surrounded and ordered by Gen. CASTRILLON to surrender,

and who did so under a promise of his protection, finding resistance any longer in vain—indeed, perfect madness. Castrillon was brave and not cruel, and disposed to save them. He marched them up to that part of the fort where stood 'his Excellency', surrounded by his murderous crew, his sycophantic officers. DAVID CROCKETT was one of the six. The steady, fearless step, and undaunted tread, together with the bold demeanor of this hardy veteran—'his firmness and noble bearing' to give the words of the narrator, had a most powerful effect on himself and Castrillon. Nothing daunted, he marched up boldly in front of Santa Anna, looked him steadfastly in the face, while Castrillon addressed 'his Excellency.' 'Sir, here are *six* prisoners I have taken alive; how shall I dispose of them?' Santa Anna looked at Castrillon fiercely, flew into a most violent rage, and replied, 'Have I not told you before how to dispose of them? Why do you bring them to me?' At the same time his brave officers drew and plunged their swords into the bosoms of their defenceless prisoners!! So anxious and intent were these blood thirsty cowards to gratify the malignity of this inveterate tyrant, that CASTRILLON barely escaped being run through in the scuffle, himself. Castrillon rushed from the scene apparently horror-struck—sought his quarters, and did not leave them for some days, and hardly ever spoke to Santa Anna after. This was the fate of poor Crockett, and in which there can be no mistake. Who the *five* others were, I have not been able to learn. Three other wounded prisoners were discovered and brought before 'his Excellency', and were ordered to be instantly shot. There are certain reasons why the name of the narrator of these events should not be made known. I will only repeat that he was an *eye witness*.

Crockett's name appears in upper case, as if to emphasize its importance to the story, and the letter focuses on Santa Anna's barbarity. The author is unidentified, as are the informant and Mexican prisoner, with no explanation for concealing their identities.[13]

A similar letter was written from Galveston on July 19, 1836, by George M. Dolson, a Texian soldier, to his brother. It appeared in the Detroit *Democratic Free Press* on September 7. The report was uncovered in 1960, although it doubtless was reprinted in other newspapers throughout the United States in the months after its first appearance, as was the journalistic custom at the time. Significantly, Dolson began with news of the May 14 treaty and the plan to release Santa Anna but noted the plan was cancelled when soldiers threatened violence if he was not held. Dolson described Santa Anna as being so terrified by the news that he swallowed a large dose of opium and "cried like a child," which mirrors descriptions by Green and Tobin of Santa Anna's behavior aboard the *Invincible*. Dolson labeled him a cold-blooded murderer who had stained Texas with the blood of slaughtered, unarmed men. Dolson claimed to be an interpreter for Colonel Morgan in Galveston and that he was asked to interpret the statement of an unidentified Mexican officer who wanted to report Santa Anna's order to execute prisoners at the Alamo. Dolson wrote that only he, Morgan, and the informant, who claimed to be an eyewitness, were present during the interview. The informant described "the fate of Colonel Crocket [sic] and his five brave companions," which occurred after the Alamo was captured:

> General Castrillon, who fell at the battle of San Jacinto, entered the back room of the Alamo, and there found Crockett and five other Americans, who had defended it until defence was useless; they appeared very much agitated when the Mexican soldiers undertook to rush in after their General, but the humane General ordered his men to keep out, and, placing his hand on one breast, said, 'here is a hand and a heart to protect you; come with me to the General-in-Chief, and you shall be saved.' Such redeeming traits, while they ennoble in our estimation this worthy officer, yet serve to show in a more hedious [sic] light the damning atrocities of the chief. The brave but unfortunate men were marched to the tent [or banner] of Santa Anna. Colonel Crockett was in the rear, had his arms folded, and appeared bold as the lion as he passed my informant. (Almonte) Santa Anna's interpreter knew Colonel Crockett, and said to my informant, 'the one behind is the famous Crockett.' When brought in the presence of Santa Anna, Castrillon said to him, 'Santa Anna, the august, I deliver up to you six brave prisoners of war.' Santa Anna replied, 'who has given you orders to take prisoners, I do not want to see those men living—shoot them.' As the monster uttered these words each officer turned his face the other way, and the hell-hounds of the tyrant [*despatched the six in his presence, and within six feet*] [sic] of his person. Such an act I consider murder of the blackest kind. Do you think that he can be released? No—exhaust all the mines of Mexico, but it will not release him. The one half, nor two thirds, nor even the whole of the republic, would not begin to ransom him. The combined powers of Europe cannot release him, for before they can come to his release, Texas will have released him of his existence; but I coincide with the secretary of war, as to the disposal to be made of him, that is, to try him as a felon. Strict justice demands it and reason sanctions it.

Dolson's focus is clearly on detaining Santa Anna and his description of Crockett's barbaric execution provides a powerful justification. Whether or not the informant's story is true, it would not have carried nearly the same propaganda value if it had involved only a few nameless victims, as the earliest press reports of the Alamo's fall did.[14]

Dolson claimed that the statement was taken down by Morgan in writing with the Mexican officer's name included. When Morgan offered to omit his name, the officer replied that he had no objection to including it and was willing to attest to the statement "in the presence of his God, and General Santa Anna, too, if necessary." But there is no such report anywhere in Morgan's papers, nor any reference to the interview or any explanation of why the officer's name was omitted from the letter if he did not object to being identified. Dolson's informant claimed that Almonte identified Crockett, but Almonte made no mention of Crockett or executions at the Alamo in his diary entry that day or afterward. Almonte may have known who Crockett was if only by reputation. While in New Orleans in 1834, he translated an article that appeared in the newspaper *Merchant Daily News* on March 19 suggesting there was broad belief in the United States that Texas was destined to be added to the union and that Mexico "would find it as hard to contain Colonel Crocket [sic] as to govern their new subjects in Texas." Almonte noted that "Colonel Crocket [sic] is a lunatic politician from the United States of America," suggesting he may have read some of the outrageous Crockett yarns in circulation at the time and perhaps negative comments about him in the Jacksonian press. Portraits of Crockett were commonly available in 1834, his autobiography was a national best seller, and he embarked on a widely publicized speaking tour of the Northeast at the time. It would have been nearly impossible for Almonte to be unaware of Crockett in 1834, but it is questionable whether he would have recognized him two years later after he endured a two-week siege and desperate battle.[15]

Attree and Dolson served in companies that Green claimed were part of his brigade, but there is little evidence that was true. Green was a flamboyant opportunist and self-promoter who had cajoled Burnet into granting him a brigadier general's commission. However, the appointment was contingent upon Green raising at least one thousand men for his unit, a goal he never reached. But that did not stop him from using the title anyway and claiming to have recruited several companies that he had not actually recruited at all, including Alonzo Bowman Sweitzer's company of Cincinnati Volunteers, which included Dolson. Attree served as a courier and dispatch rider in Abraham Marshall's company, which Green also dubiously claimed to have recruited. Green, Dolson, and Attree were vehemently opposed to releasing Santa Anna, which led historian Thomas Ricks Lindley to suspect they were involved in a conspiracy to have Santa Anna executed. Aside from similar descriptions of Santa Anna's behavior aboard the *Invincible* by Green and Dolson, there is little evidence of such a conspiracy, and no conspiracy is necessary to establish that many Texians sought the same goal. The Dolson letter is not unique in its focus on Santa Anna's crimes and the desire to hold him for trial. On July 17, 1836, only two days before Dolson's letter was written, Lydia Ann McHenry of Austin's colony wrote to her brother complaining that the new Texas cabinet, with the exceptions of Zavala and Lamar, "is perhaps the most imbecile body that ever sat in judgment on the fate of a nation. Weak, corrupt & orderlous, they were with difficulty prevented from setting Santa Anna at liberty, notwithstanding all his crimes, upon his bare word that he would pay the expenses of the War." She describes the arrival of Green's troops from New Orleans and the furor among them over the proposed release of Santa Anna, which she shared.[16]

Of course, both the Dolson and Attree accounts could have been fabricated. Neither report identifies its source and each simply says that an unidentified Mexican officer claimed to have seen the executions. The Attree report is thirdhand and claims that an unidentified "gentleman" allegedly spoke to an unidentified Mexican officer in Galveston and repeated the officer's story to an unidentified reporter. There is no corroborating evidence for either story, and we only have the two writers' word that these conversations took place. These stories served the writers' intention to inflame Texian anger at Santa Anna and prevent his release. There is no proof these reports are genuine, and the similar reports that followed their publication could have been taken from them. However, if Dolson's report was fabricated, then Morgan must have been party to the deception. If Morgan was not present during the interview, he could have contradicted Dolson's account by denying that he witnessed the interview and exposed Dolson's story as a fabrication. In any case, Dolson must have been confident that Morgan would corroborate his story.

However, there is an element of Sherlock Holmes's *The Curious Incident of the Dog in the Night-Time* about these accounts. In all the June through

December 1836 correspondence and other documents I have reviewed, including the papers of James Morgan, John J. Forbes, and David Burnet, not once are Alamo executions or atrocities mentioned, even after the June 9 and July 19 reports were published and presumably available in Texas. However, for the sake of argument, let us accept that these two reports are genuine, and look at those that followed them and could have been influenced by them.[17]

In August 1836, a modified version of the June 9 letter appeared in a fictional account of Crockett's Texas journey, *Col. Crockett's Exploits and Adventures in Texas*, purportedly "Written by Himself," but actually penned by Richard Penn Smith and commissioned by Crockett's publisher, Carey & Hart, in the wake of Crockett's death when public interest in him ran high. Smith's book includes a fictitious Crockett "diary" with entries running right up to the eve of the Alamo battle. It also contains the dramatic account of Castrillón trying to save Crockett and the other prisoners, embellished from the June 9 report and other early newspaper accounts. The modified text adds flourishes such as Crockett standing "alone in an angle of the fort, the barrel of his shattered rifle in his right hand, in his left his huge Bowie knife dripping blood. There was a frightful gash across his forehead, while around him there was a complete barrier of about twenty Mexicans, lying pell-mell, dead, and dying." When Santa Anna ordered Castrillón's prisoners killed, "Crockett, seeing the set of treachery, instantly sprang like a tiger at the ruffian chief, but before he could reach him a dozen swords were sheathed in his indomitable heart; and he fell, and died without a groan, a frown on his brow, and a smile of scorn and defiance on his lips." By adding the detail of Crockett trying to kill Santa Anna before being cut down, Smith embellished a scene that already appeared melodramatic and staged. Although a work of fiction, the novel proved durable, and Smith's account was recycled in many Crockett biographies well into the twentieth century.[18]

In 1837, Ramón Martínez Caro, Santa Anna's secretary, published his own account of the Texas campaign, which is critical of Santa Anna and reports a similar execution, but doesn't mention Crockett. According to Caro, Castrillón found five Alamo defenders "hiding after the assault" and took them to Santa Anna, who severely reprimanded him before ordering the prisoners killed. "We all witnessed this outrage," Caro wrote, "which humanity condemns but which was committed as described. This is a cruel truth, but I cannot omit it." While the Galveston letters say that six men were executed, including Crockett, Caro says there were only five and does not mention Crockett, suggesting the Mexican informants in Galveston may have added Crockett's name themselves to point an angrier, more incriminating finger at Santa Anna by portraying him as Crockett's murderer. Caro's description seems more credible than the other accounts of Castrillón's prisoner rescue. Here the Texians are found hiding after the battle and are simply hauled before Santa Anna. Caro writes as if he were a witness to this event, but he wrote his memoir a year after the battle, so he may have gotten the story from someone else or newspaper accounts that were widespread even in Mexico by then. However, if we accept that he was in the Alamo and did witness such executions, he makes a powerful witness, and one who does not name Crockett as one of the executed prisoners. However, one of the points raised by those who reject the execution accounts is that the Mexicans would not have known who Crockett was. If so, Crockett could have been among those Caro saw executed, but Caro didn't recognize him.[19]

Finally, Lt. Col. José Enrique de la Peña, who was an aide to Col. Francisco Duque, commander of the Toluca Battalion during the assault on the Alamo, offered his own account of the incident. After the war, he became an outspoken antagonist of the centralist government, Santa Anna, Filisola, and other officers responsible for the Texas campaign. He was imprisoned in 1838 for his support of Mexican federalists and "revolutionary activity" in support of General Urrea. De la Peña spent two years in prison, during which he composed a memoir of the Texas campaign based partly on his own rewritten diary (the original is lost) and supplemented by accounts provided by others. Although his is the most hotly disputed account of Crockett's alleged execution, de la Peña was very much last to the party since the accounts mentioned above all preceded his and may have been his sources. The Crockett execution story found in de la Peña's manuscript is written on a single, two-sided sheet of paper and is very likely in de la Peña's own handwriting, although several other handwritings are found in the document. The account says:

> Some seven men had survived the general slaughter [and] guided by General Castrillón, who was protecting them, they were presented to Santa Anna. Among them was one of tall stature, well formed, and of regular features, in whose face was imprinted the sense of misfortune, but in whom was noticed definite resignation and nobility which recommended him. He was the naturalist David Croket [sic], well known in North America [i.e., the United States] for some novel adventures, who

had come to examine the country and who, finding himself in Bejar in the moment of surprise, was shut in the Alamo, fearful that he would not be respected for his quality as a foreigner. Santa Anna replied to Castrillon's intervention with an expression of indignation, and addressing at once the Zapadores, who were the troops whom he had very close by, he ordered them to execute them. His chiefs and officers etc. were angry at this behavior and did not support the commands, hoping that once the first moment of rage had passed, those men would be saved, but several officers who were around the President and who perhaps had not been there in the moment of danger, were made noteworthy by an infamous action surpassing the soldiers in cruelty [when] they placed themselves in front of them, in order to gratify the cruelty of their chief, and, sword in hand, threw themselves upon those defenseless wretches in the same manner as a tiger hurls itself on its prey, and tortured them before killing them, and those unfortunates died protesting but without humbling themselves to their executioners. . . . I confess that the single memory shook me and the doleful and piercing voices of the victims ring yet in my ears.[20]

Although de la Peña's account is similar to the others, he adds the unsettling detail of Crockett not only surrendering but claiming to be a noncombatant and simply unlucky enough to find himself in Béxar when the Mexican army arrived. Fearing that he would not be treated as a foreign visitor, he took refuge in the Alamo where he hid out and, presumably, took no part in the battle. It is perhaps this detail that has made the de la Peña account the most controversial. The others portray Crockett as either fighting to the end or being persuaded to surrender before being taken prisoner. For those who refuse to believe Crockett died any way other than "fighting like a tiger," the vision of an obsequious Crockett trying to escape execution by denying any role in the battle is too much to bear. Since this detail is missing from the Galveston and Caro accounts, it raises the question of where de la Peña got the story. He admitted that his in-progress manuscript was augmented with contributions from others who claimed to have seen things that de la Peña did not witness. However, even if he had seen the other execution accounts by the time he was imprisoned, which is entirely possible, none of them include this detail. It is possible that it was added to make Santa Anna look even worse by portraying him as the murderer of a defenseless civilian. Or did the story originate somewhere else?[21]

There is another account of Crockett's execution, roundly dismissed by historians and biographers, that does include the same detail and merits a fresh look. It reportedly came from General Cós during his imprisonment and originated with William P. Zuber some seventy years after the Alamo fell. Zuber famously originated the tale of Travis's line in the sand, his dramatic speech to the Alamo garrison, and Moses Rose's escape. In 1904 Zuber wrote to Charlie Jeffries saying that Cós had told the story to George Patrick while he was a prisoner on Patrick's ranch "doubtless in hope thereby to mitigate his condition as a captive," according to Zuber, and that Patrick had repeated the story to him. Zuber said that Patrick spoke to Cós through an interpreter and "asked Cos if he saw Colonel David Crockett in the Alamo, and if he knew how he died." Cós allegedly replied:

> Yes, sir. When we thought that all the defenders were slain, I was searching the barracks, and found, alive and unhurt, a fine-looking and well-dressed man, locked up, alone, in one of the rooms, and asked him who he was. He replied: "I am David Crocket [sic], a citizen of the State of Tennessee and representative of a district of that State in the United States Congress. I have come to Texas on a visit of exploration; purposing, if permitted, to become a loyal citizen of the Republic of Mexico. I extended my visit to San Antonio and called in the Alamo to become acquainted with the officers, and learn of them what I could of the condition of affairs. Soon after my arrival, the fort was invested by government troops, whereby I have been prevented from leaving it. And here I am yet, a noncombatant and foreigner, having taken no part in the fighting. I [Cós] proposed to introduce him to the President, state his situation to him, and request him to depart in peace, to which he thankfully assented. I then conducted him to the President, to whom I introduced him in about these words.

Cós then repeated Crockett's story to Santa Anna and said:

> 'I beseech your Excellency to permit him to depart in peace.' Santa Anna heard me through, but impatiently. Then he replied sharply, 'You know your orders'; turned his back upon us and walked away. But, as he turned, Crockett drew from his bosom a dagger, with which he smote at him with a thrust, which, if not arrested, would surely have killed him; but was met by a bayonet-thrust by the hand of a soldier through the heart; he fell and soon expired.

Zuber labeled Cós's story "a gross falsehood" but bizarrely suggested that it showed "what Santa Anna would have done if it were true." It is unclear how Cós would have communicated with Crockett, who spoke no Spanish. Since Patrick needed an interpreter to talk to Cós he clearly spoke little or no English. Since Zuber did not relate the story to Jeffries until 1904, and it wasn't published until 1939, it is possible that it could have been influenced by earlier reports of Crockett's death, including the Galveston accounts. Since de la Peña's memoir was not published until 1955, neither Cós, Patrick, nor Zuber could have gotten the story from him, even as late as 1904. De la Peña was not at the Battle of San Jacinto nor a Texian prisoner and was not available to give the story to Cós in Galveston, so Cós couldn't have gotten it from him. The account claims that Crockett attempted to kill Santa Anna, a detail only seen otherwise in Smith's *Exploits*, which was not published until August or September 1836, after Cós was held at Patrick's ranch. Like de la Peña, Cós also has Crockett claiming to be a noncombatant, not mentioned in the Galveston reports, and he could not have taken it from the later de la Peña manuscript. So where did that story originate?[22]

Cós could have told the story to Patrick, as Zuber said he did, and later repeated it in Galveston, where it could have spread through the camp and later made its way to Mexico and de la Peña, who included it in his account along with other secondhand information. Attree and Dolson might have omitted mention of Crockett claiming noncombatant status because it could diminish Crockett's status as a fighting hero and reduce sympathy for him.

The Cós account has been dismissed by historians as a hard-to-believe scenario that is tainted by its connection to the unreliable Zuber. But it is fair to ask why this account is any less credible than those recorded by Attree, Dolson, and de la Peña, despite Zuber's penchant for invention. In fact, the Cós account is more credible in that it identifies the source of the story, Cós, while the other accounts do not. Cós describes Crockett as being "well dressed," and at least one source claims Crockett did call for a clean suit of clothes on the eve of the battle. The Cós account includes other accurate details, such as Crockett coming to Texas to explore, not to fight. We can only guess why anyone would say that Crockett claimed he took no part in the fighting, but each of these accounts seems to have carried an agenda, and it's likely this one did too. Perhaps the originator of the story thought that casting Crockett as a defenseless civilian would make him look even more sympathetic, and Santa Anna twice as vicious. Although there is no written version of it and despite some unlikely details, especially a well-dressed Crockett locked in a room throughout the battle, the Cós account is no more unreasonable than other reports of Crockett surviving the battle and being executed. Whether or not Cós told such a story to Patrick, or Patrick passed it on to Zuber, there is another possible connection between Cós and the Crockett execution stories.

While imprisoned in Galveston, Cós either curried favor with Colonel Morgan or Morgan became fascinated with the Mexican general and developed some sort of rapport with him, even having Cós's portrait painted. Cós was there in June and July when the Attree and Dolson letters were written, and he could have been the source of one or both reports. Dolson wrote that the Mexican officer whose statement he interpreted requested the meeting and it was not initiated by the Texians. It is possible that, given the degree of anger and tension in Galveston, Cós might have made such a statement to shield himself and the prisoners from violence by focusing Texian anger on Santa Anna. If true, however, it is puzzling that Cós would cast Castrillón as Crockett's would-be rescuer, rather than himself as Zuber claimed he did. But Cós may not have been the source of the June and July reports, and both could have been based on interviews with other Mexican officers. Neither report identifies its source. There may have been various stories about Alamo executions circulating through the Galveston prison.

Cós had good reason to fear for his life. On May 3, while at Patrick's ranch, an attempt was made to assassinate him. During the boat trip to Galveston, the prisoners were forced to lie prostrate on the deck and threatened with instant death if they raised their heads. After their arrival in Galveston, they were continually threatened by guards, who were often drunk, brawling, and insubordinate. Cós may have felt particularly vulnerable because he had violated the terms of his parole when he was permitted to leave Texas after the Battle of Béxar in December 1835. Many early news reports of the Alamo's fall included a doubtless apocryphal story that Cós had ordered Travis's slave, Joe, to point out Travis's body and then "drew his sword and mangled [Travis's] face and limbs with the malignant feeling of a Cumancie [Comanche] savage." Thus, Cós had strong motivation to present himself as a humanitarian who abhorred Crockett's murder and to place blame for it on Santa Anna alone. Despite his fears, Cós acted as a leader, advocate, and protector of the Mexican prisoners and even sought an audience with Morgan to demand protection for them, and Morgan arranged for more civil guards to reassure Cós.[23]

The scenarios casting General Castrillón as Crockett's humanitarian rescuer read like a melodrama, complete with dialog, heroes, and a consummate villain in Santa Anna. There's a touch of Hollywood in Crockett marching boldly up to Santa Anna himself, who then personally orders his brutal execution, or of Crockett making a desperate attempt on the president's life before being cut down. The choice of Castrillón as a kind of humanitarian hero, contrasted with Santa Anna's villain, is convenient in that Castrillón was dead, could not challenge the story, and left no memoir, diary, or notes.

The claim that Crockett presented himself as a noncombatant is the easiest to dismiss as his body was identified by witnesses who described it as lying, mutilated, among those of dead Mexican soldiers, rather than in a group of men who were executed together. Crockett took part in fighting during the siege and received praise for it in Travis's February 25 letter to Houston. Even most execution accounts have Crockett fighting fiercely before surrendering with others. They also have Castrillón speaking to them, although, like Cós, he spoke no English; and Crockett, even after several months in Texas, likely spoke little or no Spanish. If any of the other captives did speak Spanish, were they given time to interpret? Could Castrillón have successfully ordered his soldiers to suddenly stop fighting to spare a few Texians? The soldiers were in a killing frenzy, even shooting a cat. De la Peña describes tumult and disorder, soldiers firing in all directions, killing Mexicans as well as Texians, and "such confusion that orders could not be understood." Susanna Dickinson was shot in the leg as she was being escorted out of the Alamo by Almonte after the battle, while Mexican soldiers robbed and mutilated the Texian dead. Almonte himself was robbed by his own troops. The idea that Castrillón could suddenly stop his soldiers from killing any Texians still alive seems highly unlikely, if not impossible. Some of the Texians who bolted from the fort—at least one of whom attempted to conceal himself in some brush—were run down by lancers, and others may have tried to surrender but were killed. De la Peña describes seeing defenders trying to surrender by waving white rags or socks from windows. Bergara's earliest report, which is thirdhand, only vaguely describes some defenders being denied quarter and then killed. Zuber related similar stories of six Alamo defenders trying to surrender but being cut down, and another claiming that six men were found hiding under a bridge by some washerwomen who reported them to the Mexicans and whose execution was ordered by Santa Anna. These accounts seem a far cry from the elaborate scene described by the Galveston prisoners and de la Peña.[24]

In his memoir manuscript, de la Peña described Almonte and Castrillón as advocates of "principles regarding the rights of men, philosophical and humane principles which did them honor; they reiterated these later when General Urrea's [Goliad] prisoners were ordered executed, but their arguments were fruitless." De la Peña is the only source for these alleged statements by Castrillón and Almonte, and the statements seem designed to support the description of Castrillón as Crockett's rescuer. In his memoir, José Juan Sánchez-Navarro mentions talking to Castrillón shortly after the battle on March 6 and reminding him of a conversation they had in February when he warned Castrillón that the Texians were tenacious foes and that the Mexicans would have to "smoke [their] heads" if they were to defeat them. At that time Castrillón belittled the Texians' fighting ability, an opinion that Sánchez contradicted, based on his experience during the 1835 Battle of Béxar, and he warned Castrillón, "Now you will see, my general, how they smoke our heads." On March 6, when Sánchez reminded Castrillón of their earlier conversation, the general shrugged and said, in reference to the Texians' stiff resistance, "Who would have believed it?" There is no reference to prisoners being executed or Castrillón having any role in that. Castrillón's cavalier attitude and genuine surprise at the tenacity of the Texian defenders suggests that he had a low opinion of them and shared the view that they were mostly foreign interlopers who were trying to wrest Texas away from Mexico for the United States, a view clearly shared by Santa Anna, Almonte, and many in the Mexican government and army. It is also unlikely that Castrillón would have expected Santa Anna to spare any prisoners given the red flag he ordered to be hoisted on day one of the siege, signaling that no quarter would be given to the rebels, and the president's repeated admonitions that no prisoners were to be taken. Almonte himself replied to Alamo messengers on the first day of the siege when both Bowie and Travis tried to arrange a parley, telling the rebels they had no alternative other than surrendering at discretion if they wished to have any chance of saving their lives, and he implied that it was not proper for him to negotiate with the rebels. In fact, if the Dolson letter is accurate, Almonte witnessed the Alamo executions but said nothing in opposition to them nor did he criticize them later. He never mentioned them at all. Nor did Almonte object to Ramírez y Sesma's lancers running down and killing up to seventy Alamo defenders who fled the fort. Almonte merely notes this in his diary, quite briefly and without comment. In the Galveston accounts, Castrillón is cast as Crockett's protector because he was "not cruel" (and Santa Anna clearly was), but there is no reason to believe that Castrillón would have sought to intervene or that he took any prisoners. Prior to the Battle of San Jacinto, Col. Pedro Delgado told Castrillón of his serious misgivings about the precarious position Santa Anna had put the troops in, which the battle would soon vindicate. According to Delgado, Castrillón replied, "What can I do, my friend? I know it well, but I can not help it. You know that nothing avails here against the caprice, arbitrary will, and ignorance of that man." This attests to Castrillón's low opinion of Santa Anna's leadership, but it also shows his resignation to accepting whatever the president decided and does not suggest he would confront him with humanitarian efforts on a battlefield. Nor is it likely that he could have hoped to persuade Santa Anna to set aside the "no quarter" decree for Crockett and the other prisoners if he felt unable to advise him about military matters on the verge of a major battle.[25]

De la Peña's account of the war council before the Alamo attack differs from Almonte's. He claimed that Castrillón, Almonte, and Romero urged Santa Anna to await the arrival of the twelve-pound cannons, which were expected within a few days; use them to create a breach in the Alamo walls; and then carry out the assault. This approach would presumably make it easier to enter and secure the Alamo and might seem more humane, at least to the Mexican soldiers who would be spared a more treacherous assault on the Alamo walls. However, Almonte claimed that he, Ramírez y Sesma, and Santa Anna rejected the idea and favored an immediate assault.[26]

It is puzzling that Santa Anna would not have spared Crockett if given the opportunity if only to exhibit him as evidence that the United States was indeed behind all the trouble in Texas. What better proof could be found than the presence of a former US congressman in the Alamo? Imagine the propaganda value of parading Crockett up and down the streets of Mexico City before derisive mobs. Santa Anna sent the flag of the New Orleans Greys, who fought at the Alamo, to Mexico City as evidence of US mischief in Texas, and Mexican congressmen reportedly took turns stomping on the flag. A public exhibition of the "King of the Wild Frontier" as a war trophy would have had far greater impact. Although Santa Anna mentioned Crockett in his post-battle report, it is unlikely that he knew much about him beyond what he learned from Béxar residents who had seen Crockett in town prior to the siege or from Almonte, who had some passing knowledge of Crockett.[27]

In 1840 a rumor spread that Crockett had survived the battle and was imprisoned and enslaved in a mine near Guadalajara. Crockett's son, John Wesley Crockett, heard the rumor and requested that Powhatan Ellis, the US minister plenipotentiary to Mexico, investigate the matter. Ellis told Crockett's son that he was satisfied that Crockett had been killed in the battle, having "met the common fate of all those who were found in the

Fort on that occasion." Ellis said that his informant was "a distinguished Mexican officer who was present at the siege" who told him that "if colonel Crockett was present, he must have been killed, as no prisoners were taken."[28]

There is, of course, testimony from Alamo survivors and other witnesses regarding the deaths of Crockett and other Alamo leaders. Santa Anna reportedly asked at least three people to identify the bodies of Bowie, Travis, and Crockett: Francisco Antonio Ruiz, the alcalde of San Antonio; Travis's slave, Joe, who had seen Travis die; and Ben, Almonte's cook, who said Santa Anna and Almonte "directed me to go with them to the fort, and point out the bodies of Bowie and Travis—Whom I had known—which I did. The sight was most horrid." Another, less credible account claims that Ben had seen Crockett years earlier in Washington, DC, that he was thus able to identify Crockett's body, and that he found "no less than 16 dead Mexicans around the corpse of Colonel Crockett and one across it with the huge knife of Davy buried in the Mexican's bosom to the hilt. He stated that these three bodies were interred in the same grave separate from all the rest, and that he heard the Mexican officers say that their own loss was about 1200 men." There are clear errors in the statement, such as the number of Mexican losses and the three Alamo leaders being buried rather than burned.

Some of the first reports of Joe's testimony mention his being asked only to identify Travis's body. Others add details such as a man named Warner being the only battle survivor, his asking for quarter, but being shot on Santa Anna's order. Some reports quote Joe as saying, "Crockett and a few of the devoted friends who entered the Fort with him, were found lying together with 24 of the slain enemy around them" and that Cós mutilated Travis's body, but it's unlikely Joe could have seen that. Both he and Ben are cited as saying that Crockett "had the biggest pile" of Mexican dead around him, ranging from sixteen to twenty-four. Other press reports had Crockett surrounded by "heaps of dead Mexicans." Press accounts of their testimonies include information from other sources, such as Bowie firing through the door of his room, which none of them could have seen. Doubtless, Susanna, Joe, and Ben conversed on their way to Gonzales after the battle and their recollections could have combined what they saw with what they heard from one another. They also likely heard accounts from their Mexican captors that they included in their statements, but which press reports attributed directly to them. For example, some Mexicans knew who Bowie was and how he died, and they could have told Ben, Joe, or Susanna about that.

It is not even clear where Crockett died. Neither Joe nor Ben identified the location of Crockett's body. It's not certain that Santa Anna asked Joe to identify Crockett and some reports only say that Santa Anna "made the negro point out Col. Travis." Ruiz, on the other hand, correctly identified Bowie's body in his sick room and Travis's at the north wall cannon platform known as Fortin de Teran, exactly where Joe said Travis was killed. Ruiz was equally specific about the location of Crockett's body. "On the north battery of the fortress lay the lifeless body of Col. Travis on the gun-carriage, shot only in the forehead," Ruiz testified. "Toward the west, and in the small fort opposite the city, we found the body of Col. Crockett. Col. Bowie was found dead in his bed, in one of the rooms of the south side." In locating Crockett's body, Ruiz could have been referring to a cannon platform located near the center of the west wall, but more likely to the cannon emplacement at the northwest corner of the fort, west of where Travis died, called Fortin de Condelle. Such a location would have placed Crockett in the thick of battle as the main Mexican force pressed along the north wall. It was there he most likely died, probably early in the battle not long after Travis was killed.[29]

The suggestion that Crockett died in a semicircular entrenchment outside the center of the west wall is unlikely as archaeological excavation has shown no sign of such a structure, although it appears on some Alamo plats.

It is possible that Santa Anna ordered a group of prisoners executed without realizing that Crockett was among them until Ruiz identified the body for him. However, there is a sharp discrepancy between Ruiz locating Crockett's body on a cannon platform and the descriptions of Crockett being executed with several other men in front of Santa Anna and his officers.

Although Susanna Dickinson said she saw Crockett's mutilated body in the courtyard between the church and long barrack, even identifying his "peculiar cap," her statement was made in 1874, nearly forty years after the battle, and she said nothing about Crockett's body in any of her other statements. By 1874 she could easily have been influenced by John Sutherland's 1860 account of the siege and battle. Sutherland located Crockett's body at the palisade running between the church and low barrack on the south side of the compound, near where Susanna said she saw it, and Sutherland is the primary source for the many later accounts that place Crockett at the palisade. But Sutherland, who left the fort on the first day of the siege, evidently based his account on where Crockett was stationed on that date. Crockett might well have moved to other locations over the next two weeks, especially on the morning of the assault when the brunt of the Mexican attack came at the north wall. Since the Mexicans did not attack the palisade, it is unlikely he was there during the battle. In 1876, Susanna claimed that Crockett entered the fort during the siege but before the battle and simply that he "was killed, she believes." Despite inconsistencies and contradictions in the accounts of Ruiz, Susanna, Joe, and Ben, they all indicate that Crockett died in battle. Other than Ruiz, the witnesses were illiterate and wrote nothing of their own, thus it is difficult to tell what the witnesses said, what was paraphrased, and what was added as embellishment by newspapers or those who recorded their statements.[30]

These accounts provide no definitive conclusion about how or where Crockett died. He is mentioned in accounts that came from unidentified Mexicans who were likely in fear of their lives and anxious to tell their captors what they wanted to hear. The stories emerged from Galveston just as the fury over Santa Anna's proposed release crested and efforts to hold him for trial and execution were strongest. Texian leaders identified the Goliad massacre as his most serious crime but mentioned no atrocities or executions at the Alamo. The only references to executions before stories from Galveston appeared were in the first reports of the Alamo's fall and the newspaper stories that grew out of them. The conflating of those reports that placed Crockett among those who sought quarter could have prompted the Texians in Galveston to ask the Mexican prisoners probing or leading questions about Crockett and how he died. Those reports and Texian questions regarding Crockett's death would have spread rapidly through the camp, alerting the prisoners that Texians were curious about someone named Crockett who died at the Alamo and whom they held in high regard. Painting a sympathetic picture of Crockett, while also demonizing Santa Anna as his murderer, might provide some cover for the frightened prisoners. Crockett execution stores could have been repeated among the prisoners who passed variations of them on to the Texians, who welcomed an additional inflammatory charge against Santa Anna that tied him to the death of the revered Crockett and added to the case against his release. Years later a variation of the story reached de la Peña in prison. He then furthered the story, casting Crockett as a helpless noncombatant who was murdered by Santa Anna, which served de la Peña's purposes as a political prisoner who openly opposed the centralist government.

The de la Peña documents have been found to be genuine, disproving charges that they are forgeries. The June 9 and July 19, 1836 Galveston reports also are genuine, and for that matter, so is Richard Penn Smith's fictional account of Crockett's journey and death. That does not mean they are reliable or truthful.[31]

Of course, it is possible that Crockett was captured and executed. Some Alamo defenders clearly were, and the Tornel Decree mandated such executions, which Santa Anna was eager to carry out. Witnesses may have been told later that Crockett was among those executed and added his name to their accounts of the event. The mention of Castrillón in several accounts of Crockett's death could represent a consensus suggesting that such an incident did occur, and the minor discrepancies in the accounts strengthens their credibility and discounts arguments that they all derive from a single source or were coordinated. However, the weight of evidence suggests that, although authentic, they are not particularly reliable and relate secondhand or thirdhand accounts from unidentified informants. There is greater weight to the suggestion that the informants and those who took their statements had powerful motives for generating such a brutal account of Crockett's death. There are discrepancies, inconsistencies, and errors in the accounts of Alamo survivors as well, although their descriptions of Crockett's body suggest that his death occurred in battle.[32]

That Crockett died in the Alamo is all that we can know for sure. Where, when, and how he perished remains uncertain. We do know that his family soon received the shocking news of his death, and that his plan to explore Texas and return home had somehow gone fatally awry.

CHAPTER 8

The Promised Land

Robert Patton Crockett was at work on his Tennessee farm when word arrived of his father's death. The devastating news capped months of stress the family had endured since learning that Crockett had joined the army. "We were all greatly distressed when we heard that he had been killed," Crockett's daughter Matilda later recalled. "We could hardly believe it."[1]

The Crocketts could have learned of the Colonel's fate through newspaper reports but word of it may have reached them first by mail. Hearing of Crockett's death, Isaac N. Jones, who had traded watches with Crockett in Lost Prairie, Arkansas, wrote to Crockett's widow, Elizabeth, and enclosed Crockett's timepiece. Jones felt compelled to return it to his family and express his fond memories of the Colonel. "With his open frankness, his natural honesty of expression, his perfect want of concealment, I could not but be very much pleased," he wrote. He prized the watch as a keepsake "which would often remind me of an honest man, a good citizen and a pioneer in the cause of liberty." Jones expressed the hope that Texas would "afford to yourself and children, a home, rendered in every way comfortable, by the liberal donations of her government." That would come to pass—in time.[2]

But Elizabeth now found herself in financial difficulty with no property or means of support since Crockett left no will, possibly because he owned so little at the time. Shortly before leaving for Texas, he sold the last of his Tennessee land, including two hundred acres to his brother-in-law, Hance C. McWhorter, who allowed Elizabeth to remain on the property after the Colonel's death. But within a few months she was forced to vacate the place following a complex lawsuit that challenged McWhorter's title. In November 1837, the Weakley County Court decided to lend some assistance to the Crocketts by donating a year's worth of provisions to them including "twenty barrels of corn, six hundred pounds of pork, three hundred pounds of flour, 30 pounds of coffee, 60 pounds of sugar, one pound of spice, one pound of ginger, three bushels of salt, one cow and calf 'if on hand.'" After her daughters Rebecca and Matilda married, Elizabeth "broke up housekeeping," according to her son Robert, and moved in with her children.[3]

Before setting out for Texas, Crockett put the nineteen-year-old Robert in charge of the farm and tasked him with the care of his mother and two sisters. After learning of his father's death, Robert later recalled that he packed his "knapsack and cut out for Texas as a volunteer," leaving the family behind and doubtless creating more consternation among them. In Texas he received a first lieutenant's commission in Sidney Sherman's cavalry regiment and served nine months before resigning. He returned to Tennessee where he married.[4]

When Crockett wrote his family from San Augustine two months before his death, he saw a bright future in this new country, built on land he expected to receive for his army service. Although he did not live to reap the rewards he expected, his family did. Texas made good on its promise of land for those who fought for its independence. During the revolution, the years of independence, and US statehood that followed, Texas adopted several laws that rewarded its soldiers or their heirs with large tracts of land. Special grants were given to those who died at the Alamo and other battles for Texas independence, and Crockett's heirs received five separate land grants totaling more than eleven thousand acres.

Laws adopted during the revolution by the provisional government entitled Crockett's heirs to 1,280 acres of bounty land as reward for his service. Although he did not live to serve out his six-month enlistment, he was given full credit for it and was "honorably discharged by death," having served from January 8 to March 6, 1836. An additional 640-acre augmentation bounty grant brought the total of land given to those killed at the Alamo to 1,920 acres.[5]

Crockett's heirs received two more large land grants. The first was another 640-acre grant. The second was a headright, or league and labor of land, representing the largest prize of all, 4,605.5 acres, which brought the total to 7,165.5 acres of land issued to Crockett's heirs.[6]

Finally, on February 2, 1856, the Texas legislature added 4,428.4 acres to the Crockett holdings when it donated a league of land to Elizabeth. The legislature gave no reason for making such a generous grant, but newspapers reported that the Crocketts were living "in indigent circumstances," which was unlikely considering the amount of land they had already received. Nonetheless, a year earlier a group appealed to the state on behalf of the family for "ample relief" and claimed "the family of Davy Crockett was among us, needy and poor." Perhaps the reports, accurate or not, embarrassed the legislature into action. The donation brought the Crockett land grant total to 11,593.94 acres—far beyond anything Crockett envisioned and enough to have started him on a lucrative career as a land agent. Crockett's heirs, however, did not share that dream and would treat the lands they received far differently than Crockett would have—they sold almost all of it nearly as quickly as it came into their hands.[7]

Crockett's family was aware of the Texas land bounties long before most of the titles were issued to them, but they seemed uninterested in relocating to Texas or claiming any of the land, perhaps out of a distaste for the place that had claimed Crockett's life—a place that had tantalized him only to lure him to his death. Adjusting to their new reality, and accepting that he was gone from their lives, may have been enough for them to take in without also making decisions about land acquisitions or relocating to a new country.

By 1842, however, some of the family decided to cash in on the land bounties. On May 14, Crockett's sons, John and Robert, and his daughter Rebecca and her husband, George Kimbrow, signed an indenture in Gibson County, Tennessee, which served as a contract or deed. In this case, the Crockett children sold their entire interest in Crockett's Texas lands, including the large headright, to Richard Forester for $900, or $300 each. The selling price factored in a deduction for the costs of locating and surveying the Texas lands. In short, the three Crockett children sold *"their entire interest in all and any land in [Texas] to which they may be entitled in right of their father . . . David Crockett, on account of his military service in the Revolution that terminated in the independence of Texas, being three sixths thereof"* (italics added). The "three sixths" caveat noted that only three of Crockett's six natural children were involved in the sale, but this assessment omits his widow, Elizabeth, and his two stepchildren from Elizbeth's first marriage, George and Margaret Ann Patton. On July 6, the three appeared before Circuit Judge William R. Harris to formally enter into the indenture. The certification further stipulated that Rebecca was "privately examined separate and apart from her said husband and acknowledged that she executed [the indenture] freely and voluntarily without constraint or compulsion on the part of her said husband," suggesting that spousal coercion was of some concern at the time.

Crockett's daughter Matilda, also in Gibson County, joined her three siblings by signing a separate indenture on August 20, selling her one-sixth interest in the land to Forester, also for $300. The indenture was signed by Matilda and her husband, Thomas D. Tyson. As in the case of her sister Rebecca, the indenture certified that Matilda was examined "separate and apart from her husband" and acknowledged that she executed the agreement "freely and voluntarily without threats or constraints" on the part of her husband. Thus, John, Robert, Rebecca, and Matilda Crockett sold their share of Crockett's headright and all other lands in Texas to which they were entitled for a total of $1,200 ($43,357, or $10,839 each, in 2022 dollars).

The indenture agreements included only about 45 percent of Crockett's Texas land because only four of the nine Crockett heirs signed them. Crockett's widow, Elizabeth, and two of his children from his first marriage, William and Margaret, chose not to sell their interest in the land, and his two stepchildren from Elizabeth's first marriage were not entitled to an inheritance. The indentures overshadowed Crockett land transactions in Texas for years because they did not mention any land warrant certificates and the only specific land grant identified was the headright, by far the largest amount of land involved. Because of the open-ended nature of the indenture wording, it remained possible for Forester or his heirs to claim a large amount of *all and any* Crockett land in Texas.[8]

Aside from the 1842 indentures, the Crockett heirs took no action regarding their Texas land until 1851. It's not clear what suddenly generated this new interest, but it may have resulted from their dealings with Richard Forester, whose son, John B. Forester, a Texas attorney, became administrator of the Crockett estate in February 1851, replacing Crockett's son Robert. The Crocketts needed someone in Texas to act for them, and their hiring of Forester indicates that there was no animosity between the two families regarding the 1842 indentures. Forester's first act as estate administrator was to have the Crockett lands inventoried and appraised. He determined the family held title to four different land warrants:

1. A headright, or one league and labor of land, totaling 4,605.54 acres, appraised at $450 ($16,259 in 2022).[9]

2. A bounty claim of 1,280 acres, appraised at $128 ($4,925 in 2022).[10]

3. A bounty claim augmentation of 640 acres, appraised at $64 ($2,463 in 2022), which was added to the 1,280-acre bounty in order "to make the 1,920 acres to which

those killed at the Alamo are held to be entitled for
service during the war."[11]

4.   A donation grant of 640 acres, appraised at $64 (also
worth $2,463 in 2022).[12]

The appraisal yielded a total value of $706 for 7,165.54 acres, or about
ten cents an acre ($27,165, about $3.79 per acre, in 2022). A certificate for
the 1,280-acre bounty claim had been issued on December 23, 1837, and
Forester obtained certificates for the other three grants on March 13, 1852.
With the Bexar County Court's permission, Forester sold the two 640-acre
warrants at a public auction on July 6, 1852, for about fifteen cents per
acre (about $5.77 in 2022). The bounty augmentation warrant was sold to
Sam Maverick for ninety-six dollars ($3,694 in 2022), while the donation
certificate went to George T. Howard for one hundred dollars ($3,848 in
2022). Forester told the court the sales were necessary to recover some of
his costs as estate administrator. He also said that this was all the estate
land he had knowledge of or had come into his possession. However, he
did not fully account for the 1,280-acre grant, saying only that a certificate
was issued for it, but no patent applied to it. He also recommended that it
was not in the best interests of the estate to sell the headright at that time.[13]

Three years later, in 1855, Forester asked the Bexar County Court to be
repaid for additional expenditures he had incurred as estate administrator
totaling $688.60 ($23,450 in 2022). He noted that he had in hand only the
$196 ($6,675 in 2022) from the sale of the two land certificates he sold
in 1852. He added that the estate was indebted for court costs and other
administrative expenses, which he wished to pay off, and that he wished to
be discharged from his duties as soon as possible. He reported there were
no additional outstanding claims or debts against the estate. He again
suggested that it was not advisable for the Crocketts, whom he represented,
"or the claimants of the remaining shares of said estate" (italics added) to
seek the immediate sale of the headright. Forester said he had to remain
as administrator until he could correspond with the "other claimants to a
portion of said estate," who, he had been informed, had recently arrived in
Texas and would be able to "settle up the estate." Forester's mention of "the
claimants of the remaining shares of said estate" and "other claimants to
a portion of the estate" were references to the Foresters and the Crocketts,
each of whom claimed portions of the headright, the Foresters by virtue
of the 1842 indentures.[14]

Indeed, Elizabeth Crockett and some of her children had arrived in Texas by 1855, but before leaving Tennessee, Elizabeth took two important legal steps. Recognizing that Forester was eager to end his role as estate administrator, Elizabeth gave her power of attorney to William L. Mitchell of Ellis County, Texas, on February 23, 1854, and authorized him to act as her attorney and estate agent. Mitchell was to locate all Texas land certificates to which the Crocketts were entitled and survey and secure patents for the land. As with all her legal documents, Elizabeth signed this one with an "X," labeled as "her mark" because she was illiterate.[15]

In October 1854, while still in Tennessee, Elizabeth took the further step of transferring one-half of all her Texas lands to her five natural children. She may have done this to ensure they would own property after she was gone and not find themselves in the precarious financial situation she faced after Crockett's death. No specific land certificates were mentioned in the land transfer, nor was any money exchanged, and the document was not executed until April 1860, shortly after Elizabeth's death. The other half of the land was reserved as payment to Mitchell as part of her agreement with him, however much there might be. Mitchell also would pay all costs incurred in the process.[16]

Meanwhile, Forester was still dealing with the Texas lands although he was anxious to turn matters over to Mitchell. Since Forester had not resolved the 1837 grant for 1,280 acres, the only one that he had difficulty in securing, it may have become Mitchell's primary task, although the headright also remained unresolved. In his report to the Béxar County Court for Settlement of Estates on May 5, 1851, Forester did not fully account for the 1,280-acre grant, saying only that a certificate was issued, but no patent applied to it. Nearly four years later, on March 26, 1855, he said that the only estate property remaining in his hands was the headright, which had already been located and surveyed on the Nueces River. He remained vague about the fate of the 1,280-acre bounty claim, saying only that a warrant certificate had been issued for the land but, unlike the other Crockett warrants, had never come into his possession. Nonetheless, Forester had the land surveyed on November 27, 1851, and told the court it had been located in the vicinity of the Brazos River. He also said the land had been taken possession of by some person or persons claiming to represent the Crockett heirs, which must have been Mitchell or his representatives.[17]

The year 1854 was a busy one for the Crocketts. On February 1, Margaret Flowers, David and Polly's youngest and only surviving child, and her husband, Wiley Flowers, sold their interest in the Texas land to William Warren for $500 ($17,635 in 2022). The sale was similar to the 1842 indentures that were concluded by four other Crockett children.[18]

Soon after receiving Elizabeth's power of attorney, Mitchell set about securing title to the 1,280-acre grant, which Forester had already surveyed, and on April 6, 1855, he secured a patent on the land for the Crocketts. Just as Forester had noted years earlier, it was located on the Brazos River about eleven miles northeast of Comanche Peak, not far from Rucker Creek and near where the town of Granbury was later established, about seven miles west of Acton. By early 1855, Elizabeth, her sons Robert Crockett and George Patton, her daughter Rebecca Elvira Crockett Halford, and their families had moved to Texas. The exact date is not certain, but it was after Elizabeth had concluded the transfer of her Texas lands to her five children in October 1854 while still in Tennessee. Robert later recalled the family moved to Texas in 1854, so the move may have taken place in late autumn of that year. It is not certain where they lived when they arrived in Texas, but Mitchell may have arranged a place for them to stay until their own land claim was secured.[19]

Elizabeth, however, did not move onto this land and instead turned it over to her children. She resided instead on some 320 acres of nearby public land in the Pacific Railroad Reserve, which was adjacent to the 640 acres on which her children were living. Texas had set aside the reserve for construction of a railroad that would have run from the eastern border of Texas to El Paso but was never built. It was not unusual for people to live on public land they did not own and to construct homes and other improvements on it. The same was true in Tennessee, where many occupant farmers, or "squatters," worked and improved public land they didn't own. They could, and often were, forced off the land when it was legally claimed, but they retained the right to be paid for their improvements. Elizabeth would have been familiar with the regime as Crockett had invested much of his political career in the pursuit of legal title to Tennessee lands occupied by squatters, but she would not remain a squatter for long.

The Crockett lands increased considerably with the legislature's 1856 donation of a league of land to Elizabeth, which included the 320 acres she was living on in the Pacific Railroad Reserve, thus giving her legal title to it. Elizabeth opted to convert the acreage to cash and quickly sold all but the 320 acres she occupied to Edward S. Terrill of Tarrant County. She sold the remaining 4,108.4 acres for $1,000, or 24 cents per acre ($34,856, or about

$8.48 per acre, in 2022 dollars). Elizabeth remained on this land until her death on January 31, 1860, when it passed to her surviving children.[20]

The Crockett headright still had not been disposed of, although Forester had secured the land warrant certificate for it in 1852 and arranged to have the land located and surveyed for the Crocketts on the west bank of the Nueces River, about one hundred miles southwest of San Antonio. Before turning things over to Mitchell, he directed the Bexar County Court Clerk to secure a patent on the headright for the Crockett heirs.[21]

There was still the lingering uncertainty cast by the 1842 indentures, which entitled the Foresters to as much as 45 percent of Crockett land in Texas due to their references to *all and any* such lands. In 1859 Elizabeth decided to remove any shadow the indentures might cast over Crockett land titles and sought to avoid the volatile land situation the family had endured in Tennessee. On March 19, she paid the Forester heirs $1,200 for the lands the Crockett children had sold to Richard Forester, by then deceased, for the same price. To sweeten the deal, the Foresters bought 1,912 acres of the Crockett headright for the same $1,200 Elizabeth had paid them to kill the indentures. The deal amounted to a clever land swap that provided a way for Elizabeth to undo the indentures and was agreeable to the Foresters as well. It gave them about 42 percent of the original headright, roughly what Richard Forester purchased from the Crocketts in 1842.[22]

According to Sam S. Smith, the Bexar County Court clerk, the settlement between Elizabeth and the Foresters regarding the headright was completely amicable. In an 1867 letter to Stephen Crosby, commissioner of the Texas General Land Office, Smith attested to J. B. Forester's honesty as administrator of the Crockett estate and noted that the court authorized Forester to contract with John S. McDonald, Bexar District surveyor, to have the Crockett headright located and surveyed on the Nueces River, which was carried out for a fee of one hundred dollars. "Subsequently, after Mrs. Crockett . . . came to Texas," Smith wrote, "then Governor [John McClannahan] Crockett [no relation] of Dallas opened a correspondence for her with Forester . . . through Judge William F. Weeks, the result of which was, as I understood at the time, (1857 I believe) that the widow and heirs made no claim to said Donation and Bounty warrants so sold, but would take the donation land located in Dallas County (I believe) and that the Foresters by virtue of their transfers from the heirs should have a proper portion of the league & labor on the Nueces River. It is my impression that the whole matter has been amicably adjudicated between the parties." Although Smith's memory of dates and locations may have been faulty, his letter suggests the Crocketts were primarily interested in the 1,280-acre grant rather than the headright, although they retained a portion of that too.[23]

On May 4, 1870, still residing in Gibson County, Tennessee, Matilda Crockett Fields joined with a man named B. M. McFarland, another Tennessean who owned land in Texas, in legal action regarding the headright, some of which McFarland owned by that time. Both gave their power of attorney to J. M. Lindsay of Cooke County, Texas, who often speculated in Texas lands. A patent on the headright had been registered to H. C. Holman on January 14, 1860, but Matilda and McFarland charged that there was a conflict in the survey of the land and instructed Lindsay to procure a cancellation of the Holman patent. As "part owners of the league certificate granted to heirs of David Crockett," they authorized Lindsay to "withdraw from the Government Land Office the said league certificate and to relocate the same on the vacant public domain of Texas as early as practicable." McFarland owned other lands in Texas and authorized Lindsay "to attend to all his lands in the State of Texas as well as the Crockett interest he owns and that of the Crockett lands [of] Margaret Flowers, formerly Margaret Crockett." Margaret and Wiley Flowers had sold their interest in the Texas land to William Warren in February 1854, and at least a portion of it had been sold to McFarland, who still referred to it as Margaret Flowers' land since she was regarded as the original owner, which was common in Texas land transactions. Lindsay succeeded in having the 1860 Holman patent cancelled on February 6, 1871, when the challenge posed by Matilda and McFarland was upheld. A few months later the conflicting surveys were resolved, and a certificate was issued to Lindsay on behalf of Matilda and McFarland for relocation of the land.[24]

The Crockett children were satisfied with the 640 acres they retained from the 1,280-acre grant along Rucker Creek, half of which had gone as payment to Mitchell. Elizabeth held title to her own adjacent 320 acres, and the Crocketts retained an unknown portion of the headright. By 1885, Robert and Matilda were the only surviving Crockett children, the former residing in Granbury, Texas, the latter still in Rutherford, Tennessee, married to her third husband, Redden Fields. On December 28, 1885, Matilda wrote to Robert asking that he send her money from the sale of her land in Texas. She said she needed it because she had borrowed money intending to repay it with income from the Texas land sale. She was in a hurry and urged Robert to "Send money by express." It's not clear what Texas land belonged to her in 1885, but it was likely a portion of the headright she owned after her suit with McFarland was upheld and the Holman patent on the headright was removed.[25]

Robert Crockett also was awarded 960 acres of bounty land for his nine months of service in the Texas army from November 9, 1836, to August 24, 1837, which he promptly sold to William Ayers for $500 ($17,428 in 2022). He received an additional 1,280-acre Veteran Donation land grant in 1881, which he sold within days of receiving it for $600 ($20,914 in 2022).[26]

In all the Crockett family ultimately received 14,011 acres of Texas land, of which they retained 960 acres plus an undetermined amount of the headright. Either by design or chance, none of it lay near the Bois d'Arc Creek and Choctaw Creek area that Crockett had explored and dreamed of owning.[27]

* * * * *

David Crockett had been to the mountaintop and he had seen the promised land, but like Moses, he would never dwell in it. His family never shared his dream of a land empire and sold most of their Texas acreage. They remained satisfied with the land they kept, welcomed the security of ownership, and remained on it for the rest of their lives. It was land, Robert Crockett later remembered, "that was won by the blood of my father at the Alamo."[28]

APPENDIX 1

David Crockett's Terms in Office

*Crockett's Campaigns, Terms, and Pay
in the US House of Representatives*

1825

Election: Aug. 4–5, 1825—Defeated by Adam R. Alexander
Tennessee Ninth Congressional District

Vote Totals:
> Adam R. Alexander: 2,865—42%
> David Crockett: 2,594—38.1%
> James Ferrill: 912—13.4%
> Thomas H. Persons: 447—6.6%

1827

Election: Aug. 2–3, 1827—Defeated Adam R. Alexander, incumbent
Tennessee Ninth Congressional District

Vote Totals:
> David Crocket: 5,868—49.1%
> Adam R. Alexander: 3,646—30.5%
> William Arnold: 2,427—20.3%

Served in Twentieth Congress:

First session: Dec. 3, 1827–May 26, 1828

Second session: Dec. 1, 1828–March 3, 1829

Total pay: 269 days at eight dollars per day equals $2,152
($68,558 in 2022 dollars)

1829

Election: Aug. 6–7, 1829—Defeated Adam Alexander
Tennessee Ninth Congressional District

Vote Totals:
David Crockett: 6,783—64%
Adam R. Alexander: 3,643—34.4%

Served in Twenty-First Congress:

First session: Dec. 7, 1829–May 31, 1830
Second session: Dec. 6, 1830–March 3, 1831

Total pay: 264 days at eight dollars per day equals $2,112
($71,924 in 2022 dollars)

1831

Election: Aug. 4–5, 1831—Defeated by William Fitzgerald, incumbent
Tennessee Ninth Congressional District

Vote Totals:
William Fitzgerald: 8,534—51.8%
David Crockett: 7,948—48.2%

1833

Election: Aug. 1–2, 1833—Defeated William Fitzgerald, incumbent
Tennessee Twelfth Congressional District

Vote Totals:
David Crockett: 3,985—51.1%
William Fitzgerald: 3,812—48.9%

Served in Twenty-Third Congress:

First session: Dec. 2, 1833–June 30, 1834
Second session: Dec. 1, 1834–March 3, 1835

Total pay: 304 days at eight dollars per day equals $2,432
($81,880 in 2022 dollars)

1835

Election: Aug. 5–6, 1835—Defeated by Adam Huntsman
Tennessee Twelfth Congressional District

Vote Totals:
Adam Huntsman: 4,652—51.4%
David Crockett: 4,400—48.6%[1]

Crockett's Terms in the Tennessee General Assembly

Fourteenth General Assembly in Murfreesboro:

First session: September 17–November 17, 1821

Special session called by Governor William Carroll:
July 22–August 24, 1822

Fifteenth General Assembly in Murfreesboro:

First session: September 15–November 29, 1823
Second session: September 20–October 22, 1824

APPENDIX 2

Enlistment in Texas Volunteer Auxiliary Corps

The date of Crockett's enlistment in the Texas army is often given as January 14, 1836, because Judge John Forbes, who administered the oath of allegiance in Nacogdoches, compiled several rolls of enlistees bearing that date, including the one with Crockett's name. However, the original rolls and other enlistment documents that may have existed were lost in a fire that destroyed the adjutant general's office in Austin in 1855. All that survive are handwritten copies of the original rolls that were compiled by someone else—not Judge Forbes. The copies are not signed by the enlistees, their names simply being written by a scribe onto those copies. The lists are preceded by the oath of allegiance and, with one exception, include the preamble, "Know all men by these presents, that I have this day voluntarily enlisted myself in the Volunteer Auxiliary Corps for and during the time of six months," thus certifying the enlistees' loyalty and specifying their six-month enlistment term. The oath above the list with Crockett's name differs from all the others in two ways. First, it inserts the word "republican" before the word "government" so that it reads, "I do solemnly swear that I will bear true allegiance to the provisional government of Texas or any future *republican* government that may be hereafter declared" (italics added). Second, it is the only list where the preamble is missing from the oath at the top of the page.

Judge Forbes may have been preoccupied with rewriting the oath to suit Crockett's insistence on inserting the word "republican" and inadvertently neglected to add the preamble, but it was more likely omitted from the surviving copy by whoever wrote it. Without the preamble, the document does not actually commit Crockett or the others on that list to a specific enlistment term, so the original documents must have included the preamble and the actual signatures of Crockett and the other enlistees. The copies were compiled in accordance with a February 9, 1850, act of the Texas legislature to provide for the heirs of those who died at the Alamo, Goliad, and elsewhere during the Texas Revolution. The act instructed the Office of the Adjutant General to make copies of the enlistment rolls in their possession for that purpose, which turned out to be serendipity as these copies are all that survive, imperfect as they may be.

According to the Texas Government Land Office website, "The red, bound volume titled 'The Republic of Texas Muster Rolls' has historically been a showcase artifact for the Archives of the GLO. It has also been misrepresented over the years as to when it was made, by whom, and what it represents. All evidence points to this Muster Roll Book as being the work of the Court of Claims. It appears to be the culmination of the work done by the Court in the gathering of existing muster rolls, including the one the GLO sent to the court, and transcribed by the Court into one bound volume. In fact, at the end of the book are notations made in 1856 by Court of Claims Commissioners upon receipt of muster rolls being sent to the Court by the Governor and other individuals, as required by the law of 1856."[1]

Crockett's enlistment appears on page 114 of the surviving muster roll copies, which includes sixty-eight names, and is dated January 14, 1836, with a notation that it was signed by Judge Forbes on that date, although none of these documents actually has Forbes's signature. Again, only the copies survive, and like all the other rolls, this one simply states that the original was, "Signed' John Forbes, 1st Judge of the Municipality of Nacogdoches." Forbes's actual signature can be found on a letter dated September 22, 1837, certifying the enlistments of Daniel W. Cloud and P. J. Bailey.[2]

Other rolls appear on page 115 with ten names and a similar but not identical oath, which does include the preamble; page 116 with twenty-six names; and page 117 with thirteen names, including Micajah Autry (misspelled "M. Authey") of Tennessee, Daniel W. Cloud of Kentucky, and H. S. (Herbert Simms) Kimble of Tennessee. The oaths all have slight differences in wording and spelling. The list on page 113 includes a note from the Adjutant General's Department dated February 1, 1839, stating, "I certify that I have examined the foregoing muster rolls and carefully compared them and found them true copies of the originals, signed by P. H. Bell, Acting Adjt. Genl," and are thus copies, not originals.

Together, these lists include a total of 117 names and are all dated January 14, even though Autry wrote home to his wife on January 13 telling her he had already enlisted and that Crockett had joined his company by that date. It seems unlikely that Forbes gathered all 117 men together and administered four slightly different oaths on the same day. Also, the volunteers did not all arrive in Nacogdoches on the same day, but even if Forbes did gather everyone together on the same day there is still the problem of the differently worded oaths and the insertion of the word "republican" only on the Crockett muster roll. Why the different oaths and lists if everyone enlisted together on January 14? If they did, it is more likely that Forbes would have put all the names on a single list with one oath.

Forbes wrote to Lieutenant Governor James W. Robinson on January 12, 1836, to report his recruiting progress, but he put the letter aside and resumed writing on January 15. In the latter section of the letter, he said he had "been very busily engaged in attending to numerous volunteers from the United States, fifty-two of whom will leave here tomorrow for the frontier. Almost all are gentlemen of the best respectability and mostly hailing from Tennessee." He even mentioned that the "celebrated David Crockett is of the number." As Forbes says, he was very busy signing up recruits for several days and likely did not enlist one group of 117 on a single day.[3]

Autry doesn't say that he and his party arrived in Nacogdoches on January 13, and, in fact, notes his group was waiting for a company expected to arrive from Columbia. He also lingered a few days in San Augustine prior to that and still earlier in Natchitoches, Louisiana. He was certainly in Nacogdoches no later than January 13 when he wrote his letter and might have arrived several days earlier than that. The enlistment of Autry and Crockett likely took place earlier than January 13 but certainly no later than that, perhaps as early as January 8. Crockett wrote his own letter home on January 9, while he was visiting San Augustine, in which he clearly stated he had already taken the oath of government and enlisted as a volunteer for six months. Those are the very terms on the muster rolls, which he must have already signed.

The January 14 enlistment date is questionable for all these reasons, and there is stronger evidence suggesting that Crockett enlisted on January 8. First, Crockett's land bounty certificate No. 1295 for 1,280 acres, dated December 23, 1837, lists his dates of service as January 8 to March 6, 1836. He was credited with serving his full six-month enlistment by virtue of being killed at the Alamo. Second, Sam Houston's discharge endorsement of Peter Harper noted that Harper enlisted with Crockett on January 8 in Nacogdoches. Third, as mentioned, Micajah Autry's January 13, 1836, letter from Nacogdoches clearly stated that he'd already enlisted by that date and that Crockett had joined his company by then.

Although Crockett biographers have puzzled over the contradictory dates surrounding Crockett's enlistment, the available evidence strongly suggests that he enlisted on January 8, 1836.[4]

Notes

Introduction

1. *Register of Debates*, US House of Representatives, 20th Cong., 1st Sess., April 29, 1828, 2520.

2. Thomas Jefferson, *Notes on the State of Virginia* (Richmond: J. W. Randolph, 1853), 244. Originally written in 1781 and first published in 1784; Google Books reprint, https://www.google.com/books/edition/Notes_on_the_State_of_Virginia /z4lJAQAAMAAJ?hl=en&gbpv=1&dq=Notes+on+the+state+of+virginia&print- sec=frontcover.

3. Dennis Hodgson, "Benjamin Franklin on Population: From Policy to The- ory," *Population and Development Review*, vol. 17, no. 4 (1991). 639–61; H. W. Brands, "Why Have Americans Always Been So Obsessed with the Land?" History website, last modified March 7, 2018: https://www.history.com/news/american -land-frontier; Richard Hofstadter, "The Myth of The Happy Yeoman," *American Heritage*, vol. 7, no. 3 (April 1956); "Westward Expansion: The Louisiana Purchase," U. S. History Online Textbook, last modified 2019: http://www.ushistory.org/us /20c.asp.

4. Daniel Feller, University of Tennessee Knoxville (author of *The Public Lands in Jacksonian Politics* and editor-in-chief of *The Papers of Andrew Jackson*) in discussion with the author, July 2019.

5. Brands, "Why Have Americans Always Been So Obsessed with the Land?"

6. Steve Inskeep, "How Jackson Made a Killing in Real Estate," *Politico*, July 4, 2015: https://www.politico.com/magazine/story/2015/07/andrew-jackson-made -a-killing-in-real-estate-119727.

Chapter 1

1. *Carroll County, Tennessee, Deed Books*, Entry recorded in RG-50-Series 2- Book 29; Entry book for 1st Survey District, Book G, 1813–1815; No. 11386–14482; p. 452; also see line item in Index Book 41, p. 414. The land was surveyed May 4, 1814, Plats & Surveys, Series 3, Book 28, 2nd Surveyor's District, 596–597; Entries 3944 and 3945, Entry Book RG-50 Series 2, Book 36, 2nd Surveyor's District, Book C, 1810–1812, page 238; David Crockett, *A Narrative of the Life of David Crockett of the State of Tennessee*, eds. James A. Shackford and Stanley J. Folmsbee. (Knoxville: University of Tennessee Press, 1973), 69, footnote 23; James Atkins Shackford, *David Crockett: The Man and the Legend*, ed. John B. Shackford (Chapel Hill & London: University of North Carolina Press, 1956), 8, 295, footnote 23. The land

was surveyed May 4, 1814; *Carroll County, Tennessee, Plats & Surveys*, Series 3, Book 28, 2nd Surveyor's District, 596–97. Although Crockett left Lincoln County early in 1813, he still owned the five acres until 1814 when he lost it due to his being delinquent in tax payments. He had gone to the expense of surveying the tract, so he intended to hold onto it, perhaps to rent it out; Gert Petersen, *David Crockett, The Volunteer Rifleman: An Account of his Life, while a Resident of Franklin County, 1812–1817* (Franklin County, TN: Franklin County Historical Society, 2007), 10–11; Despite conjecture placing Margaret's birth in 1815, shortly before Polly's death, US Census records show that she was born November 22, 1812, and would have been two-and-a-half years old when Polly died, although Crockett refers to her as an infant in his autobiography; Crockett likely leased the Beans Creek land from its owner, Frances "Fanny" Gillaspie (sometimes spelled Francis Gillespie), who bought two hundred acres from Robert Bean in 1811. Bean had purchased the tract from Eliza Boddie, and it was part of Boddie's 2,500-acre tract. Crockett settled on some part of Gillespie's two-hundred-acre tract; Frances Henderson Gillaspie had strong Kentucky roots and may well have called her land "Kentuck" before Crockett's arrival there. She was born May 29, 1777, in Boonesborough, Kentucky, the oldest daughter of Samuel Henderson and Elizabeth Callaway. Boone family tradition claims that Samuel and Elizabeth were married by Daniel Boone himself, and it was said to have been the first marriage in Kentucky. I am indebted to Gert Petersen for sharing his research on Gillaspie.

2. Crockett, *Narrative*, 72–73; Bob Thompson, *Born on a Mountaintop: On the Road with Davy Crockett and the Ghosts of the Wild Frontier* (New York: Crown, 2012), 57. Thompson quotes Jim Hargrove, who said the story was handed down by his ancestors. It may be apocryphal, but its irony was not lost on Thompson, who points out that, while Crockett was off fighting Indians, a kind Cherokee may have been caring for his family at home. Peter Cozzens, *A Brutal Reckoning: Andrew Jackson, The Creek Indians, and the Epic War for the American South* (New York: Alfred A. Knopf, 2023), 140-51.

3. Crockett, *Narrative*, 87–89, 92-93; Shackford, *David Crockett*, 202; Cozzens, *A Brutal Reckoning*, 186-95; "Battle of Talladega," Encyclopedia of Alabama, last modified March 23, 2023, http://encyclopediaofalabama.org/article/h-2620.

4. Crockett, *Narrative*, 96–97; Mark Derr, *The Frontiersman: The Real Life and the Many Legends of Davy Crockett* (New York: Quill, 1993), 70–72; Thompson, *Born on a Mountaintop*, 74–75; Cozzens, *A Brutal Reckoning*, 320-24.

5. Crockett, *Narrative*, 101; Thompson, *Born on a Mountaintop*, 74.

6. Shackford, *David Crockett*, 29–32; Crockett, *Narrative*, 101–24.

7. Crockett, *Narrative*, 125–27; Thompson, *Born on a Mountaintop*, 57; Derr, *The Frontiersman*, 77.

8. Crockett, *Narrative*, 126–27; Petersen, *David Crockett, The Volunteer Rifleman*, 29–32. Born in Swannanoa, North Carolina, on May 22, 1788, Elizabeth Patton came from a well-off family. She was a widow with two small children, George and Margaret Ann (Peggy) Patton (birth dates unknown). Crockett had three children of his own, John Wesley Crockett, born July 10, 1807; William F. Crockett, born November 25, 1809; and Margaret Finley (Polly) Crockett, born November 22,

1812. David and Elizabeth's children were Robert Patton Crockett, born September 16, 1816; Rebecca Elvira Crockett, born December 25, 1818; and Matilda Crockett, born August 2, 1821. Elizabeth's $800 is the equivalent of $15,391 in 2022 dollars. For important financial transactions mentioned throughout this book, nineteenth century dollars are converted to 2022 dollars using Ian Webster's CPI Inflation Calculator website. Since 1913 the US Bureau of Labor Statistics has tracked inflation using the Consumer Price Index (CPI), but it is more difficult to track inflation prior to 1913. Webster notes that his inflation data from 1634 to 1912 "is sourced from a historical study conducted by political science professor Robert Sahr at Oregon State University and from the American Antiquarian Society." "CPI Inflation Calculator," US Official Inflation Data, Alioth Finance, accessed August 29, 2022, https://www.officialdata.org/; also see Sarah Kuta, "What Online Inflation Calculators Can—and Can't—Tell Us About the Past," *Smithsonian Magazine*, August 15, 2022: https://tinyurl.com/2znrcz6r.

9. Although war records show Crockett's rank as third sergeant, his discharge says he was a fourth sergeant; see Derr, *The Frontiersman*, 274, footnote 19. Derr puts the discrepancy down to a scribe's error, a reasonable explanation. Shackford, *David Crockett*, 34.

10. David Crockett contract, SPR158 dated January 1, 1817, Alabama Dept. of Archives and History. The rent was set at $2.50 per acre per year, but a few days later, on January 6, Crockett cut the first year's rent to two dollars per acre, or seventy-six dollars per year in exchange for Penn paying thirty dollars toward the first year's rent immediately (cash in hand). Crockett continued to rent this land out until he and Elizabeth sold it in 1833 following a lengthy lawsuit by their former landlord, Fanny Gillaspie, which Crockett won. September 15, 1833, indenture, Tennessee State Library and Archive (TSLA), provided to author by Jerry Limbaugh.

11. *Lawrence County, Tennessee, Deed Book*, entry no. 138 for 160 acres in Range 4, section 4 on Beeler Fork of Shoal Creek, based on certificate land warrant no. 894. The entry was not recorded until December 20, 1820, nearly four years after Crockett had settled on the tract and after he had begun renting it out. Such time lags in recording land transactions were not unusual on the frontier; The corporation published a notice on April 26, 1817, that it intended to petition the state legislature to form a new county, which they submitted on July 14, 1817. Lawrence County was created by the legislature on October 21, 1817, from lands formerly lying in Hickman and Giles counties. Gert Petersen, news clip dated April 26, 1817, sent to author; Gert Petersen, *David Crockett, The Public Man and Legislator: An Account of his Life, while a resident of Lawrence County, 1817–1822* (Lawrence County, TN: Lawrence County Genealogical Society, 2010), 12–15.

12. Shackford, *David Crockett*, 38–41; Crockett, *Narrative*, 133, footnote 21; Jonathan Kennon Thompson Smith, *The Land Holdings of Colonel David Crockett in West Tennessee*. (Jackson: The Mid-West Tennessee Genealogical Society, 2003), 10; Tennessee State Commission Book, No. 4, 1815–1827, page 96, (TSLA). Crockett served as a magistrate, called justices of the peace at the time. Each county was required to maintain a regiment of militia with an elected colonel as commander;

in time of war, two colonels, who were entitled to retain the title indefinitely upon good behavior. If he moved to a new county, he retained the title, although no longer the official rank of commander.

13. *Lawrence County, Tennessee, Deed Book*, Entry No. 499, February 4, 1821; Military land warrant No, 1909 purchased from Ralph Graves. The other 11 entries are Nos. 411, 412, 414, 416, 417, 419,421, 422, 424, all dated January 21, 1821; Entry No. 498, dated February 8, 1821, and Entry No. 1572, dated August 19, 1824; see also Tennessee Grant #24167, October 28, 1825; Petersen, *David Crockett, The Public Man and Legislator*, 23–29; "Life of David Crockett," Lawrence County Archives, David Crockett Folder 1, 13–14, and alternate typescript, 39–40. The entries were not registered until early 1821; one entry was made in August 1824, long after the fact but not unusual for the recording of land transactions at the time. Article 1, section 7 of the Tennessee Constitution required that candidates for the General Assembly be residents of the state for at least three years and of their county at least one, and that they own at least two hundred acres of land.

14. *Lawrence County, Tennessee, Deed Book*, Entry No. 414, January 9, 1821; Entry No. 422, January 29, 1821; Petersen, *David Crockett, The Public Man and Legislator*, 29–30; Crockett, *Narrative*, 144.

15. Smith, *Land Holdings of Colonel David Crockett in West Tennessee*, 10; Petersen, *David Crockett, The Public Man and Legislator*, 26–29. For an alternative account of Lawrence's end see Tom Halsted, "The real, shameful story behind 'Don't give up the ship!'" *Boston Globe*, May 19, 2013, https://tinyurl.com/yxefpmve.

16. Crockett to John C. McLemore, October 26, 1820, quoted in James R. Boylston and Allen J. Wiener, *David Crockett in Congress: The Rise and Fall of the Poor Man's Friend* (Houston: Bright Sky Press, 2009), 146. McLemore, one of the wealthiest and most influential men in the Memphis area, was a major landowner and speculator with vast land holdings in western Tennessee and elsewhere. He was a former partner of Andrew Jackson and the two accumulated thousands of acres of land. "John Christmas McLemore," *Tennessee Encyclopedia*, last modified March 1, 2018, https://tennesseeencyclopedia.net/entries/john-christmas-mclemore/.

17. Lawrence County Minute Book of the Court of Pleas and Quarter Sessions, January 1, 1821; Shackford, *David Crockett*, 43; Derr, *The Frontiersman*, 93, cites John L. Jacobs' letter to the *Morristown* (Tennessee) *Gazette* dated November 22, 1884, based on a typescript by Annie Bell Bryson, Franklin County, North Carolina, of a clipping in her mother's scrapbook, housed in the University of Tennessee Special Collections.

18. Crockett, *Narrative* 138–143, footnotes 6 and 10; Boylston and Wiener, *David Crockett in Congress*, 17–18; Smith, *Land Holdings of Colonel David Crockett in West Tennessee*, 10.

19. Crockett, *Narrative*, 144, footnote 12. A frequently told tale of Crockett's debut in the legislature suggests that after he gave a speech possibly dotted with colorful backwoods expressions, James C. Mitchell rose and referred to Crockett as the "Gentleman from the Cane." Crockett took it as a slur and demanded satisfaction from Mitchell, who apologized and swore that he meant no harm in his remark. Crockett accepted the apology, but later when he found a ruffle that

Mitchell had lost lying on the ground, he pinned it to his shirt and made a point of drawing attention to it by strutting into the hall and sitting next to Mitchell, which brought boisterous laughter from the assembly. If true, it showed Crockett's shrewd ability to use humor and one-upmanship. The story originated in the partly fictitious *Life and Adventures of Colonel David Crockett of West Tennessee* by James Strange French, later retitled *Sketches and Eccentricities of Col. David Crockett of West Tennessee* (New York: J & J Harper, 1833), 57–59. Shackford, *David Crockett*, identified Mitchell as Crockett's foil, 52–53. Also see Boylston and Wiener, *David Crockett in Congress*, 17.

20. Crockett, *Narrative*, 144–145, footnote 13; Smith, *Land Holdings of Colonel David Crockett in West Tennessee*, 10; Shackford, *David Crockett*, 42–43; Lawrence County *Minute Book of the Court of Pleas and Quarter Sessions*, October 5, 1821, and April 4, 1822; Morrison, John F. Jr., *Life of David Crockett in Lawrence County*, 13–14, and alternate typescript, 39–40. Article 11, section 18 of the Tennessee Constitution of 1796 stipulated that "the person of the debtor, where there is not strong presumption of fraud, shall not be continued in prison after delivering up his estate for the benefit of his creditor or creditors, in such manner as shall be prescribed by law." This would have enabled Crockett to pay his debts with his land holdings, regardless of their monetary value or how much he had actually borrowed from his creditors.

21. *Lawrence County Minute Book of the Court of Pleas and Quarter Sessions*, April 4–5, 1822, containing Crockett power of attorney to Mansil Crisp, February 26, 1822, registered April 17, 1822; *Life of David Crockett*, 13–14, and alternate typescript, 39–40, Lawrence County Archives. Ironically, a few days earlier a deed of gift from Crockett to Nancy and Ann Musgrave was certified and registered in court. Crockett had agreed to act as a go-between for Joshua Bowdry by purchasing some furniture and livestock at an auction of Thomas Musgrave's property and then donating them to the Musgrave sisters through the deed of gift. The reason for the subterfuge remains a mystery. *Lawrence County (Tennessee) Minute Book of the Court of Pleas and Quarter Sessions*, April 1, 1822; Vicky L. (Morrow) Hutchings, *Lawrence County, Tennessee, Deeds* (Mountain Press, TN, 2001), Books A-E, Aug. 1819-Jan. 1836, Vol. 1, 57, image 46. The deed was witnessed by William M. Crisp; letter from John F. Morrison to Andrew Forest Muir dated Feb. 5, 1956; "Life of David Crockett" by John F. Morrison, Jr., 1953 draft manuscript; David Crockett folder "Deeds to spring and other property," Lawrence County Archive.

22. Crockett, *Narrative*, 144–145 and footnote 13.

23. It should be noted that, although Robert Patton deeded this land to his daughter, as a married woman she had no right to the property and her husband, Hance McWhorter, actually had control over it. In the same way, Crockett held control over any land or money that Elizabeth owned as a widow prior to their marriage. However, women did have some protection under laws that required them to approve any land transactions their husband's might arrange. Since Elizabeth was illiterate, she signed documents with an "X," witnessed by one or more individuals who certified that it was "her mark." Land transactions also required that married women be interviewed privately by public officials to certify that they

had not been coerced by their husbands into signing documents against their will. Despite these remedial measures, women still lacked legal control of their own property and the law would not change substantially until the twentieth century. Margaret L. Crawford, "The Legal Status of Women in Early Tennessee: Knox, Jefferson, and Blount Counties, 1792–1843," (master's thesis, University of Tennessee, 1992), http://trace.tennessee.edu/cgi/viewcontent.cgi?article=4955&context=utk _gradthes; Jone Johnson Lewis, "A Short History of Women's Property Rights in the United States" ThoughtCo. last modified July 13, 2019, https://www.thoughtco .com/property-rights-of-women-3529578; Smith, *The Land Holdings of Colonel David Crockett in West Tennessee*, 6–16.

24. Smith, *The Land Holdings of Colonel David Crockett in West Tennessee*, 6–16; Crockett, *Narrative*, 147–154, footnotes 1, 2, 5, 10.

25. Crockett, *Narrative*, 155, footnote 14; Shackford, *David Crockett*, 57–58; Stanley J. Folmsbee and Anna Grace Catron, "The Early Career of David Crockett," *East Tennessee Historical Society's Publications* 28 (1956), 74. For a discussion of North Carolina land warrants applied to Tennessee lands, see Boylston and Wiener, *David Crockett in Congress*, 27–30.

26. Crockett, *Narrative*, 155–160.

27. Jackson resigned his Senate seat in 1825 and was replaced by Hugh Lawson White, a Jackson ally who later broke with Old Hickory. Boylston and Wiener, *David Crockett in Congress*, 18, 25, 54, 95; Crockett, *Narrative*, 170–71.

28. Crockett, *Narrative*, 167, footnote 3; Boylston and Wiener, *David Crockett in Congress*, 24, footnotes 16 and 17; Shackford, *David Crockett*, 66–68. Overton was one of the wealthiest men in Tennessee, a banker, land speculator, a lawyer who served on the Tennessee Supreme Court from 1804 to 1816, and a founder of Memphis. He was a close friend of Jackson as well as his business partner and political ally. Andrew Erwin's animosity toward Jackson dated at least from 1806, when Jackson killed Charles Dickinson, Erwin's son-in-law, in a duel. In the ensuing years the two sued each other on various grounds and accused each other of slave trading and illegal land speculation. Erwin even accused Jackson of conspiring with Aaron Burr to remove western states and the Louisiana territory from the Union. They remained bitter enemies for life, and Crockett's alignment with the Erwin faction placed him directly in Jackson's sights.

29. Crockett, *Narrative*, 193–194; Shackford, *David Crockett*, 70; Lewis C. Gray, *History of Agriculture in the Southern United States to 1860* (Washington, DC: Carnegie, 1940), II, 1027; Samuel H. Williamson, "What Is the Relative Value?" *Economic History Services* (June 2005), http://www.eh.net/hmit/compare.

30. Crockett never secured title to this tract through several court rulings that continued into 1835 and even after Crockett's death, although by then he no longer appears to have been a party to the dispute, having lost whatever claim he may have had. Reese lost his claim when he failed to pay sums ordered by the court and the land was sold at auction. Ironically, it was bought by Edwin Warren, Crockett's original buyer, for one hundred dollars. Gibson County Circuit Court Minutes, Book A, 53–54; Reese v. Crockett, 16 Tenn. 129, 8 Yer. 129 (1835), Caselaw Access Project, Harvard Law School, https://cite.case.law/tenn/16/129/; Crockett, *Narrative*, 174, footnote 1; Smith, *The Land Holdings of Colonel David Crockett in*

West Tennessee, 55–56; Shackford, *David Crockett*, 74–75. Crockett's eighty dollars equals $2,100 in 2022 dollars; $205 equals $5,375.

31. Boylston and Wiener, *David Crockett in Congress*, 20–21; Shackford, *David Crockett*, 74–79; Crockett, *Narrative*, 195–200; J. M. Keating, *History of the City of Memphis and Shelby County Tennessee*, 3 vols., I (Syracuse: D. Mason & Co., 1888), 181; James D. Davis, *History of the City of Memphis* (Memphis: Hite, Crumpton, & Kelly, 1873), 146–150.

32. Shackford, *David Crockett*, 74–80; *Gibson County Circuit Court Minute Book A*, 1824–1832, 42; Crockett, *Narrative*, 195–199 and footnotes. 1, 5; J. M. Keating, *History of the City of Memphis*, vol., I, 178–180.

33. Crockett to James Blackburn, February 5, 1828, Tennessee Historical Society, TSLA, quoted in Boylston and Wiener, *David Crockett in Congress*, 151.

34. A likely apocryphal account, written by Carson's daughter, Rebecca Carson Whitson, in 1894, sixty-seven years later, claims that "David Crockett was the first man who brought the news to Pleasant Gardens, he rode his horse almost to death, beat his hat to pieces & came dashing up yelling 'The Victory is Ours.'" This seems hardly likely as it is nearly two hundred miles from Swannanoa, N.C., to the cite of the Carson-Vance duel, which is near present-day Tuxedo, N. C. Even in the best of conditions, Crockett would have been hard-pressed to make such a journey, let alone while recovering from a serious illness. James Atkins Shackford, "David Crockett and North Carolina," *The North Carolina Historical Review* 28, no. 3 (1951): 298–315, http://www.jstor.org/stable/23515913; Shackford, *David Crockett*, 84–86; "Documents Relating to Honorable Samuel P. Carson, First Secretary of State of Republic of Texas," Sam Houston State University, Newton Gresham Library, https://digital.library.shsu.edu/digital/collection/p243coll3/id/15222. This includes the Whitson letter, also transcribed in Shackford, "David Crockett and North Carolina;" "Carson, Samuel Price," *Biographical Directory of the United States Congress: 1774—Present*, https://bioguideretro.congress.gov/Home/MemberDetails?memIndex=C000193; "Vance, Robert Brank," *Biographical Directory of the United States Congress: 1774—Present*, https://bioguideretro.congress.gov / Home/MemberDetails?memIndex=V000018.

35. Crockett, *Narrative*, 209; Andrew Jackson to James Polk, May 3, 1835, and May 12, 1835, *Correspondence of James K. Polk, Vol. 3* (Knoxville: University of Tennessee Press, 1975), 182–83, 191; Shackford, *David Crockett*, 141-42; Boylston and Wiener, *David Crockett in Congress*, 85–86, 119–120. For a summary of Crockett's campaigns and terms in office see Appendix 1. For a thorough study of Crockett's political career, including his election campaigns, terms in Congress, and his struggle for land reform, see Boylston and Wiener, *David Crockett in Congress*.

36. *Weakley County, Tennessee, Deed Book*, entry No. 934 dated June 12, 1826; land grant No. 1360 dated October 12, 1829; *Gibson County Deed Book B*, microfilm roll 69, Vol. B, 128–129; *Gibson County, Tennessee, Deed Book*, 1828–1832, page 117; *Weakley County, Tennessee, Deed Book D*, page 264, registered September 13, 1836; Weakley County, Tennessee, microfilm roll 59, Vol. D, page 264, TSLA; Smith, *Land Holdings of Colonel David Crockett in West Tennessee*, 66–67. Flowers was the future father-in-law of Crockett's daughter Margaret. Crockett's last surviving letter, written from San Augustine, Texas, January 9, 1836, was addressed

to Margaret and her husband, Wiley Flowers. Crockett's $500 equals $14,963 in 2022 dollars; $505 equals $15,113.

37. Smith, *Land Holdings of Colonel David Crockett in West Tennessee*, 7–8; Crockett to George Patton, January 27, 1829, quoted in Boylston and Wiener, *David Crockett in Congress*, 162.

38. For sale of twenty-five acres to G. Patton: *Weakley County, Tennessee, Deed Book B*, microfilm roll 58, Vol. B, 185–187; for sale of slave girl Adeline: *Weakley County, Tennessee, Deed Book B*, microfilm roll 58, Vol. B, 151; Smith, *Land Holdings of Colonel David Crockett in West Tennessee*, 42; Shackford, *David Crockett*, 122–137. Sale of the two hundred acres by Joel Henry Dyer to Crockett for eighty dollars: Smith, *Land Holdings of Colonel David Crockett in West Tennessee*, 71. For the complex history of the dispute over the two hundred acres that Crockett bought from Joel Henry Dyer, see Smith, *The Land Holdings of Colonel David Crockett in West Tennessee*, 68–98. The case was so confusing that it was ultimately dismissed before the chancellor could render a decree. Smith doesn't hazard an interpretation. September 15, 1833, indenture, provided to author by Jerry Limbaugh.

39. "Salaries of Members of Congress: Recent Actions and Historical Tables," FRASER, Discover Economic History, November 26, 2018, https://fraser.stlouisfed .org/title/salaries-members-congress-5996?start_page=19. For an assessment of Crockett's gambling see Boylston and Wiener, *David Crockett in Congress*, 16, 23, footnote 9. Crockett to Jacob Dixon, April 11, 1834, quoted in Boylston and Wiener, *David Crockett in Congress*, 245. Crockett borrowed $700 from Kentucky congressman Robert Lytle McHatton on February 17, 1829, likely to pay off gambling debts, payable in sixty days; on February 24 he signed a revised note to McHatton giving him until December 26, 1836, to pay off the $700, which equals $22,300 in 2022 dollars, rather a large debt for Crockett to pay back. February 17 note provided to author by Gert Petersen; "David Crockett [February 24] Promissory Note Signed," Heritage Auctions, https://tinyurl.com/yyzfaxhr.

40. *Jackson Gazette,* March 27, 1830 and April 10, 1830; *Register of Debates,* US House of Representatives, 21st Cong., 1st Sess., January 21–22, 1830, 551–54 and February 25, 1830, 583–84; "Congressman Davy Crockett's Resolution to Abolish the Military Academy at West Point," National Archives, https://www.doc-steach .org/documents/document/davy-crockett-abolish-west-point; Boylston and Wiener, *David Crockett in Congress*, 77–78; Shackford, *David Crockett*, 113–115; Crockett, *Narrative*, 80–82.

41. Boylston and Wiener, *David Crockett in Congress*, 38.

42. *Jackson Gazette,* January 27, 1829; Boylston and Wiener, *David Crockett in Congress*, 51.

43. Boylston and Wiener, *David Crockett in Congress*, 51–52.

44. Boylston and Wiener, *David Crockett in Congress*, 109.

45. A copy of the British edition of *Sketches and Eccentricities of Co. David Crockett of Tennessee* (1834) is on display in the Alamo in San Antonio. Also see "Biographical Sketches: David Crockett," *Chambers' Edinburgh Journal*, no. 135 (August 30, 1834): 244–245; Jim Boylston, "'Sketches' Re-Examined: The First Crockett Biography," address presented at Alamo Society Symposium, San Antonio, March 2006; Boylston and Wiener, *Crockett in Congress*, 85.

46. "*Sketches*," 115–116; Boylston, "Sketches Re-Examined: The First Crockett Biography."

47. Boylston and Wiener, *David Crockett in Congress*, 115, 124. In 1834 "Colonel Crockett's March," by H. Dielman, was published by John Cole and Son of Baltimore; a year later "Go Ahead—A March Dedicated to Colonel Crockett" (aka "The Crockett Victory March"), was published by Firth and Hall in New York. See William R. Chemerka and Allen J. Wiener, *Music of the Alamo: From 19th Century Ballads to Big-Screen Soundtracks* (Houston: Bright Sky Press, 2009), 123. Songs would continue to be written about Crockett well into the twentieth century.

48. Crockett to Henry Storrs, January 9, 1834, collection of Buffalo & Erie County Historical Society, file A00–110; Crockett to John Wesley Crockett, January 10, 1834, Thomas W. Streeter Collection of Texas Manuscripts, Yale Collection of Western Americana, Beinecke Rare Book and Manuscript Library; Boylston and Wiener, *David Crockett in Congress*, 231–232. Edward L. Carey and Abraham Hart founded their publishing company in Philadelphia, Pennsylvania, in 1829.

49. "Biographical Sketches: David Crockett," 244–245; Crockett's *Narrative* was published in England by John Limbird, 143, Strand, London; Boylston and Wiener, *David Crockett in Congress*, 121. Crockett also lent his name to the title page of *The Life of Martin Van Buren, Hair-apparent to the Government and the Appointed Successor of General Jackson*, although he had little to do with the book, which was written by Augustin Clayton and published in June 1835. The text was scathing enough for publishers Carey & Hart to remove their name from the volume out of fear of being charged with libel. William C. Davis, *Three Roads to the Alamo, The Lives and Fortunes of David Crockett, James Bowie, and William Barret Travis* (New York: Harper Collins, 1998), 402.

50. Interview with Matilda Fields, 1882, reprinted in Smith, *The Land Holdings of Colonel David Crockett in West Tennessee*, 96–98.

51. Boylston and Wiener, *David Crockett in Congress*, 121–122.

52. Interview with Matilda Fields, 1882, reprinted in Smith, *The Land Holdings of Colonel David Crockett in West Tennessee*, 96–98; *Register of Debates*, US House of Representatives, 21st Cong., 1st Sess., March 30, 1830, 717.

53. McWhorter allowed Elizabeth Crockett to remain on the land but within a few months she was forced to vacate the place following a complex lawsuit that challenged McWhorter's title to the land, after which she lived with her children on their property until moving to Texas in 1854. *Weakley County Deed Book D*, p. 264; Smith, *The Land Holdings of Colonel David Crockett in West Tennessee*, 69. Crockett had sold the same land to Henry Flowers in 1830 but it somehow came back into Crockett's hands, and he sold it a second time to Tucker. *Weakley County Deed Book B*, 128–129; Smith, *The Land Holdings of Colonel David Crockett in West Tennessee*, 66–69.

54. Crockett to John Wesley Crockett, December 24, 1834 quoted in Boylston and Wiener, *David Crockett in Congress*, 260–61; Crockett to Charles Schultz, December 25, 1834 and Crockett to John P. Ash, December 27, 1834, both quoted in Boylston and Wiener, *David Crockett in Congress*, 119, 262–63; Crockett to editor of *National Intelligencer*, August 10, 1835, published September 2, 1835, quoted in Boylston and Wiener, *David Crockett in Congress*, 122, 282.

55. Interview with Matilda Crockett Fields, 1882, reprinted in Smith, *The Land Holdings of Colonel David Crockett in West Tennessee*, 96–98; Crockett to George Patton, October 31, 1835, quoted in Boylston and Wiener, *David Crockett in Congress*, 285.

56. Interview with Matilda Crockett Fields, 1882, reprinted in Smith, *The Land Holdings of Colonel David Crockett in West Tennessee*, 97. Bran dances are described in C. W. Webber, *Wild Scenes and Song Birds*, (New York: G. P. Putnam & Co., 1853), 134–35; "Kentucky Dance 1813," Square Dancing in the 1800s, January 9, 2014, https://fredfeild.wordpress.com/tag/bran-dance/. This is not a typo but a dance different from "barn" dances. "Then there was the bran dance, which—commencing with the barbecued feast—wound up with a grand dance upon the rolled earth, sprinkled with bran beneath the arbors and in which everybody, high or low, participated with a reckless abandon of jollity. The confused jumble of all classes in this rude festival, made it more an occasion for roystering fun than refined enjoyment, and although forty years ago they were participated in by our ladies, and I remember well hearing my aunt and mother tell, many times, of dancing with the young Harry Clay at the bran dance, yet they gradually fell into disuse by the more refined."

Chapter 2

1. Richard Bruce Winders, *Sacrificed at the Alamo: Tragedy and Triumph in the Texas Revolution* (Abilene, TX: State House Press, 2004), 23; William C. Davis, *Lone Star Rising: The Revolutionary Birth of the Texas Republic* (College Station: Texas A&M University Press, 2004), 54–62.

2. Davis, *Lone Star Rising*, 66–72.

3. Jack Jackson, ed., *Texas by Terán: The Diary Kept by General Manuel de Mier y Terán on His 1828 Inspection of Texas*, trans. John Wheat (Austin: University of Texas Press, 2000), 100, 181–82.

4. The Constitution of Texas, March 17, 1836, General Provisions, Sections 6, 9, and 10, Tarlton Law Library—Jamail Center for Legal Research, https:// tarlton. law.utexas.edu/constitutions/republic-texas-1836/general-provisions; Andrew J. Torget, *Seeds of Empire: Cotton, Slavery, and the Transformation of the Texas Borderlands, 1800–1850* (Chapel Hill: University of North Carolina Press, 2015), 160–3; Paul D. Lack, *The Texas Revolutionary Experience: A Political and Social History: 1835–1836*, 264. Also see Randolph B. Campbell, *An Empire for Slavery: The Peculiar Institution in Texas* (Baton Rouge: Louisiana State University Press, 1989); Paul D. Lack, "In the Long Shadow of Eugene C. Barker: The Revolution and the Republic," in *Texas Through Time: Evolving Interpretations*. Edited by Walter L. Buenger and Robert A. Calvert (College Station: Texas A&M University Press, 1991), 134–64; and the more recent *Forget the Alamo: The Rise and Fall of an American Myth* by Bryan Burrough, Chris Tomlinson, and Jason Stanford, (New York: Penguin Publishing Group, 2021), which relies heavily on Torget. In addition to the constitutional provisions, a stricter law was adopted in 1840 that gave free Blacks two years to either leave Texas or be subject to being sold into slavery. As president,

Sam Houston suspended the law for a time, but free Blacks remained vulnerable in Texas. Douglas Hales, "Free Blacks," *Handbook of Texas Online*, accessed February 22, 2023, https://www.tshaonline.org/handbook/entries/free-blacks.

5. H. W. Brands, *Lone Star Nation: How a Ragged Army of Volunteers Won the Battle for Texas Independence and Changed America* (New York: Doubleday, 2004), 181–184.

6. Wilfred H. Callcott, "Santa Anna, Antonio Lopez de," Handbook of Texas Online, accessed October 17, 2022, https://www.tshaonline.org/handbook/entries/santa-anna-antonio-lopez-de.

7. Archie P. McDonald, "Travis, William Barret," Handbook of Texas Online, accessed October 17, 2022, https://www.tshaonline.org/handbook/entries/travis-william-barret. For a rejoinder to the charge that Travis's wife, Rosanna E. (Cato) Travis, was unfaithful see William C. Davis, *Three Roads to the Alamo: The Lives and Fortunes of David Crockett, James Bowie, and William Barret Travis* (New York: Harper Collins, 1998), 633, footnote 64. Davis offers the most thorough biography of Travis.

8. Davis, *Lone Star Rising*, 77–88; Brands, *Lone Star Nation*, 170–81.

9. Jackson and Wheat, *Texas by Terán*, 187–88.

10. Davis, *Lone Star Rising*, 90–101.

11. Brands, *Lone Star Nation*, 226–228; Davis, *Lone Star Rising*, 62, 107–09; James Donovan, *The Blood of Heroes* (New York: Little Brown, 2012), 123; Winders *Sacrificed at the Alamo*, 20.

12. Lack, *The Texas Revolutionary Experience*, 15.

13. Almonte to Secretary of State, November 25, 1834; Almonte's 1834 Secret Report, quoted in Jack Jackson, ed., *Almonte's Texas*, trans. John Wheat (Austin: Texas State Historical Association, 2003), 156; 209–22; Davis, *Lone Star Rising*, 107–20; George William Featherstonhaugh, *Excursion Through the Slave States: From Washington on the Potomac to the Frontier of Mexico: With Sketches of Popular Manners and Geological Notices, Volume 2.* (London: John Murray, 1844), 161, 183–86. Featherstonhaugh related his observations while visiting Washington, Arkansas, in December 1834, and his conviction that Houston and others, who were there at the time, were determined to achieve complete independence for Texas. "I was not desirous of remaining long at this place," he wrote. "General Houston was here, leading a mysterious sort of life, shut up in a small tavern, seeing nobody by day and sitting up all night. The world gave him credit for passing these his waking hours in the study of *trente et quarante* and *sept a lever*; but I had been in communication with too many persons of late, and had seen too much passing before my eyes, to be ignorant that this little place was the rendezvous where a much deeper game than faro or rouge-et-noir was playing. There were many persons at this time in the village from the States lying adjacent to the Mississippi, under the pretence of purchasing government lands, but whose real object was to encourage the settlers in Texas to throw off their allegiance to the Mexican government. Many of these individuals were personally acquainted with me; they knew I was not with them, and would naturally conclude I was against them. Having nothing whatever in common with their plans, and no inclination to forward or

oppose them, I perceived that the longer I staid the more they would find reason to suppose I was a spy upon their actions. . . . It had occurred to me, before I crossed Red River, that it would be prudent not to prolong my stay in Texas at this time. All the persons whom I had had any intercourse with, appeared to be of one opinion as to the expediency and propriety of occupying and detaching this province from the Mexican Government, and it was easy to see that they thought the moment for action was drawing nigh. Upon several occasions, when this important subject was earnestly discussed in my presence, I had remained silent; and as this was unusual in a quarter where all men had some plan or other to offer to accelerate their design, I was by many regarded as a spy upon them." He placed much of the blame on Mexico's poor judgment, ineffectiveness, and its own internal turmoil, observing, "The indiscreet legislation of Mexico, by which American citizens have been permitted to settle in Texas, upon condition of conforming to its laws, of adopting the Roman Catholic religion, and abolishing slavery, has already put the country into their possession; the conditions will none of them be observed, and when it is too late, Mexico will find that it would have been easier to have kept them out, than it will be to turn them out. But as Mexico is essentially a revolutionary government, and as no party will probably for a long time be strong enough to do more than attend to its own interests, it is almost self-evident that if ever she has the inclination, she will never have the power to govern––at a distance of 1800 miles––a race of active and intrepid men, who are hostile to her laws, religion, and manners. It would seem, therefore, that Mexico, in relation to the settlement of Texas, has made an irretrievable false step."

14. Travis to Burnet, May 21, 1835, quoted in Davis, *Lone Star Rising*, 125–6.

15. *New-York Spectator*, October 1, 1835; Travis to Andrew Briscoe, August 31, 1835, quoted in James H. Jenkins, ed., *Papers of the Texas Revolution, 1835–1836*, Vol. 1, (Austin, TX: Presidial Press, 1973), 380–81.

16. Lack, *The Texas Revolutionary Experience*, 110–123; Davis, *Lone Star Rising*, 134–35; Thomas W. Cutrer, "Army of the Republic of Texas," Handbook of Texas Online, accessed December 20, 2023, https://www.tshaonline.org/handbook /entries/army-of-the-republic-of-texas.

17. *Jackson Gazette*, March 27, 1830.

18. Davis, *Lone Star Rising*, 136–53; Winders, *Sacrificed at the Alamo*, 55–6.

19. *Huntsville Democrat*, September 13, 1835, reprinted in *Richmond Enquirer*, Oct. 23, 1835; *Tuscaloosa Alabama Flag of the Union*, October 31, 1835; *New Bedford Gazette & Courier*, November 2, 1835; *Connecticut Courant*, November 2, 1835; Houston's appeal, October 5, 1835, was reprinted in the *New Orleans Bee Extra*, October 13, 1835, from a *Red River Herald Extra*; Houston to Isaac Parker, October 5, 1835, and Houston's orders of October 8, 1835, quoted in Davis, *Lone Star Rising*, 146; Austin's "Circular of the Committee of Safety at San Felipe," September 19, 1835, Texas State Library and Archives Commission (TSLAC) website: https://www.tsl.texas.gov/exhibits/texas175/circular.html; Austin's September 22, 1835, broadside quoted in Frank W. Johnson, *A History of Texas, Vol. 1*, American Historical Society, 1914, 267, reprinted on *Portal of Texas History* website: https://texashistory.unt.edu/ark:/67531/metapth760581/m1/314/?q=%20 date%3A%2A-1977.

20. *Connecticut Courant*, CT, November 2, 1835; *Alexandria Gazette*, VA, November 3, 1835.

21. Winders, *Sacrificed at the Alamo*, 58; Davis, *Lone Star Rising*, 168–9; Lack, *The Texas Revolutionary Experience*, 58, 149–50.

22. Davis, *Lone Star Rising*, 192–93; Hobart Huson, "Goliad Declaration of Independence," Handbook of Texas Online, accessed October 6, 2022, https://www.tshaonline.org/handbook/entries/goliad-declaration-of-independence.

23. Winders, *Sacrificed at the Alamo*, offers a thorough discussion and analysis of citizen-soldier armies and their shortcomings; Eugene C. Barker, "The Texan Revolutionary Army," *The Quarterly of the Texas State Historical Association*, Vol. IX, No. 4 (April 1906),   227–261; *Ordinances and Decrees of the Consultation, Provisional Government of Texas and the Convention*, 76–78; Lack, *The Texas Revolutionary Experience*, 49–59, 110–11, 137–42; Davis, *Lone Star Rising*, 171; Paul D. Lack, "Consultation," Handbook of Texas Online, accessed April 5, 2020, http://www.tshaonline.org/handbook/online/articles/mjc08.

24. Martin Perfecto de Cós to Santa Anna, December 27, 1835, quoted in Wallace O. Chariton, *100 Days in Texas: The Alamo Letters* (Plano, TX: Wordware Publishing, 1990), 73–74; Davis, *Lone Star Rising*, 179–85; Winders, *Sacrificed at the Alamo*, 61–67; Alwyn Barr, "Grass Fight," Handbook of Texas Online, accessed February 2, 2020: http://www.tshaonline.org/handbook/online/articles/qfg01; William Fairfax Gray, *From Virginia to Texas, 1835: Diary of Col. Wm. F. Gray Giving Details of His Journey to Texas and Return in 1835–1836 and Second Journey to Texas in 1837* (Houston: Gray, Dillaye & Co., Printers, 1909), 111; surrender terms signed by Cós reprinted on TSLAC website: https://www.tsl.texas.gov/treasures/republic/bexar/cos1.html.

25. Edward Burleson to Provisional Governor, December 14, 1835; Smith to Houston, December 17, 1835; Houston to Bowie, December 17, 1835; F. W. Johnson to Wyatt Hanks & J. D. Clements, Members for the Committee of Military Affairs, General Council, December 24, 1835; all quoted in Chariton, *100 Days in Texas*, 33–36, 42–43, 61–62, 97–98; *Ordinances and Decrees of the Consultation, Provisional Government of Texas and the Convention*, 120; Craig H. Roell, "Matamoros Expedition of 1835–36" Handbook of Texas Online, accessed July 5, 2020: http://www.tshaonline.org/handbook/online/articles/qdm01; Barker, "The Texan Revolutionary Army," 254. Barker argues that the General Council approved the plan at least partly to keep the approximately 750 soldiers in the field from sitting idle and very likely deserting out of boredom. Also see Stuart Reid, *The Secret War for Texas* (College Station: Texas A&M University Press, 2007) for more on Grant's role and objectives in pushing for the Matamoros adventure. I am grateful to Stuart Reid for providing insight into the roots of the Matamoros expedition; Eugene C. Barker, "Land Speculation as a Cause of the Texas Revolution," *The Quarterly of the Texas State Historical Association* 10, no. 1 (July 1906): 76–95; Constitution of Texas, 1836, General Provisions, Section 10. "Constitution of Texas: 1834–1876," Tarlton Law Library—Jamail Center for Legal Research, https://tarlton.law.utexas.edu/constitutions/republic-texas-1836/general-provisions.

26. As another example of command confusion, Neill had been honorably discharged by Burleson on December 14, the day before he placed Johnson in

command of Béxar. Nonetheless, a week later Houston ordered Neill to take command. This was likely a case of orders crossing in transit as it took six days for communications to travel between San Antonio and Houston's headquarters in Washington. Houston could not have known of Johnson's appointment when he dispatched his order to Neill on December 21, and that order could not have reached Neill before December 27. By then Johnson was preparing to leave for San Felipe to secure command of the Matamoros expedition and the issue was moot. Burleson discharge of Neill, December 14, 1835; Houston to Neill, December 21, 1835, both quoted in Chariton, *100 Days in Texas*, 36, 54–55.

27. Smith to Houston, December 17, 1835; Houston to Bowie, Dec. 17, 1835; Houston to Neill, December 21, 1835; F. W. Johnson to Wyatt Hanks and J. D. Clements, December 24, 1835; Johnson to General Council, January 3, 1836 and February 3, 1836; William R. Carey to his brother and sister, January 12, 1836, all quoted in Chariton *100 Days in Texas*, 42–43, 54–55, 61–62, 100–01, 134–38, 206–07; Reid, *The Secret War for Texas*, 67–88; Davis, *Lone Star Rising*, 186–95; Davis, *Three Roads to the Alamo*, 496; Winders, *Sacrificed at the Alamo*, 78–81, 88–93; Roell, "Matamoros Expedition of 1835–36." The Alamo and San Antonio were established as the Mission San Antonio de Valero in 1718, where Spain established the Presidio San Antonio de Béxar and the town, called La Villa de Béxar, which lay west of the fort. The fort, which came to be called the Alamo, had fallen into near ruin by the time of the Texian uprising. For a complete history of the Alamo see George Nelson, *The Alamo: An Illustrated History* (Uvalde, TX: Aldine Press, third revised edition, 2009).

28. Wallace O. Chariton, *Exploring the Alamo Legends* (Plano, TX: Republic of Texas Press, 1992), 107–115. Chariton argues persuasively that some letters from Neill have been lost, including one from around January 1 to Houston reporting the actions of Grant and Johnson, how devastated the Béxar garrison was, and blaming some members of the council by name. It may have been this letter that so incensed Smith that he berated the council in the harshest terms and attempted to disband it on January 10. Smith message to council, January 10, 1836, and declaration of the council and resolutions, January 11, 1836; Council resolution January 17, 1836; Smith to L. W. Groce, January 18, 1836; Horatio A. Alsbury to Houston, December 30, 1835, all quoted in Chariton, *100 Days in Texas*, 78, 121–23, 126–28, 153, 158–59.

29. Houston to Smith, January 17 and January 30, 1836, quoted in Chariton, *100 Days in Texas*, 152–53, 180–83; Davis, *Lone Star Rising*, 191; Winders, *Sacrificed at the Alamo*, 92–93.

30. Johnson to General Council, January 3, 1836; Houston to Smith, January 17, 1836; Neill to governor and council, January 23, 1836; Houston to James Collinsworth, March 13, 1836; Fannin to acting Governor Robinson, February 4, 1836, all quoted in Chariton, *100 Days in Texas*, 100–01, 210–11, 364; Houston to Fannin, March 11, 1836; Houston to Henry Raguet, March 13, 1836; Houston to Collinsworth, March 15, 1836, all quoted in Todd Hansen, ed., *The Alamo Reader: A Study in History* (Mechanicsburg, PA: Stackpole Books, 2003), 512–14, 517–20,

656–59. Despite the conditional wording in Houston's January 17 report to Smith, a week after the Alamo's fall Houston claimed that he had "directed, on the 16th of January last, that the artillery should be removed, and the Alamo blown up; but it was prevented by the expedition upon Matamoros, the author of all our misfortunes." Houston's blaming the Matamoros expedition was a reference to Johnson and Grant removing all of the dray animals that could have hauled away the Alamo cannons, which were considered too valuable to abandon. Although Houston may have overstated his orders to Bowie, he clearly favored abandoning Béxar. It is also worth noting that, after learning of the Alamo's fall, he ordered Fannin to abandon and blow up Goliad "to prevent all future murders where our men have no alternative but to starve in forts, or remain inactive, and useless to the defence (*sic*) of the country. With our force, we can not fight the enemy ten to one in their own country--where they have every advantage." Winders, *Sacrificed at the Alamo*, 93–94, suggests that Houston was merely facing reality in advising that Béxar be abandoned.

31. Jameson to Houston, January 18, 1836, quoted in Hansen, *Alamo Reader*, 570–72.

32. Neill to Houston, January 1 and January 14, 1836; Neill to governor and council, January 6, 1836, January 14, 1836, January 23, 1836, and January 28, 1836; Neill to Smith, January 27, 1836; Pollard to Smith, January 16, 1836, all quoted in Hansen, *Alamo Reader*, 647–55, 657–59, 662–66; Lack, *The Texas Revolutionary Experience*, 54; Winders, *Sacrificed at the Alamo*, 89; John Bryant, "Alamo Cannon," *Alamo de Parras/Sons of Dewitt Colony*, http://www.sonsofdewittcolony.org/adp/ history/1836/the_battle/the_weapons/cannon.html.

33. Smith to Houston, January 29, 1836, quoted in Chariton *100 Days in Texas*, 178; Stephen Hardin, *Texian Iliad: A Military History of the Texas Revolution, 1835–1836* (Austin: University of Texas Press, 1994), 109–11; see Reid, *The Secret War for Texas*, 102–08 for a discussion of Houston's efforts in Refugio. Also see "Sam Houston's Speechwriters" in James E. Crisp, *Sleuthing the Alamo: Davy Crockett's Last Stand and Other Mysteries of the Texas Revolution* (New York: Oxford University Press, 2005), 27–60. Crisp discusses a bogus version of Houston's speech to soldiers that included racist anti-Mexican language that was inconsistent with other of Houston's words and deeds and was fabricated by Herman Ehrenberg in the German-language edition of his book *With Milam and Fannin: Adventures of a German Boy in Texas' Revolution*, trans. Charlotte Churchill (Dallas: Tardy Publishing Co., 1935), 154-55, quoted in Hansen, *Alamo Reader*, 611-12.

34. Hardin, *Texian Iliad*, 158–159; Davis, *Lone Star Rising*, 194–96; Winders, *Sacrificed at the Alamo*, 145–147. J. W. Robinson to James Tarlton, B. C. Wallace, and T. H. McIntire, January 30, 1836; Advisory committee to J. W. Robinson, February 15, 1836, both quoted in Chariton, *100 Days in Texas*, 237. On March 3, Urrea reported that forty-two Texians were killed outright, including Grant, and that two of five who took flight also were killed. See Hansen, *Alamo Reader*, 367.

35. Houston to Smith, January 30, 1836, quoted in Hansen, *Alamo Reader*, 666-67; Davis, *Lone Star Rising*, 205; Lack, *The Texas Revolutionary Experience*,

111, 215.

36. Bowie to Smith, February 2, 1836, quoted in Chariton, *100 Days in Texas*, 203–04; Davis, *Three Roads to the Alamo*, 494–96; Davis, *Lone Star Rising*, 194–96; Hardin, *Texian Iliad*, 111, 117.

37. Travis to Smith, January 28, 1836, quoted in Hansen, *Alamo Reader*, 17–18; Travis to Smith, December 3, 1835, quoted in Barker, "The Texan Revolutionary Army," 250; Davis, *Three Roads to the Alamo*, 503–14; Winders, *Sacrificed at the Alamo*, 77, 96–97.

38. Lack, *The Texas Revolutionary Experience*, 54–56, 73–74, 114–23.

39. Travis to Smith, January 29, 1836, quoted in Hansen, *Alamo Reader*, 18–19; Davis, *Three Roads to the Alamo*, 513 and footnote 43, 717. Davis offers interesting conjecture on Travis's movements in the days prior to his arrival in Béxar and his reason for changing his mind about resigning his commission. He may have become aware of the recent intelligence locating Santa Anna on the Rio Grande with thousands of troops poised to advance on San Antonio. Davis suggests that Travis and Neill saw a need for Travis's cavalry to spy on Santa Anna and disrupt his supply lines. Travis's arrival in San Antonio on February 3 is documented in his notebook entry regarding payment for corn and wood in San Antonio on that day; Chariton, *100 Days in Texas*, 206.

Chapter 3

1. For example, Houston's appeal of October 5, 1835, was reprinted in the *New Orleans Bee Extra* on October 13, taken from a *Red River Herald Extra*; Travis to J. W. Moore, August 31, 1835, quoted in Davis, *Lone Star Rising*, 133.

2. Atlas Jones to Calvin Jones, November 13, 1835, and Calvin Jones to Edmond D. Jarvis, December 2, 1835, Calvin Jones Papers, 921, Southern Historical Collection, Manuscript Department, Wilson Library, The University of North Carolina at Chapel Hill; Julian A. Smith, "Halley's Comet: Canadian Observations and Reactions, 1835–36 and 1910," *The Journal of the Royal Astronomical Society of Canada*, vol. 80, no. 1, whole no. 598 (February 1986): 2; Robert Patton Crockett to Smith Rudd, June 15, 1880, Rudd Manuscripts, Lilly Library, Manuscripts Department, Indiana University, Bloomington; Manley F. Cobia, Jr., *Journey into the Land of Trials: The Story of Davy Crockett's Expedition to the Alamo* (Franklin, TN: Hillsboro Press, 2003), 28; Davis, *Three Roads to the Alamo*, 409. Abner Burgin was married to Elizabeth Patton Crockett's sister, Margaret Ann (Patton) Burgin; Lindsey Kavender Tinkle was married to Elizabeth's niece, Rebecca Catherine McWhorter, the daughter of Elizabeth's sister, Ann Catherine (Patton) McWhorter; William Patton was Elizabeth's nephew, son of her late brother, James Patton of Mississippi. I am grateful to Gert Petersen for providing genealogical information on the Patton and Crockett families.

3. James D. Davis, *The History of the City of Memphis*, (Memphis: Hite, Crumpton & Kelly, 1873), 143. There are no contemporaneous newspaper reports of raucous behavior by Crockett's party, and Davis admitted that he was not a witness "to the big bender that occurred the night before the Colonel left." He said that he got the story secondhand from William T. Avery many years after Crockett's visit

and confessed that he embellished whatever Avery told him, admitting that he made "some additions to his [Avery's] admirable story, in reference to Col. David Crockett's last visit to Memphis." Both Davis and Avery were sixteen years old at the time, Davis's book was published nearly forty years later, and Davis notes that Avery was over fifty years old when he related the story to him. Avery did not move to Memphis until 1840, where he opened a law practice. He later won election to the Tennessee legislature and served two terms in Congress. See Avery entry in *Biographical Directory of the United States Congress* online, https://bioguideretro .congress.gov/Home/MemberDetails?memIndex=A000347. Unidentified letter dated December 7, 1835, describing Crockett's visit to Memphis, published in the Newburyport Herald, MA, January 22, 1836, titled "Correspondence of the New-buryport Herald; Memphis Dec. 7, 1835." Another story in the same newspaper describes a group that planned to invest $50,000 in the manufacturing of silk goods. After scouting locations for their proposed enterprise, they were sure they were right in undertaking the endeavor and "have adopted the motto of David Crockett—'Go Ahead.'"

4. Davis, *History of the City of Memphis*, 143. Davis may have lifted the speech from news reports of Crockett's later visit to Nacogdoches, where he gave a speech nearly identical to the one quoted by Davis. *Arkansas Gazette*, May 10, 1836; Cobia, *Journey*, 15, citing *Sunday Express* article in David Crockett file at the Daughters of the Republic of Texas (DRT) Library, San Antonio.

5. Davis, *History of the City of Memphis*, 139–40; Cobia, *Journey*, 36. See Davis, *Three Roads to the Alamo*, 693, footnote 83, for evidence that Crockett crossed by ferry, rather than boarding a steamboat down the Mississippi as many accounts claim. Also, Crockett had purchased a horse for his nephew William Patton and clearly planned to go overland by horseback. Crockett's son Robert later stated emphatically that his father left home on a large bay horse that was returned to his mother after Crockett's death. Robert Patton Crockett to Smith Rudd, June 15, 1880, Rudd Manuscripts, Lilly Library, Manuscripts Department, Indiana University, Bloomington; *Arkansas Gazette*, November 17, 1835.

6. William F. Pope, *Early Days in Arkansas* (Little Rock, Ark.: Frederick W. Allsopp, Publisher, 1895), 183–85; S. Charles Bolton, "Like a Bridge Finished to the Middle of a Stream: The Memphis Road and Internal Improvements in Antebellum Arkansas," *The Arkansas Historical Quarterly* 78, no. 4 (2019), 339–64; "Memphis to Little Rock Road," *Encyclopedia of Arkansas*, accessed May 2, 2020, https:// encyclopediaofarkansas.net/entries/memphis-to-little-rock-road-7503.

7. *Arkansas Advocate*, November 13, 1835, reprinted in *Baltimore Gazette and Daily Advertiser*, December 3, 1835; *Arkansas Gazette*, August 25, 1835, and November 17, 1835.

8. *Arkansas Advocate*, November 20, 1835.

9. Reprinted in the *New York Sun*, January 12, 1836, quoted in Gary Zaboly, *An Altar for Their Sons: The Alamo and the Texas Revolution in Contemporary Newspaper Accounts* (Buffalo Gap, TX: State House Press, 2011), 113.

10. Pope, *Early Days in Arkansas*, 185; Benjamin Perley Poore, *Perley's Remi-niscences of Sixty Years in the National Metropolis*, vol. 1 (Philadelphia: Hubbard Brothers, 1886), 152.

11. *New York Sunday Morning News*, December 6, 1835, quoted in Zaboly, *An Altar for Their Sons*, 110.

12. *Public Ledger*, Philadelphia, Pennsylvania, April 5, 1836.

13. *Boston Traveler*, February 5, 1836; *New York Sun*, January 29, 1836; *Albany Journal*, December 11, 1835; Cobia *Journey*, 54; "The Reverend Z. N. Morrell," Sons of Dewitt Colony, http://www.sonsofdewittcolony.org/morrellzn.htm.

14. *Arkansas Times and Advocate*, November 2, 1835; *Arkansas Advocate*, July 10, 1835; *Arkansas Gazette*, August 14, November 13, and November 17, 1835; Samuel P. Carson to John Branch, September 8, 1835, Tennessee State Library and Archives, Miscellaneous Collection, Box 2, C-25; Cobia, *Journey*, 53.

15. *Arkansas Gazette*, November 17, 1835.

16. Louis Kemp, *The Signers of the Texas Declaration of Independence* (Salado, Texas: Anson Jones, 1944), 48–49, 57–59; B. R. Brunson, "Swartwout, Samuel," Handbook of Texas Online, accessed May 23, 2021, https://www.tshaonline.org/handbook/entries/swartwout-samuel; Margaret S. Henson, "New Washington Association," Handbook of Texas Online, accessed May 23, 2021, https://www.tshaonline.org/handbook/entries/new-washington-association. Throughout his memoir, William Fairfax Gray refers to land transactions continuing even during the moratorium. Gray, *From Virginia to Texas*, 125–7.

17. A more frequently proposed route for Crockett suggests he took the military road from Washington, Arkansas, crossed the Red River near Fulton, Arkansas, then traveled to Fort Towson in the Indian Territory (now Oklahoma), which was about 110 miles, and Crockett could have made it in four days. From there, he would have t ten or fifteen miles south to Jonesboro and taken a ferry across the Red River, as many new arrivals did at the time. In this scenario he would have arrived in the Clarksville area by November 26. In his 1937 memoir, Judge Pat B. Clark has Crockett taking this route. However, Clark relied on recollections of conversations with his grandmother Isabella Clark and others decades after they took place and he clearly erred in some of what he wrote. It is more likely Crockett took the Dooley's Ferry route on his way into Texas, just as Featherstonhaugh had, and having already crossed the Red River there, he had no reason to go to Fort Towson or Jonesboro. However, some accounts suggest he arrived at Jones's plantation weeks later, after exploring the Red River country and while on his way to Nacogdoches. But such a detour for Crockett at that late stage of his journey makes little sense and would have taken him at least ninety miles and three or four days out of his way. Moreover, he had no reason to travel all the way to Lost Prairie at that point, having decided to go to Nacogdoches. However, he might well have had good reason to visit the plantations in the Lost Prairie area as he made his way into Texas, including Isaac Jones's place. Descriptions of the land there agree that the soil was very rich and ideal for the production of cotton. Travelers came to Dooley's Ferry and crossed the Red River there to reach the area. Another theory has Crockett escorting his traveling companions Burgin and Tinkle back as far as Lost Prairie on their way home to Tennessee, but those men had come to Texas with Crockett and would have had no trouble finding their way home by the same route they followed going in. This theory also has them crossing near Fulton

on their way in, thus it is fair to ask why they would not go home the same way. Why go via Lost Prairie, which was out of the way and, according to this scenario, an unfamiliar route? Perhaps Crockett accompanied them as far as Trammel's Trace and then headed south to Nacogdoches while his friends continued back to Tennessee. Isaac N. Jones to Mrs. David Crockett, 1836, Calvin M. McClung Historical Collection, East Tennessee History Center, Knoxville, TN, MM.1981.133; Pat B. Clark, *The History of Clarksville and Old Red River County, Texas* (Dallas: Mathis, Van Nort and Company, 1937), 4; Rex Wallace Strickland, "History of Fannin County, Texas, 1836–1843," *Southwestern Historical Quarterly* 33, no. 4, 262–98; Stephen L. Hardin, "History Davy Crockett," unpublished transcript of Pat B. Clark's two-page handwritten account of Crockett's itinerary dated May 21, 1910, from author's collection; Robin Cole-Jett, *The Red River Valley in Arkansas* (Charleston, SC: The History Press, 2014), 29–34, 49–59; Rick Tice, "Dooley Ferry–historic transit passageway," *Texas Gazette*, May 2, 1976; Texas Republic Claim no. 91, reel 15, TSLAC; Kemp, *Signers of the Texas Declaration*, 48–49; Joe E. Ericson, "Carson, Samuel Price," Handbook of Texas Online, accessed June 20, 2021, https://www.tshaonline.org/handbook/entries/carson-samuel-price. Cobia, *Journey*, 59–60, suggests four possible places where Crockett might have crossed the Red River. Among other things, the 1819 Adams-Onis Treaty established the international border between the United States and Spain along the Sabine River. After Mexico won independence from Spain, the Treaty of Limits recognized the border as defined in the Adams-Onis Treaty. The Treaty of Amity, Settlement, and Limits Between the United States of America and His Catholic Majesty, 1819 (aka the Adams-Onis Treaty), concluded February 22, 1819, ratified February 22, 1821, Lillian Goldman Law Library, Yale Law School, The Avalon Project, https://avalon .law.yale.edu/19th_century/sp1819.asp; Treaty of Limits Between the United States of America and the United Mexican States, signed at Mexico January 12, 1828; additional article signed at Mexico April 5, 1831, Library of Congress, https://www .loc.gov/law/help/us-treaties/bevans/b-mx-ust000009–0760.pdf).

18. Micajah Autry mentioned the high costs of staying at hostelries on his own journey saying he feared the outbreak of smallpox in Natchitoches, Louisiana, less than "the Tavern bill. . . . Such charges never were heard of." Crockett made similar complaints about inns along the route to Washington City during his years in Congress. Micajah Autry to Martha Autry, December 13, 1835, holograph on Rice University, Fondren Library, Woodsen Research Center Special Collections and Archives, https://hdl.handle.net/1911/76038. Isaac N. Jones to Mrs. David Crockett, 1836, MM.1981.133, Calvin M. McClung Historical Collection, East Tennessee History Center, Knoxville, TN. The thirty dollars that Jones paid Crockett for his watch is equal to $956 in 2022 dollars.

19. Crockett would have covered an average of twenty-five to thirty miles per day on horseback, allowing for weather, road conditions, rest periods, days on which he did not travel, and the uncertainty of his exact route for major parts of his journey. Throughout December Crockett explored the area near present-day Bonham, Texas, perhaps as far west as Sherman or Whitewright, about ten to twenty-five miles west of Bonham. By the end of his exploration and hunting trip,

Crockett had decided to remain in Texas and enlist in the army in Nacogdoches, so his route would have taken him there as directly as possible, or via Trammel's Trace. He would have picked up this well-known route, perhaps somewhere around present-day Maud, Texas, which is about 130 miles from Bonham, or about four days ride, a route that may have taken him through present-day Paris, Texas. It was about forty-five miles further east from Maud to Lost Prairie, which would have added at least three or four travel days to Crockett's trip, plus the day or two that he spent with Isaac Jones. There was no apparent reason for Crockett to visit Lost Prairie or go so far out of his way at that point in his journey and the route makes no sense. It is more likely Crockett traveled no further east than Trammel's Trace and took that road south to Nacogdoches. Confusion over the date of Crockett's visit to Lost Prairie lies in Isaac Jones's letter to Elizabeth Crockett in which he only says that Crockett's visit occurred "last winter" but admits he cannot recall the exact date. That has led historians to conclude that Crockett's visit occurred in the latter part of December, but given that it was an unusually mild winter in that part of Arkansas, it is possible that Jones remembered late November as "last winter." The winter was so mild that peach trees were in bloom in January. When George William Featherstonhaugh visited Isaac Jones's plantation a year earlier he observed that, "even as late as December 11, the temperature stood at 74° on a cloudless day." I am indebted to Melissa Nesbitt, archival manager at the Southwest Arkansas Regional Archives in Washington, Arkansas, for her assistance in locating Lost Prairie near the current New Zion Baptist Church, about two hundred yards west of First Old River Lake. Dooley's Ferry was located on the Red River between Lower Red Lake and Clear Lake. It is about three miles from the site of Dooley's Ferry to New Zion Baptist Church. Isaac N. Jones's plantation was west of there and was one of several large plantations in the area, including the Finn, Hervey, and Fowlkes, and the Pryor plantations. See "Lost Prairie (Miller County)," Encyclopedia of Arkansas, https://encyclopediaofarkansas.net/entries/lost-prairie-miller-county-13833/. *Monthly Weather Review*, Volume 48 (Washington, DC: US Department of Agriculture, Government Printing Office,1920), 449; Featherstonhaugh, *Excursion*, 183–88; "Dooley's Ferry," Arkansas Archeological Survey at Southern Arkansas University, https://web.saumag.edu/aas/research/dooleys-ferry/; Cole-Jett, *Red River Valley*, 49–59; Gary L. Pinkerton, *Trammel's Trace: The First Road to Texas from the North* (College Station: Texas A&M University Press, 2016), 154, 174.

20. Featherstonhaugh, *Excursion*, 188–189.

21. Mexico vacillated on the abolition of slavery throughout the period. On September 15, 1829, President Vicente Guerrero declared an end to slavery throughout Mexico, a measure strongly opposed in Texas, which was exempted from the declaration three months later. Among other things, the Law of April 6, 1830, prohibited importation of new slaves into Mexico, a measure clearly aimed at Texas, the only place in Mexico where slavery was a major economic factor. In April 1832, a new colonization law closed the "indentured servant" loophole and limited such agreements to ten years, ending the only remaining legal means of permanently importing slaves into Mexico. However, it was not until April 1837 that Mexico finally adopted a law abolishing slavery. Featherstonhaugh, *Excursion*, 188–189;

Dena White, "Slavery in Hempstead County, Arkansas" (Honors Thesis: Ouchita Baptist University, 1984), https://scholarlycommons.obu.edu/honors_theses/188. Torget, *Seeds of Empire*, 137–79; Campbell, *An Empire for Slavery*, 10–49; Lack, *The Texas Revolutionary Experience*, 238–54; Randolph B. "Mike" Campbell, "Slavery," Handbook of Texas Online, accessed August 28, 2022, https://www.tshaonline .org/handbook/entries/slavery; Burrough, Tomlinson, and Stanford, *Forget the Alamo*, which attempts to make a case for slavery being the primary cause of the Texas Revolution. For Crockett's sale of the slave girl Adeline, see *Weakley County Deed Book B*, microfilm roll 58, Vol. B, 151, TSLA; Crockett to James Blackburn, February 5, 1828, and Crockett to George Patton, January 27, 1829, both quoted in Boylston & Wiener, *David Crockett in Congress*, 151, 162; Crockett, *Narrative*, 144–5, 161, 179, 207; French, *Sketches*, 115–16; Boylston, "Sketches Re-Examined." The $300 Crockett was paid for Adeline equals $10,216 in 2022 dollars. For some examples of Crockett's views on slavery and race, see Boylston and Wiener, *David Crockett in Congress*, 13, 16, 20–21, 40, 84, 100, 152, 162, 203, 211, 214, 262.

22. Larry Mahon Beachum, "Becknell, William," Handbook of Texas Online, accessed May 25, 2020, http://www.tshaonline.org/handbook/online/articles/fbe17; Christopher Long, "Stiles, John," Handbook of Texas Online, accessed May 25, 2020, http://www.tshaonline.org/handbook/online/articles/fstbh; Clark, *The History of Clarksville*, 179.

23. Choctaw Creek extends from southwest of Sherman, Texas, and runs northeast for thirty-eight miles to its mouth on the Red River. Bois d'Arc Creek rises two miles northwest of Whitewright in southeastern Grayson County, runs northeast across Fannin County, and eventually forms a boundary between Fannin and Lamar counties before its confluence with the Red River. There is much local oral history regarding Crockett's travel through the region, some of it more credible than others. There is practically no documentation that tracks this part of Crockett's journey with the reliability of the newspaper reports that confirm his location as far as Little Rock. Many places in Texas have claimed that Crockett passed their way, but in most cases, we have only oral tradition, word of mouth, and legend to guide us, some of it recorded decades after the fact. The town of DeKalb claims that Crockett not only passed through there but gave the place its name. Thomas Henry Skidmore, not quite thirteen at the time, is said to have met Crockett as a boy and vowed to follow him to Texas. Arriving too late at their proposed meeting point, Skidmore followed the Colonel's trail into Texas, never found him, but settled in the Red River country. The least credible yarn comes from James Nichols who claimed to have met Crockett as a teen when the Colonel visited his family in an unidentified part of Arkansas and that Crockett was childhood friends with Nichols' father. Par for the course as these stories go, but Nichols goes overboard when he claims to have seen Crockett's rifle, shot pouch, and coonskin cap in San Antonio in December 1836. He recognized the rifle, of course, from having seen it during Crockett's Arkansas visit. Someone bought the artifacts but both he and the artifacts perished when the boat he sailed home on burned, killing all aboard. Another yarn has Crockett nearly being lynched for stealing horses on his way to Nacogdoches. He is saved at the last minute by Elijah Gossett, an old friend from

Tennessee. A milder version of the tale has Crockett merely visiting his old Tennessee friend, who later named the local town in Crockett's honor. Some of these legends conflicted with one another. When a 1931 *Dallas News* story claimed that Crockett never came within eighty miles of Paris, Texas, Carolyn S. Scott attempted to rebut it. The *Dallas News* story apparently relied heavily on the fictional *Col. Crockett's Exploits and Adventures in Texas*, concocted by Richard Penn Smith. But Scott's reply to it relied on Pat B. Clark's account and conflated stories that had Crockett roaming near Clarksville while "recruiting soldiers to send to Colonel Travis at Bexar," but also finding time to go on a bear hunt with Stiles, Becknell, and Stout, which according to Scott, took them through Paris, where they camped under a grove of oaks, Crockett taking time to carve his name into one of the trees. Scott adds another dodgy tale of Crockett in Texas that had the Colonel staying at the home of John Click where he constructed a contraption known as a "lizard" or "spider," which was used in hauling water. It was kept in the Paris courthouse until it was consumed by fire in 1871. Crockett then allegedly roamed far and wide looking for a trail to San Antonio, crossing Bois d'Arc Creek and Choctaw Bayou along the way, eventually making his way back to Clarksville "where the recruits were waiting for him." The story loses what credibility it has by claiming Crockett returned to Fulton, Arkansas, hopped a steamboat to Natchitoches, Louisiana, and then went on to Nacogdoches. All that can be concluded from this tale is that Crockett may have passed through present-day Paris. Crockett is also alleged to have had a broken rifle repaired in Bastrop by a gunsmith named John Berry. It is unlikely Berry would not have charged Crockett for his work, but no payment voucher to Berry exists, and by the time he reached Bastrop, Crockett and other volunteers were paying for everything from lodging to provisions with such vouchers. Andy Thomas is said to have traded rifles with Crockett somewhere north of Honey Grove, possibly near Kentucky Town. According to the story, Crockett wanted to trade his heavier rifle for a lighter one. The rifle swap may have taken place on what is now Lindsey Creek, near present-day Whitewright, which did lie on Crockett's trail. Thomas lived in Kentucky Town, which is only a few miles west of Whitewright, so this story is plausible. Zenos N. (Z. N.) Morrell claimed that he had a date with Crockett to meet at the Falls of the Brazos on Christmas Day for a bear hunt, but Crockett never showed up. By then, Crockett was making ready to leave for Nacogdoches from the Clarksville area, some 250 miles from today's Falls of the Brazos historical marker. Crockett may have made the date with Morrell but canceled it after deciding to move on to Nacogdoches. I am grateful to Ronnie Atnip for identifying and mapping Crockett locations in the Red River country. "Choctaw Creek," Handbook of Texas Online, accessed May 27, 2020, http://www.tshaonline.org/handbook/online/articles/rbcdx; Donna J. Kumler, "Bois D'arc Creek (Grayson County)," Handbook of Texas Online, accessed May 27, 2020, http://www.tshaonline.org/handbook/online/articles/rhb25; "Blackland Prairie," Partners for Conservation, https://www.partnersforconservation .org/ our-landscapes/blackland-prairie-texas/; "Texas Ecoregions," Texas Parks & Wildlife, https://tpwd.texas.gov/education/hunter-education/online-course/wildlife -conservation/texas-ecoregions; "Blackland Prairie Guerilal Droppings," Seed-Balls.

com, https://shop.seed-balls.com/products/blackland-prairie-guerrilla-droppings; Bill Cannon, *Texas: Land of Legend and Lore* (Dallas: Republic of Texas Press, 2004), 52; Cobia, *Journey*, 57, citing James W. Nichols, "Adventures of an Old Texas Ranger," *The Texas Monthly*, Dec. 1891, 73, 136–137; Zenos N. Morrell, *Flowers and Fruits in the Wilderness—Or, Forty-Six Years in Texas and Two Winters in Honduras* (Commercial Printing Co., 1882; Amazon Kindle edition, August 24, 2016), 468; Sue Flanagan, "Davy Crockett: Man & Myth," *Alcalde: The University of Texas Alumni Magazine*, March 1966, vol. LIV, no. VII, 8–11; *Daughters of the Republic of Texas: Patriot Ancestor Album Vol. II* (Paducah, KY: Turner Publishing Co., 2001), 112; *Honey Grove Signal-Citizen,* March 20, 1931.

24. Clark, *History of Clarksville*, 12; *Alexandria Gazette*, February 12, 1836; Edward Warren to his uncle, January 1, 1836, in John H. Jenkins, ed., *The General's Tight Pants: Edward Warren's Texas Tour of 1836* (Austin, TX: The Pemberton Press, 1976), unpaginated.

25. *The New Hampshire Gazette*, February 23, 1836; *The New-Bedford Mercury*, February 26, 1836; *The New York Journal of Commerce*, reprinted in *The Pennsylvanian*, March 24, 1836; *Boston Traveler/American Traveler*, February 23, 1836; *Bangor Advertiser*, March 19, 1836, quoted in Zaboly, *An Altar for Their Sons*, 114.

26. "Mrs. Ibbie Gordon––A Remarkable Lady, One of the Mothers of Texas," *Dallas Morning News*, January 6, 1894. The former Mrs. Clark was married to Dr. George Gordon at the time of the interview. Clark, *History of Clarksville*, 10–13. James Clark is said to have run into Crockett at the headwaters of the Trinity River, where he heard the story of a woman warning Crockett about danger from Comanche. "That was my wife," he is said to have replied, "for no other woman would do a thing like that." The story comes from Claude V. Hall, who said he heard it from Judge Pat B. Clark. Although he describes the headwaters as lying near present-day Dallas, they are nearer to Gainesville, about seventy miles from Dallas and 125 miles from Clarksville, so James Clark would have gone quite far in his pursuit of the Comanche if he ever did set out on such a task. The correct spelling of Becknell's name may have been Becknill. "Company order from Captain Becknill," August 7, 1836, in the James Clark Family Papers, Dolph Briscoe Center for American History, The University of Texas at Austin.

27. Clark was well versed in local politics. He was elected to the lower house of the Arkansas Territory General Assembly in 1827 and 1829, and to the upper house in 1833. He was appointed postmaster for Miller County in 1830 and made a justice of the peace in 1831. He also established the town of Clarksville in 1833. In December 1835, he led a delegation from Pecan Point to the General Council in San Felipe. He arrived in Nacogdoches by December 23 and received a letter of introduction from Judge John Forbes to Lieutenant Governor Robinson before riding on to San Felipe. It was at least 160 miles from Clarksville to Nacogdoches, or about a five-day trip. He would have left Clarksville by December 17 or 18, which would have provided a window during which he could have met Crockett, but this casts doubt on the idea that he was running down Comanches at the time. The Bois D'Arc Creek and Choctaw Creek areas were indeed fertile with an average growing season of 228 days and abundant timber. The letter of introduction for

James Clark from Judge John J. Forbes to James Robinson, dated December 23, 1835, is in William C. Binkley, ed., *Official Correspondence of the Texan Revolution, Vol. 1, 1835–36*, 231–32; The James Clark Papers: 1827–1845, Dolph Briscoe Center for American History, The University of Texas at Austin; Jeff Dunn, "Clark, James," Handbook of Texas Online, accessed December 18, 2022, https://www.tshaonline.org/handbook/entries/clark-james; Shackford, *David Crockett*, 215 and footnote 8, 313; Cole-Jett, *Red River Valley*, 11–12; Kelly Pigott, "Fannin County," Handbook of Texas Online, accessed June 6, 2020, http://www.tshaonline.org/handbook/online/articles/hcf02; Donna J. Kumler, "Grayson County," Handbook of Texas Online, accessed June 6, 2020, http://www.tshaonline.org/handbook/online/articles/hcg09; Brian Hart, "Whitewright, TX," Handbook of Texas Online, accessed June 6, 2020, http://www.tshaonline.org/handbook/online/articles/HJW10.

28. Constitution of Texas, 1836, General Provisions, Section 10. "Constitution of Texas: 1834–1876," Tarlton Law Library—Jamail Center for Legal Research, https://tarlton.law.utexas.edu/constitutions/republic-texas-1836/general-provisions.

29. The ill-named Permanent Council, which met for only twenty-one days in October 1835, closed all land offices for the duration of hostilities. The decree was formalized by the Consultation in Article XIV of the Organic Law, adopted November 13, 1835. Eugene C. Barker, "Journal of the Permanent Council (October 11–27, 1835)," *The Quarterly of the Texas. State Historical Association* 7, no. 4 (April 1904), 251–52; Article XIV of the Organic Law, adopted by the provisional government November 13, 1835; "An Ordinance and Decree to organize and establish an Auxiliary Volunteer Corps to the Army of Texas and other purposes," adopted by the provisional government on December 5, 1835, in *Ordinances and Decrees of the Consultation*, 8–9, 47–50; the *Laws of Texas*, 1822–1897 Volume 1 page 895, "Proceedings of the Convention at Washington," 75; Lack, *Texas Revolutionary Experience*, 40–41; Davis, *Lone Star Rising*, 162–63.

30. Daniel Cloud to John B. Cloud, December 26, 1835, Micajah Autry to Martha Autry, January 13, 1836, both quoted in Chariton, *100 Days in Texas*, 71–74, 142–143; "Daniel Cloud's Letter," MyKindred.com website: https://mykindred.com/cloud/documents/DanielCloud.php; Davis, *Three Roads to the Alamo*, 420–432.

31. "The Heirs of Col. Davy Crockett," *Houma Ceres*, Houma, Terrebonne Parish, Louisiana, January 31, 1856, reprinted from the *Dallas Herald*; Tom Kailbourn provided a copy of the newspaper to the author.

32. Like many acts of the disorganized Texas government, there was no clear provision for volunteer terms of enlistment other than a reference to volunteers "who shall tender their services for a less time than during the war, agreeably to what [the governor or the commander-in-chief of the army] shall think the defence [*sic*] of the country and the good of the service may require." Volunteers were to get the same pay for the "less time" but no land bounty. An ordinance passed on December 11, 1835, added 640 acres to the heirs of anyone killed in battle or who died while in honorable service, which was among the land that ultimately went to Crockett's heirs. One labor is 177.14 acres; one league is 4,428.50 acres, or 25 labors; a league and a labor is 4,605.64 acres or 26 labors. In their letters home

Crockett and Autry misestimated the acreage, but they were close to the one league number, which is all they may have been aware of. Crockett was off by only ten acres, telling his family that he stood to gain 4,438 acres; Autry said it was 4,444. This accounts for much of the land that Crockett's heirs later received for his service and death at the Alamo. Later Texas laws added additional bounties to heirs of those killed during the war. Crockett's Texas land certificate no. 125 entitled his heirs to a league and labor under a law passed on February 9, 1850. They did not receive the league and labor they would have under the colonization laws because Crockett did not survive to move his family to Texas, but the 1850 law granted that amount of land to heirs. Texas Government Land Office, certificate 125, March 13, 1852; "An Ordinance and Decree to organize and establish an Auxiliary Volunteer Corps to the Army of Texas, and other purposes," Section 7; adopted December 5, 1835. In The *Laws of Texas*, 1822–1897 Volume 1, page 895, "Proceedings of the Convention at Washington," the government stipulated that grants to heirs of soldiers killed in the Texas war for independence were to receive the same amount of land "which would have been due the deceased under the colonization laws, as established by the laws of the land had he survived, and that is to say, one league and labor (_______ acres) for a man of family and one-third of a league (_______ acres) for a single man." "Proceedings to the Convention at Washington," Portal of Texas History, https://texashistory.unt.edu/ark:/67531/metapth5872/m1/903 /zoom/?q=League&resolution=3&lat=2952&lon=600.

The Tornel Decree was named for the Mexican Minister of War, José María Tornel y Mendivil, who issued it. The decree reads in part, "Foreigners landing on the coast of the republic or invading its territory by land, armed with the intention of attacking our country, will be deemed pirates and dealt with as such, being citizens of no nation presently at war with the republic, and fighting under no recognized flag." Chariton, *100 Days in Texas*, 79–80.

Chapter 4

1. Millard served as a recruiting officer in Nacogdoches for a time and later fought at San Jacinto. Gray, *From Virginia to Texas*, 89–92; Judith Linsley and Ellen Rienstra, "Millard Henry," Handbook of Texas Online, accessed June 02, 2020, http://www.tshaonline.org/handbook/online/articles/fmi10.

2. Houston to Smith, January 17 and January 30, 1836, quoted in Chariton, *100 Days in Texas*, 152–53, 180–83; Reid, *Secret War for Texas*, 71–72. Apparently, the belief that Anglo Texian forces could defeat larger numbers of Mexicans was fairly common, doubtless fueled by early Texian military success, especially their victory at Béxar. Edward Warren, who had traveled with Houston during the first week of January 1836, wrote his uncle in Maine that Mexico's army "can be repelled by a force of one tenth their [Texian] number, so superior are the Texians or Americans to them in arms." Edward Warren to his uncle, February 1, 1836, in Jenkins, *The General's Tight Pants*.

3. *Niles' Weekly Register*, April 9, 1836, taken from the *Louisville Journal*; H. [Henderson K.] Yoakum, *History of Texas from Its First Settlement in 1685 to Its*

Annexation to the United States in 1846, Vol I (New York: Redfield, 1855; facsimile edition by Steck-Vaughn Company, Austin), 70. Yoakum cites the January 16, 1836, issue of *Emigrant's Guide.*

4. Micajah Autry to Martha Autry, January 13, 1836, quoted in Chariton, *100 Days in Texas*, 142–43; Adéle B. Looscan, "Micajah Autry, A Soldier of the Alamo," *The Quarterly of the Texas State Historical Association* 14, no. 4, 319–320.

5. See Appendix 2 for an analysis of Crockett's enlistment date.

6. Crockett to Margaret and Wiley Flowers, January 9, 1836. Doubts have been raised about the authenticity of this, his only letter written from Texas. No original holograph of the letter in Crockett's hand has ever been located, and the letter exists only in transcripts, versions handwritten by someone else, or photocopies of those versions. The earliest mention of a personal Crockett letter from Texas that might be related to the Flowers letter was recorded in an unidentified 1882 newspaper interview with Crockett's daughter Matilda Fields. She mentioned that a letter brought the unwelcome news that Crockett had joined the army, which is mentioned in the Flowers letter. The first transcript of the Flowers letter was published in the *Dallas Morning News* on June 1, 1913, which quoted the letter in full. The article stated the letter was transcribed from a copy owned by Martha M. Parks of Granbury, Texas. Constance Rourke quoted the same letter in her 1934 book, *Davy Crockett*, and identified the owner as Mrs. T. M. Hiner of Granbury, Texas. Crockett biographer James Shackford contacted Mrs. Hiner but was informed that she had never owned the original of the letter, only a transcript copy. Mrs. Hiner and Mrs. Parks were both granddaughters of Crockett's and both likely had copies of the same document. This letter includes spelling and punctuation corrections. This version is referred to as The Texas Letter, and its text and spelling is nearly the same as that contained in the handwritten letter that was nearly purchased by The Texas Historical Commission in 2007. The June 5, 1955, edition of the *Memphis Commercial Appeal* included a story about a handwritten copy of the Flowers letter and said the original was owned by J. D. Pate, a Crockett descendant from Martin, Tennessee. The article stated that the reverse of the letter was inscribed, "Memphis Feb. 3 Mr. Wiley Flowers, Crockett P. O. Gibson County, Tenn." It's not clear what the February 3 date refers to, but it may have been a postmark copied from the original letter. The *Commercial Appeal* quoted the letter in full, but the text differs from the letter quoted in the *Dallas Morning News* forty-two years earlier. The transcript published in the *Commercial Appeal*, however, is nearly identical to the text found in photocopies of a handwritten Flowers letter that is in collections at the University of Tennessee, Knoxville, the DRT Library at the Alamo, and the Tennessee State Library and Archives. This letter is seen in a photo that accompanied the article, which shows Louise Pate holding the letter, covered in protective clear plastic and housed in a black frame. Other photocopies of this letter appear to have been made from this one and were seen by Crockett biographers, including Shackford. The letter is not in Crockett's hand, but shows grammar, punctuation, and spelling errors more typical of Crockett's other letters, such as, "this is the first I have had an opertunity." This version is known as The Tennessee Letter.

On December 8, 2007, a handwritten letter purported to be the original Flowers letter was offered for sale to the Texas Historical Commission. The commission eventually declined to purchase the letter when Federal Forensic Associates, Inc., with whom it had contracted to analyze the document, was unable to confirm the letter's authenticity. This letter bears no physical resemblance to The Tennessee Letter, but the text is very similar to that of the letter printed in the 1913 *Dallas Morning News* article and shows the same spelling and other corrections found in that version. It could very well have been copied from that text and presented as an original, but the handwriting is not Crockett's, and the paper and forensic tests showed that the ink and paper dated from the mid- to late-twentieth century. It seems likely this letter is a clumsy attempt at forgery with text copied from the 1913 newspaper story. This letter can be called The Second Texas Letter, which is the subject of "What a Crockett!" by Gregory Curtis, published in the January 2008 edition of *Texas Monthly*.

Unlike the 2007 letter, it is doubtful the earlier versions were attempts at forgery. If they were, it is fair to ask why no one tried to sell the letter, since gain is the usual objective of a forger. There was no attempt to copy Crockett's handwriting in either version, as a forger would surely try to do, and it is unlikely that a forger would do such a sloppy job, clearly in someone else's handwriting, if they were trying to create a convincing forgery. Nor would a forger create two distinctly different versions of the letter if they sought to establish its authenticity. The alleged forger would also have to undertake considerable research to find some of the information in the letter, including the fact that Crockett's enlistment took place prior to January 9, especially given that his biographers have uniformly accepted the date as January 14; where he in Texas and details regarding the landscape; the idea that he would be a delegate to the 1836 Convention; and his suggestion that he was being sent to the Rio Grande. A forger is unlikely to have included the passing reference to his sons John and William. In the letter, Crockett says "I have not wrote to William but have requested John to direct him what to do." This may have been a reference to the unfinished business of settling the estate of Crockett's father-in-law, Robert Patton. Crockett had taken on this task but was unable to complete it before leaving for Texas. His son John Wesley Crockett was asked to finish the job.

Much that is in the letter is consistent with Crockett's movements and actions in Texas. He did explore the Red River country; he did enlist on January 8; and he was in San Augustine on January 9. Additionally, at least one person, James Gaines, wrote to Lieutenant Governor James W. Robinson on January 9 saying that Crockett was to represent San Augustine at the Convention of 1836, as Crockett's letter also suggests. The land bounties offered to enlistees that Crockett mentions are essentially correct. Also, Crockett did have reason to believe that he would be sent to the Rio Grande since preparations for the ill-fated Matamoros Expedition were still underway when he wrote the letter. Much of this could have been learned by a forger years later and used to craft a fake letter, but why would anyone forge such a letter unless they intended to sell it? Virtually all of Crockett's biographers and Texas historians have used the letter because the facts therein are substantially correct, and it contains much information that is verifiable elsewhere.

The tone and style of the letter differ from earlier Crockett letters. He is unusually descriptive and appears to be writing a sales pitch for his planned land business in the Red River country. However, Crockett may have intended to paint an attractive picture of what he hoped would be his family's new home and to play down the danger of his army enlistment, which he mentions only in passing. Most of his earlier letters deal with political or business issues, but this one describes the land he found in Texas and the promise of a brighter future that it offered. Crockett's optimism and the different subject matter could account for the apparent difference in writing style.

A reasonable explanation is that the letter was received by Margaret and Wiley Flowers in Tennessee and was immediately shared with Elizabeth and the rest of the family. Once they learned that Crockett had been killed, the letter took on greater significance for the family, and family members made one or more copies to keep. When Elizabeth and some of her children moved to Texas, they took a copy with them, which could have been copied again there. However, it is odd that the family went to the trouble of preserving copies but lost the original, and it is curious that the letter was not published in newspapers at the time. By contrast, a letter from Isaac Jones to Elizabeth Crockett, written shortly after Crockett's death, was published in full in the *Jackson Truth Teller* and printed in the *National Banner and Nashville Whig* on August 12, 1836. It is puzzling that so many Crockett letters were found and sold at auction for years prior to this letter's first appearance in 1913.

The Curtis article in *Texas Monthly* focuses on the 2007 letter and appears to conflate the Tennessee and Texas Letters, or Curtis was unaware of the two earlier letters. He also hasn't distinguished between the authenticity of the document itself and its contents. Curtis interviewed James R. Boylston, my co-author on *David Crockett in Congress*, at some length, and Mr. Boylston told him that he had researched the letter and examined all the copies, including the 2007 letter, and concluded that it was not in Crockett's handwriting and was likely a forgery. Mr. Boylston was the first to establish that neither letter is in Crockett's hand and that there is no proof that an original letter ever existed. However, he conceded that the existence of two versions of the letter suggests there was likely an original source for them, and Crockett's daughter Matilda confirms the family did receive such a letter. I am indebted to Jim Boylston for sharing his analysis of the letter with me.

The two surviving versions of Crockett's letter are quoted in Boylston and Wiener, *David Crockett in Congress*, 286–88. The headright referred to in the letter was actually 4,605.5 acres. Crockett's phonetic spelling of Bois d'Arc as "Bodark" is likely the pronunciation he heard used in the Red River country and refers to today's Bois d'Arc Creek. The Choctaw Bayou was in the vicinity of today's Choctaw Creek. Micajah Autry to Martha Autry, January 13, 1836, quoted in Chariton, *100 Days in Texas*, 142–43.

7. Interview with Matilda Fields, 1882, reprinted in Smith, *The Land Holdings of Colonel David Crockett in West Tennessee*, 96–98.

8. Crockett to Margaret and Wiley Flowers, January 9, 1836, quoted in Boylston and Wiener, *David Crockett in Congress*, 286–88. Crockett's reference to "being elected a member to form a Constitution for this province" has been misinterpreted to mean that he hoped to represent San Augustine at the upcoming convention, but he only referred to forming a constitution for the *province of*

Texas and representing volunteer soldiers, not San Augustine. Gaines similarly erred in writing that Crockett was to represent San Augustine, perhaps based on hyperbole surrounding the Colonel's visit. It's entirely possible that enthusiastic residents made such a suggestion, but no one took it seriously, and Crockett, an experienced politician, would not have made such a presumption. James Gaines to J. W. Robinson, January 9–10, 1836, quoted in Chariton, *100 Days in Texas,* 118; Jenkins, *Papers of the Texas Revolution,* Vol. 2, 236; *Ordinances and Decrees of the Consultation, Provisional Government of Texas and the Convention,* 76–78. Known only as Washington at the time, the town would later be called Washington-on-the-Brazos. The election of convention delegates in Béxar on February 1 resulted in the election of Antonio Navarro, Erasmo Seguin, Francisco Ruiz (the Alcalde's father), and Gaspar Flores. However, the garrison in the Alamo complained that it should have two of those seats and only Ruiz and Navarro were sent; the other two were replaced by Samuel A. Maverick and Jesse B. Badgett, who were elected by the garrison. See excerpts from *Remember the Alamo* by Albert Curtis (1961) quoted in Todd Hansen, *The Alamo Reader,* 602–04.

9. Micajah Autry to Martha Autry, January 13, 1836, quoted in Chariton, *100 Days in Texas,* 142; Smith, *The Land Holdings of Colonel David Crockett in West Tennessee,* 98.

10. Micajah Autry to Martha Autry, December 13, 1835, quoted in Chariton, *100 Days in Texas,* 31.

11. Daniel Cloud to a friend, December 25, 1835; Cloud to his brother, John B. Cloud, December 26, 1835, both quoted in Chariton, *100 Days in Texas,* 67–68, 71–74. Cloud mentioned he was low on writing paper and unable to go into Natchitoches to buy some because of an outbreak of smallpox there. Micajah Autry to Martha Autry, January 13, 1836, quoted in Chariton, *100 Days in Texas,* 142–143. Also see Thompson, *Born on a Mountaintop,* 74; "Micajah Autry's Letter," MyKindred.com, https://mykindred.com/cloud/documents/mautry.php; "Daniel Cloud's Letter," MyKindred.com, https://mykindred.com/cloud/documents/DanielCloud .php.

12. Crockett to John P. Ash, December 27, 1834, quoted in Boylston and Wiener, *David Crockett in Congress,* 263; Micajah Autry to Martha Autry, January 13, 1836, quoted in Chariton, *100 Days in Texas,* 142; Travis to David Burnet, April 11, 1835, quoted in Jenkins, *Papers of the Texas Revolution,* Vol. 1, 63–64. Houston may have seen annexation as the end game, and no doubt Jackson shared that goal. It was another Jackson Tennessee protege, and Crockett enemy, James K. Polk, who rose to the presidency in 1845, annexed Texas, and brought on the Mexican-American War. Under the terms of the Treaty of Guadalupe Hidalgo, signed on February 2, 1848, which ended the war, Mexico ceded 55 percent of its territory, including the present-day states of California, Nevada, Utah, New Mexico, most of Arizona and Colorado, and parts of Oklahoma, Kansas, and Wyoming. Mexico also relinquished all claims to Texas and recognized the Rio Grande as the southern boundary with the United States. "Treaty of Guadalupe Hidalgo," National Archives, https://www.archives.gov/milestone-documents/treaty-of-guadalupe -hidalgo#:~:text=This%20treaty%2C%20signed%20on%20February, Oklahoma% 2C%20Kansas %2C%20and%20Wyoming.

13. Crockett to John Wesley Crockett, December 24, 1834; Crockett to Charles Schultz, December 25, 1834; Crockett to John P. Ash, December 27, 1834; Crockett to editor of *National Intelligencer,* August 10, 1835, published September 2, 1835, all quoted in Boylston and Wiener, *David Crockett in Congress,* 119, 122, 282, 260–63.

14. Crockett's son Robert collected the $240 on behalf of the estate on August 22, 1837. Although part of the compensation was for the use of Crockett's horse in the war effort, Robert later said that his father's horse was returned to the family; Republic Claim no. 3196, reel 21, TSLAC; a facsimile of the check issued to Crockett's estate is in the collection of the Tennessee State Museum. On January 15, 1836, Thomas Rusk certified that he purchased two rifles from Crockett for sixty dollars, but Crockett was paid only $2.50, the balance to be paid to him later. After arriving in Béxar, Crockett asked Colonel Neill to endorse the claim, which he did on February 11, signing as commandant of Béxar. On February 13, Crockett wrote a note to the auditor asking that he validate the claim and pay Horace (aka Horatio) Alsbury, the bearer of his note, the amount due to Crockett. It is the last surviving item signed by Crockett. On December 5, 1836, in Columbia, Texas, Alsbury filed for and received a draft for the $57.50 on behalf of Crockett's estate. Republic Claim no. 1358, reel 21; Republic Claim no. 3196, reel 21: https://www.tsl.texas.gov/apps/arc/repclaims/viewdetails/15821. The cited Republic Claims are archived in the TSLAC. The sixty dollars Crockett was paid for his rifles equals $1,911 in 2022 dollars; the $240 claim equals $7,646; Jenkins, *Papers of the Texas Revolution,* Vol. 4, 66.

15. In his January 12–15 letter to Lieutenant Governor Robinson, Judge Forbes reported enlisting "numerous Volunteers from the States fifty-two of whom will leave here tomorrow for the frontier . . . I trust that hereafter the Volunteers will take the route by sea to Matagordo or Copono [Matagorda or Copano], as Provisions are scarce." Forbes gives no reason for suggesting the volunteers would head so far south to the coastal ports, but he must have thought their ultimate destination was likely to be Matamoros. Matagorda and Copano are close to Goliad and would be the logical ports to land at if the recruits were being sent by sea to Goliad, where the Matamoros expedition was forming up and Houston was trying to squelch it. He also seemed to think the men would first make their way to San Felipe and specifically recommended "Captain Kimble, Major Autry, and Major Gilmore" to Robinson, adding, "I hear that these are on the road for this place," by which he must have meant San Felipe as they had been in Nacogdoches for some time and were not on their way there. Forbes seems to have expected that Robinson would meet them in San Felipe and it is possible that the men did intend to go there, but they got no farther than Washington before being directed to San Antonio. Forbes to J. W. Robinson, January 12–15, 1836, quoted in Jenkins, *Papers of the Texas Revolution,* Vol. 3, 496–98; Houston to Gov. Smith, January 17, 1836, and January 30, 1836, both quoted in Chariton, *100 Days in Texas,* 152–53, 180–83; Gray, *From Virginia to Texas,* 107.

16. The Alamo website says the Nacogdoches party included Crockett, Patton, Autry, Cloud, Peter Harper, Jesse Benton, B. Archer Thomas, and perhaps a dozen others, which would have included William B. Harrison and H. S. Kimble. Kimble,

Benton, and Harper left the group at Washington and did not go to San Antonio. Benton and Harper joined other units, but Kimble remained in Washington where he served as secretary of the convention that convened there on March 1. Kimble should not be confused with George C. Kimbell, a member of the Gonzalez Ranging Company, who died at the Alamo. Davis, *Three Roads to the Alamo*, 416; Anonymous, "Kimble, Herbert Simms," Handbook of Texas Online, accessed December 29, 2023, https://www.tshaonline.org/handbook/entries/kimble-herbert-simms. Bruce Winders, "David Crockett in Texas: Myths & Legends of the Texas Revolution," from The Alamo website, https://medium.com/@OfficialAlamo /david-crockett-in-texas-e01f2ac4fd2a#_edn1; William B. Harrison to John Eblin, January 31, 1836, Republic Claim No. 208, reel 28: https://www.tsl.texas.gov/apps /arc/repclaims/viewdetails/19948; B. M. Thomas to John Lott, January 24, 1836, Republic Claim No. 617, reel 62: https://www.tsl.texas.gov/apps/arc/repclaims /viewdetails/34493; all Republic Claims from TSLAC. Enlistment dates on land grant certificates issued posthumously to Alamo defenders are not always reliable. One of Harrison's certificates for 1,920 acres gives his enlistment date as February 1, 1836; Republic Claim certificate 3290, May 10, 1838, TSLAC. Micajah Autry's pay certification dated May 8, 1839, gives his enlistment date as February 10, 1836, as does bounty certificate 9104, also dated May 8, 1839; Claim No. 9163, reel 4, Texas Government Land Office (GLO) website, https://s3.glo.texas.gov/ncu/SCANDOCS /archives_webfiles/arcmaps/webfiles/landgrants/PDFs/1/5/2/152084.pdf; https://s3 .glo.texas.gov/ncu/SCANDOCS/archives_webfiles/arcmaps/webfiles/landgrants /PDFs/3/3/7/337476.pdf; Edward Warren to his uncle, January 1, 1836, in Jenkins, *The General's Tight Pants*.

There is little evidence that Capt. William B. Harrison's company was referred to as the "Tennessee Mounted Volunteers," although a receipt he signed on his way to San Antonio on January 31, 1836, to John Eblin for provisions says the supplies were furnished to the "Tennessee Volunteer Company." A number of companies were referred to as mounted volunteers during the war. For example, William Becknell, who traveled with Crockett for a time in the Red River country, mustered a company of mounted volunteers known as the Red River Blues in July 1836. Texas Republic claims and other documents pertaining to various men who enlisted with Crockett do refer to their units as mounted volunteers, or Captain Harrison's mounted volunteers. For example, A. L. Harrison left Washington with Harrison, but did not die in the Alamo and later fought at San Jacinto. Shortly after that battle, Dr. William P. Smith certified that "A. L. Harrison was a member of Capt. William B. Harrison's company of mounted volunteers when the company left Washington for San Antonio about the 15th of last January—said A. L. Harrison was likewise under my medical care as surgeon in the army of Texas." Col. Sidney Sherman later certified that A. L. Harrison was part of a group of "mounted volunteers," enlisted December 1, 1835, and had a horse appraised by Captain W. Harrison, Crockett, and Lieutenant Robert Campbell at $85 and a gun valued at $35, and that his property was lost at the Alamo. Another certification from Dr. William P. Smith appears on a separate sheet of paper in the same file stating that "A. L. Harrison was a member of William B. Harrison's company of Mounted

Volunteers when that company left Washington for San Antonio about January 20, last. He fell sick and was likewise under my medical care as a surgeon of the army of Texas." Apparently, A. L. Harrison fell ill on the way to San Antonio and was left behind, although he donated his horse and gun to Capt. Harrison's company and later claimed compensation for their loss at the Alamo. The phrase "Tennessee Mounted Volunteers" appears to have originated with Amelia Williams, "A Critical Study of the Siege of the Alamo and of the Personnel of Its Defenders," *The Southwestern Historical Quarterly,* Vol. 37 (July 1933-April 1934), 251–52, 165–67, 299; However, none of the records that Williams referred to in that study include the term "Tennessee Mounted Volunteers," although several refer to "mounted volunteers," and the Eblin receipt refers to the "Tennessee Volunteer Company." In any case, it is not clear who comprised Crockett and Harrison's group of mounted volunteers since the men quickly broke into several separate groups and did not travel from Nacogdoches as a single unit. Nor were all of them mounted. Several men in Autry's group traveled by foot and later purchased a buggy to carry their baggage on the road to San Antonio. Command is equally unclear. Although Captain Harrison may have nominally been in command of the group, or some portion of it, others may have regarded Crockett as their leader. As noted above, A. L. Harrison had three officers certify the value of his horse and gun; Captain Harrison, Colonel Crockett, and Lieutenant Campbell, suggesting all of them enjoyed some form of leadership status among the volunteers. Despite his official rank of private, Crockett retained his militia title of colonel, and it is possible that some of the men traveled with Crockett and called themselves the Tennessee Mounted Volunteers in his honor. Captain Harrison, a young officer, may have deferred to the celebrated Crockett as well and was happy to travel with the Colonel at least as far as Washington. In any case, Crockett clearly enjoyed a role far greater than that of a simple private throughout his time in the Texas army. Wm. B. Harrison, Capt., to John Eblin, January 31, 1836, Republic Claim No. 208, reel 28, TSLAC, https://www.tsl.texas.gov/apps/arc/repclaims/viewdetails/19948; Larry Mahon Beachum, "Becknell, William," Handbook of Texas Online, accessed May 25, 2020, http://www.tshaonline.org/handbook/online/articles/fbe17; Amelia Williams, "A Critical Study of the Siege of the Alamo and of the Personnel of Its Defenders," *The Southwestern Historical Quarterly,* Vol. 37 (July 1933-April 1934), 251–52, 165–67, 299; Unnumbered Republic Claim 01, reel No. 41, April 24, 1836, TSLAC, https://www.tsl.texas.gov/apps/arc/repclaims/viewdetails/26780; B. M. Thomas to John Lott, January 24, 1836, Republic Claim No. 617, reel 62, TSLAC, https://www.tsl.texas.gov/apps/arc/repclaims/viewdetails/34493.

17. Edward Warren to his uncle, January 1, 1836, in Jenkins, *The General's Tight Pants.*

18. B. B. (Benjamin) Goodrich to General Council, December 20, 1835, quoted in Chariton *100 Days in Texas,* 49; Donovan, *Blood of Heroes,* 414. Reimbursement to John Lott for his service as Commissary in Washington during the war of $414.44. Nov 27, 1838, claim filed by Lott May 7, 1838. John Lott file, unnumbered claim 01, reel 62: https://www.tsl.texas.gov/apps/arc/repclaims/viewdetails/34519, TSLAC.

19. Crockett to John Lott January 23, 1836; Republic Claim No. 617, reel 62; John Lott file, https://www.tsl.texas.gov/apps/arc/repclaims/storage/republic_media/imgs/62/view_06200311.jpg, TSLAC, also quoted in Hansen, *The Alamo Reader*, 659. Hansen notes the document is missing from the Republic Claims file, but it is found there in the John Lott file. William B. Harrison to John Lott January 23, 1836, Republic Claim No. 617, reel 62, TSLAC, https://www.tsl.texas.gov/apps/arc/repclaims/viewdetails/34492; the claim was for four dollars for lodging and provisions for Harrison and Joseph Kerr and two horses; B. M. Thomas to John Lott, January 24, 1836, Republic Claim No. 617, reel 62, TSLAC, https://www.tsl.texas.gov/apps/arc/repclaims/viewdetails/34493. Crockett could have reached Washington by January 22 if he left Nacogdoches early on January 18, although most sources suggest he left on January 16. Edward Warren wrote that he covered the distance in five days only a few weeks earlier. Edward Warren to his uncle, January 1, 1836, in Jenkins, *The General's Tight Pants*. A man named A. L. Harrison was with Captain Harrison when he left Washington but was not killed at the Alamo. He was under the care of Dr. William P. Smith on or before April 24, 1836, possibly for wounds received at San Jacinto. Republic claim unnumbered 01, reel No. 41, April 24, 1836, TSLAC, https://www.tsl.texas.gov/apps/arc/repclaims/viewdetails/26780.

20. Autry's group departed Washington on February 2 after paying Roberts forty-five dollars. Voucher to Roberts dated February 2, 1836, signed by Autry, Cloud, and Bailey "on the part of the squad". The squad of eight men was still en route on February 11, nine days later, when they received lodging and provisions from John Y. Criswell. Autry and Cloud signed a claim for Criswell "as agents for the squad." Republic claim No. 7486, reel 21, February 11, 1836, Republic claim No. 4109, reel 4, TSLAC. On the same day they purchased nine dollars' worth of corn from Zadock Woods; Republic claim No. 4244, reel 118, February 11, 1836, TSLAC. Several members of the party appear to have traveled on foot as Autry had for much of his journey from Tennessee. If they had, in fact, procured a wagon or buggy they may have taken turns riding in it, the others walking or sharing the four horses the ten men had when they reached Washington in a state of exhaustion. A buggy would have made slower time than men on horseback. Kimble left Autry's group and remained in Washington where he later ran into Horace Alsbury, who was on his way from Béxar to Nacogdoches. Kimble asked if Alsbury had seen the small group of volunteers and Alsbury said he had seen them shortly after leaving Béxar and noted that they traveled with a carryall. Two weeks later Kimble saw a man arriving in Washington from Béxar who was driving the same carryall. The man said he had purchased it from a group of volunteers who arrived in Béxar around February 21. Herbert Simms Kimble letter dated September 5, 1836, DRT Library, William Irving Lewis file. Republic Claim No. 1361, reel 88, TSLAC, https://www.tsl.texas.gov/apps/arc/repclaims/viewdetails/89047. Full Text: "Washington Feby 2nd 1836. This is to certify to the provisional government of Texas that a squad of ten of us volunteers for six months have been fed with our horses four in number for five days by S. R. Roberts Esq. upon his own responsibility there being no possible provisions at this point for the soldiers. Our circumstances after a long march made it necessary for us to remain here that length of time. We do hope

that the government in its liberality will make full remuneration to him who may have sustained the soldiers upon his own responsibility in these times of peculiar (?) in the country. Very Respectfully—M. Autry, D. W. Cloud, P. J. Bailey—On the part of the squad."

21. John M. Swisher, *The Swisher Memoirs*, ed. Rena Maverick Green (Delhi, India: Facsimile, 2019, originally published in 1932), 19–22. Not everyone enjoyed Crockett's talking. Henry Clay's son-in-law, James Erwin, reported that "Col. Crockett is perhaps the most illiterate Man, that you have ever met in congress Hall he is not only illiterate but he is rough & uncouth, talks much & loudly, and is by far, more in his proper place, when hunting a Bear, in a Cane Brake, than he will be in the Capital, yet he is a man worth attending to, he is independent and fearless & has a popularity at home that is unaccountable." Quoted in Boylston and Wiener, *David Crockett in Congress*, 22–23.

22. Swisher, *The Swisher Memoirs*, 21.

23. There is little information about Patton's movements after his enlistment in Nacogdoches. He likely accompanied his uncle to Washington, but Swisher makes no mention of Patton being at Gay Hill. It is not certain that he ever went to San Antonio or was in the Alamo. Another man named William Hester Patton from Hopkinsville, Kentucky, was at the Alamo but left prior to the siege and may have been an early messenger sent out by Travis. He later became Houston's aide de camp, fought at San Jacinto, and was placed in charge of guarding Santa Anna and other high-level Mexican prisoners afterward. Crockett's nephew also may have been an early Alamo messenger, but there is no evidence of that. Although he enlisted with Crockett, he was mustered into Capt. Henry Teal's company, commanded by Lt. Col. Henry Millard, on March 17, 1836, and later served with several other units. In August 1836, *Niles' Weekly Register* reported that he arrived in Galveston in mid-July and may have been among the troops guarding Mexican prisoners there. Around the same time, he met briefly with Robert Patton Crockett, who had come to Texas after learning of his father's death and later enlisted in the Texas army. William Patton was discharged on December 13, 1837, and received a bounty land grant for 1,280 acres the following day. He sold it eight days later for $200 (about $6,372 in 2022 dollars). Thomas W. Cutrer, "Patton, William Hester," Handbook of Texas Online, accessed July 10, 2020, http://www.tshaonline.org /handbook/online/articles/fpa54; Copies of the original Texas volunteer muster rolls are available on the Texas General Land Office (GLO) website, https://s3 .glo.texas.gov/ncu/SCANDOCS/archives_webfiles/arcmaps/webfiles/landgrants /PDFs/3/1/9/319742_109.pdf; https://s3.glo.texas.gov/ncu/SCANDOCS/archives _webfiles/arcmaps/webfiles/landgrants/PDFs/3/1/9/319742_118.pdf; https://s3 .glo.texas.gov/ncu/SCANDOCS/archives_webfiles/arcmaps/webfiles/landgrants /PDFs/3/1/9/319742_167.pdf; https://s3.glo.texas.gov/ncu/SCANDOCS/archives _webfiles/arcmaps/webfiles/landgrants/PDFs/3/1/9/319742_168.pdf; Republic Claims No. 5579, reel 8, and Claim No. 5772, reel 81, TSLAC, https://www.tsl .texas.gov/apps/arc/repclaims/viewdetails/40388; https://www.tsl.texas.gov/apps /arc/repclaims/viewdetails/40389; William Patton's bounty land grant no. 979,

December 14, 1837, Texas GLO website: https://s3.glo.texas.gov/ncu/SCANDOCS /archives_webfiles/arcmaps/webfiles/landgrants/PDFs/1/5/2/152073.pdf; Patton family genealogy website, http://genforum.genealogy.com/patton/messages/5626 .html; anonymous letter from Galveston dated July 21, 1836 quoted in *Niles' Weekly Register* of August 20, 1836. I am grateful to Wade Dillon for providing a copy of the August 20, 1836, *Niles' Weekly Register*.

24. Edward Warren to his uncle, January 1, 1836, in Jenkins, *The General's Tight Pants*. The town was officially named Bastrop in 1832 but the name was changed to Mina in 1834, then permanently back to Bastrop in 1837. I have chosen to call it Bastrop to more easily identify its location today. "History, Bastrop, Texas," Bastrop, Texas Network website, https://www.bastroptexas.net/history/bastrop.htm. Donovan, *The Blood of Heroes*, 415, cites *An Early History of Fayette County* by Leonie Rummell Weyand and Houston Wade (LaGrange, TX: LaGrange Journal, 1936), 283, as evidence that Lester was serving as a recruiter in Bastrop in January and February 1836, and that he met Crockett there and ordered him to Béxar, further evidence that volunteers were being sent there at the time. But Crockett and the others had already been directed to Béxar by John Lott in Washington and were on their way there in any case. Although it's possible that Crocket could have reached San Antonio from Bastrop in as little as four days, apparently the journey was a difficult one. "Origins of the Camino Real in Texas," Texas Almanac, https:// texasalmanac.com/topics/history/origins-camino-real-texas; "El Camino Real de los Tejas", US National Park Service website: https://www.nps.gov/elte/planyour-visit/places-to-go.htm. Neill to Provisional Government, January 28, 1836; Travis to Smith, Jan. 29, 1836; Green B. Jameson to Smith, February 11, 1836, all quoted in Chariton, *100 Days in Texas*, 175, 179, 222–23. Republic Claims, Pension application, August 13, 1870, Fayette County, Texas, TSLAC; James Seaton Lester file, unnumbered claim; reel 225, images 2, 3, and 4 (images 369, 370, 371), TSLAC, https://www.tsl.texas.gov/apps/arc/repclaims/viewdetails /73448; Republic claim no. 1361, reel 88, TSLAC, https://www.tsl.texas.gov/apps/arc/repclaims/viewdetails /89047; William B. Harrison to James Gotcher, January 30, 1836, Republic Claim No. 226, reel 36, TSLAC, https://www.tsl.texas.gov/apps/arc/repclaims/viewdetails /24333; William P. Kerr claim No.1442, reel 56, January 28, 1836, TSLAC, https:// www.tsl.texas.gov/apps/arc/repclaims/viewdetails/33773; Harrison to John Eblin, January 31, 1836, Republic Claim No. 208, reel 28, TSLAC: https://www.tsl.texas .gov/apps/arc/repclaims/viewdetails/19948. Gotcher's name is also found under the spellings Gotier, Goacher, and Goucher, but is filed under Gotcher in the Republic Claims files, TSLAC. In 1831 or 1832 Gotcher built Gotier's Trace, a road that ran from San Felipe to Bastrop, which is named for him with that spelling. In 1835 he moved his family to Bastrop County. Gotcher, his wife, two sons, and son-in-law were killed in an Indian raid in 1837. His daughter and her two children were captured but later released. Vivian Elizabeth Smyrl, "Gotier's Trace," Handbook of Texas Online, accessed June 19, 2020: http://www.tshaonline.org/handbook /online/articles/exg01; "Gotier, James," Handbook of Texas Online, accessed June 19, 2020: http://www.tshaonline.org/handbook/online/articles/fgo01.

Chapter 5

1. Crockett likely left Bastrop between January 30 and February 1 and could have covered the ninety miles in three or four days, but that estimate does not account for days he didn't travel due to bad weather, hunting or foraging for food, or just resting. In any case he did not arrive in San Antonio until late in the first week of February, probably a few days after Travis's February 3 arrival. This calculation is based on Crockett leaving Gay Hill between January 26–28, arriving in Bastrop January 28–30, leaving Bastrop January 30-February 1, and spending five to seven days on the trail. Sutherland noted that Crockett arrived a few days after Travis, thus February 7 seems a likely date for Crockett's arrival; Sutherland quoted in Hansen, *Alamo Reader*, 140.

2. Charles Ramsdell, *San Antonio: A Historical and Pictorial Guide* (Austin: University of Texas Press, 1959); Davis, *Three Roads to the Alamo*, 513; Cobia, *Journey*, 165–6; George Nelson, *The Alamo: An Illustrated History* (Third Revised Edition, Uvalde, TX: Aldine Press, 2009), 35–46; Jackson and Wheat, *Texas by Terán*, 16–27.

3. Dr. John Sutherland, *The Alamo* (ca. 1860), John S. Ford Papers, published by Sutherland's granddaughter, Annie Sutherland, in a rare 1936 pamphlet, 18–25, quoted in Hansen, *Alamo Reader*, 140. Apparently following the same route taken by Crockett and Harrison, Autry's group was ten miles from modern-day Smithville and another fifteen from Bastrop. If they reached Bastrop on February 11 and left there within two days, they could have reached Béxar by February 18, nearly two weeks after Crockett arrived. Jenkins, "Documents of the Texian Revolution," *The Alamo Journal* (February 1995) includes a typescript of Harrison's certification that Cloud and Bailey were in San Antonio by February 18 under his command, documents provided to *The Alamo Journal* by Thomas R. Lindley. The original Harrison certification of Cloud's arrival in San Antonio is missing from the TSLAC online database. Republic Claim No. 402, reel 127; Claim No. 7486, reel 21; Claim No. 4244, reel 118; Republic Claim No. 4109, reel 4, TSLAC: https://www.tsl .texas. gov/apps/arc/repclaims/viewdetails/104092; https://www.tsl.texas.gov/apps/arc /repclaims/viewdetails/16616; https://www.tsl.texas.gov/apps/arc/repclaims/view- details/99933; https://www.tsl.texas.gov/apps/arc/repclaims/viewdetails/4660; https://www.tsl.texas.gov/apps/arc/repclaims/storage/republic_media/pdfs/21 /02100601.pdf. Paul N. Spellman, "Woods, Zadock," Handbook of Texas Online, accessed June 30, 2020, http://www.tshaonline.org/handbook/online/articles/fwo17.

4. Timothy Matovina and Jesús F. de la Teja, eds., with collaborator Justin Poché, *Recollections of a Tejano Life: Antonio Menchaca in Texas History* (Austin: University of Texas Press, 2013), 64–6. Menchaca left San Antonio prior to the Alamo siege. In his memoir, written decades later, he claimed that Bowie encouraged him to leave because of the danger he would face as a Tejano rebel, but the same was true of all Tejanos who stood against Santa Anna. It is more likely that Menchaca left just prior to the arrival of Santa Anna's army along with at least eleven other Tejanos. His memoir was written long after the Alamo was enshrined in mythology and Menchaca, by then a man of considerable prestige in Texas, would understandably

have been reluctant to say he had left Béxar prior to the siege. Crockett's claim to being only a "high private" is from Sutherland, *The Alamo*. A second version of the manuscript, transcribed by Amelia Williams, quotes Crockett saying, "I have come to assist Travis as a high private," adding that "me and my Tennessee boys have come to Help Texas as privates--and will try to do our duty," quoted in Hansen, *Alamo Reader*, 140, 178. For a thorough analysis and text of the Forbes and Williams versions of Sutherland, see Hansen, *Alamo Reader*, 138–191. Sutherland was at the Alamo prior to the siege, served during the war, and received two land grants for his service; Texas GLO, certificates 82 and 204, TSLAC Sutherland claim No. 1262, reel 102, with William H. Patton's certification of expenditures through February 19 in Béxar and February 25 in Gonzales on the same reel, TSLAC website: https://www.tsl.texas.gov/apps/arc/repclaims/viewdetails/94340; April 9, 1836, certification by John W. Smith for John Sutherland valuing a horse, saddle, and bridle used in the service of the army for $175, Claim 1262, reel 102, TSLAC, https://www.tsl.texas.gov/apps/arc/repclaims/viewdetails/94339. Sutherland's list of expenses show he was in Béxar as late as February 19 but was in Gonzales on February 25; Stephen L. Hardin, "Efficient in the Cause," in Gerald E. Poyo, ed, *Tejano Journey: 1770–1850* (Austin: University of Texas Press, 1996), 67–8.

5. Sutherland, *The Alamo*, quoted in Hansen, *Alamo Reader*, 142; Matovina and Teja, *Recollections,* 64–6. The Menchaca and Sutherland accounts differ in key respects. Menchaca says the messenger arrived during the ball on February 10, but it is more likely the ball took place after Neill left, possibly the evening of February 11, since he was still post commander until that date and any messages would have been taken to him if he were still in Béxar. Menchaca's account is a bit suspicious in that he places himself, rather than Seguin, in the central role of receiving the messenger's report. But Sutherland's dates also seem confused. He says Herrera arrived on February 20 but also says Travis arrived only two days before that, yet we know that Travis was in Béxar by February 3. Despite that error, Sutherland appears to have accurately conveyed Herrera's report and his February 20 arrival date seems reasonable. Santa Anna did cross the Rio Grande around February 16, and advance units did reach the Medina River by February 22. Jackson and Wheat, *Almonte's Texas*, 349–59, 362–74. *The Constitutional Advocate and Texas Public Advertiser* in Brazoria, Texas, published a review of the Crockett bio on June 15, 1833, French, *Life and Adventures of Colonel David Crockett of West Tennessee.*

6. Travis to Henry Smith, February 13, 1836, quoted in Hansen, *Alamo Reader*, 24. Travis wrote that he was enclosing Crockett's statement, but it has been lost. John J. Baugh to Henry Smith, February 13, 1836, quoted in Hansen, *Alamo Reader*, 673–5.

7. Crockett's note to the auditor, entrusted to Alsbury, is the last surviving document signed by him. On December 5, 1836, in Columbia, Texas, Alsbury filed for and received a draft for $57.50 on behalf of Crockett's estate. TSLAC, Republic Claim No. 1358, reel 21: https://www.tsl.texas.gov/apps/arc/repclaims/viewdetails/15815; Claim No. 3196, reel 21: https://www.tsl.texas.gov/apps/arc/repclaims/viewdetails/15821. Alsbury's first name is often given as "Horatio." In 1832 Juana Alsbury married Alejo Pérez Ramigio, with whom she had a son,

Alejo. Perez died in 1834 and Juana married Alsbury around January 1836. Crystal Sasse Ragsdale, "Alsbury, Juana Gertrudis Navarro," Handbook of Texas Online, accessed December 21, 2020, https://www.tshaonline.org/handbook/entries/ alsbury-juana-gertrudis-navarro; Davis, *Three Roads to the Alamo*, 362–3.

8. Travis to Smith, February 12, 1836, quoted in Hansen, *Alamo Reader*, 21–22; Winders, *Sacrificed at the Alamo*, 107; Travis to unknown recipient, misdated January 17, 1836, quoted in Hansen, *Alamo Reader*, 16, taken from Yoakum, *History of Texas*. Stephen Hardin estimated that, prior to Santa Anna's arrival, when Neill still commanded Béxar, the entire Texian army numbered "some 790 citizen-soldiers dispersed over a 150-mile front, without unity of command or concentration of force" facing an enemy of 6,000 men. Numbers were fluid with commanders never certain how many men they had on any given day since men were free to come and go as they pleased. Stephen L. Hardin, *The Alamo 1836: Santa Anna's Texas Campaign* (Osceola, WI.: Osprey, 2001), 20.

9. Stephen L. Hardin, "J. C. Neill: The Forgotten Alamo Commander," Alamo de Parras website: http://www.sonsofdewittcolony.org//adp/archives/feature/neill /neill.html; Davis, *Three Roads to the Alamo*, 720. Sutherland suggested that Travis offered Crockett a command of some kind, possibly shortly after his arrival, but that Crockett declined, issuing his oft-quoted preference to serve only as a private. It is possible that some of the volunteers who refused to vote for Bowie asked Crockett to offer himself as a candidate, but as an enlistee in the Auxiliary Volunteer Corps, he served under Travis, a regular army officer, and would have been obliged to refuse. It is unlikely that Crockett would have accepted in any case as he had clearly tried to steer a neutral course between the feuding Alamo leaders. Sutherland, *The Alamo*, quoted in Hansen, *Alamo Reader*, 140.

10. Green B. Jameson to Henry Smith, February 11, 1836; Travis to Smith, February 13, 1836; Baugh to Smith, February 13, 1836. All quoted in Hansen, *Alamo Reader*, 22–4, 572, 673–5; Chariton, *100 Days in Texas*, 222–29; Winders, *Sacrificed at the Alamo*, 107. Jameson's letter of February 11 says the garrison was "one hundred and fifty strong Col Crockett & Col Travis both here & Col Bowie in command of volunteer forces," so the election must have occurred that day shortly after Neill left. See Cobia, *Journey*, 179–183, regarding the possibility that some volunteers may have asked Crockett to run against Bowie. Sutherland says that, upon his arrival, Crockett was "immediately offered a command by Col. Travis and called upon by the crowd for a speech," but Sutherland seems to have compressed several events into a single day. Travis to Smith, December 3, 1835, quoted in Barker, "The Texan Revolutionary Army," 250.

11. Travis to Smith, February 12, 1836, and February 13, 1836; Baugh to Smith, February 13, 1836, all quoted in Chariton, *100 Days in Texas*, 225–9; Travis and Bowie to Smith, February 14, 1836, quoted in Hansen, 22–23; Davis, *Three Roads to the Alamo*, 210–11; Winders, *Sacrificed at the Alamo*, 110.

12. Cole-Jett, *The Red River Valley in Arkansas*, 33. For a biography of Bowie that details his land schemes and illicit slave trading see Davis, *Three Roads to the Alamo*.

13. Travis and Bowie to Smith, February 14, 1836, quoted in Hansen, *Alamo Reader*, 22–23; *Ordinances and Decrees of the Consultation, Provisional Government*

of Texas and the Convention, 76–8; Winders, *Sacrificed at the Alamo,* 110; David Harman [Harmon] affidavit, dated February 18, 1885, in Voucher File for land grant certificate no. 1205, veterans donation of 1,280 acres; Texas GLO, https://s3 .glo.texas.gov/ncu/SCANDOCS/archives_webfiles/arcmaps/webfiles/landgrants /PDFs/1/6/2/162462.pdf.

14. Harman and Bland were friends from Vermillion Bayou, Louisiana, who moved to Orange County, Texas, around 1828, and both enlisted in the Texas army in October 1835. The time frames in Harman's statement are confused and compressed. He said he left San Felipe the day the General Council called for the convention to convene on March 1 and set election of delegates for February 1. Those events occurred on December 10, 1835, long before Bowie could have sent him on his mission. Harman says the volunteers he raised "immediately left for San Antonio and joined the army under General Burleson, I think [he] was in command," but Burleson left San Antonio on December 15. Even if Harman left San Felipe on December 10 (although the December 10 seems more likely) it would have taken five days to cover the 150 miles to San Antonio. The earliest he could have gotten there is December 15, the day Burleson left Béxar and Johnson took command. Harman's statement is more problematic when he tells of meeting Crockett only days after arriving in Béxar. Crockett did not arrive in San Antonio until February 7, weeks after Harman says he got there. His statement includes references to his raising a reinforcement, of running into Houston's army and being directed away from Béxar and back to Washington, and of being at the Battle of San Jacinto but not taking part in it. His account of meeting Crockett and Bowie in Béxar seems genuine, as do the other events he describes, but the statement reads as if they all happened within days or weeks of each other, which cannot have been Harman's intention. He dictated the statement on February 18, 1885, at age sixty-nine, nearly a half-century after the fact, and his recollections might have understandably been fogged by time, thus explaining the time compression in his statement. The statement's clear handwriting does not match Harman's more rudimentary, somewhat shaky signature, indicating it was dictated to someone else who could have distorted the time sequences. His encounter with Crockett must have taken place after the volunteers had elected Bowie their commander and before Bowie fell ill and passed command to Travis. Bowie signed himself, in a shaky hand, "Commander of the Volunteers of Béxar," his February 23 message to the Mexican commander, so he did not fully relinquish that command to Travis until the following day. Harman received a land grant of 1,280 acres for his service from October 1835 until May 1836. Neither Harman nor Bland appear on Neill's January 15 muster roll or the February 1 roster of men voting for convention delegates, although George (Robert) Evans does. Thus, despite considerable confusion in time frames in Harman's 1885 statement, he was not in Béxar until after February 1 and his encounter with Crockett and Bowie likely took place after February 14, when Travis and Bowie reconciled and Bowie was still physically able to share command, or in any case sometime between February 14 and February 23 when Mexican troops arrived in Béxar. See Donovan, *Blood of Heroes,* 418–22 for a discussion of when Bowie became bedridden and Travis took sole command. David Harman affidavit, dated February 18, 1885, in Voucher

File for land grant certificate 1205, veterans donation of 1,280 acres; Texas GLO, https://s3.glo.texas.gov/ncu/SCANDOCS/archives_webfiles/arcmaps/webfiles/landgrants/PDFs/1/6/2/162462.pdf. The file includes several affidavits attesting to Harman's service. Note that Harman's name is often misspelled "Harmon," but his signature clearly reads "Harman." Harman also qualified for a pension for his war service, which was stipulated in unnumbered Republic Claim, David Harman file, reel 219, TSLAC, https://www.tsl.texas.gov/apps/arc/repclaims/viewdetails/70569. Background information on Payton Bland, who later married Harman's sister, is found on the Texas Historical Marker website, https://www.txhistoricalmarker.com/marker/11119. Burleson to Smith, January 14, 1836, quoted in Chariton, *100 Days in Texas*, 33–6; Travis to Smith, February 13, 1836, and Baugh to Smith, February 13, 1836, quoted in Hansen, *Alamo Reader*, 673–75; Travis and Bowie to Smith, February 14, 1836, quoted in Hansen, *Alamo Reader*, 24–5. Neill's January 15, 1836, Alamo muster roll is found in Chariton, *100 Days in Texas*, 148–9; the Alamo roster, February 1, 1836, election of delegates to the convention, often referred to as the Alamo muster roll, is found on the TSLAC website, https://www.tsl.texas.gov/treasures/republic/alamo/election-1.html; Bowie to commander of Mexican Army of Texas, February 23, 1836, quoted in Hansen, *Alamo Reader*, 31; original Bowie holograph reproduced in Chariton, *100 Days in Texas*, 264.

15. Winders, *Sacrificed at the Alamo*, 108–9; Davis, *Three Roads to the Alamo*, 210–13; Sutherland, *The Alamo*, quoted in Hansen, 143–4; Thomas Ricks Lindley, *Alamo Traces: New Evidence and New Conclusions* (Lanham, MD: Republic of Texas Press, 2003), 323.

16. Gen. Vicente Filisola, *Memoirs for the History of the War in Texas*, 1849, quoted in Hansen, *Alamo Reader*, 387; James E. Ivey, "Archaeological Evidence for the Defenses of the Alamo," *The Alamo Journal* 117 (June 2000): 1–8; James E. Ivey, "Estrada or Navarro? The José Juan Sánchez Vista and Plano of the Alamo," The Second Flying Company of Alamo DeParras Website, last modified June 2000, http://www.sonsofdewittcolony.org//adp/archives/feature/sanchez.html; Susan Prendergast Schoelwer. "The Artist's Alamo: A Reappraisal of Pictorial Evidence, 1836–1850," *The Southwestern Historical Quarterly,* vol. 91, no. 4 (April 1988): 404–5; Winders, *Sacrificed at the Alamo*, 116–17; Davis, *Three Roads to the Alamo*, 538–40; Kevin R. Young, "Where Were the Bathrooms? An Informal Look at Sanitation in the 1836 Alamo," The Second Flying Company of Alamo DeParras website, http://www.sonsofdewittcolony.org/adp/history/archaeology/bano/frameset.html. Although several maps and plats of the 1836 Alamo exist, only one, the Labastida map, matches the results of archaeological excavations. Alamo archaeologist James E. Ivey produced an archeological map of his findings and pointed out that it "doesn't look at all like the Green Jameson map created by Adina de Zavala and Jane Briscoe about 1911, using Briscoe's memory and a tracing of one of Giraud's plans as its basis. Nor does it resemble the maps made by Reuben Marmaduke Potter in the 1840s, or the John Sutherland map of the 1860s, supposedly two of the best sketches of the defenses of the Alamo, nor is it like the drawings of José Juan Sánchez. What it looks like is the Ignacio Labastida plan. In fact, only the Labastida plan shows all the trenches on our archaeological

plan of the Alamo, and does not show ditches where we found none. As a result of the archaeology, then, we can say that the Alamo defenses followed the standard military field fortification practices of the 1830s, and that they were fairly accurately recorded by the Labastida plan, but not on any other known map." James E. Ivey's observations are contained in his unpublished manuscript, "Notes on the construction of the defenses of the Alamo." I am grateful to Mr. Ivey for sharing this manuscript with me.

17. Jameson to Houston, January 18, 1836, and Jameson to Smith, February 16, 1836, quoted in Hansen, *Alamo Reader*, 570–3; Travis to Smith, February 16, 1836, quoted in Hansen, *Alamo Reader*, 26. For a full discussion and illustrations of Jameson's and other plats see Hansen, *Alamo Reader*, 570–90. Alamo archeologist James E. Ivey has labeled the surviving Jameson's plat as a bogus "fictional concoction put together by Adina de Zavala and Jane Briscoe about 1911." Ivey, "Archaeological Evidence," 3; James E. Ivey, "Another Look at Storming the Alamo Walls," *Alamo Journal* 120 (March 2001); Sutherland, *The Alamo*, quoted in Hansen, 145–6. See Nelson, *The Alamo: An Illustrated History*, for Alamo plats by Col. Jose Juan Sanchez Estrada and Col. Ygnacio de Labastida, 58–61, and the reconstructed Jameson plat, 43. Nelson's renditions of the Alamo's appearance from 1745–1861 are on 8–17.

18. Stuart Reid, "What Ails You Jim, Exactly?" *The Alamo Journal*, 143 (December 2006); Stuart Reid email to author, July 27, 2020. For an analysis of when Bowie likely fell ill and his Sandbar injuries see Donovan, *Blood of Heroes*, 44–5, 392, 418–20. Bowie was effectively removed from any command by February 19, when Travis wrote to the provisional government and signed himself "Lt. Col. Comdt." In the February 14 letter, signed jointly with Bowie, he gave his title as "Comdt of Cavalry" while Bowie signed as "Comandant of volunteers at Bexar." Hansen, *Alamo Reader*, 24–7.

19. Travis to Smith, February 16, 1836; Travis to Vaughan, February 19, 1836, both quoted in Hansen, *Alamo Reader*, 26–7.

20. Fannin to Robinson, February 7–8, 1836; Robinson to Fannin, February 13, 1836; Advisory Council to the People of Texas, February 13, 1836; Fannin to Robinson, February 14, 1836; Advisory Council to the People of Texas, February 14, 1836; Advisory Council to Robinson, February 15, 1836, all quoted in Chariton, *100 Days in Texas*, 216–20, 230–3, 237.

21. Robinson to Fannin, February 13, 1836; Fannin to Robinson and council, February 14, 1836, both quoted in Chariton, *100 Days in Texas*, 230–3. Travis to convention, March 3, 1836, quoted in Chariton, *100 Days in Texas*, 304–6; Chariton, *Exploring Alamo Legends*, 132; Wm. N. Bonham, "James Butler Bonham," Internet Archive, Last modified October 19, 1999, https://web.archive.org/web/20060912183516/http://home.att.net/~wnbonham/james.htm. No written February 16 message to Fannin has survived, and there is no record of Fannin's response to that appeal.

22. Cloud and Bailey enlistment certification, Republic Claim 4108, reel 18, TSLAC; Patton's certification that Bailey served under him in Béxar, Republic Claim 4109, reel 4, TSLAC; Patton certification that Cloud "was in my command

about the 18th of Feby, or about six days previous to the fall of the Alamo, and the said young gentleman fell in the Alamo," dated December 31, 1836, missing from the TSLAC online database but reprinted by Thomas R. Lindley in *Alamo Journal* No. 95 (February 1995). Bailey and Cloud left Autry's group and arrived a few days before them. Travis to Ponton, February 23, 1836, quoted in Hansen, *Alamo Reader*, 28; Sutherland, *The Fall of the Alamo*, ca. 1860, reprinted in Hansen, *Alamo Reader*, 179. Sutherland said there were 187 men killed in the Alamo and forty of them were on the sick list when he left on February 23.

Although some sources claim that Dr. Horace Alsbury was sent out of the Alamo as a messenger on February 23, no convincing evidence of that has been found. Instead, there is considerable evidence that he left prior to the siege. Herbert S. Kimble, who left Autry's group in Washington, later saw Alsbury there while Alsbury was on his way from Béxar to Nacogdoches. Alsbury had left his wife, Juana, her infant son, Alejo, and her sister Gertrudes in San Antonio and hoped to find a safe haven for them in East Texas before the Mexican army arrived. Kimble asked if Alsbury had seen the small group of volunteers along the trail and Alsbury said he had seen them shortly after leaving Béxar and noted that they traveled with a carryall, or buggy, indicating this was the Autry group. Two weeks later Kimble saw a man from Béxar drive the same buggy into Washington. The man said he had purchased it from a group of volunteers who arrived in Béxar around February 21, which indicates that Alsbury, who passed the group on the road, had left the Alamo by that date. Juana Alsbury confirmed that her husband left Béxar before the siege, saying, "When the news of Santa Anna's approach at the head of a considerable force, was verified" he left to "procure means to remove his family, expecting to return before Santa Anna could reach the city," but he failed to do so. Dr. Joseph Henry Barnard, who was in San Antonio after the war, noted in his diary entry for May 17, 1836, that "Dr. Alsbury came in town to-da. . . . He has come in order to look after his family." Kimble, who never left Washington, was appointed secretary of the convention on March 1, 1836. Kimble to Cave Johnson, September 5, 1836, DRT Library, in William Irvine Lewis file; Juana Alsbury, undated interview by John S. Ford, quoted in Hansen, *Alamo Reader*, 87; Barnard's journal, quoted in Hansen, *Alamo Reader*, 613. See Donovan, *Blood of Heroes*, 426–28, for a discussion of sources placing Alsbury on the road out of San Antonio prior to February 23.

23. Francisco Becerra 1875 interview, quoted in Hansen, 453–5; José Enrique De La Peña, *With Santa Anna in Texas: A Personal Narrative of the Revolution*. Translated by Carmen Perry. Introduction by James E. Crisp (College Station: Texas A&M University Press, 1975; Expanded edition, 1997), 57; also see Donovan, *Blood of Heroes*, 416–17, 424.

24. Sutherland, *The Alamo*, quoted in Hansen, *Alamo Reader*, 140–5; Davis, *Three Roads to the Alamo*, 212–17; Winders, *Sacrificed at the Alamo*, 114.

25. Susanna (Dickinson) Hannig, in James M. Morphis, *History of Texas from Its Discovery and Settlement* (New York: United States publishing Co., 1874), 168–77, quoted in Hansen, *Alamo Reader*, 45–6; Susanna Belles (formerly Dickinson) deposition, November 21, 1853, Court of Claims file C-7115, Texas GLO, quoted in Hansen, *Alamo Reader*, 43; "Mrs. Alsbury's Recollections of the Alamo,"

conducted by John S. Ford, manuscript account (in Ford's handwriting) in the John S. Ford Memoirs (ca. 1880), Center for American History, University of Texas, Austin, 102–4, quoted in Timothy M. Matovina, *The Alamo Remembered* (Austin: University of Texas Press, 1995), 45-8, and Hansen, *Alamo Reader*, 87–8; November 10, 1901, Adina de Zavala interview of Enrique Esparza, *San Antonio Light*, quoted in Hansen, *Alamo Reader*, 94–6; May 12–19, 1907, *San Antonio Daily Express* interview with Enrique Esparza, quoted in Hansen, *Alamo Reader*, 101–10; William Groneman, "Alamo Noncombatants," Handbook of Texas Online, accessed December 21, 2020, https://www.tshaonline.org/handbook/entries/alamo-noncombatants.

26. Sutherland, *The Alamo*, quoted in Hansen, *Alamo Reader*, 145; Travis to San Felipe, February 24, 1836, quoted in Hansen, *Alamo Reader*, 32–3; Michael R. Green, "To the People of Texas & All Americans in the World," *The Southwestern Historical Quarterly*, 91, no. 4 (April 1988) 492, footnote 31.

27. There are conflicting accounts of the events of February 23. Sutherland says the Mexicans first presented a white flag, called for the parley, and met with Martin, who carried the surrender demand to Travis, after which Travis fired the Alamo cannon. He doesn't mention Bowie's note or the Mexicans firing grenades. Almonte doesn't mention Travis firing the cannon; he says the Mexicans fired grenades first and then ceased fire when the Texians raised a white flag. He then met first with Jameson and then with Martin, after which firing ceased. The San Luis *Potosi* Battalion journal says Travis fired the Alamo cannon and the Mexicans responded with four grenades. The Texians then sent the two messengers under white flags, both of whom were told to surrender at discretion. Sutherland, *The Alamo*, quoted in Hansen, *Alamo Reader*, 148, 179; Jackson and Wheat, *Almonte's Texas*, 367; "Batallón Activo de San Luis, Itinerario de las jornadas que han hecho el espresado cuerpo desde la ciudad de San Luis Potosí el dia 17 de Noviembre de 1835," manuscript copy in the José Enrique de la Peña Collection, Briscoe Center for American History, University of Texas at Austin, with comments by Tom Kailbourn to the author, February 20, 2008, and December 22, 2010; David McDonald, transcriber and translator, "The Siege of the Alamo: A Mexican Army Journal," Edited by Kevin R. Young, *Journal of the Alamo Battlefield Association* 3, no. 1 (1998); Bowie to Commander of the Army of Texas, February 23, 1836, quoted in Chariton, *100 Days in Texas*, 263; José Batres to Bowie, February 23, 1836, quoted in Hansen, *Alamo Reader*, 331–2. On December 7, 1835, Santa Anna issued orders to General Ramírez y Sesma classifying the Texians as foreigners who were warring on Mexico, violating all laws and who were thus not deserving of "any consideration, and for that reason no quarter will be given them." He claimed that the rebels had "with audacity, declared a war of extermination to the Mexicans, and they should be treated the same way." Santa Anna to Ramírez y Sesma, December 7, 1835, quoted in Hansen, *Alamo Reader*, 330–1.

28. Bowie and Travis to Fannin, February 23, 1836, quoted in Hansen, *Alamo Reader*, 31–2 and in Chariton, *100 Days in Texas*, 263. Sutherland claimed the February 23 courier to Goliad was a man named Johnson, and Tom Lindley suggested that it was likely John Johnson. Sutherland, *The Alamo*, quoted in Hansen, *Alamo*

Reader, 146; Lindley, *Alamo Traces*, 19–20, 109, footnote 20; Donovan, *Blood of Heroes*, 196 and 425, identifies John B. Johnson as the express rider to Goliad.

29. Personal communication with Stuart Reid, who first compared the Alamo under siege to a lifeboat. Travis to Ponton, February 23, 1836, quoted in Hansen, *Alamo Reader*, 236–7; Sutherland, *The Alamo*, quoted in Hansen, 149.

Chapter 6

1. "Travis to the People of Texas & All Americans in the World," February 24, 1836, quoted in Jenkins, *Papers of the Texas Revolution*, Vol. 4, 423.

2. Launcelot Smither to All Inhabitants of Texas, February 24, 1836, quoted in Hansen, *Alamo Reader*, 236–8; Travis to San Felipe, February 24, 1836, including postscripts by Martin and Smither, quoted in Hansen, *Alamo Reader*, 32–3; Michael R. Green, "To the People of Texas & All Americans in the World," *The Southwestern Historical Quarterly*, Vol. 91, no. 4 (April 1988): 483–508. "I shall never surrender or retreat" was underlined; "Victory of Death" was underlined three times. Jackson, and Wheat, *Almonte's Texas*, 369. Almonte's diary records that "in the night, according to the statement of a spy, thirty men arrived at the fort from Gonzales." There is no other record of such a force reaching the Alamo on this date, and Travis only later referred to the group of thirty-two men from Gonzales who arrived on March 1; Bill Groneman, "Smither, Launcelot," Handbook of Texas Online, accessed March 15, 2020, https://www.tshaonline.org/handbook /entries/smither-launcelot. Smither's name is sometimes spelled "Smithers."

3. Susanna Dickinson deposition, July 16, 1857, quoted in Hansen, *Alamo Reader*, 43–4; Travis to Houston, February 25, 1836, quoted in Hansen, 34; *Daily Pennsylvanian*, Philadelphia, Pennsylvania, April 4, 1836; *Baltimore Gazette and Daily Advertiser*, April 6, 1836; Jackson and Wheat, *Almonte's Texas*, 369–70; also see Hansen, *Alamo Reader*, 362–7, 388–9. Almonte does not say how many soldiers were involved in the operation, but Travis put the total at from two hundred to three hundred and claimed that "many of the enemy were killed and wounded."

4. Charles Merritt Barnes interview with Enrique Esparza, *San Antonio Daily Express*, May 1907, quoted in Hansen, *Alamo Reader*, 103–4.

5. Jackson and Wheat, *Almonte's Texas*, 370.

6. John Sowers Brooks to Mary Ann Brooks, February 25, 1836; Brooks to father, February 25, 1836; Fannin to Robinson, February 25, 1836, all quoted in Chariton, *100 Days in Texas*, 271–5; Burr H. Duval to his father, March 9, 1836, quoted in Hansen, *Alamo Reader*, 607–8; Fannin to Robinson, February 27, 1836, quoted in Chariton, *100 Days in Texas*, 282–3, which Chariton says was misdated February 29 in Henry Stuart Foote, *Texas and the Texans*, Volume 2, 225–6 (Philadelphia: Thomas, Cowperthwait & Co., 1841), and in Yoakum, *History of Texas*, which was likely taken from Foote; quoted in Hansen, *Alamo Reader*, 600–1, 691. Fannin estimated that his force had gone a mere two hundred yards before turning back.

7. Fannin to Robinson, February 27, 1836, and February 28, 1836, both quoted in Chariton, *100 Days in Texas*, 282–5; Jackson and Wheat, *Almonte's Texas*, 371. Apparently, Fannin's express to Gonzales left Goliad on February 27, but his

February 27 letter to Robinson was not dispatched until the following day, carried by Colonel Ferris, before Fannin wrote his follow-up letter to Robinson on February 28. Hardin, *Texian Iliad*, 158–9; Davis, *Lone Star Rising*, 194–6; Winders, *Sacrificed at the Alamo*, 145–7.

8. John Sowers Brooks to his mother, March 2, 1836, quoted in Chariton, *100 Days in Texas*, 297–9, and in Hansen, *Alamo Reader*, 604–5.

9. Gray, *From Virginia to Texas*, 119; Williamson to governor and General Council, February 25, 1836; Williamson to Tomlinson, February 25, 1836, quoted in Chariton, *100 Days in Texas*, 275–6; John A. Wharton to citizens of Brazoria, February 28, 1836, quoted in Chariton, *100 Days in Texas*, 286.

10. The date of Seguín's departure and his movements afterward are unclear and a matter of some dispute, See Hansen, *Alamo Reader*, 192–208, 225–9; Donovan, *Blood of Heroes*, 219–20, 429; Juan Seguín, "Personal Memoirs of John S. Seguín," 1858, quoted in Hansen, *Alamo Reader*, 193.

11. Sutherland, Seguín, and Horace Alsbury, whose wife, Juana, remained in the Alamo, continued recruiting efforts in Gonzales and were encouraged by the prospect of some three hundred men from Goliad joining them. Fannin had sent Captains Francis DeSauque and John Chenowith ahead with a company of men to Seguín's ranch near San Antonio to gather provisions and beef, but they hastily retreated back to Cibolo Creek when they learned the Mexicans were in pursuit of them. Sutherland and Alsbury gathered ten more men and joined a company of twenty-four Tejanos led by Seguín. Maj. Robert Williamson was also organizing a company in Gonzales, but there is no information regarding its size or if he ever actually raised one at that time. Although the exact numbers are not known, the combined strength of these groups was likely no more than one hundred men who assembled on the Cibolo and waited for Fannin. After learning he had turned back to Goliad, they returned to Gonzales. Sutherland mistakenly says that Smith rode from the Alamo to Gonzales with Travis's March 3 letter, but it was addressed to the convention in Washington, and that is where Smith took it, arriving there on the morning of March 6, before hurrying on to Gonzales. Once there, he joined the others in trying to assemble another reinforcement but failed to gather more than twenty-five men. Although one hundred initially volunteered, seventy-five eventually dropped out. Smith led the small group out of Gonzales on March 6, but the Alamo had fallen that morning. Travis told Smith he would fire a signal gun several times a day if the Alamo still held out. When Smith failed to hear the signal guns, he sent a scouting party to San Antonio, which hastened back to the Cibolo when they learned that Mexican cavalry had spotted them. The admirable efforts of these few men to bring relief to the Alamo resulted in a force far too small to have made any difference in the Alamo's fate. Thomas Ricks Lindley fashioned an untenable theory that far more men were raised to relieve the Alamo and some of them were actually led by Crockett, but his scenario is based on supposition and lacks solid evidence. In any case, the small number of men involved in these efforts would not have made any difference in the outcome at the Alamo. On March 3, George W. Poe wrote to Governor Henry Smith from Velasco saying there were two companies there: Captain Turner's, with forty-three men, and Captain Roman's

with thirty-five men, or about eighty men in all. Combined with the likely total of men at the Cibolo at this time with Sutherland, Smith, Chenowith, DeSauque, Tomlinson, and Seguin, plus whoever Williamson had with him (assuming he had any of his own men), and Fannin's 450, the total of all units then in the field who might have gone to Travis comprised something like six hundred to seven hundred men. Turner had received an order from Lieutenant Governor James W. Robinson, "self styled Commander in Chief of the Army to proceed immediately to Bexar--Capt. Roman is also ordered & this place will be left defenseless--Turner's Commission comes from Robinson & Roman has received none yet." Poe, commander of the post, said his troops would only obey Governor Smith and asked for orders. He feared an attack by sea and land, and told Smith, "I will obey your orders if they are to march to the devil but the thing the other governor [Robinson] I will not." Adding to the uncertainty regarding the number of volunteers is an account in John Swisher's memoir claiming that some two hundred volunteers, in several uncoordinated companies, had arrived in Gonzales by March 5 but thought their numbers too small to provide meaningful relief for the Alamo and waited for more troops to arrive. George Poe to Henry Smith, March 3, 1836; Robinson to Houston, February 27, 1836; Smith to fellow citizens and countrymen, February 27, 1836; Advisory Committee to J. W. Robinson, February 27, 1836; Fannin to Robinson and General Council, March 1, 1836; Fannin to Robinson, February 25, 1836; Fannin to DeSauque and Chenowith, March 1, 1836, all quoted in Chariton, *100 Days in Texas*, 271–72, 277–78, 280, 292–94, 307; Sutherland, *The Alamo*, quoted in Hansen, *Alamo Reader*, 152, 179–81; Gray, *From Virginia to Texas*, 145; Lack, *The Texas Revolutionary Experience*, 54–6, 73–4, 111–23, 215; Boyce House, *City of Flaming Adventure, A Chronicle of San Antonio* (San Antonio: Naylor Company, 1949); Zelime Vance Gillespie II, "John William Smith: Soldier, Messenger, Patriot," Sons of DeWitt Colony Texas website: http://www.sonsofdewittcolony.org//smith-johnwilliam.htm; Swisher and Green, ed., *The Swisher Memoirs*, 29. For Lindley's second reinforcement theory see Lindley, *Alamo Traces*, 104–46, but also see Stuart Reid's rejoinder, "The Second Reinforcement: A Re-appraisal of the Evidence," *Alamo Journal*, no. 137 (June 2005): 16, and Phil Guarnieri, "Some Thoughts on the 'Second Reinforcement Theory,'" *Alamo Journal*, no. 138, (September 2005): 9. Also see Donovan's discussion of the Gonzales reinforcement in *Blood of Heroes*, 431–5.

12. Gray, *From Virginia to Texas*, 120; Lack, *The Texas Revolutionary Experience*, 121–24. Lack estimates that only slightly more than nine hundred men, total, served in Béxar and Goliad between January and March 1836, reflecting a decline in participation since the earlier victories of 1835.

13. Esparza interview found in Howard R. Driggs and Sarah S. King, *Rise of the Lone Star*, (New York: Frederick A. Stokes Co., 1936), 213–31, quoted in Hansen, *Alamo Reader*, 112–19; Susanna (Dickinson) Hannig interview in Morphis, *History of Texas*, quoted in Hansen, *Alamo Reader*, 45–6; Dickinson grandchildren Interviews, quoted in Hansen, *Alamo Reader*, 57–60; Looscan, "Micajah Autry," 323; Charles K. Wolfe, "Davy Crockett's Dance and Old Hickory's Fandango," *The Devil's Box* 16 (September 1982) 34–41. William Groneman III, "Fiddling with

History: David Crockett and the 'Devil's Box,'" *True West*, March 2007, 58–61, casts doubt on the tales of Crockett's fiddling and McGregor's piping in the Alamo. Groneman points out no other Alamo survivor mentioned anyone playing such musical instruments. Although there is no evidence that Crockett ever played the fiddle, Micajah Autry did. His daughter, Mary Autry Greer, remembered her father had "a fine ear for music, played well on the violin, and sketched striking pictures." Susanna Dickinson often told of the duels between Crockett and McGregor, but she appears to have confused Crockett with Autry when she described him in one interview as "a performer on the violin."

14. Jackson and Wheat, *Almonte's Texas*, 370–3; "Mrs. Alsbury's Recollections of the Alamo," quoted in Hansen, *Alamo Reader*, 87–8. William Fairfax Gray described a "norther" as "a hard and cold blow from the north. It generally lasts for two or three days, and is sometimes so excessively cold that persons have been known to freeze to death in crossing the plains. Long observation has taught them to expect a norther between the 20th of February and 1st of March, and that generally closes the winter." Gray, *From Virginia to Texas*, 119; Young, "Where Were the Bathrooms?" I am grateful to Tom Kailbourn for his observations regarding living conditions in the Alamo and their impact on the garrison.

15. Jackson and Wheat, *Almonte's Texas*, 371; Sutherland, *The Alamo*, quoted in Hansen, *Alamo Reader*, 147; Enrique Esparza interview in Driggs and King, *Rise of the Lone Star*, 213–31, quoted in Hansen, *Alamo Reader*, 112–19.

16. Robert McAlpin Williams to Travis, March 1, 1836, quoted in Hansen, *Alamo Reader*, 601; also see Hansen's commentary, 616–17. The letter was confiscated by Santa Anna and sent back to Mexico for the government to "make whatever use of [it] that is seen fit," but if he had other letters, he did not mention them, and they are lost. Williamson's original letter is lost, but a Spanish-language translation of it was found among documents in Mexico's Archivo Historico Militar, Expediente 18909:8–9, and is the only surviving correspondence that arrived in the Alamo. Todd Hansen has pointed out that the surviving version, an official copy signed by Santa Anna, may be an inaccurate translation, done either deliberately or accidentally, possibly for political purposes. Sutherland also mentioned that two messages from Fannin had arrived in Gonzales on the same day only an hour apart; Sutherland, *The Alamo*, quoted in Hansen, *Alamo Reader*, 181; Todd Hansen email to author, January 24, 2021; Fannin to Francis DeSauque and John Chenowith, March 1, 1836, quoted in Chariton, *100 Days in Texas*, 293–95; Yoakum, *History of Texas Vol 2*, p. 68; "Veteran Bios, John A. Wharton," San Jacinto Museum of History website, https://www.sanjacinto-museum.org/Library/Veteran_Bios/Bio _page/?id=879&army=Texian; Sutherland, *The Alamo*, quoted in Hansen, *Alamo Reader*, 181; Wharton was one of two men Houston sent to New Orleans to procure supplies. He returned to Velasco on January 31, 1836, with provisions, but there is no indication he attempted to transport them to Goliad, Gonzales, or Béxar, nor that he commanded a company of 270 men. In fact, Fannin had ordered Wharton to move the supplies to Copano, but Houston ordered them to Matagorda. Fannin claimed that Wharton had "270 men and 9 carts with about 70 barrels flour," which Fannin thought he was taking to Béxar. It's not clear if Fannin thought Wharton

was going directly to Béxar or attempting to join the reinforcement assembling on the Cibolo, but he wasn't actually going anywhere and wrote to Houston informing him that he would wait in Matagorda, as Houston had ordered him to, and believed that Fannin's order conflicted with Houston's, adding, "I perceive that there are more commanders-in-chief than one." In his March 1 letter, Fannin said Wharton had left Victoria and crossed the Guadalupe on February 27. Fannin's February 27 express to Gonzales is lost, but it's possible he mentioned that Wharton was on his way with 270 men and Williamson included them in his estimates of reinforcements in his March 1 letter to Travis. Wharton was commissioned a colonel in the Texas army in September 1835 but resigned two months later. He served primarily as a diplomat and did some work for the army including transporting provisions. He did not receive a land bounty for military service, but his heirs were granted a headright for his status as a head of a family and his immigration to Texas prior to 1830. Republic Claims Nos. 1474 and 8,250, reel 113, TSLAC; head right certificate No. 21/120, Texas GLO.

17. Gray, *From Virginia to Texas*, 113–24.

18. There is some uncertainty about Bonham's service as an Alamo courier. It is believed he left the Alamo on February 16 and arrived in Goliad two days later. In his March 3 letter to the convention, Travis mentions that Bonham "my special messenger, arrived at Labahia [Goliad] fourteen days ago [or February 18] with a request for aid." But earlier in the letter he says that "Col. J. B. Bonham (a courier from Gonzales) got in this morning at eleven o'clock," indicating that Bonham might have been sent out a second time on a separate mission to Gonzales. But if Bonham was only sent out once, on February 16, it is not clear where he went after leaving Goliad until he reached Gonzales at the end of February. One theory suggests he returned to the Alamo from Goliad, possibly around February 23, and was sent out a second time on February 26 or 27 to Gonzales. Sutherland says a courier named Johnson, who was on his way to Goliad on February 23, saw Bonham racing for the Alamo, possibly on his way back from Goliad, but Sutherland got everything else about Bonham wrong, and his information regarding Johnson is secondhand at best. Sutherland claimed that Bonham came to Texas to purchase land, "had not attached himself to the army," and was prospecting for land when the Mexicans arrived on February 23. But we know that Bonham was commissioned a second lieutenant in the Texas cavalry on December 20, 1835, and that Houston recommended he be promoted to major on January 11, 1836. It is likely Bonham went to Béxar under Bowie's command in January. He was an unsuccessful candidate for delegate to the convention on February 1. He offered his services to the rebellion without compensation or land bounty, indicating he would hardly have been out scouting land on February 23. Bonham was not a land speculator but a lawyer who had opened a law office in Brazoria on January 2, 1836. Bonham's younger brother, Milledge Luke Bonham, insisted that Bonham went out only once, to Goliad, and returned to the Alamo on March 3 believing that neither Fannin nor any other reinforcements were coming. Thus, Bonham would have known that he was going to his death when he returned to the Alamo on March 3. The younger Bonham suggests his brother went to several other places on his way back from

Goliad in a vain attempt to gather reinforcements, ending up in Gonzales some time before March 1, likely around the same time Williamson got there. Jackson and Wheat, *Almonte's Texas*, 372; Travis to convention, March 3, 1836, quoted in Hansen, *Alamo Reader*, 35–8; de la Peña, *With Santa Anna in Texas*, 37; Sutherland, *The Alamo*, quoted in Hansen, *Alamo Reader*, 146–50; Donovan, *Blood of Heroes*, 268; Anonymous letter, thought to be Milledge Luke Bonham, "Col. Jas. Butler Bonham," in John Henry Brown family papers, Dolph Briscoe Center for American History, The University of Texas at Austin, quoted in Hansen, *Alamo Reader* 705–6, 717; Bill Groneman, "Bonham, James Butler," Handbook of Texas Online, accessed February 9, 2021, https://www.tshaonline.org/handbook/entries /bonham-james-butler; Williams, "A Critical Study," 25–6, footnote 58; Wm. N. Bonham, "James Butler Bonham," October 19, 1999, Internet Archive, https://web .archive.org/web/20060912183516/http://home.att.net/~wnbonham/james.htm; Stephen L. Hardin, "Where Was Bonham?" Alamo de Parras website, last modified circa 2005, http://www.sonsofdewittcolony.org/adp/archives/feature/bonham. html; Harbert Davenport and Craig H. Roell, "Goliad Campaign of 1836," Handbook of Texas Online, accessed February 23, 2023, https://www.tshaonline.org /handbook/entries/goliad-campaign-of-1836; author's email exchanges with Todd Hansen, January 2021.

19. Sutherland, *The Alamo*, quoted in Hansen, 150; Jackson and Wheat, *Almonte's Texas*, 372; de la Peña, *With Santa Anna in Texas*, 37; J. W. Robinson to James Tarleton, B. C. Wallace, and T. H. McIntire, January 30, 1836; Advisory Committee to J. W. Robinson, February 15, 1836, both quoted in Chariton, *100 Days in Texas*, 183–4, 237. On February 27 Urrea reported that sixteen Texians were killed and twenty-one taken prisoner, including Johnson, who later escaped with two other captives. On March 3 Urrea wrote in his diary that forty-one Texians were killed outright at Agua Dulce Creek, including Grant, and that six prisoners were captured. On the same day Santa Anna wrote to Urrea to remind him that no prisoners were to be taken and that all "foreigners invading the republic . . . shall be judged and treated as pirates" as should all Mexicans who joined in the rebellion; all were to be executed as mandated by the Tornel Decree. Santa Anna to Filisola, February 27, 1836; Urrea to Santa Anna, February 27, 1836; Urrea diary entry, March 2, 1836; Santa Anna to Urrea, March 3, 1836, all quoted in Chariton, *100 Days in Texas*, 278–80, 283, 299, 309.

20. Travis to convention, Travis to Jesse Grimes, March 3, 1836, quoted in Jenkins, *Papers of the Texas Revolution*, vol. 4, 501–04. In a 1902 interview Enrique Esparza said that about seven days into the siege, or around February 29, a three-day armistice was declared by Santa Anna, ostensibly to discuss surrender terms. According to Esparza, who was about eight years old at the time, Crockett, who he referred to as "Don Benito," "had conferences every day with Santa Anna. Badio [Juan A. Badillo], the interpreter, was a close friend of my father and I heard him tell my father in the quarters that Santa Anna had offered to let the Americans go with their lives if they would surrender, but the Mexicans would be treated as rebels. . . . Only one person went out during the armistice, a woman named Trinidad Saucedo. . . . Crockett . . . assembled the men on the last day and told them Santa

Anna's terms, but none of them believed that anyone who surrendered would get out alive, so they all said as they would have to die any how they would fight it out." In a 1907 interview Esparza, then nearly eighty years old, again referred to an "all too short armistice" but says that it was the ill Bowie who "one day" announced to the garrison, "All of you who desire to leave here may go in safety. Santa Anna has just sent a message to Travis saying there will be an armistice for three days to give us time to deliberate on surrendering. During those three days all who desire to do so may go out of here. Travis has sent me a message and told me to tell those near me. When Bowie said this quite a number left." Esparza also says that Bowie asked his father, Gregorio Esparza, if he wanted to take advantage of the armistice and leave, but his father chose to remain with the garrison. Hardin, "Efficient in the Cause," in Poyo, ed., *Tejano Journey,* 49–71, footnote 28, 143; "Alamo's Only Survivor," *San Antonio Daily Express*, May 12, 1907, quoted in Hansen, *Alamo Reader*, 104; Matovina, *The Alamo Remembered*, 70; Hansen, *Alamo Reader*, 98–104; Charles Merritt interview with Enrique Esparza, *San Antonio Daily Express*, May 12 and 19, 1907, quoted in Hansen, *Alamo Reader*, 101–10; "Heroes Who Died Fighting for Freedom," The Alamo website, https://www.thealamo.org/remember /history/defenders/index.html.

Travis had no need to transmit messages through Bowie, a very sick man, rather than simply addressing the men himself, especially since he had been in sole command throughout the siege. There is a huge difference in these two Esparza stories, especially in the casting of Crockett in the role of negotiator in one version and leaving out mention of negotiations in the other. Esparza also claimed Crockett was the real leader in the Alamo and that he "seemed to be the leading spirit. He was everywhere. He went to every exposed point and personally directed the fighting. Travis was chief in command, but he depended more upon the judgment of Crockett and that brave man's intrepidity than upon his own." No doubt Travis relied on Crockett's leadership skills to motivate the men and keep their spirits up, but there is no question that Travis was very much in command and considered himself to be. Moreover, it is highly doubtful that Santa Anna would have offered such an amnesty when all of his communications emphasized the unequivocal necessity to kill all rebels as foreign pirates and all Mexicans who joined them as traitors. The red flag over San Fernando Church, the Mexican refusal to even talk to the Alamo commanders on the first day of the siege, the Mexican demand for unconditional surrender, and the playing of "El Degüello," the bugle call signaling no quarter—as well as Santa Anna's communications on this question—all suggest it is highly unlikely that he would offer such an armistice for no apparent reason. However, this did not stop Santa Anna from later claiming that he did, in fact, offer the Texian defenders amnesty. In his 1837 *Manifesto*, he claimed that, even after he saw advantages to attacking the Alamo, "I still wanted to try a generous measure, characteristic of Mexican kindness, and I offered life to the defendants who would surrender their arms and retire under oath not to take them up again against Mexico. Colonel Don Juan Nepomuceno Almonte, through whom this generous offer was made, transmitted to me their reply which stated that they would let us know if they accepted and if not, they would renew the fire at a given hour. They decided on the latter course and their decision irrevocably sealed their fate." In a footnote, Santa Anna added that Travis replied to proposals to surrender "always that every man under his command preferred to die rather than surrender the fort to the Mexicans." This statement was clearly an attempt to rewrite history and make Santa Anna look more humane than he was. It is contradicted by Almonte and Santa Anna's actions during the siege and throughout the war. *Manifesto Which General Antonio Lopez de Santa-Anna Addresses to His Fellow-Citizens Relative to His Operations During the Texas Campaign and His Capture 10 of May 1837*, quoted in Carlos E. Casteñeda, *The Mexican Side of the Texas Revolution [1836]* (Washington, DC: Documentary Publications, 1971), 13–14;

In his March 3 letter, Travis complained that most of the Tejanos had deserted and that only three remained in the fort, although the official list of Alamo dead includes the names of at least eight Tejanos. It is possible some Tejanos and perhaps Louis Rose, who is discussed later, simply deserted. If so, Esparza may have wanted to conceal that fact and invented the story of an armistice to cover the desertions. There is no proof Esparza did so, but he is the only one who ever mentioned an armistice. By the early twentieth century Esparza may have sought to conceal such a desertion to protect the image of Tejano defenders and those who fought throughout the war. Evidence suggests that at least eleven Tejano soldiers in Juan Seguin's company left the Alamo on February 20 and 21, only days before Santa Anna's arrival. In his 1907 account, Esparza named six more, including Antonio Menchaca, who he said departed during an armistice but who more likely left with Seguin's men. Decades after the Alamo fell, in a Texas dominated by Anglos and after the Alamo dead were elevated to martyrdom, Menchaca and Esparza had reason to obscure any hint that these Tejanos were deserters, although they are very likely the ones Travis referred to in his March 3 letter.

In addition to his awareness of anti-Mexican prejudice, Esparza may also have been caught up in the dispute between Adina De Zavala and Clara Driscoll over the preservation of the Alamo, which was ongoing at the time of the Esparza interviews. De Zavala wanted to preserve and emphasize the importance of the *convento*, or Long Barrack building, while Driscoll wanted the church to be the center of the Alamo site. De Zavala's grandfather, Lorenzo De Zavala, signed the Texas Declaration of Independence and was the first vice president of the Republic of Texas. Esparza could have been concerned that negative images of Tejano Alamo defenders might hurt De Zavala's case, and like Santa Anna, he may have been attempting to rewrite history. L. Robert Ables, "Zavala, Adina Emilia De," Handbook of Texas Online, accessed February 2, 2021, https://www.tshaonline.org/handbook/entries/zavala-adina-emilia-de.

Tejanos were divided on the best course in the Texas revolt. Some supported the centralists, others opposed Santa Anna and wanted to return to the Constitution of 1824 rather than separate from Mexico, and some supported full independence. Some may have deserted Béxar when they learned Santa Anna was near rather than remain in what they regarded as a hopeless situation, but many fought bravely throughout the war. Although Travis also railed against the civilian Tejanos in Béxar, they had done much to support the Texians and provided them with provisions prior to the siege. Once they found themselves occupied by Santa Anna's army, their reluctance to offer open opposition is understandable. Jesús F. de la Teja, "Tejanos and the Siege and Battle of the Alamo," Handbook of Texas Online, accessed February 2, 2021, https://www.tshaonline.org/handbook/entries/tejanos-and-the-siege-and-battle-of-the-alamo; Raymond Estep, "Zavala, Lorenzo de," Handbook of Texas Online, accessed February 2, 2021, https://www.tshaonline.org/handbook/entries/zavala-lorenzo-de.

John Sutherland claimed that "very few of the Mexican citizens of the Republic were friendly to the cause of Texas. Some were openly hostile, and had gone to Mexico to join Santa Anna, while a majority occupied a kind of half-way ground, yet eager to follow the dominant party. It was said that between a thousand and fifteen hundred of them joined Santa Anna, during his stay in Bexar, and whilst on the march from that place to the Colorado." It was Sutherland who also pointed out the reluctance of the garrison commanders to accept the word of Tejano spies who accurately reported Santa Anna's movements prior to the siege, and Sutherland himself referred to them as "a degraded class of 'Greasers.'" Finally, Sutherland said that by March 3, "nearly all of the Mexicans, who had joined the garrison at the beginning of the siege, had left it. They had joined believing that Travis would receive re-inforcements sufficient to enable him to maintain the fort, when they would be on the safe side, but being disappointed in this their hearts failed in view of the fate which they must unavoidably suffer should they stand up to their first resolves. They knew both the weakness of the garrison and the strength of the enemy. Only three of them remained true to our cause." Sutherland's account supports the idea that several Tejanos did desert the Alamo, but Sutherland left the Alamo on the first day of the siege and could only have gotten this information second hand, possibly from Travis's March 3 letter, from Smith, who was in the Alamo until late on the night of March 3, or from Susanna Dickinson or Joe, who he says spoke to him after the battle. However, it was not the desertion of a few Tejanos that determined Travis's fate but rather the inability of Texas to assemble a credible relief force for the Alamo. Sutherland, *The Alamo*, quoted in Hansen, *Alamo Reader*, 46, 58, 141–2, 151.

Susanna Dickinson later testified that a "Mexican woman deserted us one night, and going over to the enemy informed them of our very inferior numbers, which Col. Travis said made them confident of success and emboldened them to make the final assault, which they did at early dawn the morning of the 6th of March." Susanna's granddaughter, Mrs. Susan Sterling, told Amelia Williams that her grandmother always said the woman was Juana Alsbury. But Esparza and others later testified that Juana remained in the fort throughout the siege and battle. Nor would much information about conditions in the Alamo have been news to Santa Anna, particularly the garrison's inferior numbers, or affected his plans. The illiterate Susanna appears to have shared anti-Tejano sentiments with other Anglos and perhaps mistook Trinidad Saucedo, who Esparza said left the fort, for Juana Alsbury. In 1849, Mexican General Vicente Filisola wrote that on the evening of March 5 Travis, "through the intermediary of a woman, proposed to the general in chief that they would surrender arms and fort with everybody in it with the only condition of saving his life and that of all his comrades in arms. However, the answer had come back that they should surrender unconditionally, without guarantees, not even of life itself, since there should be no guarantees for traitors. With this reply it is clear that all were determined to lose their existence, selling it as dearly as possible." However, Filisola was not at the Alamo and could only have gotten his information secondhand. His description seems to conflate events on the first day of the siege, when the Texians sought to parlay, and accounts of events later in the siege. Susanna (Dickinson) Hannig interview in Morphis, *History of Texas*, 174–77, quoted in Hansen, *Alamo Reader*, 45-6; Filisola, *Memoirs*, quoted in Hansen, *Alamo Reader*, 391–2. See Davis, *Three Roads to the Alamo*, 729–30, footnote 83, for an evaluation of reports of a woman leaving the Alamo and rumors that Travis proposed surrendering to Santa Anna.

21. Travis to David Ayers, March 3, 1836, quoted in Jenkins, *Papers of the Texas Revolution*, Vol. 4, 501.

22. No letters written by Alamo defenders during the siege have survived other than Travis's, although it seems certain that at least some personal letters must have gone out with Smith or other Alamo couriers. However, it is also possible that a lack of writing paper may have prevented the defenders from sending written messages. See Hansen, *Alamo Reader*, 136–37, 190–91, for a discussion of Alamo letters. Sutherland, *The Alamo*, quoted in Hansen, *Alamo Reader*, 151; Chariton, *100 Days in Texas*, 303–4; Wallace O. Chariton, *Exploring the Alamo Legends* (Plano: Republic of Texas Press, 1992), 185–7; Winders, *Sacrificed at the Alamo*, 106; Jackson and Wheat, *Almonte's Texas*, 372. Crockett's participation in the sortie on the sugar mill is based on Susanna Dickinson's recollection that "3 of our spys who entered 3 days before the assault & were all killed. Col. Crockett was one of the 3 men who came into the Fort during the siege & before the assault." *The Journal of the San Luis Potosí Battalion de San Luis Potosí* entry for March 6 says Crockett "succeeded in getting in three nights before," but that information could have come from Susanna, who was interrogated by the Mexicans after the battle. September 23, 1876, interview with Susanna (Dickinson) Hannig by Adjutant General, quoted in Hansen, *Alamo Reader*, 47–8; "Batallón Activo de San Luis, Itinerario de las jornadas." Tom Lindley's "second reinforcement theory" contends that Crockett left the Alamo and led fifty reinforcements back in. This is largely unsubstantiated and based on questionable sources, but the *Arkansas Gazette* of April 12, 1836, curiously reported that "Col. Crockett, with about 50 resolute volunteers, had cut their way into the garrison, through the Mexican troops only a few days before the fall of San Antonio." The source of that report is unknown.

23. Susanna (Dickinson) Hannig interview in Morphis, *History of Texas*, quoted in Hansen, *Alamo Reader*, 44–6. Susanna Dickinson also quoted Henry Warnell as saying that he, too, "had much rather be out in the open prairie, than to be pent up in that manner." Susanna Hannig deposition, March 8, 1860, Texas GLO Court of Claims file C-8490, quoted in Hansen, *Alamo Reader*, 44–5. Warnell is thought to have been wounded, but survived the battle and escaped, only to die later of his wounds. Other accounts say he was found hiding among the Alamo dead and then executed. Still other sources claim he was a messenger who was wounded while

leaving the Alamo, later dying of his wounds. He is sometimes mistakenly referred to as "Warner." See Groneman, *Alamo Defenders*, 118–119; Hansen, *Alamo Reader*, 240, 324; Donovan, *Blood of Heroes*, 453.

24. Journal of Capt. José Juan Sánchez Navarro y Estrada, quoted in Hansen, *Alamo Reader*, 410–12; Jackson and Wheat, *Almonte's Texas*, 372–3; Sutherland, *The Alamo*, quoted in Hansen, 152; Donovan, *Blood of Heroes*, 269.

25. Jackson and Wheat, *Almonte's Texas*, 362–7. It is not certain Allen was the messenger sent out on March 5, but that is a minor point. Regardless of who the courier was, the message carried to Fannin conveyed the same information. For a discussion of Allen's identification see Donovan, *Blood of Heroes*, 271–2, 387–8, 437; Groneman, *Alamo Defenders*, 4; Robert H. Davis, "Bob Davis Uncovers an Untold Story About the Alamo," Fort Worth *Star-Telegram*, February 28, 1932; James L. Allen biographical papers, 1932, Center for American History, quoted in Hansen, *Alamo Reader*, 219–20; Williams, "A Critical Study," quoted in Hansen, *Alamo Reader*, 221. Also see Hansen's "Commentaries," 242–3, and 617 regarding Allen; John Sowers Brooks to James Hagerty, March 9, 1836, and Brooks to A. H. Brooks, March 10, 1836, both quoted in Hansen, *Alamo Reader*, 605–7.

26. Susanna (Dickinson) Hannig later testified that Almonte told her a man who tried to escape had been shot and he offered to show her the body, an offer she declined. Hannig interview by the adjutant general, September 1877, quoted in Hansen, *Alamo Reader*, 48; de la Peña, *With Santa Anna in Texas*, 44.

27. There is a powerful legend that Travis made an emotional speech to his men a few days prior to the battle, telling them that all hope of reinforcement was gone and that they must perish. He then drew a line on the ground with his sword and asked those who would stay to cross over. All but one, Louis Rose, who was called "Moses," crossed. Rose made his way through the Mexican lines that night and ended up at the home of William P. Zuber's parents, Abraham and Mary Zuber, his legs badly injured by cactus thorns, and Rose told them the story of his escape.

The Rose story is a thirdhand account with little or no confirmation from other witnesses. However, in the years that followed, Rose's testimony in support of the heirs of the Alamo dead was accepted by land commissioners, which is offered as proof that he was in the Alamo. He may have been, but Rose never received a land grant for military service himself and was given only one-third of a league of land, which all men were entitled to if they were residents prior to March 2, 1836, the day Texas independence was declared. Zuber published Rose's story in 1873 and revised or amended it several times afterward. He claimed Rose told the story to his parents, who didn't write it down but that his mother, who had a photographic memory, repeated it to him verbally countless times and that he then wrote it down. He admitted he invented at least part of Travis's alleged speech and that his mother's account did not call it a speech at all. Regardless of the veracity of Zuber's story, Rose's existence and his service in the Alamo were confirmed by Robert Bruce Blake, whose painstaking research of countless private and public documents, including Nacogdoches records, proved that Rose did leave the Alamo and openly spoke of it. The documents also attest to Rose's honesty and document his sixteen appearances as a witness regarding land claims of heirs of Alamo defenders that were upheld based at least partly on his testimony. However, Rose claimed to have left the Alamo on March 3, which indicates that Travis addressed his men on that day, but Travis made no mention of it in his final letters, which were sent out that night, nor did messenger John W. Smith, who left the fort around midnight on March 3, ever mention it. It is possible that Travis addressed the men after that in the early hours of March 4 and that Rose simply remembered it as March 3. Charles Merritt Barnes, "Alamo's Only Survivor," *San Antonio Daily Express*, May 12 and 19, 1907, quoted in Hansen, *Alamo Reader*, 101–10; Donovan, *Blood of Heroes*, 351–74; Chariton, *100 Days in Texas*, 205. For discussion of the Rose story see Hansen, *Alamo Reader*, 245–94; the Blake report on "Documents from Nacogdoches County Records Relating to Moses (Louis) Rose," is found on 274–282; Davis, *Three Roads to the Alamo*, 731–32, footnote 99.

Susanna Dickinson supported Zuber's story, but her statements were all recorded after Zuber's account was published, and she could have been influenced by it. Other accounts were handed down to her grandchildren who repeated them to interviewers but are, at best, hearsay. However, in *Blood of Heroes*, James Donovan revealed more persuasive evidence that an event like this did take place, although less melodramatic than the Zuber account. First, Frank Johnson, a leader of the ill-fated Matamoros expedition, read the 1873 Zuber account to Susanna, who said she didn't know Rose personally but recalled that Travis did assemble the men and addressed them, and that one man escaped from the fort. She recalled the men saying they didn't think he would survive his escape attempt. Although she didn't endorse Zuber's description of the event, she acknowledged that something like it did take place but, again, she could have been influenced by the Zuber story once she had heard it. In 1853 she testified that James M. Rose was the only man named Rose that she knew of in the Alamo. She thought Rose and Crockett were friends and recalled hearing Rose relate to her husband that he had a narrow escape from a Mexican officer during a skirmish. She made no mention of Louis or Moses Rose or of Rose having a foreign accent, which Louis Rose, a Frenchman, had. Second, however, Donovan also cites a 1901 interview with David S. H. Darst, whose father, Jacob Darst, was one of the thirty-two volunteers from Gonzales who died in the Alamo. Darst the younger was a former mayor of Gonzales and founded the *Inquirer* in 1851. He said he actually met Rose in 1840, long before the Zuber account was published, and that Rose essentially confirmed the story. He told Darst that when it became clear that no help was coming, Travis drew a line and asked all who would stay to cross over to him. Rose told Darst he was the only man who refused to cross the line and that he escaped from the fort that night. The Darst account is the most persuasive and lends strength to the idea that Travis took some action of this kind even if it was not the scene Zuber constructed. Donovan also cites Amelia Williams's handwritten notes regarding interviews with Susanna Dickinson's grandson, A. D. Griffith, that relate Griffith being told the Rose story in the 1860s, before the Zuber account was published. Donovan also points out that it would have been a lot easier for Rose to simply claim he was sent out as a messenger and somehow got injured and ended up at the Zuber place. Who could have contradicted him? The noncombatant survivors didn't know who all the couriers were or when they went out. And it would have been far easier for Rose to simply never mention that he'd been in the Alamo at all and avoid being labeled a coward, as he was in the years that followed. And it is fair to ask why Rose, who admittedly abandoned his comrades, would dictate a Travis speech that cast him in the worst possible light. Zuber's story has all the men, including Bowie and the sick, dragging themselves across the line in a courageous act of self-sacrifice and Rose is identified as the sole deserter. He must have known that such a moving, patriotic tableau would make him look bad, which makes Zuber's story regarding Travis's speech even less credible. Donovan, *Blood of Heroes*, 351–74; Chariton, *100 Days in Texas*, 205. For discussion of the Rose story see Hansen, *Alamo Reader*, 245–94.

In an early twentieth century account, Enrique Esparza said he saw Travis draw a line and that all of the men "jumped across." By then, any testimony about the event could have simply been repeated from other sources, including Zuber. Esparza was a child during the siege and these statements were made more than a half-century later when he enjoyed being a local celebrity who spun yarns for tourists and journalists, but whose memory was clearly clouded by the years. Neither Juana Alsbury nor her sister, Gertrudis Navarro, nor other survivors mentioned it, aside from Susanna Dickinson. There is no record of James Allen or any other Alamo messenger relating such a story, although no written communication from March 5 survives, and we have only Brooks's recollection of the message Allen carried to Goliad.

It is also possible that, rather than asking the men who would stay in the Alamo to cross the line, Travis asked those who wanted to *leave* to cross over or simply step out of ranks. In an 1877 interview, Susanna Dickinson said Travis "asked the command that if any desired to escape, now was the time, to let it be known, and to step out of the ranks. But one stepped out. His name to the best of my recollection was Ross. The next morning he was missing." This was likely a reference to Louis Rose since there is no one named Ross included among lists of Alamo defenders. It is possible that she simply pronounced Rose as "Ross," or was heard to by whoever recorded the interview. It is curious that Susanna only mentioned James Rose in her earlier interviews and said he was the only man named Rose in the Alamo, but in 1877, after hearing the Zuber account, she said that the only man who chose to leave the fort was named "Ross." Susanna told essentially the same story in an 1881 interview saying that Travis told those who wanted to *leave* to cross the line ("who crosses the line that I have drawn, shall go!"). She did not mention Rose or Ross. It's quite a different matter to actively signal to your comrades that, by crossing the line, you are quitting rather than staying and, in this scenario, Rose seems to be the only one who did so. Although some of her interviews sound embellished by those who transcribed them, this one sounds more straightforward and is comparable to the version Darst says Rose related to him. De la Peña claimed Travis's agreement to surrender or seek escape came when the men became highly agitated after realizing no help was coming. He wrote that "these facts were given to us by a lady from Béjar, a Negro who was the only male who escaped [no doubt a reference to Travis's slave Joe, who survived the battle], and several women who were found inside and were rescued by Colonels Morales and Miñón. The enemy was in communication with some of the Béjar townspeople who were their sympathizers, and it was said as a fact during those days that the president-general had known of Travis's decision and that it was for this reason that he precipitated the assault." "Survivor of the Alamo," San Antonio *Daily Express*, April 8, 1881, quoted in Hansen, *Alamo Reader*, 51–4; Susanna Belles, formerly Dickinson, deposition, November 21, 1853, and deposition, July 16, 1857, James Rose Court of Claims file C-7115, Texas General Land Office, quoted in Hansen, *Alamo Reader*, 43–4; Susanna (Dickinson) Hannig, interview, September 16–30, 1877, adjutant general correspondence, quoted in Hansen, *Alamo Reader*, 48; Driggs and King, *Rise of the Lone Star*, quoted in Hansen, *Alamo Reader*, 112–19; Adina De Zavala interview with Enrique Esparza, *San Antonio Light*, November 10, 1901, quoted in Hansen, *Alamo Reader*, 94–6; Charles Merritt Barnes, "Alamo's Only Survivor," *San Antonio Daily Express*, May 12 and 19, 1907, quoted in Hansen, *Alamo Reader*, 101–10; the Blake report on "Documents from Nacogdoches County Records Relating to Moses (Louis) Rose," is found on 274–282; Davis, *Three Roads to the Alamo*, 731–32, footnote 99; Chariton, *Exploring the Alamo Legends*, 175–206; Lindley, *Alamo Traces*, 173–248; De La Peña, *With Santa Anna in Texas*, 44.

28. Santa Anna's Military Order, March 5, 1836, translation from Filisola, *Memoirs*, are quoted in Hansen, *Alamo Reader*, 337–8. For details regarding Santa Anna's orders see Jackson and Wheat, *Almonte's Texas*, 372–3; De la Peña, *With Santa Anna in Texas*, 45–6; Carlos Sánchez-Navarro, *La Guerra de Texas: Memorias de un Soldado* (Mexico: Editorial Jus, S.A., 1960), translations of excerpts, 82-86, by Tom Kailbourn provided to the author, February 2008, revised December 23, 2010; McDonald, "Siege of the Alamo, a Mexican Army Journal," 31–6.

29. *Jackson Gazette*, February 7, 1829; Dr. J. H. Barnard letter to *Missouri Argus*, August 26, 1836, quoted in Donovan, *Blood of Heroes*, 441; Micajah Autry to Martha Autry, January 13, 1836, quoted in Chariton, *100 Days in Texas*, 142–3; Daniel Cloud to John B. Cloud, December 26, 1835, quoted in Chariton, *100 Days in Texas*, 73; Interview with Joe, Frankfort *Commmonwealth*, May 25, 1836, quoted in Hansen, *Alamo Reader*, 74; anonymous, "Col. Jas. Butler Bonham," in John Henry Brown family papers, Dolph Briscoe Center for American History, The University of Texas at Austin, quoted in Hansen, *Alamo Reader*, 706; Hansen presents evidence that the author is Bonham's brother, Milledge Luke Bonham, *Alamo Reader*, 717.

30. C. Newell, interview of Ben, 1838, *History of the Revolution in Texas, Particularly of the War of 1835 & '36* (New York: Wiley & Putnam, 1838), quoted in Hansen, *Alamo Reader*, 473. Ben, a free Black man, was Almonte's body servant, but served as cook to both Almonte and Santa Anna during the siege. Robert L. Durham, *African Americans and the Fight for the Alamo*, Alamo de Parras website, 1996: http://www.sonsofdewittcolony.org/adp/history/1836/blacks/durham.html.

31. "Batallón Activo de San Luis, Itinerario de las jornadas"; McDonald, "Siege of the Alamo," 31–6; de la Peña, *With Santa Anna*, 45–53; Newell, interview of Ben, 1838, *History of the Revolution*, quoted in Hansen, *Alamo Reader*, 473. Details of

the battle are found in a March 7, 1836, account written by an unidentified Mexican soldier, which was published in *El Mosquito Mexicano* (newspaper) on April 5, 1836, quoted in Hansen, *Alamo Reader*, 486–87, translated by John Wheat.

32. Interview with Joe, New Orleans *Commercial Bulletin*, April 11, 1836; interview with Joe, *Memphis Enquirer*, April 12, 1836; another version of the interview is in *National Intelligencer*, April 30, 1836; interview with Joe, Frankfort *Commmonwealth*, May 25, 1836, all quoted in Hansen, *Alamo Reader*, 70–8; Gray, *From Virginia to Texas*, 136.

33. De la Peña, *With Santa Anna in Texas*, 51.

34. De la Peña, *With Santa Anna in Texas*, 51; Santa Anna, *Manifesto*, quoted in Casteñeda, *The Mexican Side of the Texas Revolution*, 13; March 7, 1836, account by unidentified Mexican soldier, published in *El Mosquito Mexicano* April 5, 1836, quoted in Hansen, *Alamo Reader*, 486–87. There are many reports of Bowie's death, but perhaps the most reliable was contained in a letter dated March 7, 1836, published in the Mexico City newspaper *El Mosquito Mexicano* on April 5, 1836, quoted in Davis, *Three Roads to the Alamo*, as part of a broad discussion of Bowie's death, 734-36. For discussion of Bowie's death, also see Hansen, *Alamo Reader*, 786–91.

35. Killing the sick and wounded may have been done under the Tornel Decree, which mandated that no foreigners bearing arms be taken prisoner, even if they had surrendered or, presumably, were among the sick or wounded. Richard Bruce Winders, "'This Is a Cruel Truth, But I Cannot Omit It': The Origin and Effect of Mexico's No Quarter Policy in the Texas Revolution," *Southwestern Historical Quarterly* 120, no. 4 (2017): 426.

36. In one interview Susanna claimed that her rescuer was Almonte, and he confirmed her report years later. However, in another interview she says it was Colonel Black, an Englishman. One of Susanna's grandchildren told Amelia Williams that the wife of Ramón Músquiz, who was a friend of Susanna's, pleaded with Santa Anna to spare her life and that an unidentified officer was told to find her and bring her out of the fort, hence her being called for by name. Susanna (Dickinson) Hannig quoted in Morphis, *History of Texas*, 168–77; interview with Susanna by adjutant general, September 23, 1876, in Rena Maverick Green, *Memoirs of Mary A. Maverick* (Lincoln: University of Nebraska Press, 1989); *San Antonio Express*, February 24, 1929; San Antonio *Daily Express*, April 28, 1881; Williams, "Critical Study," all quoted in Hansen, *Alamo Reader*, 45–9, 51, 55, 59; Jackson and Wheat, *Almonte's Texas*, 373–4, 421.

37. Susanna (Dickinson) Hannig, quoted in Morphis, *History of Texas*, 168–77; *San Antonio Express*, February 24, 1929; San Antonio *Daily Express*, April 28, 1881; "Mrs. Alsbury's Recollections of the Alamo," all quoted in Hansen, *Alamo Reader*, 45–6, 49–51, 87–88.

38. Interview with Joe, New Orleans *Commercial Bulletin*, April 11, 1836; interview with Joe, *Memphis Enquirer*, April 12, 1836; another version of the interview is in *National Intelligencer*, April 30, 1836; interview with Joe, Frankfort *Commmonwealth*, May 25, 1836, all quoted in Hansen, *Alamo Reader*, 70–78; Gray, *From Virginia to Texas*, 136. Joe thought the officer who saved him was a

Captain Baragan; Ben interview by Newell, *History of the Revolution*, quoted in Hansen, *Alamo Reader*, 473; Edward Stiff interview of Ben, *The Texan Emigrant*, 1840, quoted in Hansen, *Alamo Reader*, 474; De la Peña, *With Santa Anna in Texas*, 46–55; Tom Kailbourn, transcriber and translator, "Lt. Col. Pedro Ampudia's After-action Report of the Siege and Capture of the Alamo," *Alamo Journal*, issue 159, Dec. 2010; McDonald, "The Siege of the Alamo," 31–6; General Joaquin Ramírez y Sesma, after-action report of Battle of the Alamo, March 6, 1836, to Santa Anna, Arroyo del Salado, Texas, March 11, 1836, Secretaria de Guerra y Marina, Archivo General de México, Book No. 335, 166–68, typescript copy, Dolph Briscoe Center for American History, University of Texas at Austin, translation by Tom Kailbourn, September 18, 2005, provided to the author; Filisola, *Memoirs*, quoted in Hansen, *Alamo Reader*, 390–3; Ramon Martinez Caro, "A True Account of the First Texas Campaign" (Mexico: Imprenta de Santiago Perez, 1837) quoted in Castañeda, *The Mexican Side of the Texas Revolution*, 102–4; Francis Antonio Ruiz, "Fall of the Alamo, and Massacre of Travis and His Brave Associates," *Texas Almanac* (1860): 80–2, quoted in Hansen, *Alamo Reader*, 500–3; Ruiz Court of Claims deposition, April 16, 1861, Texas GLO file 5026; Sutherland, *The Alamo*, quoted in Hansen, *Alamo Reader*, 152–3; Newell interview of Ben, *History of the Revolution*, quoted in Hansen, *Alamo Reader*, 473; Donovan, *Blood of Heroes*, 273–8, 443; Winders, *Sacrificed at the Alamo*, 111–12. In an 1840 interview with Ben by Edward Stiff for *The Texan Emigrant*, which sounds highly embellished, Ben is said to have identified Crockett's body and added that no less than sixteen Mexican dead surrounded it. Several accounts portray Crockett surrounded by Mexican dead in double digits but estimates of the number of Mexicans killed at the Alamo, some including those who died of their wounds later, range from seventy to 150. Thus, if Crockett himself really had killed that many Mexicans himself, it would give him from 10 to 23 percent of the total. Quoted in Hansen, *Alamo Reader*, 474, 778–782; Donovan, *Blood of Heroes*, 455–6; Santa Anna to Citizens, March 7, 1836, quoted in Jenkins, *Papers of the Texas Revolution*, Vol. 5, 20–21.

39. Gray, *From Virginia to Texas*, 127.

40. Gray, *From Virginia to Texas*, 125–7. Word of the Alamo's fall did not reach Washington until March 15.

41. Brooks to James Hagerty, March 9, 1836, quoted in Chariton, *100 Days in Texas*, 352.

42. Gray, *From Virginia to Texas*, 125–7. Gray was apparently referring to Ramón Músquiz of San Antonio, who assisted Francisco Ruiz in gathering the Alamo dead and identifying the bodies of Travis, Bowie, and Crockett on March 6. J. W. Robinson to Fannin, March 6, 1836; Parmer to wife, March 6, 1836; Robinson to Fannin, March 6, 1836, all quoted in Chariton, *100 Days in Texas*, 315–17; James C. Neill receipt to Horace Eggleston, March 6, 1836, Republic Claim No. 446, reel 28, TSLAC; Hardin, *Texian Iliad*, 162; reward for Joe dated May 21, 1837, published in *Telegraph and Texas Register*, August 24, 1837.

Chapter 7

1. De la Peña, *With Santa Anna in Texas*; David B. Gracy II, "'Just as I Have Written It': A Study of the Authenticity of the Manuscript of José Enrique de la Peña's Account of the Texas Campaign," *The Southwestern Historical Quarterly* 105, no. 2 (October 2001); Dan Kilgore, *How Did Davy Die?* (College Station: Texas A&M University Press, 1978). Also see William C. Davis, "How Davy Probably Didn't Die," *Journal of the Alamo Battlefield Association* 2, no. 1 (Fall 1997), a critical survey of the Crockett death accounts.

2. Susanna (Dickinson) Hannig interview by adjutant general, September 23, 1876; Santa Anna's military report, March 6, 1836; Santa Anna to Jose Maria Tornel, March 6, 1836, quoted in Todd Hansen, *Alamo Reader*, 47–48, 339–41, 369–71, 402–412; Jackson and Wheat, *Almonte's Texas*, 373–4; José Juan Sánchez-Navarro, "Año de 1836: Indice de la correspondencia dirigida por el Señor Comandante general e Inspector de los Departamentos de Nuevo Leon y Tamaulipas, al Ayudante de los mismos," José Juan Sánchez-Navarro Papers, Dolph Briscoe Center for American History, University of Texas at Austin, translations of excerpts by Tom Kailbourn provided to the author, February 2008, revised December 23, 2010; Kailbourn, "Lt. Col. Pedro Ampudia's After-action Report;" Sesma, after-action report to Santa Anna, March 11, 1836, Dolph Briscoe Center for American History, University of Texas at Austin, translation provided by Tom Kailbourn; McDonald, "Siege of the Alamo," 31–36.

3. Hansen, *Alamo Reader*, 194; 508–13; 517; Thomas Ricks Lindley, "Killing Crockett, Lindley's Opinion," *Alamo Journal*, no. 98 (1995); *Telegraph and Texas Register*, March 24, 1836; Hansen, *Alamo Reader*, 240, 324, and Donovan, *Blood of Heroes*, 453. For a discussion of the shortcomings and contradictions in statements made by Alamo survivors, see Davis, "How Davy Probably Didn't Die." For discussion of Henry Warnell, see Hansen, *Alamo Reader*, 324, and Groneman, *Alamo Defenders*, 118–119.

4. *Telegraph and Texas Register*, March 24, 1836, *New Orleans True American*, March 27, 1836, *Louisiana Advertiser*, March 28, 1836, *New Orleans Commercial Bulletin*, March 28, 1836, *Arkansas Gazette*, April 12, 1836, all quoted in Hansen, *Alamo Reader*, 551-61; *New Orleans Advertiser*, March 28, 1836; *Natchez Courier*, March 31, 1836, reprinted in *New York Commercial Advertiser*, April 18, 1836. Also see Davis, "How Davy Probably Didn't Die," 15–16.

5. José Urrea, *Diary of the Military Operations*, 1838, reprinted in Castañeda, *The Mexican Side of the Texas Revolution*, 234–37; Jackson and Wheat, *Almonte's Texas*, 388–90; Chariton, *100 Days in Texas*, 79–80.

6. The Treaties of Velasco are found on the Texas State Library and Archives Commission website, https://www.tsl.texas.gov/treasures/republic/velasco-01.html#:~:text=The%20public%20treaty%20provided%20that,prisoners%20on%20an%20equal%20basis. This includes photocopies of the treaty documents; also available on Lone Star Junction website, http://www.lsjunction.com/docs/velasco.htm. Mexico refused to ratify the treaties because Santa Anna was a prisoner when he signed them. The treaties never took effect and Mexico did not recognize

Texas independence until the Mexican-American War ended with the Treaty of Guadalupe Hidalgo in 1848. Margaret Swett Henson, "Politics and the Treatment of the Mexican Prisoners after the Battle of San Jacinto," *The Southwestern Historical Quarterly*, 94 (1990): 198-203, found online at the Portal of Texas History, http://texashistory.unt.edu/ark:/67531/metapth101214/m1/233/.

7. George H. Tobin correspondence, *New Orleans Daily Delta*, April 30, 1847; Gen. T. J. Green, *Journal of the Texian Expedition Against Mier* (New York: Harper and Bros., 1845), Appendix IX, 284-87. https://www.google.com/books/edition/Journal_of_the_Texian_Expedition_Against/dzkVAAAAYAAJ?hl=en&gbpv=1.

8. Rusk to Burnet, June 14, 1836, James Morgan Papers, File 36, Box 4ff36, item 3, Dolph Briscoe Center for American History, University of Texas at Austin; Lamar to Burnet, July 17, 1836, Mirabeau B. Lamar Papers 414, Archives and Information Services Division, TSLAC; "Giants of History: Lorenzo de Zavala," TSLAC website, https://www.tsl.texas.gov/treasures/giants/zavala-01.html; Green, *Journal of the Texian Expedition Against Mier*, 248–50; Henson, "Politics and the Treatment of the Mexican Prisoners," 198–203; Col. Pedro Delgado, "Mexican Account of the Battle of San Jacinto," in William Carey Crane, *Life and Select Literary Remains of Sam Houston of Texas* (Philadelphia: J. B. Lippincott & Co., 1884), 651–58; Marilyn McAdams Sibley, "Thomas Jefferson Green: Recruiter for the Texas Army, 1836," *Texas Military History* 3, no. 3 (1963): 129.

9. Santa Anna to Burnet, June 9, 1836; Burnet to Santa Anna, June 10, 1836; Burnet to Citizen Soldiers of the Army of Texas, June 11, 1836; Morgan Papers, File 36, Box 4ff36, item 3, MS 278; Dolph Briscoe Center for American History, University of Texas at Austin; https://cdm16018.contentdm.oclc.org/digital/collection/p15125coll9/search/searchterm/james%20morgan; https://cdm16018.contentdm.oclc.org/digital/collection/p15125coll9/id/8251/rec/22; https://cdm16018.contentdm.oclc.org/digital/collection/p15125coll9/id/8259/rec/23; https://cdm16018.contentdm.oclc.org/digital/collection/p15125coll9/id/8272/rec/24. Caro later said the brutal execution of the Goliad prisoners was the main reason Mexican prisoners were in danger from their Texian captors. Caro, *A True Account of the First Texas Campaign and the Events Subsequent to the Battle of San Jacinto* (Mexico: 1837), reprinted in Casteñeda, *The Mexican Side of the Texan Revolution*, 104.

10. "Charges and Specifications preferred against David G. Burnet Esquire a Citizen of Texas by E L R Whelock [sic] for himself and the Citizens of Texas," typescript in John Forbes Papers, Dolph Briscoe Center for American History, University of Texas at Austin, Box 2Q510; Mary Foster Hutchinson, "Wheelock, Eleazar Louis Ripley," Handbook of Texas Online, accessed Oct. 22, 2020, https://www.tshaonline.org/handbook/entries/wheelock-eleazar-louis-ripley; Margaret Swett Henson, "Burnet, David Gouverneur," Handbook of Texas Online, accessed Nov. 5, 2020, https://www.tshaonline.org/handbook/entries/burnet-david-gouverneur.

11. Rusk to Morgan, June 14, 1836, Morgan Papers, Box 4, File 4–36, Dolph Briscoe Center for American History, University of Texas at Austin; *Richmond Enquirer*, July 15, 1836. On November 30, Santa Anna, Almonte and their entourage were released from Texian custody and left for Washington, DC, where they were to meet with President Jackson. Henson, "Politics and the Treatment of the Mexican Prisoners,"

189–221; Santa Anna to Andrew Jackson, July 4, 1836, and Jackson to Santa Anna, September 4, 1836, in the Andrew Jackson Papers, 1775–1874, Library of Congress Manuscript Division, viewable on the website, https://www.loc.gov/resource/maj.01095_0016_0026/?st=text; and https://www .loc.gov/resource/maj.01096_0089_0096/?st=text.

12. De la Peña, *With Santa Anna in Texas*, 165–191; Henson, "Politics and the Treatment of the Mexican Prisoners," 209–211; William C. Binkley, "The Activities of the Texan Revolutionary Army after San Jacinto," *Journal of Southern History* Vol. 6, no. 3 (August 1940): 341–43; Morgan Papers, Box 4, files 31 and 32, Dolph Briscoe Center for American History, University of Texas at Austin. Mexican prisoners might have found kindred spirits of sorts among the Texas colonists who had fled their settlements in panic after learning of the Alamo's fall. Some had begun evacuating even before that. Houston pulled his small army out of Gonzales and ordered the town evacuated and burned to the ground. Colonists throughout Texas were terrified that Santa Anna's army would soon sweep through their settlements. They packed what they could and fled eastward toward the United States border in what came to be known as "The Runaway Scrape." As many as thirty thousand Texians, most on foot––some barefoot–– fled through miserable cold and rain traversing mud-soaked roads and surging rivers, a route soon littered with abandoned wagons and possessions. Thousands bunched up waiting as long as three days to cross the San Jacinto River aboard Lynch's Ferry, little more than a wooden raft that held only a few dozen people and goods per trip. Many became ill and some died from various diseases before learning that Houston had defeated Santa Anna at San Jacinto on April 21, 1836. More hazards lie along the path back to their burned settlements amid continuing fear of a new Mexican invasion. Julia Robinson, "The Runaway Scrape: Exodus of Texians Is an Unsung Episode of the Texas War for Independence," *Texas Co-op Power*, April 2021, https://tinyurl.com /2v8asur2.

13. *Morning Courier and New York Enquirer*, July 9, 1836, reprinted in the *Phoenix Civilian*, July 23, 1836, attributed to "the correspondence of the New York Courier & Inquirer;" also in the Baltimore *American and Commercial Daily Advertiser*, July 12, 1836, and in Hansen, *Alamo Reader*, 563–65. William Groneman, *Eyewitness to the Alamo* (Lanham, MD: Republic of Texas Press, 2001), 47–48.

14. George M. Dolson to brother, July 19, 1836, *Democratic Free Press* [Detroit], in Hansen, *Alamo Reader*, 608–610; Thomas Lawrence Connelly, "Did David Crockett Surrender at the Alamo? A Contemporary Letter," *Journal of Southern History* 26, no. 3 (August 1960): 368–76; Davis, "How Davy Probably Didn't Die," 28.

15. Jackson and Wheat, *Almonte's Texas*, 87, 208; Boylston and Wiener, *David Crockett in Congress*, 118; Hansen, *Alamo Reader*, 609.

16. Green, *Journal of the Texian Expedition Against Mier*, vii–x, 248–50; Sibley, "Thomas Jefferson Green: Recruiter for the Texas Army, 1836," 129–44; Marilyn McAdams Sibley, "Letters from the Texas Army, Autumn, 1836: Leon Dyer to Thomas J. Green," *Southwestern Historical Quarterly* 72, no. 3 (1969): 371–84; George R. Nielsen, "Lydia Ann McHenry and Revolutionary Texas," *Southwestern Historical Quarterly*, 74, no. 3 (1971): 404–408; Jackson and Wheat, *Almonte's Texas*, 416–418. The William H. Attree file, Audited Military Claims collection, Archives

Division, Texas State Library, Austin, Texas. The file contains two documents that verify Attree's service with Green's brigade: an expense record for Attree's courier service and a receipt showing that Green purchased Attree's equipment on August 30, 1836. Both documents were written and signed by Green and are found in the Texas GLO Court of Claims file 000266, filed August 27, 1858, and can be viewed on the GLO website, https://s3.glo.texas.gov/ncu/SCANDOCS/archives_webfiles /arcmaps/webfiles/landgrants/PDFs/1/8/9/189861.pdf. Green's signed certification of Attree's service as a dispatch rider and courier is dated September 9, 1836. Attree was in Capt. Abraham Marshall's company. Dolson appears on the July 12, 1836, muster roll of Capt. Alonzo B. Sweitzer's company, Texas GLO website, https:// s3.glo.texas.gov/ncu/SCANDOCS/archives_webfiles /arcmaps/webfiles/landgrants/PDFs/3/1/9/319742_062.pdf. A man named Dolson appears on the June 6, 1836, Fort Travis muster role, viewable on UTSA Libraries Digital Collections website, https://cdm16018.contentdm.oclc.org/digital/collec-tion/p15125coll9/id/8245. Although Green claimed to have recruited many volun-teers, including Sweitzer's company, he did not. Sweitzer's company of Cincinnati Volunteers was recruited in Ohio, and as late as July 10 Sweitzer was not sure his company was even in Green's brigade. Although much maligned, Green also had his defenders, ultimately including Burnet.

17. In Arthur Conan Doyle's 1892 story *The Adventure of Silver Blaze*, Sherlock Holmes comments that, although a crime was committed, a dog that was present never barked. The John J. Forbes, James Morgan, and David G. Burnet papers are in the Dolph Briscoe Center for American History, University of Texas at Austin. It has been suggested the Dolson and Attree accounts may have been partly intended to attract volunteers from the United States as a check on a renewed Mexican attack and to secure Texas for American land speculators. Jackson and Wheat, *Almonte's Texas*, 416–17.

18. Richard Penn Smith, *"On to the Alamo" Col. Crockett's Exploits and Ad-ventures in Texas*, edited with an introduction and notes by John Seelye (New York: Penguin Classics, 2003), 118–19. Carey and Hart did not publish the book under its own name, but rather the fictitious publishing firm of "T. K. and P. G. Collins"; Crisp, *Sleuthing The Alamo*, 69; *Georgetown Metropolitan*, May 11, 1836; William Bedford Clark, "Col. Crockett's Exploits and Adventures in Texas: Death and Transfiguration," *Studies in American Humor New Series 2*, no. 1 (June 1982): 66–76; Shackford, *David Crockett*, 273–81.

19. Caro, *A True Account of the First Texas Campaign*, reprinted in Casteñeda, *The Mexican Side of the Texan Revolution*, 103–104; Winders, "This Is a Cruel Truth," 426. Winders places Caro in the Alamo with Santa Anna after the battle.

20. José Enrique de la Peña, narrative, 1836, José Enrique de la Peña Collec-tion, Dolph Briscoe Center for American History, University of Texas at Austin, extract of an account of the capture and execution of "David Croket," transcribed and translated by Tom Kailbourn, June 2, 2012, provided to the author; Crisp, *Sleuthing the Alamo*, 114.

21. For detailed accounts of the de la Peña manuscript, see Crisp, *Sleuthing the Alamo*, 65–138; David B. Gracy II, "'Just as I Have Written It': A Study of the Authenticity of the Manuscript of José Enrique de la Peña's Account of the Texas

Campaign," *The Southwestern Historical Quarterly* 105 (2001): 255–91.

22. Advertisements for *Col. Crockett's Exploits and Adventures in Texas*, printed in the *National Banner and Nashville Whig*, September 21, 1836.

23. William P. Zuber to Charlie Jeffries, August 17, 1904, in J. Frank Dobie, *In the Shadow of History* (Austin: Texas Folklore Society, 1939), 42–47, reprinted in Hansen, *Alamo Reader*, 268–71; Henson, "Politics and the Treatment of the Mexican Prisoners," 199; *New Orleans True American*, March 27, 1836; Delgado, "Mexican Account of the Battle of San Jacinto," 651; Crisp, *Sleuthing the Alamo*, 119–122.

24. De la Peña, *With Santa Anna in Texas*, 51; Zuber to Jeffries, August 17, 1904, reprinted in Hansen, *Alamo Reader*, 268–71.

25. Sánchez-Navarro, *La Guerra de Tejas*, 7, 85, translated by Tom Kailbourn, February 2008; Delgado "Mexican Account of the Battle of San Jacinto," 651.

26. Hansen, *Alamo Reader*, 401–12; Jackson and Wheat, *Almonte's Texas*, 373–374; De la Peña, narrative, Dolph Briscoe Center, excerpt transcribed and translated by Tom Kailbourn, June 2, 2012; de la Peña, *With Santa Anna in Texas*, 43–44; Hansen, *Alamo Reader*, 401–12.

27. Bruce Winders makes a similar point by noting that Santa Anna made no mention of Crockett being executed in his post battle reports, when identifying a former US congressman among the rebel casualties would have provided strong evidence for his claim that foreigners were aiding the rebellion. Winders also traces the implementation of the no quarter policy and shows that Santa Anna alone was not responsible for it, although he was clearly a zealous advocate of it. Winders, "'This Is a Cruel Truth,'" 427; Jackson and Wheat, *Almonte's Texas*, 378.

28. Powhatan Ellis to US Secretary of State John Forsyth, July 6, 1840, quoted in Jackson and Wheat, *Almonte's Texas*, 418. The authors concluded that Ellis's informant was Almonte. Ellis served as US chargé d'affaires to Mexico, May 11, 1836–December 28, 1836, and as envoy extraordinary and minister plenipotentiary, July 7, 1839–April 21, 1842.

29. Hansen, *Alamo Reader*, 74–78.

30. Susanna Dickinson statements quoted in Hansen, *Alamo Reader*, 41–51. Her statement identifying Crockett and his cap near the church is found in Morphis, *History of Texas*, 174–77. Hansen points out that it is difficult to separate Susanna's own statements from contributions or embellishments by Morphis, who could have added the location of Crockett's body based on Sutherland's 1860 account. Morphis also has Susanna describing Bowie's death, which she could not have seen, and incorrectly locating Travis's body with her husband's on the church cannon emplacement. Still, Hansen believes her statement about Crockett's body is really her own. It is, however, significant that she never mentioned it in any other statement, nor did her grandchildren relate hearing such an account from her. In his 1874 book, Morphis doesn't say where Crockett died and relies heavily on Susanna's account of the siege and battle, quotations from Travis's letters, and Zuber's account of Travis drawing a line on the ground. In an 1878 interview, Susanna mentions being well acquainted with Crockett, seeing him during the siege, and a man named Wolff being the only one to call for quarter and being killed. She

also mentioned the killing of two boys, ages eleven and twelve, in her room along with Walker, and being rescued by Almonte and shot in the leg on her way out, but she doesn't mention seeing Crockett's body. Ivey, "Archaeological Evidence for the Defenses of the Alamo," 3; Ruiz, "Fall of the Alamo," quoted in Hansen, *Alamo Reader* 500–503; Ruiz Court of Claims deposition, April 16, 1861, Texas GLO file 5026. Ruiz is corroborated by Reuben Potter in "The Fall of the Alamo," *Magazine of American History* 2 (January 1971): 1–21, reprinted in Hansen, *Alamo Reader*, 694–705. Potter has Crockett dying on a gun platform located at the center of the west wall, which housed a twelve-pound cannon. It is possible that Ruiz was referring to that emplacement and Crockett might have died there. 1838 interview with Ben, in Newell, *History of the Revolution*, quoted in Hansen, *Alamo Reader*, 473; account attributed to Ben, in Edward Stiff interview, *The Texan Emigrant* (Cincinnati: George Conclin, 1840), quoted in Hansen, *Alamo Reader*, 474–5; interview with Joe, Frankfort *Commonwealth*, May 25, 1836, quoted in Hansen, *Alamo Reader*, 74; interview with Joe, New Orleans *Commercial Bulletin*, April 11, 1836; interview with Joe, *Memphis Enquirer*, April 12, 1836; another version of the interview is in *National Intelligencer*, April 30, 1836, quoted in Hansen, *Alamo Reader*, 70–78; Gray, *From Virginia to Texas*, 136. Sutherland's location of Crockett's body is in Sutherland, *The Alamo*, quoted in Hansen, *Alamo Reader*, 145, 176. Also see Davis, "How Davy Probably Didn't Die," 19–21; Mary Helm, *Scraps of Early Texas History* (Austin: B. R. Warner, 1884), 56, quoted in Hansen, *Alamo Reader*, 83. Although Ruiz's account seems more persuasive and straightforward than those of Susanna Dickinson, it is not without problems. His accounts of identifying the bodies of Crockett, Travis, and Bowie are persuasive and consistent, but his 1860 account also contains serious inaccuracies, including the number of Mexican dead. His original statement is lost, and the only surviving version is an 1860 English translation published in the *Texas Almanac*. See Jackson and Wheat, *Almonte's Texas*, 402, footnote 139; Hansen, *Alamo Reader*, 542–43, 783–98; Davis, "How Davy Probably Didn't Die," 31. An alternative scenario has Crockett at the palisade at the start of the attack but moving to a location along the west wall after the Mexicans broke off their attack on the palisade. Donovan, *Blood of Heroes*, 282.

31. Gracy, "'Just as I Have Written It,'" 255–91; Crisp, *Sleuthing the Alamo*, 65–138; Davis, "How Davy Probably Didn't Die," 21–25 includes a discussion of prison camp dynamics.

32. For a discussion of the Tornel Decree and the role Santa Anna played in carrying it out, see Winders, "'This Is a Cruel Truth,'" 412–39.

Chapter 8

1. Robert Crockett to Smith Rudd, December 30, 1879, and June 15, 1880, Rudd Manuscripts, Lilly Library, Manuscripts Department, Indiana University, Bloomington; 1882 interview with Matilda Crockett, quoted in Smith, *The Land Holdings of Colonel David Crockett in West Tennessee*, 96–101.

2. Isaac N. Jones to Mrs. David Crockett, 1836., MM.1981.133, Calvin M. Mc-Clung Historical Collection, East Tennessee History Center, Knoxville.

3. Smith, *The Land Holdings of Colonel David Crockett in West Tennessee*, 96–101; Robert Crockett to Smith Rudd, December 30, 1879, and June 15, 1880, Rudd Manuscripts, Lilly Library, Manuscripts Department, Indiana University, Bloomington. For the convoluted history of the two hundred acres Crockett sold to McWhorter before leaving Tennessee, see Smith, *The Land Holdings of Colonel David Crockett in West Tennessee*, 68–94; James R. Boylston, "'Give My Love to Mother': The Crockett-Patton Marriage," *The Alamo Studies Review: A Journal of the Texas Revolution*, Vol.1, no. 1 (Summer 2012): 83. According to Robert Crockett, the family moved to Texas some time in 1854, but they were still in Tennessee as late as mid-October 1854. In his June 15, 1880, letter to Rudd, Robert also claimed the bay horse Crockett rode to Texas was returned to the family after Crockett's death, suggesting that, like the horse Comanche, which survived the Battle of Little Big Horn, Crockett's mount may have survived the assault on the Alamo. Crockett's family likely learned of his death by April. Newspaper reports of the Alamo's fall and Crockett's death appeared in Nashville and Memphis by then. Micajah Autry's family received word of his death at the Alamo in April, and they lived in Jackson, Tennessee, not far from the Crockett homestead. However, earlier newspaper reports of Crockett's death appeared within weeks of the Alamo's fall, and those reports may have reached the Crocketts. Autry's daughter, Mary, later recalled that the news arrived "one lovely April morning, when snowy white dogwood blossoms and the red bud trees spotted the tender green of the forest that surrounded the house. My little playmate and I were striving to gather the lovely white and pink flowers . . . when a voice near us said to me: 'You must come to the house. Your father has been killed, and your mother half dead with the news.'" Isaac N. Jones to Mrs. David Crockett, 1836., MM.1981.133, Calvin M. McClung Historical Collection, East Tennessee History Center, Knoxville; Micajah Autry to Martha Autry, December 13, 1835, from Natchitoches, LA., holograph at Rice University Fondren Library website: https://hdl.handle.net/1911/76038; *National Banner & Nashville Whig*, April 8, 1836, reprinted in *New Orleans True American*, March 29, 1936; *Memphis Enquirer*, April 12, 1836, quoted in Hansen, *Alamo Reader*, 71–72; Looscan, "Micajah Autry, A Soldier of the Alamo," 318–19.

4. Texas General Land Office (GLO), Austin; land warrant certificate 525.

5. Texas GLO land warrant certificate no. 1295 for 1,280 acres bounty land, issued December 23, 1837; GLO files nos. 609, 1558, 1471. The certificate does not cite a specific act or resolution under which the grant was issued, only that Crockett had served from January 8 to March 6, 1836, and was "honorably discharged by death." For the 640-acre augmentation donation grant, issued March 13, 1852, see GLO warrant certificate no. 1065, file 1558.

6. Texas GLO headright certificate 125, files 1249 and 1709, issued March 13, 1852, under a law passed on February 9, 1850, a revision of a resolution adopted on May 24, 1838, granting a headright to the heirs of those who had fallen in battles at the Alamo, Goliad, and elsewhere during the revolution. The 640-acre donation grant certificate 428, files 0003, 1471, 1308, and 1286, also was issued on March 13, 1852. A May 3, 1838, report by the clerk of the Board of Land Commissioners for Bexar County listed Crockett's headright (certificate/line number 499) and

stipulated Crockett was an "Emigrant previous to March 1836," and named Robert P. Crockett as administrator of the estate. The clerk's report only confirms that Texas acknowledged Crockett's heirs' claim to the headright and was completed prior to the May 24, 1838, resolution and the 1850 law governing headrights. The actual headright certificate (125) was issued under the 1850 law.

7. Texas GLO land warrant certificate 4/15, issued February 4, 1856, file 1121. By 1856, Crockett had passed from life into mythology as the Alamo's most preeminent martyr and the legislature may have sought to erase any hint of callousness toward his family. "The Heirs of Col. Davy Crockett," *Houma Ceres*, Houma, Terrebonne Parish, Louisiana, January 31, 1856, reprinted from the *Dallas Herald*; copy of newspaper provided by Tom Kailbourn.

8. Texas GLO file 1249. Aside from the headright, no specific plots of land and no specific Texas land certificates are mentioned in these indentures. Nonetheless, the Crocketts were aware of the land bounties that Texas had awarded to its veterans or their heirs, and the four Crockett children involved in the indentures were willing to sell their interest in them, bringing about twenty-six cents an acre for the headright. Land prices in Texas were quite low at the time, considerably below the average price of one dollar per acre for public lands in the United States. The indenture signed by the three Crockett children on May 14, 1842, was registered in Gibson County, Tennessee, by Registrar L. B. Gilchrist on October 22, 1850. Sam S. Smith, Bexar County Court clerk, filed the indentures in Bexar County, Texas, on September 30, 1851, and they were recorded the next day and certified June 2, 1855. On August 23, 1842, Joshua D. Hill, chairman and presiding justice of Gibson County Court, certified the indenture agreement signed by Matilda and her husband. On October 22, 1850, Gilchrist certified that the "foregoing deed and the certificates thereto" were duly registered in his office. It was recorded in Bexar County, Texas, by Smith on October 1, 1851, and had been filed in his office the previous day.

9. Texas GLO warrant certificate 125; Aldon S. Lang and Christopher Long, "Land Grants," Texas Handbook Online, https://tshaonline.org/handbook/online /articles/mpl01; Texas Land Measures website, https://www.independencetitle .com/wp-content/uploads/TXLandMeasures.pdf. One labor of land is 177.14 acres; one league is 4,428.40 acres, or twenty-five labors. A league and a labor equals 4,605.54 acres, or twenty-six labors.

10. Texas GLO land warrant certificate 1295 issued December 23, 1837.

11. Texas GLO land warrant certificate 1065 issued March 13, 1852.

12. Texas GLO land warrant certificate 428, March 13, 1852. Robert Crockett was acting as the family's agent as late as August 1837 when he signed an auditor's authorization to act as agent for the Crockett heirs in collecting the twenty-four dollars pay due to Crockett and conducting other business for the family. He also was serving in the Texas army through August 24, 1827. Texas State Library and Archive, Republic Claim No. 3196, reel 21: https://www.tsl.texas.gov/apps/arc /repclaims/viewdetails/15823; https://www.tsl.texas.gov/apps/arc/repclaims/stor- age/republic_media/pdfs/21/02100677.pdf; https://www.tsl.texas.gov/apps/arc /repclaims/storage/republic_media/pdfs/21/02100678.pdf.

13. Texas GLO land warrant certificate 125 for twenty-six labors of land (a league and a labor), GLO file 0296; survey 426. J. B. Forester's actual title was administrator *de bonis non* (or *de bonis non administratis*), Latin for "of goods not administered." It is a legal term for assets remaining in an estate after the death or removal of the estate administrator. The second administrator, or administrator *de bonis non*, distributes the remaining assets. This was Forester's role after he replaced Robert Crockett as administrator of the estate. It is not clear why Robert was replaced, but he would have found it difficult to attend to affairs in Texas efficiently while still living in Tennessee. He, his mother, Elizabeth, his sister, Rebecca Elvira, and his half-brother, George Patton, did not move to Texas until 1854 or 1855. Forester filed a petition to replace Robert on February 26, 1851, and on April 4 the Bexar Probate Court approved it without objection.

14. Texas GLO file 0296.

15. Elizabeth Crockett power of attorney dated February 23, 1854, Republic claim 3149, reel 147, 35–9, TSLAC, https://www.tsl.texas.gov/apps/arc/repclaims /viewdetails.php?id=116561&set=1#viewSet. Also see Boylston, "Give My Love to Mother," 83, which suggests that Elizabeth, finding herself destitute after Crockett's death, took steps to ensure the same fate did not befall her children in Texas. The article also lays to rest the frequently repeated false assertion that Crockett and Elizabeth were estranged. The power of attorney also includes an affidavit certifying that David and Elizabeth had lived together as husband and wife for many years.

16. Johnson County, Texas, land records, key no. 446913, 334, transfer; RP/ 0000A/334. The land transfer document dated October 16, 1854, was not actually filed until April 30, 1860, three months after Elizabeth's death on January 31, 1860. Elizabeth's two children by her first husband, James Patton, were George Patton and Margaret "Peggy" Ann Patton. The three children from her marriage to Crockett were Robert P. Crockett, Rebecca Elvira Crockett (later Kimbro and still later Halford), and Matilda Crockett (later Tyson, still later Wilson, and finally Fields). Two of David and Polly Crockett's children, John and William, were dead by the time the 1854 documents were concluded, although their daughter, Margaret, survived until 1860. The document transferred Elizabeth's "entire interest in all the lands belonging to the estate of my said husband in the state of Texas," but added, "I do hereby bind myself, my heirs to warrant and defend the title to my interest of one entire half of all the lands belonging to the estate of my said husband the said David Crockett, deceased, in the said state of Texas to" the five children named. She certified that she had never sold land in Texas before, except to pay off Mitchell with half the land he secured, located, surveyed, and patented for her. She also signed this document with an "X," identified as "her mark."

17. Texas GLO warrant certificate 1295, December 23, 1837, for 1,280 acres, files 609, 1558, 1471, and 0296. Although no records exist supporting the claim, some Crockett family oral history holds that the family arrived in 1852 and stayed for a time in Waxahachie, in Ellis County, until their own land was secured on the Brazos, then part of Johnson County, which adjoins Ellis County but is now part of Hood County. See Smith, *The Land Holdings of Colonel David Crockett in West Tennessee*, 101, footnote 5. Robert P. Crockett's son Ashley Wilson Crockett is

quoted as saying that the Crocketts were in Ellis County for two years. According to Ashley, his father, Robert, built at least two cabins along Rucker Creek during the 1850s.

18. Johnson County, Texas, Court Clerk Records, Warranty Deed, document 302782; RP/0000D/40. Some records spell Flowers' first name as "Wilie."

19. Texas GLO land warrant certificate 1295, file 609; Johnson County, Texas, land records, key 447573, patent 1025, filed March 31, 1859, RP/0000C/616. Robert Crockett to Smith Rudd, December 30, 1879, Rudd Manuscripts, Lilly Library, Manuscripts Department, Indiana University, Bloomington; Thomas W. Cutrer, "Raymond, James Hervey," Handbook of Texas Online, https://tshaonline.org/handbook/online/articles/fra51. On February 3, 1855, Adjutant General James S. Gillett officially approved Crockett's 1837 warrant certificate for 1,280 acres and on March 6, Texas Treasurer James H. Raymond certified that Elizabeth was Crockett's widow and that he had on file her power of attorney issued to Mitchell, authorizing him to carry out all business affairs pertaining to Crockett's estate. Under Elizabeth's agreement with Mitchell, one half of the 1,280 acres went to him while the Crockett heirs divided the remaining 640 acres among themselves.

20. Republic of Texas bounty warrant certificate 1295, December 23, 1837, Texas GLO file 0609; patent 1025, April 6, 1855, for 1,280 acres; Texas GLO land warrant certificate no. 4/15, February 4, 1856, file 1121; Johnson County, Texas, Land Records, key 447229, July 27, 1857, warranty deed filed July 28, 1857, RP/0000C/209; Johnson County, Texas, land records, key 447573, land patent filed March 31, 1859, RP/0000C/616; Johnson County land records, key 446913, land transfer; RP/0000A/334, filed April 30, 1860; Hood County, Texas, Deed Records, Vol. M, page 477, Proof of Heirs of David Crockett; Hood County, Texas, land records, 280AC, D. Crockett survey; Robert Crockett to Smith Rudd, December 30, 1879, Rudd Manuscripts, Lilly Library, Manuscripts Department, Indiana University, Bloomington; Richard Elam, "Johnson County," Handbook of Texas Online, https://www.tshaonline.org/handbook/entries/johnson-county; Cutrer, "Raymond, James Hervey." On March 5, 1857, Elizabeth filed an application to locate the 320 acres she was living on along Rucker Creek near the 640 acres that her children occupied. The special legislation granting her a league of land specified she could locate part of the land there. The timing of the Crocketts arrival in Texas is somewhat murky. Some Crockett descendants recall being told Elizabeth arrived with her son Robert, his wife, Matilda Porter Crockett, and their three children; Elizabeth's daughter, Rebecca, her second husband, James Halford, and their five children; and Elizabeth's son, George Patton, from her first marriage and his family. Family oral history suggests the Crocketts stayed in Ellis County upon their arrival, which is possible since William L. Mitchell lived there, and he was hired by Elizabeth to locate her Texas land. Perhaps he arranged a place for them to stay before they were able to move onto their own land. Robert Crockett later recalled that he, his mother, his sister Rebecca, and his half-brother George Patton, moved to Texas in 1854. According to Hood County, Texas, voter rolls dated August 24, 1867, Robert claimed to have been in Texas for twelve years and in Hood County (in an area formerly part of Johnson County) for eleven years.

It is possible the Crocketts lived in Ellis County prior to securing their land in April 1855, or twelve years prior to 1867, when Robert's voter roll information was recorded. However, the shifting county boundaries in Texas have resulted in some confusion as to where the Crocketts lived upon their arrival in Texas and afterward. Their land claim was located in what was then Johnson County, which was carved out of parts of Ellis, Navarro, and Hill counties in 1854, perhaps around the time the Crocketts moved to Texas, resulting in the belief that they originally lived in Ellis County. In 1867, the western portion of Johnson County, including the Crockett land, was incorporated into Hood County. Thus, the Crocketts may have resided in the same general location while their land was legally shifted from one county to another. By the time they settled in Texas, the only surviving Crockett children were Robert, Rebecca, and Matilda from David and Elizabeth's marriage, and Margaret from David and Polly's marriage. Elizabeth's two children by James Patton, George and Margaret ("Peggy"), also survived. Since Elizabeth had transferred all of her interest in the Texas lands to her five natural children in 1854, the family's 640 acres were divided equally among those children, giving each of them 128 acres. It's possible Elizabeth lived with one of her children as she had done during her final years in Tennessee, prior to moving onto the 320 acres she later occupied. However, her 1854 land transfer to her children was not filed in Texas until April 30, 1860, three months after her death, so she may have held part of the 640 acres for herself during her lifetime. On July 27, 1857, Mitchell transferred 280 acres of his share of the land to Mariah L. Rucker, land on which she was then residing, including the improvements she had made on it. This was part of the 640 acres Mitchell was paid for having located, surveyed, and patented it. Mitchell's land transfer to Mariah Rucker was signed by Elizabeth, Robert, and Matilda Crockett, Rebecca E. Halford (nee Crockett) and her husband, J. M. Halford, and by George Patton and his wife, Rhoda Ann Patton.

21. Texas GLO land warrant certificate 125 and files 0296, 1249, and 1709; survey 426, Bexar County, Texas, County Clerk land records, file 99991866159. On March 18, 1852, a survey was completed and on December 29, 1852, Forester, represented by his attorney, William F. Weeks, appeared before the Bexar County Court for Settlement of Estates and petitioned for permission to locate the certificate for a league and labor for the Crockett heirs. On October 31, 1854, around the time that Elizabeth Crockett moved to Texas, Forester reported the survey that had been completed by Young and Morales on February 10, 1853. On January 14, 1854, the Bexar District surveyor relocated the headright land, under the same warrant certificate, 125, but the record does not say where. On January 20, 1855, the certificate was reentered. There seems to have been a challenge to the original survey that claimed it conflicted in part with another survey, thus requiring the land to be relocated in order to correct the error. The Crockett headright land still remained in the same area of the Nueces River throughout this process.

22. Clerk of Johnson County, Texas, land records, warranty deed 406262, 620–21; RP/0000C/620; Bexar County Clerk's land records, instrument 99991866159; Texas GLO land warrant certificate 125.

23. Johnson County land records, key 406262, 620–21, RP/0000C/620, warranty deed filed and certified March 31, 1859, by the Johnson County Court clerk and

recorded June 21, 1859. The Smith letter is found in Texas GLO file 1244. Smith was clearing the way for a subsequent sale of the two 640-acre grants, which J. B. Forester had originally sold in 1852, and added his recollections of the disposition of the Crockett headright, which conveyed some portion of that land to the Foresters. Smith assured Commissioner Crosby that "you will be safe in issuing the patents to the parties claiming under said sale. If you should after an examination of the proofs filed in the Adjutant General's office at the time, you can write to our friend Gov. Crockett [no relation to David] upon the subject who I see was at Galveston a few days ago." Smith erred in referring to the land he thought was in Dallas County as "donation land," since he was referring to the 1,280-acre bounty grant Crockett had received. The terms "donation" and "bounty" were often mistakenly used interchangeably. For details regarding Texas land practices see Thomas Lloyd Miller, *The Public Lands of Texas, 1519–1970* (Norman: University of Oklahoma Press, 1972), and Thomas Lloyd Miller, *Bounty and Donation Land Grants of Texas, 1835–1888* (Austin: University of Texas Press, 1967).

The records are unclear regarding how much Crockett land the Foresters ultimately owned. As late as August 28, 1860, J. B. Forester purchased 1,494 acres of the original Crockett headright from Richard Forester's other heirs (Charles, Henry, George, and William Forester) for $2,000 ($71,392 in 2022), likely part of the 1,912 acres Elizabeth had sold the Foresters in 1859, but the Foresters may have owned additional Crockett land that was paid to J. B Forester for his work as estate administrator. On May 11, 1874, Henry Forester sought to secure all of the Crockett lands to which he was entitled from his father and brothers' estates. In 1876 and 1877, in separate actions, Charles, George, Henry and J. B. Forester each gave their power of attorney to Thomas M. Harwood to perfect title to their headright land and apply for and receive a patent for it so that they could sell it. Harwood was also to carry out the sale for the Foresters. Texas GLO files 0296, 1249, 1709, and 1490; GLO survey 426.

24. Texas GLO land warrant certificate 125, GLO files 0648, 1149, 1249, 1490, 042764, 042785 and others showing J. M. Lindsay of Cooke County, Texas, as the patentee or grantee of various land certificates. McFarland owned other lands in Texas. On November 1, 1853, while residing in Weakley County, Tennessee, he paid $500 for 1,280 acres of Texas land from George D. Hendricks. It is not surprising that McFarland would refer to some of his lands as "Margaret Flowers'" land. Texas land warrant certificates are referred to by the name of the original grantee in perpetuity, so that land warrants originally issued to Crockett or his heirs are referred to as "David Crockett's" forever, even long after the Crockett family disposed of them. For example, in 1852, J. B. Forester sold two 640-acre plots granted to Crockett's heirs in two separate certificates, so the Crocketts had no claim to these lands from that date onward, yet surveys and other documents pertaining to later sales or transfers of those lands continued to refer to them as the David Crockett bounty or donation grant and incorporated the original certificate number. So, absent any additional documentation, it is fair to conclude that the land Margaret and Wiley Flowers sold for $500 in 1854 had somehow come into McFarland's possession. The original Crockett headright remained a source of contention. A survey of 184 acres, thought to be part of the headright land, was

carried out on February 5, 1873, and located in Cooke County. Records show the land was later "abandoned" and that the certificate "floated." In a letter dated July 24, 1933, acting GLO Commissioner J. H. Walker notified M. M. Yeakley, a surveyor, that the survey was abandoned and the certificate floated and relocated for one league and one labor in Hemphill County (in the Texas Panhandle) and patented to the heirs of David Crockett on March 23, 1877. The Hemphill County survey covered the entire amount of the headright, thus the 1860 Cooke County tract would have no standing. In filing her power of attorney to pursue her protest with McFarland, Matilda was questioned by the court clerk and the acting justice of the peace apart from her husband, Redden Fields, and confirmed that she made the power of attorney of her own free will. The Crocketts continued to make land deals in Texas. On January 29, 1869, Robert Crockett bought an unspecified parcel of land from Edward Visant, a resident of Arkansas, for one hundred dollars. On September 20, 1872, McFarland sold 1,280 acres to Robert Crockett; Hood County, Texas, Clerk's land records, page 373. Page 372 is missing so there's no surviving record of how much Robert paid for this land.

25. "Letter from Matilda Field to Robert Crockett, December 28, 1885," The Portal of Texas History website, https://texashistory.unt.edu/ark:/67531/metapth38988/m1/1/. The description of the Matilda Fields holograph on the website reads, "This letter is part of the collection entitled Where the West Begins: Capturing Fort Worth's Historic Treasures and was provided by the Log Cabin Village to The Portal to Texas History, a digital repository hosted by the UNT [University of North Texas] Libraries."

26. Texas GLO land warrant certificates 1294, issued December 23, 1837, and 525, issued, August 4, 1881, under an act passed March 15, 1881; Texas GLO file 1730.

27. Texas GLO files 0296, 1249, 1709, 1490; GLO survey 426.

28. Robert Crockett to Smith Rudd, December 30, 1879, Rudd Manuscripts, Lilly Library, Manuscripts Department, Indiana University, Bloomington.

Appendix 1

1. John L. Moore, Jon P. Preimesberger, and David R. Tarr, eds., *Congressional Quarterly's Guide to U. S. Elections*, 4th edition, volume II (Washington, DC: CQ Press, 2001), 831–47. Members of Congress were paid eight dollars per day throughout Crockett's three terms, during which his total salary was $6,696.00, equal to approximately $225,439 in 2022 dollars. "Salaries of Members of Congress: Recent Actions and Historical Tables," FRASER Discover Economic History, https://fraser.stlouisfed.org/title/salaries-members-congress-5996?start_page=19.

Appendix 2

1. Republic Claim no. 4108, reel 18, TSLAC: https://www.tsl.texas.gov/apps/arc/repclaims/viewdetails/14898; *The Muster Roll Book (The Red Book)*, GLO website: http://glorrg.pbworks.com/w/page/67129275/Muster%20Rolls#footnote-2. See *Telegraph & Texas Register*, April 28, 1838, for Judge Forbes's account of Crockett telling him to insert the word "republican" into the oath.

2. Daniel W. Cloud, Republic Claim no. 4108, reel 18, September 22, 1837, TSLAC, https://www.tsl.texas.gov/apps/arc/repclaims/viewdetails/14899.

3. John Forbes to Lieutenant Governor Robinson, January 12–15, 1836, quoted in Jenkins, *Papers of the Texas Revolution*, Vol. 3, 496–8.

4. "Republic of Texas Muster Rolls," 114–17, Archives and Records Program, Texas General Land Office, Austin, sometimes referred to as the *Red Book*, http://www.glo.texas.gov/ncu/SCANDOCS/archives_webfiles/arcmaps/webfiles/arc-maps/pdfs/9/4/94246.pdf.

Crockett's Texas land certificate 1295 for 1,280 acres, dated December 23, 1837, is in Files 609, 1558, and 1471 in the Texas General Land Office and can be retrieved on the GLO website, https://s3.glo.texas.gov/ncu/SCANDOCS/archives_webfiles/arcmaps/webfiles/landgrants/PDFs/3/3/9/339941.pdf. Peter Harper's discharge file is in the Texas State Library and Archives Commission, Republic of Texas Claims, Claim No. 540, Reel 41, Frame 350, part of a set of frames 350–53, https://www.tsl.texas.gov/apps/arc/repclaims/viewdetails.php?id=26579&set=1&img=04100350#04100350. Micajah Autry's letter is in *The Southwestern Historical Quarterly*, Volume 14, 1910–1911, the Texas State Historical Association, and reprinted on the My Kindred Home website, http://mykindred.com/cloud/documents/mautry.php. Also see Thomas R. Lindley's unpublished chronology of Crockett's Texas journey hand dated October 25, 1991, shared with the author by the late Kevin Young.

The Auxiliary Volunteer Corps that Crockett joined was established by "An Ordinance and Decree to organize and establish an Auxiliary Volunteer Corps to the Army of Texas and other purposes," adopted by the provisional government on December 5, 1835. Section 5 of the ordinance provided that volunteers were entitled to one square mile or 640 acres of land for their service, which would descend to their heirs should they die during their enlistment. Section 10 stipulates that "all volunteers for three months . . . shall be entitled to a bounty of three hundred and twenty acres of land after receiving an honorable discharge." Crockett and the others with him in Nacogdoches signed up for six months and were entitled to 640 acres of land under Section 5 of the ordinance, which does not stipulate a specific term of enlistment. But Section 7 stipulates that "it shall be the duty of the Governor or the Commander-in-Chief to accept all volunteers who shall tender their services for a less time than during the war, agreeably to what he shall think the defence of the county and the good of the service may require." This vague wording could imply that volunteers were free to choose their own terms of enlistment, but Crockett and those with him clearly enlisted for six months, entitling them or their heirs to 640 acres. These bounties were separate of the league and labor of land that men like Crockett and Autry could have claimed once they permanently moved their families to Texas. *Ordinance and Decrees of the Consultation, Provisional Government of Texas and the Convention, Which Assembled at Washington March 1, 1836* (Houston: National Banner Office–Niles & Co., 1838) and reprinted in the database *Making of the Modern Law, FCIL, 1600–1926*, 47–50.

It has been suggested that Crockett began writing his letter in San Augustine on January 9 but did not complete it until after he returned to Nacogdoches, and that he enlisted after returning there, sometime after January 9. He then completed the letter and mentioned his enlistment. However, if true, Crockett would most likely have begun the latter part of his letter with a new paragraph on a separate line. But both surviving copies of his letter show that he continued writing on the same line, not with a new paragraph, suggesting he wrote continually, without a break, while in San Augustine on January 9. It was also common to put two dates on a letter that was begun on one date and finished on another, as with Judge Forbes's letter to Lieutenant Governor Robinson of January 12 and 15.

Two surviving versions of Crockett's January 9, 1836, letter are quoted in Boylston and Wiener, *David Crockett in Congress*, 286–8. The original letter has never been found.

BIBLIOGRAPHY

Barker, Eugene C. "The Texan Revolutionary Army." *The Quarterly of the Texas State Historical Association* 9, no. 4 (April 1906): 227–61.

———. "Journal of the Permanent Council (October 11–27, 1835)." *The Quarterly of the Texas State Historical Association* 7, No. 4 (April 1904): 249–78.

———. "Land Speculation as a Cause of the Texas Revolution." *The Quarterly of the Texas State Historical Association* 10, no. 1 (July 1906): 76–95.

Belfiglio, Valentine J. "The Indian Policy of Stephen F. Austin." *East Texas Historical Journal*, 31, no. 2 (1993): 15–22. https://scholarworks.sfasu.edu/ethj/vol31/iss2/6.

Beyer, Dr. Gerry W. "Intestate Succession: What Every Texas Legal Professional Needs to Know." Probate Academy, Texas Association of Counties, Lubbock, Texas, May 8, 2019, (Spring 2019). Accessed online: https://www.county.org/TAC/media/TACMedia/Education/Event%20Presentation%20Materials/2019/Probate-Academy/5a-Beyer-Intestate-Succession.pdf.

Binkley, William C. "The Activities of the Texan Revolutionary Army after San Jacinto." *The Journal of Southern History* 6, no. 3 (August 1940): 331–46.

Bonham, William N. "James Butler Bonham." Internet Archive, last modified October 19, 1999, https://web.archive.org/web/20060912183516/http://home.att.net/~wnbonham/james.htm.

Boylston, James R. "Another Look at the Perry Account." *Alamo Journal*, no. 139 (December 2005): 6–11.

———. "Crockett and Bunce: A Fable Examined." *The Crockett Chronicle*, no. 6 (November 2004).

———. "'Give My Love to Mother': The Crockett-Patton Marriage." *The Alamo Studies Review: A Journal of the Texas Revolution* 1, no. 1 (Summer 2012): 73–84.

———. "Not Yours to Give: A Fable Re-Examined." *Jim's Corner* website, last modified October 20, 2009, http://crockettincongress.blogspot.com/2009/10/not-yours-to-give-fable-re-examined.html.

———. "Sketches Re-Examined: The First Crockett Biography." Address presented at Alamo Society Symposium, San Antonio, Texas, March 2006.

Boylston, James R. and Allen J. Wiener. *David Crockett in Congress: The Rise and Fall of the Poor Man's Friend.* Houston: Bright Sky Press, 2009.

———. "David Crockett—Indian Defender." *The Crockett Chronicle*, no. 25 (August 2009).

Brands, H. W. *Lone Star Nation: How a Ragged Army of Volunteers Won the Battle for Texas Independence--and Changed America.* New York: Doubleday, 2004.

Brear, Holly Beachley. *Inherit the Alamo: Myth and Ritual at an American Shrine.* Austin: University of Texas Press, 1995.

Burrough, Bryan, Chris Tomlinson, and Jason Stanford. *Forget the Alamo: The Rise and Fall of an American Myth.* New York: Penguin Publishing Group, 2021.

Campbell, Randolph B. *An Empire for Slavery: The Peculiar Institution in Texas.* Baton Rouge: Louisiana State University Press, 1989.

Carlson-Drexler, Carl G. "Crossroads of Conflict: Archaeology at Dooley's Ferry, Hempstead County, Arkansas." Paper presented at the 41st Annual Conference of the Society for Historical Archaeology, Albuquerque, NM, 2008.

Castañeda, Carlos E. *The Mexican Side of the Texas Revolution by the Chief Mexican Participants.* Washington, D.C.: Documentary Publications, 1971.

Chariton, Wallace O. *100 Days in Texas: The Alamo Letters.* Plano, TX: Wordware Publishing, Inc., 1990.

———. *Exploring the Alamo Legends.* Plano, TX: Republic of Texas Press, 1992.

Chemerka, William R. and Allen J. Wiener. *Music of the Alamo: From 19th Century Ballads to Big Screen Soundtracks.* Houston: Bright Sky Press, 2009.

Clark, Pat B. *The History of Clarksville and Old Red River County.* Dallas: Mathis, Van Nort & Co., 1937.

Clark, William Bedford. "Col. Crockett's Exploits and Adventures in Texas: Death and Transfiguration." *Studies in American Humor New Series 2* 1, no. 1 (June 1982): 66–76.

Cobia, Manley F., Jr. *Journey into the Land of Trials: The Story of Davy Crockett's Expedition to the Alamo.* Franklin, TN: Hillsboro Press, 2003.

Connelly, Thomas Lawrence. "Did David Crockett Surrender at the Alamo? A Contemporary Letter." *The Journal of Southern History* 26, no. 3. (August 1960): 368–76.

Covner, Craig R. "Before 1850: A New Look at the Alamo Through Art and Imagery." Part 1: *Alamo Journal,* no. 70 (March 1990); Part 2: *Alamo Journal,* no. 73 (November 1990).

Cozzens, Peter. *A Brutal Reckoning: Andrew Jackson, The Creek Indians, and the Epic War for the American South.* New York: Alfred A. Knopf, 2023.

Crane, William Carey. *Life and Select Literary Remains of Sam Houston of Texas.* Philadelphia: J. B. Lippincott & Co., 1884.

Crisp, James E. *Sleuthing the Alamo: Davy Crockett's Last Stand and Other Mysteries of the Texas Revolution.* New York: Oxford University Press, 2005.

———. "Back to Basics: Conspiracies, Common Sense, And Occam's Razor." *Alamo Journal* no. 100 (March 1996).

———. "Davy in Freeze-Frame: Methodology or Madness?" *Alamo Journal* no. 98 (October 1995).

———. "Documenting Davy's Death: The Problematic 'Dolson Letter' from Texas, 1836." *Journal of the West* 46, no. 2 (Spring 2007): 22–28.

———. "The Little Book That Wasn't There: The Myth and Mystery of the De La Peña Diary." *The Southwestern Historical Quarterly* 98, no. 2 (1994): 260–96.

———. "Trashing Dolson: The Perils of Tendentious Interpretation." *Alamo Journal* no. 99 (December 1995).

———. "Truth, Confusion, and the de la Peña Controversy: A Final Reply." *Military History of the West* 26, no. 1 (Spring 1996): 99–104.

———. "When Revision Becomes Obsession: Bill Groneman and the de la Peña Diary." *Military History of the West* 25, no. 2 (Fall 1995): 143–155.

Crisp, James E. Sleuthing and William Groneman. "Crockett Controversy Continues." *The Wilson Quarterly* 22, no. 2 (1998): 7–10.

Crockett, David. *A Narrative of the Life of David Crockett of the State of Tennessee.* A Facsimile Edition with Annotations and an Introduction by James A. Shackford and Stanley J. Folmsbee. Knoxville: University of Tennessee Press, 1973.

Daughters of the Republic of Texas. *The Alamo Long Barrack Museum.* Dallas: Taylor Publishing Co., 1986.

Davis, Curtis Carrol. "A Legend at Full-Length: Mr. Chapman Paints Colonel Crockett—and Tells About It." *Proceedings of the American Antiquarian Society* (1960): 155–74.

Davis, James D. *History of Memphis.* Memphis, TN: Hite, Crumpton & Kelly, 1873. Facsimile edition published by Andesite Press.

Davis, William C. *Three Roads to the Alamo: The Lives and Fortunes of David Crockett, James Bowie, and William Barret Travis.* New York: Harper Collins, 1998.

———. *Lone Star Rising: The Revolutionary Birth of the Texas Republic.* College Station: Texas A&M University Press, 2004.

———. "How Davy Probably *Didn't* Die." *Journal of the Alamo Battlefield Association* 2, no. 1 (Fall 1997): 11–37.

Delgado, Pedro. "Mexican Account of the Battle of San Jacinto" in William Care Crane, *Life and Select Literary Remains of Sam Houston of Texas.* Philadelphia: J. B. Lippincott & Co, 1884. 648-61.

Derr, Mark. *The Frontiersman: The Real Life and the Many Legends of Davy Crockett.* New York: Quill, 1993.

Donovan, James. *The Blood of Heroes: The 13-Day Struggle for the Alamo and the Sacrifice That Forged America.* New York: Little, Brown & Co., 2012.

Drexler, Carl G. "Dooley's Ferry." *Arkansas Archeological Survey, Magnolia* no. 378 (May-June 2014).

Durham, Robert L. "Once More Against the North Wall: An Analysis of the Struggle for Control of the Alamo's North Wall." *Journal of the Alamo Battlefield Association* 3, no. 1 (Fall 1998): 21–29.

———. (transcription), Helen Hunnicut (translation). "Memoirs of a Veteran of the Two Battles of the Alamo." *The Library Chronicle* 4, no. 2, archived on Second Flying Company of Alamo de Parras website. Last modified March 8, 2000, http://www.sonsofdewittcolony.org/adp/archives/maps/sanchezdoc.html.

———. "African Americans and the Fight for the Alamo." Alamo de Parras website. Undated. http://www.sonsofdewittcolony.org/adp/history/1836/blacks/durham.html.

Featherstonhaugh, G. W. *Excursion Through the Slave States: From Washington on the Potomac to the Frontier of Mexico: with Sketches of Popular Manners and Geological Notices, Volume II.* London: John Murray, 1844.

Feller, Daniel. *The Public Lands in Jacksonian Politics.* Madison: University of Wisconsin Press, 1984.

Field, Joseph E. *Three Years in Texas: Including a View of the Texan Revolution, and an Account of the Principle Battles, Together with Descriptions of the Soil, Commercial and Agricultural Advantages, &c.* Greenfield, MA: Justin Jones, 1836.

Folmsbee, Stanley J. "David Crockett and West Tennessee." *West Tennessee Historical Society Papers* 28 (1974): 5–24.

———. "David Crockett: Congressman." *East Tennessee Historical Society's Publications* 29 (1957): 40–78.

———. "David Crockett in Texas." *East Tennessee Historical Society's Publications* 30 (1958): 48–74.

Folmsbee, Stanley J., and Anna Grace Catron. "The Early Career of David Crockett." *East Tennessee Historical Society's Publications* 28 (1956): 58–85.

Foote, Henry Stuart. *Texas and the Texans; or Advance of the Anglo-Americans to the South-West; Including a History of Leading Events in Mexico, from the Conquest by Fernando Cortes to the Termination of the Texan Revolution, Volume II.* Philadelphia: Thomas, Cowperthwait & Co., 1841.

Foreman, Gary L. *Crockett: The Gentleman from the Cane.* Dallas: Taylor Publishing Co., undated.

French, James Strange. *Sketches and Eccentricities of Col. David Crockett, of West Tennessee.* New York: J. & J. Harper, 1833. (Originally published anonymously.)

Giles, Bascom. *History and Disposition of the Texas Public Domain.* Austin: Texas General Land Office, 1945.

Gracy II, David B. "'Just as I Have Written It': A Study of the Authenticity of the Manuscript of José Enrique de la Peña's Account of the Texas Campaign." *The Southwestern Historical Quarterly* 105, no. 2 (October 2001): 255–91.

Gray, William F. *From Virginia to Texas, 1835: Diary of Col. Wm. F. Gray, Giving Details of His Journey to Texas and Return in 1835–1836 and Second Journey to Texas in 1837.* Houston: Fletcher Young Publishing Co., 1965; originally published by Gray, Dillaye & Co., Houston, 1909.

Green, Michael R. "To the People of Texas & All Americans in the World." *The Southwestern Historical Quarterly* 91, no. 4 (April 1988): 483–508.

Groneman, William. *Alamo Defenders: A Genealogy: The People and Their Words.* Austin: Eakin Press, 1990.

———. "A Last Final Reply Or, How I Learned to Stop Worrying and Love Jim Crisp." *Military History of the West* 26, no. 1 (Spring 1996): 105–06.

———. "A Rejoinder—Publish Rather Than Perish-Regardless: Jim Crisp and the de la Peña 'Diary.'" *Military History of the West* 25, no. 2 (Fall 1995): 157–65.

———. "Colonel Crockett's Exploits and Adventures in Texas." *The Crockett Chronicle,* no. 26 (November 2009): 3–6.

———. *Death of a Legend: The Myth and Mystery Surrounding the Death of Davy Crockett*. Plano: Republic of Texas Press, 1999.

———. *Defense of a Legend: Crockett and the de la Peña Diary*. Plano: Republic of Texas Press, 1994.

———. *Eyewitness to the Alamo*. Lanham, MD: Republic of Texas Press, 2001.

———. "Fiddling with History: David Crockett and the 'Devil's Box.'" *True West* 54, no. 3 (March 2007): 58–61.

———. "Some Problems With the 'Urriza' Account." *Alamo Journal*, no. 87 (July 1993).

———. "The Controversial Alleged Account of José Enrique de la Peña." *Military History of the West* 25, no. 2 (Fall 1995): 129–42.

Guarnieri, Phil. "Some Thoughts on the 'Second Reinforcement Theory.'" *Alamo Journal*, no. 138 (September 2005): 9–11.

Hansen, Todd, ed. *The Alamo Reader: A Study in History*. Mechanicsburg, PA: Stackpole Books, 2003.

Hansen, Todd. "Some Changes to *The Alamo Reader*: A Study in History." *Alamo Journal*, no. 154 (September 2009).

Hardin, Stephen L. "Dressed Like a Gentleman." Unpublished, longer version of "Gallery: David Crockett." *Military Illustrated*, no. 23 (February-March 1990): 28–35.

———. "Efficient in the Cause." In Gerald E. Poyo, ed., *Tejano Journey: 1770–1850*. Austin: University of Texas Press (1996): 49–71.

———. "Gallery: David Crockett." *Military Illustrated*, no. 23 (February-March 1990): 28–35.

———. "History Davy Crockett." Unpublished transcription of Judge Pat Clark's two-page handwritten manuscript describing Crockett's alleged route through Texas, dated May 21, 1910.

———. *Texian Iliad: A Military History of the Texas Revolution*. Austin: University of Texas Press, 1994.

———. *The Alamo 1836: Santa Anna's Texas Campaign*. Osceola, WI: Osprey, 2001.

Hardin, Stephen L., ed. "The Félix Nuñez Account and the Siege of the Alamo: A Critical Appraisal." *Southwestern Historical Quarterly* 94, no. 1 (July 1990): 65–84.

Harrigan, Stephen. "The Last Days of David Crockett." *American History* 46, no. 1 (April 2011): 28–35.

Henson, Margaret Swett. "Politics and the Treatment of the Mexican Prisoners after the Battle of San Jacinto." *The Southwestern Historical Quarterly* 94, no. 2 (October 1990): 189–230.

Hirsch, Mark. "Davy Crockett's Finest Hour." *American Indian* 8, no. 4 (Winter 2007): 52–54.

Holley, Mary Austin. *Texas*. Austin: Texas State Historical Association, 1990.

Ivey, James E. "Estrada or Navarro? The José Juan Sánchez Vista and Plano of the Alamo." Second Flying Company of Alamo de Parras website. Last modified June 2000. http://www.sonsofdewittcolony.org//adp/archives/feature/sanchez.html.

———. "Archaeological Evidence for the Defenses of the Alamo." *Alamo Journal*, no. 117 (June 2000): 1–8.

———. "Another Look at Storming the Alamo Walls." *Alamo Journal*, no. 120 (March 2001): 9–16.

———. "Notes on the Construction of the Defenses of the Alamo." Unpublished manuscript.

Jackson, Jack and James E. Ivey, "Mystery Artist of the Alamo: José Juan Sánchez." *Southwestern Historical Quarterly* 105, no. 2 (October 2001): 207–253.

Jackson, Jack, ed. and John Wheat, translator. *Texas by Terán: The Diary Kept by General Manuel de Mier y Terán on His 1828 Inspection of Texas*. Austin: University of Texas Press, 2000.

———. *Almonte's Texas*. Austin: Texas State Historical Association, 2003.

Jenkins, John H., ed. *Papers of the Texas Revolution 1835–1836*. Austin: Presidial Press, 1973.

———. *The General's Tight Pants: Edward Warren's Texas Tour of 1836*. Austin: The Pemberton Press, 1976.

Jones, Rendell. *In the Footsteps of Davy Crockett*. Winston-Salem, NC: John F. Blair, 2006.

Keating, John McLeod. *History of the City of Memphis and Shelby County, Tennessee, Volume 1*. Syracuse, NY: D. Mason & Co., 1888.

Kelly, James C. *Davy Crockett: Gentleman from the Cane. An Exhibition Commemorating Crockett's Life and Legend on the 200th Anniversary of His Birth*. Washington, DC and Nashville, TN: National Portrait Gallery and Tennessee State Museum, 1986.

Kemp, Louis Wiltz. *The Signers of the Texas Declaration of Independence*. Houston: The Anson Jones Press, 1944.

Kilgore, Dan. *How Did Davy Die?* College Station: Texas A&M University Press, 1978.

———. *How Did Davy Die? And Why Do We Care So Much?* College Station: Texas A&M University Press, 2010. Includes original 1978 edition with new essay by James E. Crisp.

Lack, Paul D. "In the Long Shadow of Eugene C. Barker: The Revolution and the Republic," in *Texas Through Time: Evolving Interpretations*. Edited by Walter L. Buenger and Robert A. Calvert. College Station: Texas A&M University Press, 1991. 134–64.

———. "Slavery and the Texas Revolution." *The Southwestern Historical Quarterly*, 89, No. 2 (1985): 181–202.

———. *The Texas Revolutionary Experience: A Political and Social History: 1835–1836*. College Station: Texas A&M University Press, 1992.

Lang, Aldon Socrates. *Financial History of the Public Lands in Texas*. Baylor Bulletin 35.3. Waco: Baylor University, 1932.

Lind, Michael. "The Death of David Crockett." *The Wilson Quarterly* 22, no. 1 (1998): 50–57.

Lindley, Thomas Ricks. *Alamo Traces: New Evidence and New Conclusions*. Lanham, MD: Republic of Texas Press, 2003.

———. "Analysis of the 'Lancer' Account of David Crockett's Death." *Alamo Journal*, no. 138 (September 2005): 3–8.

———. "David Crockett's Road to Texas." Unpublished itinerary, October 25, 1991.

———. "Killing Crockett: It's All in the Execution." *Alamo Journal*, no. 96 (May 1995).

———. "Killing Crockett, Lindley's Opinion." *Alamo Journal*, no. 98 (October 1995).

———. "Theory Being Paraded as Truth." *Alamo Journal*, no. 97 (July 1995).

Looscan, Adéle B. "Micajah Autry, A Soldier of the Alamo." *The Quarterly of the Texas State Historical Association* 14, no. 4 (April 1911): 315–24.

Lord, Walter. *A Time to Stand:* The Epic of the Alamo. New York: Harper & Brothers, 1961.

———. "Myths & Realities of the Alamo" in *The Republic of Texas*. Edited by Stephen B. Oates. Palo Alto, CA: American West Publishing Company, 1968.

Matovina, Timothy M., ed. *The Alamo Remembered: Tejano Accounts and Perspectives*. Austin: University of Texas Press, 1995.

Matovina, Timothy M., and Jesús F. de la Teja, eds. with collaborator Justin Poché. *Recollections of a Tejano Life: Antonio Menchaca in Texas History*. Austin: University of Texas Press, 2013.

McCullough, Bruce Welker. *The Life and Writings of Richard Penn Smith with a Reprint of his Play, 'The Deformed,' 1830*. Menasha, WI: The Collegiate Press/George Banta Publishing Co., 1917.

McDonald, David, transcription and translation. "The Siege of the Alamo: A Mexican Army Journal." Edited by Kevin R. Young. *Journal of the Alamo Battlefield Association* 3, no. 1 (Fall 1998): 31–36.

McKitrick, Reuben. *The Public Land System of Texas, 1823–1910*. Bulletin of the University of Wisconsin, Economics and Political Science Series 9.1, February 1918. Reprint, New York: Arno Press, 1979.

Miller, Thomas Lloyd. *Bounty and Donation Land Grants of Texas, 1835–1888*. Austin: University of Texas Press, 1967.

———. *The Public Lands of Texas, 1519–1970*. Norman: University of Oklahoma Press, 1972.

Moore, John L., Jon P. Preimesberger and David R. Tarr, eds. *Congressional Quarterly's Guide to U.S. Elections, 4th edition*. Washington, DC: CQ Press, 2001.

Morphis, J. M. *History of Texas: From Its Discovery and Settlement, with a Description of Its Principal Cities and Counties and the Agricultural, Mineral, and Material Resources of the State*. New York: United States Publishing Company, 1874.

Morrell, Z. [Zenos] N. *Flowers and Fruits in the Wilderness or, Forty-Six Years in Texas and Two Winters in Honduras*. Boston: Gould and Lincoln, 1873.

Morrison, Judge John and Col. Bob Hamsley. *The Real David Crockett*. Lawrenceburg, TN: The Democratic Union, 1955.

Morrison, John F., Jr. *Life of David Crockett in Lawrence County*. Nashville: Tennessee Department of Conservation Division of State Parks, undated.

"Mrs. Ibbie Gordon—A Remarkable Lady, One of the mothers of Texas." *Dallas Morning News*. (January 6, 1894).

Muckleroy, Anna. "The Indian Policy of the Republic of Texas." *The Southwestern Historical Quarterly* 25, no. 4 (April 1922): 229–60.

Nielsen, George R. "Lydia Ann McHenry and Revolutionary Texas." *The Southwestern Historical Quarterly* 74, no. 3 (January 1971): 393–408.

Nelson, George. *The Alamo: An Illustrated History. Third Revised Edition.* Uvalde, TX: Aldine Press, 2009.

Ordinances and Decrees of the Consultation, Provisional Government of Texas and the Convention, which Assembled at Washington March 1, 1836: Houston: National Banner Office––Niles & Co., 1838. Undated reprint: BiblioLife Network, Making of Modern Law collection.

Palmquist, Bob. "A Home or Perish." *Wild West* 29, no. 5 (February 2017): 38–43.

De La Peña, José Enrique. *With Santa Anna in Texas: A Personal Narrative of the Revolution.* Translated by Carmen Perry. Introduction by James E. Crisp. College Station: Texas A&M University Press, 1975. Expanded edition, 1997.

Petersen, Gert. *David Crockett, The Volunteer Rifleman: An Account of His Life, While a Resident of Franklin County, 1812–1817.* Winchester, TN: Franklin County Historical Society, 2008.

———. *David Crockett, The Public Man and Legislator: An Account of His Life, While a Resident of Lawrence County, 1817–1822.* Lawrence County, TN: Lawrence County Genealogical Society, 2010.

Pinkerton, Gary L. *Trammel's Trace: The First Road to Texas from the North.* College Station: Texas A&M University Press, 2016.

Pope, Judge William F. *Early Days in Arkansas: Being for the Most Part the Personal Recollections of an Old Settler.* Little Rock, AR: Frederick W. Allsopp, 1895.

Potter, Rueben M. *The Fall of the Alamo: A Reminiscence of the Revolution of Texas.* San Antonio: The Herald Steam Press, 1860. Reprint edition, Bryan, TX: Fuller Printing Company, 1979.

———. "The Defense of the Alamo in 1836." Clearfield, PA *Democratic Banner* (November 6, 1846).

———. "The Fall of the Alamo." *San Antonio Herald* (1860). Accessed at National Center for Public Policy Research: https://nationalcenter.org/ncppr/2001/11/03/fall-of-the-alamo-1836/.

———. "The Fall of the Alamo." *Magazine of American History* 2, no. 1 (January 1878). Second Flying Company of Alamo de Parras. Last modified March 8, 2000. http://www.sonsofdewittcolony.org/adp/history/1836/accounts/potter/frameset.html.

Ragsdale, Crystal Sasse. *Women & Children of the Alamo.* Austin: State House Press, 1994.

Ramsdell, Charles. *San Antonio: A Historical and Pictorial Guide.* Austin: University of Texas Press, 1959.

Ray, Frederic. *The Story of the Alamo: An Illustrated History of the Siege and Fall of the Alamo.* San Antonio: Daughters of the Republic of Texas Library Committee, 1955.

Reid, Stuart. "The Second Reinforcement: A Re-appraisal of the Evidence." *Alamo Journal,* no. 137 (June 2005).

———. *The Secret War for Texas*. College Station: Texas A&M University Press, 2007.

———. "What Ails You Jim, Exactly?" *Alamo Journal*, no. 143 (December 2006).

Remini, Robert V. *Andrew Jackson and His Indian Wars*. New York: Viking, 2001.

Reséndez, Andrés. "North American Peonage." *Journal of the Civil War Era* 7, no. 4 (December 2017): 597–619.

Robinson, Julia. "The Runaway Scrape: Exodus of Texians is an Unsung Episode of the Texas War for Independence." Texas Co-op Power website. Last modified April 2021. https://tinyurl.com/2v8asur2.

Santos, Richard G. *Santa Anna's Campaign Against Texas: 1835–1836*. Salisbury, NC: Documentary Publications, 1968.

Schlereth, Eric R. "Voluntary Mexicans: Allegiance and the Origin of the Texas Revolution" in *Contested Empire: Rethinking the Texas Revolution*. Edited by Sam W. Haynes and Gerald D. Saxon. College Station: Texas A&M University Press, 2015. 11–41.

Schoelwer, Susan Prendergast. *Alamo Images: Changing Perceptions of a Texas Experience*. Dallas, TX: DeGolyer Library and Southern Methodist Press, 1985.

———. "The Artist's Alamo: A Reappraisal of Pictorial Evidence, 1836–1850." *The Southwestern Historical Quarterly* 91, no. 4 (April 1988): 403–56.

Scruggs, Thomas E. "Davy Crockett and the Thieves of Jericho: An Analysis of the Shackford-Parrington Conspiracy Theory." *Journal of the Early Republic* 19 (Fall 1999): 481–98.

Shackford, James A. *David Crockett: The Man and the Legend*. Edited by John B. Shackford. Chapel Hill: University of North Carolina Press, 1956.

Shackford, James Atkins. "David Crockett and North Carolina." *The North Carolina Historical Review*, 28, No. 3 (July 1951): 298–315.

Sibley, Marilyn McAdams, ed. "Letters from the Texas Army, Autumn, 1836: Leon Dyer to Thomas J. Green." *The Southwestern Historical Quarterly* 72, no. 3 (January 1969): 371–84.

Smith, Jonathan Kennon Thompson. *The Land Holdings of Colonel David Crockett in West Tennessee*. Jackson: The Mid-West Tennessee Genealogical Society, 2004.

Smith, Richard Penn. *"On to the Alamo" Col. Crockett's Exploits and Adventures in Texas*, Edited with an introduction and notes by John Seelye. New York: Penguin Classics, 2003. Includes the original manuscript published in Philadelphia in 1836.

Steely, Skipper. "David Crockett's Visit to the Red River Valley." *East Texas Historical Journal* 37, no. 1, Article 7 (1999).

Steen, Ralph W. "Analysis of the Work of the General Council, Provisional Government of Texas, 1835–1836, Parts 1–3." *The Southwestern Historical Quarterly* 40, no. 4 (April 1937): 309–33 (part 1); 41, no. 3 (January 1938): 225–40 (part 2); 41, no. 4 (April 1938): 324–48 (part 3).

Strickland, Rex Wallace. "History of Fannin County, Texas, 1836–1843." *The Southwestern Historical Quarterly 33, no. 4* (April 1930): 262–98.

Sutherland, Dr. John. *The Fall of the Alamo*. San Antonio: Naylor Company, 1936.

Swisher, John M. *The Swisher Memoirs*. Edited by Rena Maverick Green. Delhi, India: Facsimile Publisher, 2019. Originally published in 1932.

Thompson, Bob. *Born on a Mountaintop: On the Road with Davy Crockett and the Ghosts of the Wild Frontier*. New York: Crown, 2012.

Thompson, Ernest T. *The Fabulous David Crockett: His Life and Times in Gibson County, Tenn. Including Tall Tales and Anecdotes of the Western Wilds*. Rutherford, TN: David Crockett Memorial Association, and Trenton, TN: Beta Graphic Arts, Inc., 1956.

Tice, Rick. "Dooley Ferry—Historic Transit Passageway." *Texas Gazette*, May 2, 1976.

Timanus, Rod. *On the Crockett Trail*. Union City, TN.: Pioneer Press, 1999.

Todish, Tim J. and Terry S. Todish. *Alamo Sourcebook 1836: A Comprehensive Guide to the Alamo and the Texas Revolution*. Austin: Eakin Press, 1998.

Torget, Andrew J. *Seeds of Empire: Cotton, Slavery, and the Transformation of the Texas Borderlands, 1800–1850*. Chapel Hill: University of North Carolina Press, 2015.

Tucker, Phillip T. "Motivations of United States Volunteers During the Texas Revolution, 1835-1836." *East Texas Historical Journal* 29, no. 1(1991) 25-34.

Voss, Frederick S. "Portraying an American Original: The Likenesses of Davy Crockett." *The Southwestern Historical Quarterly* 91, no. 4 (April 1988): 457–82.

Wallace, Ernest, and E. Adamson Hoebel. *The Comanches: Lords of the South Plains. The Civilization of the American Indian Series Book 34*. Norman: University of Oklahoma Press, 1969.

Wallis, Michael. *David Crockett: The Lion of the West*. New York: W. W. Norton & Co., 2011.

Widener, Helen Ogden, and Tad Browning. *Scraps of Life: Elizabeth Patton Crockett, Wife of Alamo Hero David Crockett*. Irving, TX: Pine Mountain Books, 2008.

Wiener, Allen J. "Who Cares How Davy Died?" *Alamo Journal*, no. 112 (March 1999).

Williams, Amelia. "A Critical Study of the Siege of the Alamo and of the Personnel of Its Defenders." *The Southwestern Historical Quarterly* 36, no. 4 (1933): 251-87.

———. "A Critical Study of the Siege of the Alamo and of the Personnel of Its Defenders: Chapter II. Santa Anna's Invasion of Texas, and His Investment and Final Assault of the Alamo." *The Southwestern Historical Quarterly* 37, no. 1 (1933): 1-44.

———. "A Critical Study of the Siege of the Alamo and of the Personnel of Its Defenders: III. The Leaders at the Alamo." *The Southwestern Historical Quarterly* 37, no. 2 (1933): 79-115.

———. "A Critical Study of the Siege of the Alamo and of the Personnel of Its Defenders: IV. Historical Problems Relating to the Alamo." *The Southwestern Historical Quarterly* 37, no. 3 (1934): 157-84.

———. "A Critical Study of the Siege of the Alamo and of the Personnel of Its Defenders: V. Historical Problems Relating to the Alamo." *The Southwestern Historical Quarterly* 37, no. 4 (1934): 237-312.

Williams, Elgin. *The Animating Pursuits of Speculation: Land Traffic in the Annexation of Texas*. New York: Columbia University Press, 1949.

Winders, Richard Bruce. *Sacrificed at the Alamo: Tragedy and Triumph in the Texas Revolution.* Abilene, TX: State House Press, 2004.

———. "'This Is a Cruel Truth, But I Cannot Omit It': The Origin and Effect of Mexico's No Quarter Policy in the Texas Revolution." *Southwestern Historical Quarterly* 120, no. 4 (April 2017): 412–39.

Winkler, E. W. "Some Historical Activities of the Texas Library and Historical Commission." *The Quarterly of the Texas State Historical Association* 14, no. 4 (April 1911): 294–304.

Winston, James E. "New Orleans Newspapers and the Texas Question, 1835–1837." *The Southwestern Historical Quarterly* 36, no. 2 (October 1932): 109–29.

Wolfe, Charles K. "Davy Crockett's Dance and Old Hickory's Fandango." *The Devil's Box* 16, (September 1982): 34–41.

Yoakum, H. [Henderson K.], Esq. *History of Texas from Its First Settlement in 1685 to Its Annexation to the United States in 1846, Vols. I & II.* New York: Redfield, 1855.

Young, Kevin R. "A Re-Evaluation of a Re-Evaluation." *Alamo Journal*, no. 89 (December 1993).

———. "Where Were the Bathrooms? An Informal Look at Sanitation in the 1836 Alamo." The Second Flying Company of Alamo De Parras website. Undated. http://www.sonsofdewittcolony.org/adp/history/archaeology/bano/frameset.html.

Zaboly, Gary. *An Altar for Their Sons: The Alamo and the Texas Revolution in Contemporary Newspaper Accounts.* Buffalo Gap, TX: State House Press, 2011.

———. "Crockett Goes to Texas: A Newspaper Chronology." *Journal of the Alamo Battlefield Association* 1, No. 1 (Summer 1995): 5–18.

Document Sources

Texas General Land Office

Tennessee State Library and Archives (TSLA)

Texas State Library and Archives Commission (TSLAC)

Texas Handbook Online

Johnson and Hood County, Texas Land Offices

Library of Congress Periodicals Reading Room

National Archives

Lilly Library, Indiana University, Bloomington

Franklin County, Tennessee, Historical Society

Lawrence County, Tennessee, Archives

Dolph Briscoe Center for American History, University of Texas at Austin

East Texas Research Center, Stephen F. Austin State University

Alabama Department of Archives & History

Research & Instructional Services Department, Louis Round Wilson Special Collections Library, The University of North Carolina at Chapel Hill

Sons of DeWitt Colony Texas website

Second Flying Company of Alamo de Parras website

Southwest Arkansas Regional Archives, Washington, Arkansas

INDEX

Italicized page numbers indicate illustrations.